CHANCE for LOVE

Gene and Marian shortly after his return in 1945.

CHANCE for LOVE

The World War II Letters of Marian Elizabeth Smith
and Lt. Eugene T. Petersen, USMCR

Edited by

Eugene T. Petersen

Michigan State University Press
East Lansing

Copyright© 1998 Eugene T. Petersen

∞ The paper used in this publication meets the minimum requirements of
ANSI/NISO Z39.48.1992 (R 1997) (Permanence of Paper).

Michigan State University Press
East Lansing, Michigan 48823-5202

06 05 04 03 02 01 00 99 98 1 2 3 4 5 6 7 8 9 10 11 12

Library of Congress Cataloging-in-Publications Data

Smith, Marian Elizabeth, 1921-
    A chance for love: the World War II letters of Marian Elizabeth Smith and
Lt. Eugene T. Petersen, USMCR / edited by Eugene T. Petersen.
        p.   cm.
    ISBN 0-87013-490-6 (alk. Paper)/ cloth
    ISBN 0-87013-524-4 (alk. Paper)/ paperback
    1. Smith, Marian Elizabeth, 1921-—correspondence. 2. Petersen, Eugene
T.—correspondence. 3. World War, 1939-1945—Personal narratives, Amer-
ican. 4. Women—United States—Biography. 5. United States. 6. Marine
Corps—. 7. Soldiers—United States—Biography. I. Petersen, Eugene T.
II. Title.
D811.5.S5867 1999   98-050191
940.53/092/2 21   CIP

Cover design by Michael Smith of View Two Plus
Book design by Nicolette Rose

Visit Michigan State University Press on the World-Wide Web at:
    http://www.msu.edu/unit/msupress

Contents

Foreword

IT IS A pleasure to have the opportunity to introduce Gene Petersen's World War II letters to and from his friend, Marian Smith. The correspondence evokes a time, an outlook, and circumstances long gone and widely forgotten. This book is a love story, a war story, as well as a diary of hardships and pleasures large and small.

Falling in love by letter is, perhaps, more intimate in some ways than the same process in person. Like Gene, I shared this experience in letters mailed from the European front to my future wife, Helen Wallbank. And like Gene and Marian, we endured the delayed reaction to questions and observations as letters crossed the thousands of miles from the front and home.

At a distance of fifty years, their letters highlight how utterly different was daily life in the 1940s from today, and at the same time, how ageless is human emotion. The gradual deepening of Gene and Marian's developing relationship permeates the two-year collection of letters sent between the Pacific theater and Chicago.

Marian's accounts of her daily routine remind us of an earlier America—a time when meat was scarce and a pork chop made an extravagant gift; when film was unloaded in a closet and prints required a ten-day wait; when young women in downtown Chicago walked home from the movies freely at any hour of the night.

The contrast between home front and Pacific theater is especially sharp. Gene's letters vividly convey the alternating boredom and tension of waiting for events to develop, and the confusion and fear of combat. Gene was among the Marines who took Iwo Jima in a three-week battle of immense proportions. Indulging an interest in history that would become his life work, Gene somehow found occasional moments to record his impressions.

Feb 24 (1945) 0800, landed with the 1st Bn. 9th Marines—Mortar fire close—dove in shell hole with dead Jap—scared—orders to go to first air-field—shelling heavy on our location—dump afire 50 yards north—shell hit 10 yards from foxhole—worked all night.

Feb 27, almost froze to death last night—still shelling beach and ammo dump—4th Marines held up on ridge for 5 days now—terrific arty [artillery] barrage today—Japs still hold high ground—hot coffee this morning tasted good—getting used to it now but it's still hell . . . .

March 6. The Army Air Corps is here! Do they look good! What a change in this place from the first night! Am beginning to smile again—big push on today by the 3rd—should secure the island soon—shaved for the 2nd time in 13 days today—had a nice beard. Marines won't forget this place.

Indeed, the Marines did not forget Iwo Jima, nor did a grateful country. Yet most of Gene's letters are not about the terrors of combat or good friends lost. He and Marian exchanged views on their expectations of life after the war, on the remarkable number of the same movies each had seen and the same articles in *Time* each read, and on their shared and earnestly held political views.

Shaped by youth and idealism, their philosophies represented a generation of Americans who hoped to make the world a better place. While many of their opinions proved either touchingly naive or downright mistaken, they worked hard at developing a thoughtful and productive approach for the post-war lives. Their interest in making a difference—wonderfully fulfilled by Gene's historical writings and restorations in Michigan—is evident in the strong intellectual kinship of these youthful letters.

Gene and Marian tried out their feelings, their beliefs, and their dreams on each other by mail for nearly two years. As a fellow veteran (and participant in the air raids over Ploesti, Romania, from which Marian's brother never returned), the memories these letters revive are particularly poignant for me. But for a younger generation, they serve as a well-preserved time capsule delivering a message from an earlier time.

Gene and Marian did their growing up in the cauldron of war at the front and sacrifice at home. I am delighted to recommend their remarkable record of this experience at once unique to them and universal to our generation.

William G. Milliken
8 August 1996

Preface

THESE LETTERS, WRITTEN during a twenty-three month period, have survived against all odds. Some of them have even gone through a war or at least a battle. In the spring of 1946, in more peaceful times, they were jammed into a box that was taped shut and placed in deepest storage. During a dozen moves and many housecleanings, they managed to stay intact, and it was not until fifty years had elapsed that the tape was removed, and they were spread out on the floor to be examined at leisure. Physically, they seemed to have survived remarkably well; at least the mice did not find them or perhaps were not interested. In due time they were entered into my Macintosh computer, and with some comfort I could read, for the first time since I had written them, my words and thoughts recorded during World War II.

My letters filled less than half of the box and I am not sure they would have survived in themselves. The others were written by Marian Smith, a young lady I met in the course of wartime travel. After a rather shaky start our correspondence became a record of wartime events that shaped our lives and revealed much about our personalities. In a very real sense the letters are personal diaries that we chose to share with one another. And because they became love letters, we believed it worthwhile to preserve them, not with the thought of publication or even revealing them to anyone else, but as a reminder at some future date of a time when we shared, through the courtesy of the United States postal service, intimate words and thoughts of war and love.

War stories have a tendency to dwell on heroism, bravery, blood, and sometimes victory. National pride and often national salvation are at stake. It is a time to raise the flag and salute. However, for the participant it is less a time of exhilaration and more a sobering experience wherein he appreciates the value of his life when others around him are losing theirs. It was inevitable that there would be some reflection on that in my letters from Iwo Jima, but they more frequently reinforce Civil War veteran Justice Oliver Wendell Holmes's view that war is mostly boring.

We are reminded that history is the sum of little ordinary events. I told Marian what I ate, described my tent and tent-mates, how much whiskey I drank, how many packages of Philip Morris I smoked, and, in between, how lonely I was. I made my views known on British imperialism and tried to see some good in our wartime allies, the Soviet Union, and the Chinese communists in their struggle with Chiang Kai-shek's Nationalist forces. I expounded on what my friends and I thought of the acting skills and other traits of Hollywood actors and actresses. I reviewed well-acted and intelligently directed movies, as well as blatant propaganda films with insipid war themes that were produced less to paint an accurate picture of service life than to entertain the home front. With a bit of irony I noted that we watched a few of the latter on Iwo Jima; even as men were being killed a few hundred yards away, I described a live but ill-suited music-hall type USO show staged to raise our morale but succeeding only in bringing down our scorn. Of course, like other Marines, I freely expressed my opinions on Marine Corps' bureaucracy and on the insufferable national hero, General Douglas MacArthur. In short, anything that happened to be on my mind is in these letters.

As my thoughts made their way to Chicago, Marian's letters found me in the Pacific. Like mine, they contain her equally frank opinions on national and world politics, as well as glimpses of wartime life on the home front as experienced by a young woman working for a defense manufacturer. Her kitchenette apartment had a living room that doubled as a bedroom, thanks to "Murphy beds" she and her friend Gale pulled down from the wall. She told me about train travel home to northern Wisconsin under trying conditions; shortages of certain food, especially meat; long lines at movie theatres; and working for less-than-enlightened superiors. And in each letter were expressions of hope that when all this was over we might share the future. In retrospect some of our opinions on politics and evaluations of contemporary national leaders proved naive or inaccurate, and our youthful idealism sometimes blinded us to reality, but in 1945, like so many others who were suffering the anguish of separation and the fear of death, we hoped this great war would be the last our generation or any generation would have to fight.

But you have been listening to just one voice long enough; it is time that I let Marian have a chance to speak in her own words:

This is a love story. As one of the principals, I was reluctant to make it public. But it is more than a love story. It tells what life was like during World War II, both on the home front and in the military and what it meant to be young in those times.

For me, as a product of the prevailing culture, marriage and children were givens. In my mother, Ottilie Ruppenthal Smith, I had an example of a woman who believed liberation was not only unnecessary but non-sense. She had been orphaned at thirteen, became a teacher, fiercely independent, but set aside that independence (partially) to become a wife and, more importantly, a partner to my father, helping him in his daily work and sometimes goading him to greater achievements. He often said to me, "If I had as much crust as your ma, I'd be a millionaire."

Well, I am too much like my father for that, but like my mother I certainly wanted to be an equal, not a subservient, partner. However, I will let Gene and our letters tell you how that scenario became reality.

To which I can only reply: The last thing in the world I wanted to do in 1944 was to fall in love. As a United States Marine who had signed up "for the duration plus six months," and as a child of divorced parents, I was very wary of commitments. My objectives, if I survived the war, were to obtain an advanced degree in history and a college teaching job that hopefully would help overcome my profound lack of confidence. After that, I could think about romance. But as you can see, fate had a different plan.

Historians generally believe that for contemporary accounts to have value as historical records they must be presented exactly as they were written and we have tried to do that with these letters. The transcriptions include misspellings, such as "viset" for visit, not all of which are identified with "sic." They are arranged in the chronological order in which they were written, but of course with address changes and the vagaries of wartime postal service they did not always reach the recipient so orderly. In a very few cases, indicated by ellipsis, a word or phrase has been eliminated to avoid repetition, and some names have been changed. Where clarification of the text was advisable, we placed these additions within brackets. When the writer refers to a letter date, he or she uses either the envelope postmark or author's date. Finally, background information is supplied in chapter introductions, narrations between the letters, and footnotes.

February 28, '45.

Dear Lt. Sweetheart:

Do you know that today
we have known each other
a year & 10 days, exactly. That
makes it sound quite respectable,
doesn't it? Seven days out
of 375 isn't a very good percentage,
though. It seems longer than
that to me — longer than the
7 days, I mean. Postal service
is a wonderful thing!

At home this weekend,
I spent quite a lot of time
going through Franklin's things.
There were so many of interest
that it didn't make me feel

Introduction

IT COULD HAVE been scripted in Hollywood. As a matter of fact, it began not far from the film capital, which in the 1940s was the fount of all romanticism. At 11:18 A.M. in Los Angeles, on 18 February 1944, I made my way down the aisle of a railroad coach on Santa Fe's *El Capitan*, carrying my military suitcase in one hand and a ticket with assigned seat 51 in the other. I had paid $54.05 for a reserved seat on the the train, which was about to begin its forty-two-hour run to Chicago. A young lady was seated in window seat 49. I figured the aisle seat must be 51, but in politeness asked her and she confirmed it. Our eyes met and our expressions changed from apprehension to mild surprise. Neither of us had looked forward to sitting next to a stranger for the long trip.

She wore a green gabardine business suit that severely hid her feminine physical features, but I could not help noticing an attractive brown hat that seemed to go well with her pretty dark eyes and medium length black hair. I removed my hat and Sam Browne belt, and put them alongside my suitcase in the overhead rack. Before sitting down I unbuttoned my forest green officer's blouse. She drew up her legs, which seemed extraordinarily shapely, and on her lap was the latest issue of *Time*, the weekly news magazine.

She told me her name was Marian Smith and that she came from Wittenberg, a small town in northern Wisconsin where her father owned a furniture and undertaking business. She had spent the last few months working in California to be near her brother, Franklin, a lieutenant in the Army Air Forces. Since he had been transferred overseas to a north African base, Marian decided to go back east to look for a secretarial job in Chicago. She was twenty-two years old and unmarried, although she was seeing a man named Cal Merrill, a Chicago art director.

I was age twenty-three and also came from Wisconsin, but my home was in Milwaukee. I explained to Marian that a benevolent draft board had allowed me to graduate from Marquette University in June, 1942, with a bachelor's degree in history. But before I was drafted, I had enlisted as a private in the Marines and had gone through boot camp and radio school in San Diego. After a year I was accepted for officers' training at Quantico, Virginia. Most recently I had been stationed in Los Angeles, where I had just completed a Navy and Marine officers' course in shipboard communication. The Marine Corps was sending me east for a month's Quartermaster training in Philadelphia before attending an Army Signal Corps class at Fort Monmouth, New Jersey.

The copy of *Time*, my favorite magazine, led to an easy conversation. To our mutual satisfaction we discovered a common liberal political philosophy and a strong interest in international relations. My grandfather, with whom I had lived since my parents' divorce in 1924, was active in Milwaukee's Socialist Party and had instilled in me a strong sense of social justice. Marian had formed her liberal convictions on her own, for her parents were conservative Republicans. We both admired President Franklin Roosevelt; looked benignly upon Russia, our military ally; and shared a deep distrust of Republicans, whose recent conversion to internationalism was suspect.

Politics gave way to a discussion of service life over a leisurely dinner. We laughed about my effort to pull the door open between the cars until a soldier showed me it should be pushed, because by then I had told her what the Marines thought of dogfaces. She wore a set of silver wings on her jacket, and that led into a discussion of aircraft. Her brother flew a P-38 fighter and I mentioned I had often seen the double-tailed planes at the Marines' Camp Mathews rifle range near San Diego. They came over at tree-top level at unbelievable speed and then suddenly banked upward and disappeared, leaving behind a distinctive whistle. Marian knew all this, but it was another thing we had in common.

We stood alone on the narrow outside platform of the last car in some privacy and close enough to hold hands. The rhythmic clickity-clack so familiar to train riders was punctuated only by an occasional and distant mournful whistle from the locomotive. The Rocky Mountains, many of them snow-covered, receded as we entered the Great Plains. I told Marian how my grandfather, whom I called Marty, had taken me to California on the Union Pacific in 1936 after my grandmother died. I was only sixteen, but I never forgot the thrill of first seeing the mountains near Colorado Springs. We visited San Francisco, joined in the city's celebration of the opening of the Golden Gate and Bay bridges, and watched *San Francisco*, a good movie starring Clark Gable and Jeanette MacDonald.

Marian, too, shared pieces of her life with me. She was born in Spokane, Washington, but during the depression her father lost his job and moved the family back to Wittenberg, where he took over her grandfather's undertaking business. As valedictorian of her class, she won a scholarship to a teachers' college in Stevens Point, but after a semester decided she would prefer office work and went to Miss Brown's Business School in Milwaukee. She was close to her older brother, Franklin, who wanted to fly commercial aircraft after the war despite her father's desire to see him carry on the family business. She liked California and hated to leave, but her roommate had sent her off with assurances she would probably "sit next to a handsome Marine." Marian thought it unbelievably prophetic and I was flattered. As the car lights dimmed, most of the passengers made fitful attempts to sleep. During one interval I looked steadily into her eyes, leaned over and kissed her lightly, and then kissed her again. When Marian put her head on my shoulder, I put my arm around her and we passed the night contentedly.

All too soon we reached Chicago and the Midwestern winter. The conductor said it was cold. Low dark clouds hid the sun, and the snow, which we had last seen sparkling atop the Rockies, had turned black. Whoever invented the word "dreary" had certainly been in Chicago in late February. We retrieved our baggage, took one last look at the *El Capitan*, where we had spent such an enjoyable forty-two hours, and emerged into the huge station. Breakfast had not been served on the train, so we sat at the station counter and ate a miserable farewell meal in silence.

Marian was going to stay with some friends while looking for a job but indicated she might seek employment in New York instead. She gave me her temporary Chicago address and we promised to write, but then people always did that. During one of our long talks, I mentioned that I had dated a couple of "Marions," and she reminded me with a smile that she spelled her name with an "a." We said good-bye, sealing the moment with a kiss. I turned and headed for my Milwaukee train, my family, and hometown girl.

When traveling across the country between military assignments, service personnel could usually squeeze out a few extra days "travel time" before reporting to a new station. Milwaukee was only a couple of hours north of Chicago, and, after six months in California, I looked forward to a brief visit with my grandfather, Martin Petersen, and my mother, Irene Trapp, who lived in nearby Waukesha. Thor, my father, had enlisted in the Navy after I left home and was now at a shore station somewhere in the South Pacific. I had to divide my precious leave time between relatives on both sides of the family, which left very little time for Marion, a girl I dated before the war and with whom I was exchanging letters.

I knew I had to see Marian again, and we arranged to meet in the Union Station between trains on my way to Philadelphia. Even in the cold, gray light of Chicago, she looked as good as I remembered. For a half hour we sat on the uncomfortable wooden benches of the station, held hands, and, with incessant announcements of train arrivals and departures interrupting our conversation, relished the memories of our first meeting. We laughed about how we had waited, not so patiently, for the car lights to dim and about overhearing an older man call us "nice kids." When it was time for me to leave, we promised again to write, and Marian sounded optimistic about finding work in New York.

In her letters to Franklin in March she mentioned the "handsome Marine." Her brother replied with some disgust, "I see you are still a confirmed romantic." She recovered quickly and backed away from her glowing report: "Well, some of his Milwaukee English annoys me, but while he's not stupid by any means, I haven't been able to figure out if he's very smart." Then she added:

> I asked several questions about his ideas on this and that and flattered him
> a bit by saying that with his background in history, he surely would know

a lot more than I do about world problems, and would he please make an attempt to educate me on a few of them. Of course I made it more specific but that was the general idea.

But Franklin knew his sister. In an immediate reply, he cautioned her, as he had done before, "Don't show him how smart you are right away, because you know it just scares them away." So, as we entered the spring of 1944, she may have been swept off her feet by "the handsome Marine," but not entirely.

1

". . . a wonderful chance for a love . . ."

ALTHOUGH WE DID *write as promised, our correspondence did not get off to a very good start. The few letters I wrote from Philadelphia and Fort Monmouth were cynical, complaining, and flippant, certainly not designed to stir a young lady's heart. If she expected to be enlightened on national and international affairs, she had to be disappointed. While I had some nice things to say about her, I did not save her letters, and when she decided not to come east to seek employment, I lost interest and quit writing. In a late June letter, Marian told me that Franklin's plane was missing after a big June 10th raid on the Ploesti, Romania oil refineries by the Fifteenth Air Force. I was obviously embarrassed about not writing.*

In mid-October I finished the communications course at Fort Monmouth and the Marine Corps promptly issued me orders to Camp Pendleton in California after a two-week leave. While in Milwaukee I wrote a short note to Marian and suggested a meeting. After our on-again off-again summer correspondence, I did not expect much, but she replied promptly and offered to come up to Milwaukee for a weekend. In two dates we talked lightly about the future, and I explained I was going to graduate school after the war and this ruled out serious commitments. Marian said she was in love (or had been, I wasn't sure) with Cal. I said I was not in love with anybody. She would like to come to California while I was there, but I did not encourage her because I was probably going overseas. We exchanged pictures and I said I hoped we could "get into some sort of correspondence arrangement."

Feb. 26, 1944
[Philadelphia]

Dear Marian,

Well here I am in Philly after a very uneventful trip. I did sit next to a girl (or lady) but we didn't say a word to each other all the time. I didn't even attempt to fall asleep and put my head on her shoulder—so you see I'm not a wolf 100% of the time. I wasn't even a patient gentleman—maybe I was tired and maybe it was you, but at any rate I behaved nobly.

I wish you were here tho especially round about sleeping time so I could put my head on your shoulder, look into your pretty brown eyes and generally feel very contented. Honestly tho I doubt more every minute I will see you again unless you come east. I wish that you would very much.

The train to Phil. was very dirty and stuff and no water. Reported in today to find I was technically 4 days A.W.O.L. The First Sergeant is a swell fellow so I decided to plead innocent. Everything is OK now but they could have made it miserable for me had they chose to do so.

I am staying at this place temporary but will move to the "Y" soon. The address will be

Lt. E. T. Petersen
117 No. 15 St.
Phil. Pa.

so file it and make use of it. I do really miss you darling and if it is at all possible I wish you could come to N.Y. or Atlantic City. Of course do what you think is right. I don't want to influence you too much but I think that we could have some swell fun together. Better close now so please write soon and say hello to everybody in Wittenberg (That shouldn't take too long) Till next time

Love, Gene

❧

1 March, 1944
Phil. Pa.

My dear Marian,

Received your letter today and I really was waiting patiently. I'm glad you wrote so soon. It is now 4:30 and I just got home from work or school. They usually let us go at 4:00 now but up to the time I arrived the fellows were just coming and going as they pleased. One fellow was (and is) on his honeymoon so he really had it nice. Now it's a different story as we have to be there from 8:30 to 4:00. It's a lot better than that crazy naval school in LA with all the stinking ground, shore-based so-called navy officers. I hate them.

I was sorry to hear that you probably wont be coming east as I was looking forward to seeing you very much. But you know what's best. If you ever decide to come you know that I will be waiting. Where do you think that you'll work? In Chicago I suppose. I'm glad you feel that way about me cause I am pretty much convinced that the feeling is mutual. However absence does not make the heart grow fonder. There are exceptions I suppose and I hope so in our case. I know that I liked you a whole lot in the little time I knew you. I will continue to write so let me know your next address.

Have to close for now Marian (see!) and do a little homework. Remember write soon and I'll see you again soon. I leave Phil. next Thurs for New Jersey.

Did I ever tell you I had a wonderful time that last night at the Schroeder? Somehow I don't think it was the rum either. I just hope there'll be more like it with you. Regardless of my other faults I am sincere. Till next time,

Lots of love, Gene

MORE LATER, IN CLASS—THIS IS AN EXAMPLE OF X MY TYPING BUT PLEASE EXCUSE IT. YUP, I READ THAT LETTER TO THE EDITOR BY THAT MARINE CAPTAIN.,SURE WAS SURPRISED THAT THE POEM WAS WRITTEN BY HIM. IT SURE DIDN'T DO THE MARINES JUSTICE BUT THE FAULT REALLY WAS WITH "YANK" INSOMUCH AS THEY DIDN'T PRINT THE WHOLE THING. ABOUT THE FIRST THING THAT I READ IN "TIME" IS THE LETTERS TO THE EDITORS. KINDA SURPRISING WHO WRITES SOME OF THEM. OH! IN THIS WEEK THE FUNNIEST THING IN MY ESTIMATION OCCURED IN THE XXX COLUMN ENTITLED "PEOPLE" IT SAID—ERROL FLYNN, WELL KNOWN HOLLYWOOD YACHTMAN—KINDA NAUGHTY BUT APPRO DON'T YOU THINK?

❧

March 12
Fort Monmouth [New Jersey]

My dear Marian,

Thought that you had forgotten about me when I didn't hear from you for about a week. I was glad to get your letter last week tho. I waited till now to write as I was in the midst of changing my address to Ft. Monmouth again. I am now among the "stinking army officers" and O boy are there droves of them here. As in combat the Marines here are outnumbered about 1000 to 1 but we still can hold our own. They do have respect for us from what I hear.

Despite the lapse of time since I saw you I still wish you were here in the east within range. Your last letter indicates you really do a little thinking—I mean about our international affairs. That interests me—It is my favorite subject and I have a lot of views on it but not much time now to air them.

I want to get across simply because I am (1) tired of service schools (they stink) (2) I have been living a life of ease and carefreeness for 2 years (3) I am tired of seeing fellows wear ribbons (4) I want to see just what it's like (5) I don't think that I am actually doing my duty (tho I can't help it) staying over here where it's safe (6) My father is over there (7) I want to say after the war that I was over there.

It looks like I'll be here for at least 6 months so write soon and tell me where I can write to you at your new address. You are still my favorite traveling companion. More later on politics and Monmouth and you.

Love, Gene

✤

May 26, 1944
Dogface Land

Dearest Marian,

For some reason those in charge of the Army of the United States gave us a couple of days off this week so being an eager beaver I set off for N.Y.C. It was only the second time I had been there in my life. Thought I had better see what it is all about. But didn't have too good a time.

However, I did make certain observations (1) The city is clean in general so that should please you. (2) It is quite big (3) It is crowded. That's about all I accomplished. Wanted some tickets to "Oklahoma" but got there a little late. If you come we'll get some hey? We as officers (even Marines) can get tickets to practically anything without too much trouble. Heard a couple AAF men were flying around here without wire staves in their hats and they were grounded $25.00 worth by our stinking line officer general. Oh—did I laugh.

Have a nice fellow staying in my room for awhile though. He's from L.A. so we have something in common. Also he can wear my underwear—which he is doing at present. He's kinda funny and always talking about his wife and baby in Lacuna Beach. That's all for now—gotta go to class again for awhile more later.

Love, Gene U.S.M.C.

✤

June 27, 1944
Ft. Monmouth

Dear Marian:

Don't know exactly how to start this as I feel like a rat and suppose that I am. I apologize for not writing before this and since I received your last letter a few minutes ago I feel worse than ever.

I have reference to your brother and I think that I can understand just how you feel. I always realized how close you were and it amazed me—not having any sisters or brothers. So I can understand somewhat of how you feel now. There isn't much that you can do Marian but hope and pray that he is a prisoner!!! On the whole I believe that the American prisoners are fairly well treated by the Axis. At least he is still a prisoner there is much to hope for. Be sure to let me know any late developments.

I have been busy lately with school which is really becoming a problem. At present we are in vacuum tubes and radio. The course is as tough as anything that I have ever taken. At least it has me overwhelmed about 90% of the time. Not being in the least bit of a technical nature I have my problems. Wish sometimes we were taking a course in history or Pol. science so I could regain a little self confidence. But I am learning a lot and it is interesting but Oh brother! what strain and pain. Manage to give us 4 hrs of homework every night. Actually it doesn't make any difference whether we pass or not but you do hate to flunk everything. Got the first "D" in my life in the final in Math and still was plenty lucky.

I was very disappointed in the fact that you are not coming east to go to school. I guess that maybe is the reason I didn't write. Not that I hold it against you for not coming because only you know what's best but I did want to see you. Guess that I felt that way ever since seeing you in Chicago last May. Still regret that I didn't spend a few days there but that's the way it goes. So you see that you have made a very good impression on me. Have to close now and study again.

(Over)Love, Gene

Followed the Rep. Convention in your dirty city. Any simalarity to the kind of politics the Rep's are going to play this fall and your dirty city—is not purely coincidental—appro place to hold their gum-beating. Dear old "Time" sure got some letters denouncing the N. Y Daily News article on why people read that "lousy" newspaper. Felt like writing myself. I buy it too but only to follow "Terry" and "Dick Tracy." Their editorials are not unlike these comic magazines you see sometimes and have about as much sense. However I can understand the "Batman" etc.—

October 14, 1944
[Chicago]

Hello Gene!

I was very glad to hear from you again and especially to hear that you are at home. Of course I'd like to see you, and I hope you'll be here more than an hour or two this time.

I've been planning to spend a weekend in Milwaukee soon and could just as well make it the 21st and 22nd. Then, perhaps, if you have no other plans, we might spend some time together. I think it would be fun. Do you?

Are you going back to California now? Lucky you, if you are.

As ever, Marian

Ten days later on the way to California I sent a picture postcard of the "Santa Fe Streamliner Crossing Johnson's Canyon, Arizona" and wrote: "Hello Mari-anne, Been thinking of you as we go thru these scenic places that I didn't see last time. Quiet trip. Love (?) Gene."

Marian was thinking of me too and wrote, as she later said, "to an indefinite address at Camp Pendleton." However, the United States Marine Corps didn't like "indefinite addresses," and it would be four months before this letter caught up with me.

Sunday Oct. 29 '44
[Chicago]

Darling Gene,

It is pleasant to find your smiling face before me whenever I come home. I simply love having this picture of you. It does interfere, though, with such occupations as reading and letter-writing, which require concentration.

The more I think of going back to California, the more anxious I am to be there. You may be sure I won't change my mind this time! I'm just waiting to hear what sort of assignment you have before making definite plans. I have a week's vacation coming, but if you think you may go overseas soon, I'll just take a couple more weeks and spend them in California. Otherwise, I'll go home for a week now and come to L.A. right after Christmas—for a long time, I hope.

Did you hear Roosevelt's speech from Chicago last night? I certainly enjoy the sarcastic remarks he makes about the Rep. "Me too" campaign and about quoting figures <u>correctly</u>.

Just the morning after you left, one of the dumb Republicans at the office came out with this typically "dopey" argument. "Just look at the huge nat'l debt!! After the war's over, the govt. will repudiate all your War Bonds."

"Oh, who told you that?" I said in extreme disgust.

"Well just wait and see!" was her reply. With that I was so furious I had to walk away to avoid ruining forever the comparative peace of the Midwest.

What really concerns me, though, is that so many people I know who greatly favor Roosevelt are considering voting for [Thomas] Dewey because they're afraid Roosevelt will die and leave Truman in the White House. What can you do with people like that?

Gene, dear, I have been thinking a lot about something you said about always having to be afraid I was still in love with someone else. I cannot say that I won't always be very fond of Cal. but, Gene, there are so many different kinds of love. Have I ever told you that favorite quotation of mine from the French flyer, St. Exupery.[3] "Love does not consist in gazing at each other," he said, "but in looking outward together in the same direction." You and I have such a wonderful chance for a love like that. With Cal, though, the circumstances of our lives would make it impossible even if he were not married.

Sometimes it seems when I try to explain all this to you, it only becomes more confused. Probably because I'm confused. I only know how relieved and how very glad I'd be to forget the whole thing. And that, perhaps, is the best indication that it can be done.

Think I'll write to Ginny[4] now and ask her if she has half a room to spare. See you soon, dear.

Love, Marian

�֍

October 31, 1944
[Camp Pendleton, California]

Dear Marian,

Well, I have finally got some sort of an assignment and got squared away in my new quarters. Temporarily I am in a company waiting further assignment to another outfit in which I will go overseas. Don't know when that will be but I hope not until after Xmas—in case you do decide to come out I would like to see you very much before I leave as the last visit (as with all the others) was too short. Was hoping that you would have been with me when I arrived in LA. But I thought of you particularly as we pulled into the station and I remembered the first time we had met there. It's nice to look back at pleasant experiences. I guess I can do plenty of that in the time to come. I may go to the 6th Marine Div. which is being organized in Guadal[canal] (Secret) But you can read all about me in "Time" which generally is favorable toward the Marines. Got my overseas physical & some shots for everything today. Now my arm is sore.

Spent Sat night in L.A. and attempted to get drunk with a Naval flier. Didn't succeed at Wilshire & Western (Melody Lane) so went to Lindys, Zephyr Room & Brown Derby. By the time I hit the last place I was in a good mood but when some dope civilian tried to tell me to vote for "Tom" [Dewey]. I proceeded to get in the hotest political argument ever. After it ended (it was good—he was a smart man) he introduced himself as the mgr. of the Beverly

Hills hotel. (interuption politics again with some fellow from Milw.) Anyway we parted friends and he invited me to his home and a trip through the studios.

Got to stop now as my arm doesnt feel too good. Anyway write soon and tell me all the news about yourself. So long and

Love, Gene

✢

Nov. 4, 1944
[Chicago]

Gene, dear,

It seemed to me as if I waited nearly forever for your letter. What were you doing with it between the 31st and the 2nd when it was postmarked? All right, I'll forgive. I guess it only seemed a long time because the week was long. I spent a couple of disgusting days at home with a cold and wasn't busy enough at the office the rest of the week.

Your Saturday night in Los Angeles makes me positively green with envy. Gene, I'll see you in exactly three weeks from yesterday. I've written to Ginny to see if I can stay with her, as I mentioned in my other letter. Did you get it, by the way? I wondered if you would as the address was not too explicit. Monday I shall tell Paul[5] that I'm leaving in two weeks. I always feel guilty about quitting a job, especially in times like these. If they want to give me a leave of absence for a couple of months, perhaps that would be a good idea.

Anyway, on Saturday, the 18th, I'm going home, and then I'll come back here Tuesday and take the El Capitan if possible, to Los Angeles. Oh, those wonderful palm trees and <u>clean</u> white buildings—and you! I suppose it's very unwise to become elated over the prospect as your orders might at any time destroy the whole thing. Will you wire me, Gene, if any such thing appears imminent? I could easily dispense with the formality of this two weeks' notice if you think you might leave soon. We may as well have as much time as possible for a change.

I had a letter this week from Lt. Jim Tipton, whom I knew last year in California & who went to Italy with Al.[6] He's been back since August and is an instructor now at Ontario, one of the fields where they were last fall. He has written quite often since Al has been missing and I've been hoping for a chance to talk to him, as you can well imagine. Al never exactly approved of Tip as his interests appeared to be limited to liquor, women and flying. I enjoy his letters and his company, but beyond that I agree with Al. I'm telling you all this so that you will know the "whys" & "wherefores" of the situation when we're in L.A.

While seeing Tip is another good reason for me to come, it's important to me only because of his association with Al. I'm sure you'll say I don't need to explain this to you, but I'd rather like to think you might be a little jealous if I didn't-(?)

Didn't you love Time for that article this week on Truman? I'd like to have a law requiring every voter to read it before Tuesday. I was happy too about that footnote regarding the Hearst press' "16 inch campaign smear guns." Clever! Wouldn't you like to meet Henry Luce[7] ? Ilka Chase said in one of her books that she didn't like him because he says he's never met anyone whose intelligence equals his own. That is obnoxious, but I think I'd be almost willing to grant he was being truthful, if not tactful.

I'd better quit rambling on before you get bored and tell me not to come.

All my love, Marian

&

Thursday [Nov. 2, 1944]
[Camp Pendleton]

My dear Marian,

Never figured I'd have to write a letter saying I couldn't see you but the way the situation is at present I expect orders momentarily and will probably be gone Sat. or Sunday of this week. I have purposely delayed writing till now as I expected the final word any minute but the indications are that I will be here only hours instead of weeks.

Just received your letter and I figured I better get the word to you without delay. I am going to wire also this noon

Got stuck with a Company commanders job last Monday & am up to my neck in troubles and grief.

So that's the way things stand at present <u>but</u> if you come I will be extremely happy to see you every available minute however I can't even promise a thing now. If I am the only real reason you are coming at this time, (and I flatter myself) I would urge you to delay it temporarily at least. I don't want you to come and find me gone but on the other hand I want to see you. It's fouled up completely. Will write more very soon.

Much love, Gene

&

November 7, 1944
[Chicago]

Hello, dear,

Have you started planning what we're going to do that first day in Los Angeles? You'll have to move the date ahead a week. I got to thinking about what I said in that last letter about having as much time as possible for a change and decided it was a waste of that valuable time to stay here two weeks. So I talked to Paul yesterday and everything's all set. I'm going home Saturday and will come back here to take the Tuesday night train. I think it's the Challenger, Union Pacific. No chance for a reservation. If I remember correctly, the train arrives in Los Angeles about 10 or 11 AM, Fri. Nov. 17. I'll give you more definite information after I get my ticket.

No doubt it would be sheer fantasy to imagine you might be able to meet the train. Just now I don't know where I'll stay, either, as I haven't heard from Ginny yet. Her address, though, is: Virginia Wilson, 1244 West 101st Street. I asked her to send her phone number and will let you know if she does. If I can't stay with her, I'm sure that for a few days, at least, I can stay with Al's girl friend and her folks. Her name is Muriel Neilson and they live at 3682 Lanfranes Street. Write to me in care of Virginia, anyway, as I'll surely see her Friday. Let me know when you can come up and perhaps I can meet your train.

Love, Marian

_____

WESTERN UNION

1944 NOV 9
OCEANSIDE CALIF
MISS MARION SMITH=
42 EAST SUPERIOR ST=

EXPECT ORDERS MOMENTARILY URGE TO DELAY VISIT LOVE=
GENE

_____

Saturday, Nov. 11, 1944
[Camp Pendleton]

Dearest Marian,

Guess this will have to be good-bye & farewell and all that. I will always go on wishing that we could have known each other better. I have told myself and you that I could really "fall" for someone with your qualifications. This is not an idle gesture or because I can smell the salt air but I really am sincere. Probably too much so and undtedly [*sic*] I have missed many opportunities. Maybe Romance is one of them. I have come to connect you & "Time" closely together and every time I read an unusual article I'll wonder if you had read it too & what you thought of it. I have a subscription but it will probably be some time before I start getting it "over there." Maybe when you read of something the Marines have done in the So. Pac. you can think of me too. I'll be wondering if it has appeared in "Time." Maybe too I'll be able to see how accurate their news-reporting is.

It is now 2:00 AM and time to start moving. Not much security in this letter but then, til later,

I remain, Gene
address overseas will be
28th Replacement Draft c/o Fleet Postmaster
San Francisco, Calif.
any time after

❧

November 13, 1944
Aboard Ship

Dearest Marian,

Have read and re-read the last issue of "Time" till I practically have it memorized. Tomorrow I'll start on the advertisements. But it's not too bad. We are out at sea and living conditions are very good considering. Four officers to a stateroom about as big as your room in Chicago. Hot and cold running water and a swell officers' lounge which I am in at present. Also a radio and in general everything to make the trip pleasant.

I have a Company of men to care for so that has kept me more or less busy. There is always something to be done but as time goes on I suppose I'll be mighty glad to get ashore. The enlisted mens' quarters are far from ideal and for sure I am glad of the bars. Hope the telegram stopped you in time. I didn't realize it was this close or would have emphasized my leaving more in the wire. Also

I might add again I'm sorry we didn't have some time together in L.A. or anywhere for that matter. Did you like "Time's" write-up on the election? I thought
it was excellent but that letter to the editor by that one Catholic in which he
advocates the Catholics boycotting the magazine shows the ignorant intolerance
that still persists in some circles—the Catholic Church not being the least
offender—Well such is life I suppose Have to close for tonight. Write soon &

Love, Gene
Lt. E. T. Petersen
Lt. USMCR.

❦

Nov. 21, 1944
[Central Pacific]

My dear Marian,
    Been wondering just what you have done. Hope that I didn't confuse you
too much by indicating I'd be on the West coast for some time yet. Got off in
such a hurry that I didn't have time to send another telegram. You received my
first one I presume. Am anxious to know what you are doing and hope you still
feel the same as your last letter indicated.
    By now you should have received a letter describing the first days aboard
ship. I am sending these to Chicago in hopes you are still there.
    Well time is passing despite the fact that it is monotony and not much else.
Have tried about everything but good hard work to pass the hours. This consisted of arguments mostly with the other 3 fellows in my stateroom. Political,
economic, and religious ah yes—philosophy, too. Yesterday we argued
Descartes till I was practically blue in the face. One of the fellows likes him. I
don't—probably the Catholic influence at Marquette—at least they had some
good arguments to defeat his line of reasoning. Read detective stories too in
great numbers for the first time in my life—Can't say I'd like a steady diet of
them however. Also read a book by Lewis Browne called "This Believing
World" The author is a Jew and aetheist. Kinda interesting but I can't say that
it impressed me too much. His history of religion is interesting and probably
quite accurate. Supposed to know the History of the Jews cold.
    I'd give $5 for a late issue of <u>Time</u> and I'm not kidding. Hope I can get the
pony "Express" [very much reduced size] issue over here. Still am not sure
where I'm going but will get the word to you somehow.
    By the way, I have been censoring letters too which is a novel experience to say
the least. Anyone could probably write a book on the subject. One letter was sent
to a neighbor of my mother's in Waukesha [Wisconsin] so I added a postscript.

Censoring should make one an authority in the art of writing "Love letters." To change the subject again—I'm glad I saw the final election results before I left. Incidently write and tell me how Mo. went in your next letter. Will you? If it turned out to be Democratic I have to collect $10 from some Lt. over here somewhere. I'll never forget election night. This other Lt. and myself got two choice seats next to the radio at 5:00 P.M. and never left until 12:30 except to go to the bar for Bourbon & Ginger Ale. By that time we both were ___ only he was sad and I very happy. Oh what a thrill—it was worth all the mud slinging of the campaign we had to read about just for that one night. Got a thrill when one station conceded to Roosevelt and then broadcast Willkie's election night speech in 1940 also conceding to FDR. I liked it. Enough of that—

I wrote almost all of my sentiments in my last letter and of course I mean them. Wish we could get in some sort of correspondence arrangement. I enjoy writing to you very much but of course that doesn't cover all of it. We will be able to see each other after I get back if you are still agreeable. Would surely like some more nights like the one at the Schroeder and Black Hawk. So write soon and often <u>please</u> and if you don't hear from me for intervals <u>don't</u> take it for granted I've stopped writing. Don't know what your Romantic interests are at present but I hope they are still largely with your brother. and—despite the impersonal parts of these letters, I don't look upon you merely as a sister or something if such a foolish thought has struck you.

Someone once said—"you are passionate"

Love, Gene

✤

Nov. 9, 1944
[Chicago]

Gene Darling,

I don't know what to say—I can't tell you how disappointed I am. All those wonderful plans! But of course I know it's what we have to expect.

I wanted so much to hoard lots of memories so that while you were gone I could remember and be sure that it isn't only in my imagination that you're so dear to me. Since you were here this last time, it seems that every time I think of you I like you better. But the longer you are gone (especially when you write only <u>once</u> in three weeks), the more it seems that that's an odd thing to say to someone you've known no longer than 65 hours.

That remark about the letters is not very kind, but I'd certainly hate to have to depend on Time for all the news of you. I should like to get lots of long, long letters. There are such millions of things I'd like to talk to you about. I'd even enjoy a correspondence course in radio. Right now, especially. The darn thing is being temperamental again. It wouldn't even work election night.

It was a lovely election, wasn't it? I had every good intention of being a gracious winner and not gloating the morning after, but one of the most repulsive Republicans in the office made some crack about, "Just wait and see how things go to ruin," so I couldn't resist calling him a poor, disappointed Rep. and from then on, I gloated! The Chicago Times headline Nov 8 was, "Oh, what a beautiful morning!" Didn't it seem that way to you?

I hope you can read this letter. This isn't a very good pencil, but I packed my pen away somewhere & can't dig it out. They have already rented my room to someone else so I'm going home for a couple weeks and when I come back I'll stay with June[8] & [Gale] Murph[y] again at 14 W. Elm, Apt 1303. In the meantime, please write to me at Wittenberg.

With all my heart, Gene, I wish you luck and hope that you'll be back safely very soon.

Love, Marian

⚜

Nov. 14, 1944
[Wittenberg]

Gene darling,

Our one and only theater in Wittenberg was showing Guadalcanal Diary tonight, so just for a little Marine atmosphere I went. All I can say is I wish this damn war could end before you ever get into something like that.

I have a long and amazing story to tell you, dear, about my trip to California. Friday morning I told Paul about your wire and said I'd decided not to go, but to go home for a while instead. "Why don't you fly?" he asked. Well, there was hardly any need to answer that. He had lunch at noon with the Pres. & V.P. & Asst. to the Pres. (impressive, isn't it?) and when he came back he said, "How would you like to go to Los Angeles on business. We'll pay your round trip plane fare and all you need to do is spend a couple of days telling Mitchell (our L.A. representative) about turnbuckles." What I could tell him about turnbuckles that he doesn't know already, you could put on a penny postcard. I just couldn't believe it! I was so amazed at such an offer and so anxious to go that my no-thank-you's were not at all convincing. So they gave me a check for $230 and at 6:00 Fri. night my reservation was confirmed on Flight #19 leaving at 6:25 Sat. A.M. You never saw anyone so excited in your life. I was actually ill from excitement. Couldn't eat. Couldn't sleep. About four in the morning I felt so awful that I called and cancelled the reservation. It sounds insane, doesn't it? I still don't know what made me do it really, except that it must have been an extreme aversion to allowing myself to become involved in the mental obligations entailed in accepting such generosity. My God, I'd have to work for Reliable the rest of my life to make up for it!

Anyway, about eight o'clock, your special delivery letter came saying you might be gone Sat. or Sun., so I was glad I didn't go. Life is a merry-go-round, isn't it?

You should have seen my mother and dad when I got home Sun. night. I had written them that I was taking that plane & they thought I was in Los Angeles. I think it was the first time I've ever seen my dad really surprised. Ordinarily he says practically nothing at all, but he just couldn't get over how often I could change my mind. That's nothing new to you, is it, dear?

Speaking of my dad, I may as well warn you now never to talk politics with him. Boy, what a Republican! He was complaining about Truman last night, and I said that what Truman did in his Senate Investigating Comm. was exactly what dad would want done if he were in Washington. "Oh that's all part of the plan to put Communism in effect," he says. He has us all saying "Heil Roosevelt!" and the OPA is already Gestapo. At that point the lights went out quite unexpectedly. Of course we all laughed and said they must be at work already, but dad couldn't refrain from adding that he wouldn't put it past them. So you see it's wise to avoid the subject.

Wednesday morning:

Your letter of the 11th came this morning. I'm glad you said everything you did. It's good to be reassured that you feel that way, too. Perhaps we're wrong in thinking that we've lost our chance again to get better acquainted. Haven't you often found it true that you learned to know someone better after you had to write letters to them than you ever had before? It always seems easier to me to write my most sincere thoughts than to talk about them. It surely worked that way with Franklin and me. We were never so close when we were both at home as when we were apart. It's a paradox, isn't it?

Gene, I hope the color of this ink doesn't blind you. [violet] Gaudy, isn't it? It's supposed to be good for shorthand because it flows faster & dries quicker than other colors. We used to use it for court reporting class. Guess I'd better quit writing & give your eyes a rest. Mine, too.

I hope this reaches you before next summer. How's the Marine Corps mail service?

All my love, Marian

✤

Monday, Nov. 20, '44

Dearest Gene,

I was surprised to get the letter you wrote last week aboard ship. They really whisked you off in a hurry, didn't they? It was interesting to read your comments on your quarters, etc. All I ever heard from Al about his trip across was that it was <u>crowded</u>. I guess he thought that was enough said.

Since you have that issue of <u>Time</u> memorized, I suppose it's hardly necessary to send you this clipping. Perhaps by the time it reaches you, though, you will have forgotten. What do you think of T. E. Lawrence's comment? Does it seem to you that the same thing is happening again? When I read about the "Western Bloc" and Russia's "Sphere of Influence" developing, it smells awfully like the old power politics again and I don't like it at all. My only objection to Roosevelt is that he seems to back up the imperialism of Churchill. Maybe he has to—I don't know. It does seem that the "old men" are going back to the old way of living, though. And the young people who are not too busy fighting seem to be either bewildered, as I am, or apathetic, as the majority here in Wittenberg are. Ye gods, are they dull!

I saw "Tunisian Victory "the other night. (There were some gorgeous shots of P-38's.) Have you seen it? As you probably know, it's a U.S.-British Ministry of Information film. In one sequence, Joe, the Britisher, goes sentimental about the Moroccan villagers returning to their homes. "I had a buddy killed the other day," he said, "and it made me mad. But somehow seeing all these poor blokes goin' home, it all kinda makes sense." Perhaps it's pure stubbornness that makes me dislike such propaganda, but I hate the way we and the British act so good! Maybe we treat the natives a little better, but we exploit them just the same & I refuse to believe we're fighting any battles for love of the underprivileged. Not while we're so afraid of the Communists.

Do you think it would be a bad thing, Gene, for the Communist parties to gain control in all or most of the European countries, in Italy or in France? I'm inclined to be in sympathy with them although I don't know enough about the situation to have any definite opinion.

I'm looking forward to a good argument on that subject with Peg [Margaret Borrebek]. She's invited me to her home in Galesville for Thanksgiving. It'll be so nice to see her. I'm going down Wednesday. Takes almost all day to get there by bus, what with waiting around here & there to make connections.

On the whole my vacation in Wittenberg has been much more pleasant than I could have hoped. I've been so busy sewing that I haven't even seen all the people I ought to visit. You should see the purdy stuff I made. Two blouses & a dress. They'd have been so nice to wear in California. Darn the Marine Corps!

Then, of course, we spent a few evenings trying to beat my dad at sheephead. Do you play, Gene? Dad is an old shark. We're lucky once in a while, though. It's fun to play with him because playing cards is the one & only thing he really enjoys & it makes quite a charming person of him for a time.

Gene, dear if you ever want anything at all, please tell me and I'll be only too glad to send it. Perhaps you'd like some books or magazines or something. Reminds me of the cartoon I saw recently of a girl at the parcel post window with a mailing tag on her wrist. The clerk looked astonished and the girl was saying, "But I have his request right here!" Might try that myself if there were any chance it might work. Provided, of course, I had a request.

Lots of love, Marian

⚜

Tuesday, Nov. 28
[Chicago]

Gene, darling,

This has been such a busy week I've hardly had time to sit still long enough to write. I've thought of you often, though, and wondered every day where you might be.

Peg and I had a grand time. Her folks were so nice to me. We just talked and ate and slept and played. Galesville, her home town, is a pretty little place. It's built on a ridge overlooking a lake. We went for a hike one afternoon along the lake and thought of what a contrast there was between that peaceful day and the hikes the infantry men are taking overseas.

After a long, long discussion of the Communist situation, particularly as it pertains to China, the only conclusion we could arrive at was that we hadn't the slightest idea what it's all about or who's right or why. The news tonight is that Madame Chiang & the Generalissimo have separated & she is going to live over here somewhere. Amazing, isn't it?

What do you think of Stettinius as successor to Cordell Hull[9]? I had hoped they might get Sumner Welles back, but I guess Stettinius is supposed to be a brilliant man.

I'm staying with June & Murph again at 14 W. Elm, as I had given up my room on Superior before I went home two weeks ago. Of course, I don't like it as well here—you know the complaints Peg & I have made about the gloomy atmosphere—but it is economical. June is planning quite definitely on entering the Nurses Cadets in March, so I guess I'll stay here until she leaves & then Murph & I will have to go room hunting again.

Gene, have you read much about the influence of Business on newspapers? A friend of mine has been urging me to read a book called "Lords of the Press." It sounds interesting.

I'm hoping to hear from you in another week or so. Hope everything's OK.

Love, Marian

P.S. Peg told me that a fellow from Galesville who was lost over Romania in April had just made his way back home a couple weeks ago. That was really encouraging.

Did I tell you what Mother said about your picture? "Well, yes, he has a nice smile, but your brother is better looking." Honestly, Gene, I think if he does come back & you meet him some day, you'll be disappointed after all this build-up.

✤

November 30 '44
[Chicago]

Gene, dear,

Your letter of the 21st came today & I enjoyed it so much. Just at the moment I can't tell you how Missouri went in the election. Haven't the faintest idea. But I shall try to find out before I mail this tomorrow. You know, dear, I can see right now that it's going to be a liberal education for me trying to write intelligent letters to you, to say nothing of studying up on the things you write about. Descartes, for instance. It's wonderful to have such an incentive, though. I've often wanted to learn something about philosophy, but could never study it in night school as all the courses req'd. Soph. or Junior credits, which I haven't.

Perhaps I've told you that Peg & I visited two friends of mine in Winona Sunday. They are both girls I used to live with in Milw. One of them, Donna Loughrey, used to have Peg's present teaching job, and the other was secy to Rev. Hjortland at Ascension when we were in Milw. Her name is Ruth [Borge] Senjem. She was telling us that she worked for a college professor last year who was obsessed with the idea that teachers belong the poor class, being grossly underpaid, and that he used to wear overalls and carry a lunch pail "to live within his means." I got to thinking about the basic truth behind his ideas & thought maybe I ought to try harder to talk you into the furniture business. But when I think how much more stimulating life would be for a professor than for a store-keeper & fixer of corpses, it does seem that even the security of a good business is hardly worth it. My dad would say that's foolish. Perhaps he's right, but I'm inclined to prefer being foolish and making the most of life to being sensible and dull. Aren't you?

Changing the subject, I imagine it is an interesting experience being a censor. Must be rather fun at times. Don't you feel awfully impolite, though, reading other people's mail?

Back to the election again, my radio wasn't working that night—or did I tell you before? I was rather glad of it, to tell the truth, as I don't believe I could have stood the excitement. A Captain who's a friend of Murph's just came in for a few minutes & he happens to be from Missouri. So, of course, I asked him what the returns were there & he says the state was definitely for Roosevelt altho the Senatorial & Gubernatorial elections are still undecided. I hope you collect the $10.00. My usual commission, of course, is 10 per cent.

As for my "romantic interests," darling, you know all there is to know about them. While I have been known to fall in love with a handsome Marine in less than 42 hours, you may be sure it's not a habit, nor is it likely to happen again.

Goodnight, dear. Marian

❀

December 7, 1944
[Chicago]

Gene, darling,

There are so many things I've been wanting to write you about that now that I've a chance to get started I should really make two or three letters of it. I'm sending a couple pages from the Chicago Sun including some good editorials on foreign policy. This is the sort of thing I was thinking of when I asked you about the Communists. The enclosed editorial by Samuel Grafton is along the same lines as the others I'm sending you. Perhaps by the time you get them they'll be old stuff. I hope not too old to be interesting. I was surely delighted with Stettinius' declaration condemning the British policy in Italy, etc. Time said that there seemed to be no doubt that with Stettinius the real Sec. of State would continue to be F.D.R. If he keeps that up, it's ok with me.

Thought you'd enjoy Gracie Allen's comments on our friend Mrs. Luce. Also the clipping from Time, you ignorant ruffian!

Here's something I can't remember whether I've told you about or not. I'll have to tell you again to get it off my mind. Remember when you told me Tyrone Power was a Marine Lt.? One of the girls who lived at 14 West Elm has friend who's an Ensign stationed in Fla. Jim is his name. One night he was sitting in a bar and a Marine Lt. came up and asked if he could join him. They talked for several hours & Jim mentioned he hadn't been able to find a hotel room. So the Marine offered to share his with Jim. When they got there, Jim found out it was Tyrone Power.[10] Said he was a nice fellow & not bad looking, but he snores! Disillusioning isn't it?

What do you hear from your dad, Gene? Do you think there's any chance you might see him down there? A friend of Al's named Bob Sadler is over there somewhere. Air forces ground crew, I think. His wife wrote a short time ago & told me Bob had met her brother over there. They had never seen each other before, but now they're only a short ferry boat ride apart. Odd, isn't it?

Well, dear, it's time for me to take care of my domestic duties. I'm the cook this week & it's a long job every evening. I'll write some more this weekend.

Much love, Marian

&

Sunday, Dec. 10 '44

Hi, darling,

I wish you could see the blizzard we're having today. It isn't so cold, but it's been snowing all day & the wind is blowing furiously. I walked to the lake front a while ago—or rather I fought my way over & blew back. It was fun watching the breakers & everything.

Speaking of the weather, I just bought a fur coat this week. I really had to. Thought I could get along with an old one I had bought a couple years ago from one of my roommates in Milwaukee, but I couldn't even get it cleaned. They were afraid it would fall apart! I'm delighted with the new one, of course. It's beaver-dyed mouton, the kind of fur they use for <u>aviator's</u> flying suits.

Next weekend my friend Margie [Thompson] from Racine is coming down and we're going to see "Winged Victory." Her brother is in the Air Force, too, B-29.

Gene, now that you have probably reached your destination, can you tell me where you sailed from? Point Loma? We could see Point Loma from where we stayed in San Diego three years ago & it always seemed an exciting place to me. Romantic in the sense of adventure, etc.

Margie lived in Los Angeles several months, too, and we have a lot of fun talking about it. She loved it, too. We decided next time we'd like to go out together. Just missed each other before.

Isn't it a disgraceful situation in Greece?[11] I get so disgusted with the British.

"Time" had a good long article about Stettinius in this week's issue Background & all that stuff, you know. Guess I'll send it to you. It may arrive sooner than your own copies.

About "Time," Greta [Marcotte] told me the other day that Don (That's the composer of "Tico Tico" and his wife, you know.) couldn't decide whether he wanted a subscription to Newsweek or Time. Said he liked Time's news coverage, but Newsweek's style was not so "la de da." I get a kick out of that.

You know, dear, in that last letter you said something about its impersonal tone. If mine seem that way, too, sometimes, it's only that I can't think of a good way to say what I'd like to say. It seems silly to say I miss you when we've spent so little time together, but I do. And the star on my horizon is the day you come back.

Love, Marian

�֍

December 14, 1944

Dearest Gene,

Since the weekend will undoubtedly be a busy one, thought I'd write tonight while there's one quiet spot in the apt.—namely the kitchen. Murph and I turned the radio off a while ago when June had gone out for a few minutes, but it went right back on again when she came in, so there's no peace in the living room. Gee, I get so tired of mystery stories. They're as bad on the air as in books. Well, that takes care of the complaint department.

One of the girls at the office has a friend who just returned from the Pacific & he is so noisily disgusted with complaining civilians that I was almost afraid to write that first paragraph. I thought you should be entitled to some explanation, though, of the lack of concentration which must be evident in these letters.

For the same reason, the most serious reading I've done since I've been back here (outside of Time, which I read on the street car) has been a book called "Topper" [Thorne Smith], which is absolutely fantastic & ridiculous but very entertaining. Perhaps you've read it or seen one of the movies.

Speaking of movies reminds me that we saw a television program Tuesday eve. A young elect. engineer and his wife, Marge and Ed Dervishion, who are friends of the girls, live in this building, and they have just recently acquired a television set of their own. The programs were not very good, but it was interesting to see. I was thinking you'd probably enjoy knowing Ed. He seems to have a lively interest in almost everything & likes to talk. That isn't a very good explanation of why I thought you'd like him, but perhaps you can be psychic & figure out what I mean.

The youngest girl in our office has a brother who's a gunner on a bomber & has been in Italy for two or three months. He was reported missing a few days ago. I felt so sad about it. Then June and I went to the show Mon., "Story of Vernon and Irene Castle." He was killed in a plane crash in the last war. So we had a good cry & felt much better the next day. It really was an excellent picture, though.

I'm glad you said in that last letter that I shouldn't worry about your having stopped writing if I didn't hear from you for a while, dear. It makes it much easier to wait.

With love, Marian

❖

Gene dear,

I feel rather self-conscious about this. [*Atlantic Monthly*] Hope you don't mind. I wanted to send you something and couldn't think of anything else sensible. Thought you might like Harper's better, but they don't send it overseas.

With love, Marian

❖

[*Christmas card*]

Thought you might enjoy at least a picture of a white Christmas, dear. I'd give anything to share mine with you.

With love, Marian

❖

Dec. 18, 1944

Hi Darling,

Every night since Friday I've been wishing you could be here. We had such a wonderful weekend, Margie and I. Guess I told you before that she was coming down. We've known each other ever since we were about 15, but hadn't seen each other more than once or twice in the last three years. And it's been so much fun getting acquainted again. We seem to have been living in the same world, which doesn't seem so true of many other friends of mine. Well, the best part of it is that I think Margie will come down here to work in February & we can share an apartment. I'm delighted. It just solves so many problems and imagine having someone around again who has the ambition to go out bowling & whatnot and who likes poetry and music and art and airplanes! It's wonderful.

But I wanted to tell you all the things we did and all the times I wished you were there. Friday night we mostly talked & drank martinis. Sat. afternoon we saw "Winged Victory." Oh, Gene, it was terrific. Made me so sad I could have wept even when it was funny. It was almost like living over those three months when Al was in training, except that it was like being there instead of just reading his letters about it.

Saturday night Margie wanted to dance so we went to the Aragon [Ballroom]. Incidentally you were right in that little discussion we had with Jerry. They do say in their radio broadcasts that the Aragon is on Chicago's "Near North Side." It's a fabulous place. Really quite beautiful in an ostentatious way. It seems bigger than the Palladium. I think the dance floor must be larger, but there's less room around the edges. I hate to go dancing like that without a date. I like to watch people, though, and the atmosphere is exciting. It was fun to think of what a lovely evening we could spend there together.

Sunday afternoon (no need to mention where we spent Sunday morning!) we went to the Art Institute. Margie wanted to look at the furniture, & in looking for it we came across some exhibits of Oriental art, vases, and tiny little jars of carved jade, amber and turquoise. They were gorgeous. One kind of jade is white & has little bits of green in it. They call it "moss in ice." Poetic, isn't it?

To come down to a more prosaic subject, my boss has been working on a new price sheet, and in the process of typing it (32 pages of the stuff) I've been getting quite an education in power-line and telephone equipment. Here's a sample of the copy, of which I'd like an explanation. "Heat coil fuse . . . will operate within 210 seconds on .5 ampere in an ambient temperature of 68 degrees F." What puzzles me is that "ambient temperature." Can you explain it in half a letter? Or less.

Goodnight, dear. I hope everything's ok.
Love, Marian

⚜

December 23, 1944

Dearest Gene,

In the mailbox the other night was the Pacific Pony Edition of Time which you mailed Nov. 24. You really gave me a dose of my own medicine, dear. Here I was worrying about some of those clippings I had sent you and thinking what a mean trick it was to send a letter that wasn't a letter! But I don't feel sorry for you anymore. Seriously I did enjoy seeing the "Pony Edition," and, as Murph says, it proves you were thinking of me at least. Wouldn't you like a magnifying glass to read your copies?

I feel rather frustrated this morning. Had expected to be in Wittenberg by this time, but the train that left at 1:50 this morning was so crowded I couldn't get near it. And I had planned to take it because I thought very few others would care to start out at such an hour & on such a train. I called Daddy this morning and suggested that we have Christmas next week, but he ignored that & just kept asking when was the next train. So I shall go down this aft. an hour early & try to find standing room, at least, on the "400." Honestly, people who travel over holidays are crazy!

Mrs. Cook, our president's charming young wife, gave all the office girls a party last night at the Racquet Club, which is quite an exclusive place a couple blocks from our apt. We had a wonderful steak dinner & lots of fun. Some of the kids were pretty gay from the afternoon's festivities. These business offices really discard their dignity the last day before Christmas. There's a bottle in every corner and the men run around trying to kiss all the girls & some of the girls do the same. It's not only embarrassing but at times disgusting. I went up to the engineering lab to talk to Greta and escape the mele, but I ran into a sorry game of tag in the factory on the way. They didn't catch me, thank goodness!

The company was notified this week that we have been awarded the Army Navy E.[12] I'm quite pleased about it. It's good to think that possibly a few things I'm doing may be helping to shorten the war. The presentation is being made at a party Monday evening, Jan. 8. We may each bring a guest if we wish. Please come with me, won't you? Darling, how I wish you could!

Love, Marian

❧

December 26, 1944
Wittenberg

Hi, honey m'love-

Your V-Mail[13] of the 15th was here when I came home Saturday night. Can't say that I like V-Mail much either, but it does seem to get through in a hurry and that's a cardinal virtue! I hope that by Christmas day you had arrived at a peaceful destination and received a nice stack of mail.

One of the girls here in town is married to an ensign in the Merchant Marine. He just came home after a trip to the Phillipines and various southern islands on a C-2. I saw them yesterday & we were discussing the possibilities of your travels and your comments on the quarters aboard ship. John said they carried troops from Morotai to Halmahera or someplace around there—a week's trip anyway—in the hold of their ship. They had to ration water, so they rigged up salt-water showers, & when it rained, everyone went up on deck & took a bath. That must have been a heck of a trip.

Speaking of trips, I expected to have both legs and arms broken before we got through the gate & onto the train in Chicago Sat. night. What a mess! After we changed trains at Appleton, I stood up in a cattle car for sixty miles. We had a pretty nice Christmas, though, considering everything. It was worth it.

Dad had two or three magnifying glasses down in his office & he gave me one which you may have if you'd like it to read Time's pony editions.

I managed to get into a couple of arguments again with these darned stuffy Republicans around here. There's a Mrs. Snyder, who thinks she knows every-thing. First she said the boys in the service should rebel and refuse to go overseas— should have in the very beginning. And five minutes later she's complaining about labor union strikes & saying "where would we be if our boys in uniform went on strike?" Such brilliance! I didn't argue much with her. No point in it. But she made me angry enough to feel like throwing a nutcracker at her. There are more stubborn people around here. Mostly Norwegians and Germans. By the way, what nationality are you, Gene? Norwegian? I've been wondering about that. Not about your being stubborn—purely curiosity. There are a million silly questions like that I'd like to ask you just because it's so nice to know you that I want to know everything about you.

Love, Marian

❀

December 15, 1944
[Central Pacific]

Dearest Marian,

I am hoping there will be some letters from you when I finally reach my destination. I am still aboard ship out here in the central Pacific. Things are going on as usual. We have been getting the news regularly but I'd still give a lot for an issue of "Time." This is the first V-Mail I've used and I don't think I'll like it too much. Am anxious to find out where you are at present. I'll send this to Wittenberg and they will forward to you, I presume.

Been thinking that inasmuch as you are my favorite traveling companion I'd like having you aboard. We would carry on where we left off last Feb. Hope you have received some of the letters I've written since I left. I have been able to get ahold of some good books here among them is [Gene] Fowler's Goodnight Sweet Prince which I am reading at present. That's all for now. Please write soon and I'll reply.

Love, Gene

❀

22 December 1944

My dear Marian,

"Oh what a glorious morning" for today we had mail call for the first time in a month. Received about six letters from you which was not the least of my joy. Kinda cleared up a few things insomuch as I had not received the letters you had written to Pendleton during the "last days" explaining the outcome of your proposed trip to California. I'm glad you didn't fly out altho I can well imagine how I would have felt if I had been there at the time. I knew I was leaving but couldn't word it any more strongly than I did in the letter or telegram without telling the exact date of departure. At any rate all turned out for the best which it usually does—however at the time it is hard to see it that way.

Had to laugh at you trying to explain "turnbuckles" in Los Angeles but you can talk to me anytime about them—or anything for that matter. It has dawned on me also that we can figure our length of acquaintance in hours. Whenever we saw each other we were either coming or going. I agree with you about the future of a teacher but unfortunately I believe that I am sensible and Dull. I do not say this proudly but rather reluctantly. The other traits—that is—making the most of life and being foolish I can admire in anyone—This is honestly what I believe.

There is much I admire in you—if you will excuse a few comments I probably shouldn't make. I think it is, above all, your ability to talk along the line that interests me most. I do get that feeling that I could enjoy living with you even after the honeymoon which may be vulgar but if it were always the case there would be more truth in "true love."

Well I started out to write a note tonight telling you some of the essentials and cut it short in order that I may get it in tomorrow's mail so that you would get it before summer so—

I'll write soon and often so please keep writing—the delay between letters may not be our fault now.

My love, Gene

P.S. After building up "Time" to my grandfather for 8 months he finally discovered Mrs. Luce's spouse is none other than the editor-in-chief. Now I have to fight on two fronts—and the Japs have nothing on him. Here's off to pacify grandpop.

Dec 26, 1944
At Sea

Dearest Marian,

Tis the day after Xmas—and I am very happy to say that we are near our destination. Can now reveal where we have been all this time. We left from you know where—stopped at San Francisco and then proceeded to Pearl Harbor. Thence to the Marshalls—Eniwetok exactly and now are nearing our final destination. I can see no reason why we can't say where that is but that is supposed to be the rule so I'll abide.

I was surprised that they let us say that much. I was rather amazed at living conditions on the latter island. They had a radio station broadcasting to the whole area—called it the Pacific network. A beautiful officers' club with all kinds of liquor also was surprising. Perfect swimming on a swell beach too.

So far the trip hasn't been bad—at least we have had many advantages that I never expected. Everyone managed to bring liquor aboard so there have been some wild parties. That seemed to be the favorite way to celebrate Christmas eve. I have had about 3 drinks since I came aboard. I never cared too much for the taste of it myself and certainly do not care to drink just for the sake of drinking. We have one Marine Gunner aboard that almost has to have a quart a day. Feel sorry for him. I had to laugh however when he said he had 19 qts in his locker box—in fact <u>that's all</u> he is carrying. We don't get our lockers till we arrive there so he'll probably have a gay time for the first 20 days—what he'll do then I don't know.

I am waiting for some more mail from you. I hope you've received the letters I've sent to Wittenberg and Superior st. So far mail delivery has been surprisingly good and should be better on the return trip. I haven't received my "Time" as yet but I'm still hoping.

Don't forget to write often. Yes—I do likewise so till later.

Much love, Gene

⚜

Jan. 1, 1945
Central Pac.

Dearest Marian,

Delayed writing for a few days because we have landed finally—and I was busy getting everything in order so that we might have most of the comforts of home.

I am now in the 3rd Marine Division so be alert for news from this outfit. It certainly is a fighting organization with a good record behind them. Refer to "Time" dates (?) But anyhow I am in the field on this island and so far have found several surprises to say the least. Living conditions are very good, considering—The island is beautiful and I really mean it—plenty of natives who are both intelligent and ultra friendly. They wear modern clothes example—saddle shoes, and ankle socks—snoods [hair net or cloth]—colored dresses—saw one who looked like she might be a coed. The girls are unusually pretty. There seems to be no shortage of liquor and beer. Last night I got pretty high at the division hdqs officers' club.

The Japs have been here which is about all I can say.

Mail delivery is good, about 7 days here and likewise going back I hear.

I met one of my best friends here who is in Jasco [Joint Assault Signal Company] and he took me for a ride all over the southern part of the island. Stopped in at a couple native homes for lemonade and ho-made cake. Also went swimming and shell hunting.

As yet I am unassigned but expect to be shortly. I want a Jasco most of all but there are no openings at present.

Hope you have the minimum of trouble reading this but I'm trying to write this while sitting on a cot.

Time out to eat a coconut. Walter just opened one so that's what we are doing now. Sure tastes good but I imagine that we'll soon get sick of them.

By the way thanks for all the letters—I particularly enjoyed the clippings. Guess I'll post the one on Marines on the bulletin board. I never realized there could be so much hatred against anyone as there is here in the 3rd toward the Japs. It really is brutal. I wonder if it's going to end with the armistice. I've not that attitude yet but probably will feel a little different after the first campaign. I don't know too much about the Greek situation, but the British have no desire for any type of Communism which is the old story again. But we'd do the same—particularly the Republicans. It is a hellava mess and sometimes it makes you want to forget everything—get the war over with—and come home. That's like saying—to hell with "the peace." Too many feel that way tho and if we're not careful the people will demand just that. The work will begin after the armistice but do the people realize that? I doubt it. They'll sacrifice any chance for a final peace if their son can come home a month sooner.

Well dear I have to close now and secure the tent. Looks like rain. I'll write regularly to you because I like to. Hope you can bear with me through a mass of uninteresting material till I find something that is more readable. Till later.

Much love and a Happy New Year, Gene

❖

Jan. 3, 1945 Central Pac.

Dearest Marian,

A few lines tonight before it gets dark. We are getting organized gradually and it begins to look more like home all the time. I am work in Hdqs Co. now and haven't too many duties. I am waiting for an assignment but it will be some time yet I'm afraid. Meantime I am in the 28th yet. Met so many fellows I know here that it's like old home week. I usually get invited to lunch every day by the Jasco's or Engineers. Guess I told you about Jasco in the last letter. It's a little rough but interesting. Would give a lot to get into one. It's quite new.

Just received letter from you dated Dec. 23. I'm terribly sorry about the "Pony Edition." I know exactly how you feel. Something like getting a bill — only worse. But now you can see what they are like. Haven't seen any since that one. Wish my subscription would catch me.

It is now Jan 3 — everybody is saying that "in the next letter we'll hear about Xmas at home." Before I go any farther I must apologize for this messy letter but it is good honest-to-goodness sweat mixed in with a little — mud. Sorry I can't tell you where I'm at But I am in the 3rd division. If you have been reading "Time" —

Have seen so much that would be interesting to write about but I guess it's out. My dad is definitely nowhere near here so I'll probably not get to see him. Met two fellows I graduated from M.U. with — also expect to make 1st Lt. in about 4 months. This seniority is a pain — been in grade 16 months now. Have to close as darkness is falling. Your letters are (1) Extremely welcome (2) Interesting and (3) Very much like <u>you</u>.

Much love, Gene

�֍

Jan. 5, 1945
Central

Dearest Marian,

Your letters are arriving at regular intervals — am getting so that I look forward to them rather than wonder if there'll be another. Can't vouch for the grammar in that last sentence but the thought should be clear.

One of the most amusing things we've noticed since we arrived here is the great amount of bitterness in the men. I have long since ceased to regard that with alarm and we laugh now when some cynic shouts something during an ardent love scene in the movies. Don't know if we are getting into a rut of thorough disbelieving ourselves. Some of these fellows have been here (in the Pacific) for 2 years now which partially explains their actions I suppose. The morale is good <u>because</u> the men are proud to be Marines in their own particular way. They fight so good because they believe their organization is the best not because they are liberty lovers or any of that. There is a great deal of spirit. I suppose the Air Corps has it too but only overseas does it really amount to anything. It surprised me —

Jan 6

Will have to finish this letter now before inspection. Since yesterday I dug a foxhole which proves officers do dig their own. Got a monthly beer allotment of one case which I am sitting on at present. Also got a pen finally. So long for a while darling.

Love, Gene

✣

January 1, 1945
[Chicago]

Happy New Year, darling!

That seems rather a silly thing to say, but then I suppose it could be a happy year—surely I hope most sincerely that it will be.

June and Murph think it will <u>have</u> to be better than '44, as that, for them, was an all-time low. In a way, I feel the same, and yet there were many pleasant things happening during the year to offset in some degree its tragedy. You, for instance.

There's a new song called "What a Difference a Day Makes." I don't know how new it is—perhaps you've heard it, perhaps not. But I'm sure you'll agree, just from the title, that it's very appropriate. I like it.

Your letter of the 22nd was here Thursday, the 28th. Isn't that excellent time? None of us remembered to pick up the mail that evening. We called after dinner to ask the desk clerk if there was any and she said yes, but no one wanted to go after it. I said there were only two letters I'd be willing to go down there for—one from Franklin or one from you—and I <u>knew</u> it wouldn't be either. So you can imagine how foolish I felt the next morning when I found your letter there. Then I was so anxious to read it that I forgot to ask for a transfer on the street car and had to pay two fares. Serves me right!

After reading your letter I've been wondering if perhaps my comments on teaching & on being sensible or foolish were not quite clear. What I meant to say was that while it might be foolish to teach inasmuch as it is not a well-paid profession, it would be a far more stimulating life than that of a small town businessman. Incidentally, you may be sensible, dear, but you are far from dull.

How did you spend New Year's Eve? June and I went to a show—"Gaslight." It's a bit on the hair-raising side. Afterward, we came home & greeted the New Year quite gaily with the aid of a bottle of bourbon someone had given to Murph.

I made a chicken dinner yesterday, and we all feel ok today, so it couldn't have been so bad.

I'm glad you feel that way about living together "after the honeymoon." I do, too. It would not be vulgar, I think, unless we felt differently.

Love, Marian

❖

January 5, 1945

Gene dear,

The comment in your letter of Dec. 26 about the beach and the perfect swimming at Eniwetok really made me wish I had been traveling with you about that time. It's been below-zero here the last few days and evidently our apt. manager is seriously practicing fuel conservation. Even my new fur coat doesn't help in that situation. Oh—good old L.A!

I was rather surprised that you were able to tell so much of where you'd been before arriving at your final destination. I'm glad it has been comparatively pleasant. John Hyland, the Merchant Marine ensign I mentioned once before whose wife is a friend of mine in W'berg, told me he thought you might be going to Bougainville as that is a staging area. It does seem exasperating sometimes not to be able to know, but if there is even a slight possibility that it may make a difference in your safety, I shall surely not complain.

I told June and Murph about the gunner who needs a quart a day and we've been wondering how such an alcoholic managed to get into the Marine Corps. Or did he acquire the habit afterward? Has he been in combat before? I feel sorry, too, for anyone who is so unstable. It makes me a little angry sometimes when people criticize them or act patronizing. My mother does!

Time out—June and I just took 64 cents worth of beer & soda bottles back to the liquor store. Sounds bad, doesn't it? Actually they've been accumulating for a long time. We brought back some port and zinfandel wine. Did you ever have the two mixed? It's a delicious drink. Wish you could have one with us.

I also wish you were here & could fix my radio. That fellow in the shop doesn't seem to be able to figure out what's wrong. He thinks it's fixed & I bring it home & it doesn't work & I take it back, etc. etc. Tiresome to say the least.

How did you like "Goodnight Sweet Prince"? I've been wondering if it's worth reading. It takes me so long to finish a book that I have to choose them carefully. Am just starting "Presidential Agent." Have you read any of the books in that series by [Upton] Sinclair?

I'm still looking for the book called "Lords of the Press." That reminds me—the Sun has contracted with Milton Caniff for "a new comic strip as soon as his present agreement with another newspaper syndicate expires." Good, hmm? I'd love to see the Sun take every last reader away from the Tribune.

Last night I felt like hearing a good concert, so went all by myself to Orchestra Hall where the Chicago Symphony was playing. I really enjoyed it, altho the critics say the Chicago Symphony is not what it used to be. Thinking of the time you told me about that concert in L.A. which you attended so reluctantly, I wondered if you might have felt like the man on the enclosed cartoon.

It's from a book of drawings by William Steig. I think they're marvelous, & this is one of my favorites. The one on the other side of this page, "A kind of love," I don't understand. If you can figure it out, please explain it to me.

See you later darling,

Love, Marian

✂

January 10, 1945

Dearest Gene,

You would never in a million years guess what sort of person escorted me to dinner, etc. at our Army Navy E party! No less than the <u>Lt. Colonel A/C</u> from Wright Field who was here to make the official presentation. He was rather a funny looking man with a waxed mustache (horrible isn't it?), but I think I was extremely fortunate. He happens to be a very good friend of all the company executives, and I spent the evening somewhat like Cinderella. After the dinner was over & the dancing waned, we went downstairs to the cocktail lounge (This was in the Hotel Continental which used to be the Medinah Club—quite a sumptuous place) with Paul Rhoads (my boss), his wife, Mr. Ripley (asst. to the Pres.) and his wife. Later John Brown Cook and Marian, (the pres. and wife) joined us. We were highly entertained by John Brown, who is quite an accomplished magician, and by the Colonel & Mrs. Rhoads, who were telling each other stories of varying degrees of vulgarity. After one of them which I tried not to hear, I told Paul I wished I could blush, because I thought I ought to at that point. A little later, we were talking about getting to work in the morning & Mrs. Rhoads asked me if I had someone to wake me or I had to depend on an alarm clock. Before I could answer, the Colonel said, "Oh, I'll just nudge her!" Then I did blush!! Everyone <u>else</u> enjoyed it.

Your letters of the 1st & 3rd came yesterday. I know where you are, dear, I'm sure, but I shall not mention it even to you. The good-looking natives and the college gal clothes gave me the first idea and then I looked in a July issue of Time to confirm it.

It's swell that you've met so many friends there. I hope you can be assigned to a Jasco, although I don't like the "rough" part. What do they do? Set up ship-to-shore communications & that sort of thing?

Since you enjoyed the clippings, I shall enclose another with this letter. Sometime ago our engineers developed some special cable grips for Wright Field to be used on nylon rope, & I suspect they were for the project mentioned in this article.

That reminds me—I was asking the Colonel what he thought of the Air Wacs etc., and telling him I had been more than usually concerned of late about the insignificance of my own "war effort." It made me feel pretty good to hear him say what I am doing here is more important than what I might find to do in the service. Unless I should join the Cadet Nurse Corps. Perhaps I ought to. What would you think of it?

You know, it's really an effort to keep my pen in check & write this small. I had only a page & this piece of a page left, though, and so many things to say.

It was real sweet of you to tell me you enjoy these letters. I'm glad dear. Need I add that yours mean very much to me.

Perhaps you would be interested to know that I saw Cal last night for the first time in nearly a month, and he is thinking quite seriously of going to New York to work. He gets that idea about every six months, but this time there seems to be no new prospect in Chicago sufficiently interesting to dissuade him. Of course I'd miss him, but I think it would be a fine thing. It's really marvelous, Gene, how easy it is now not to mind the long intervals between the times I see Cal.

Have been meaning to ask you what your dad does in the Navy. And this I've asked before, I think, but have forgotten—how long has he been in the Navy? That's for the Dept. of Vital Statistics.

The Society for the Promotion of Adult Education is now insisting that I get busy with my homework, which consists of that Sinclair book. See you later, dear.

Love and stuff- Marian

❖

1-12-45 [Chicago]

Hi darling:

Thought I'd send you a piece of Time again since you said yours hasn't caught up. It's hard to resist sending the whole thing, but I thought you'd rather have a little now than all later when the news is too old to be interesting, & mail seems to travel faster when it's light. That's a complicated explanation. Just wanted something to write a note about so it wouldn't seem too much like "getting a bill."

I like you, Marian

❖

Jan. 14, 1945

Dearest Gene:

At last I've finished reading that book and still have a little time tonight to write a brief note. Tomorrow a friend of mine is coming over for dinner, but Tuesday I promise to write a long, long letter.

Here is an indication that your ideas were correct regarding the people's willingness to sacrifice the Peace to the immediate security of their personal interests. It's very disheartening, isn't it? Of course, the publicity given in the Sun is hardly favorable, but I can picture the nods of approval with which the idea would be greeted by the old wives of Wittenberg, for example. It seems to me, however, that those people who have been least affected by the war are most eager to agree with "We, the Mothers." Those to whom it has brought suffering are more inclined to realize the importance of making a peace which will assure that that suffering has not been without purpose.

Gene, dear, I love you for the ideals you have, and that is not all — Marian

✿

Jan. 16, 1945
[Chicago]

Gene darling,

Those three letters from you last week were marvelous. I'm still enjoying them. Did I tell you the one you wrote Jan. 6 arrived the 10th? I was simply amazed. It's almost as if you were in California, except that the passenger trains are not so good between here and there!

I was amused at your saying you thought there must be somewhat the same spirit in the Air Corps as in the Marine. Sweet of you to make that concession. I imagine it is true in a way, but it seems to me the morale in the Air Corps is good largely because those fellows are so in love with their planes. Reminds me of a discussion Peg & I had one time about the meaning of the word "morale." (Peg's boy friend, Ray [Meininger], has presumably sailed from New York or thereabouts within the last week or so.) Somewhere she had read that the true definition of morale is "confidence in one's ability to solve whatever problems may arise or to overcome obstacles." In that sense, the Marines surely have morale. That's what you said, isn't it!

It has occurred to me that from the same point of view morale has a great deal to do with happiness in ordinary life. It has for me, at least. Nothing can be so destructive to my peace of mind as the feeling that I am confronted with a situation I don't know what to do with. Incidentally, June and I were talking about crossword puzzles tonight, and they are among the things that ruin my morale! They drive me crazy because I never can master them!

Mother wrote that Franklin's belongings had been sent home last week. She has washed and pressed them all as if she thought he'd need them any day. He had bought some cameos in Italy which he was anxious for us to see, but of course they were missing. I can hear the barrage of invective he'd give out with if he knew they were gone.

Bob Hope just came on. He's at Fort Monmouth tonight. That's an ice box with barracks, he says. Must be as cold as Chicago. He's so funny. I wish you could read my shorthand. I'd try to take down a few of his jokes.

To change the subject, now that I've finished Presidential Agent, I'd like to tell you a little about it. Have you read any of [Upton] Sinclair's "Lanny Budd" series? They're really fascinating. Maybe I've asked you before, as I read Dragon's Teeth last spring. Time says no author can make a current history so vivid and so readable, & 'tis true, 'tis true! I actually feel personally acquainted with all the prominent persons with whom Lanny visits in these books. "P.A." besides being a good novel, is quite an effective apology for Roosevelt's foreign policy around '38 and '39. It gave the impression that he'd like to have taken more drastic steps to halt the dictators, but was unable to go against public opinion, which of course was pacifist and isolationist at that time. Sinclair lays the blame for the war squarely upon the shoulders of big business and intimates that the capitalist lords in this country would gladly have put a Joe McWilliams or Gerald Smith in power, & in fact tried hard to do it. He just about convinces me that the Communists or the "Pinks" are the only decent people when I get to wondering if it isn't just a battle of the worker versus the employer in which either one who wins will exploit whomever he can. How do you know <u>what</u> to believe?

Do you remember dear, how I told you I felt the first time you touched my hand? When I read at the end of your letter, "So long for a while darling," it makes me feel just the same.

Love, Marian

Jan.17, '45
[Guam]

Dearest Marian,

Just finished your lastest letter of Jan. 10 and really enjoyed it as much as any letter I have received. No fooling!

Decided to take time out and answer it right away as it seems that is the way to write a more intelligent reply. Writing paper is still scarce, hence this old variety of a few months back. I may have to use something more drastic than this old stuff so standby.

Everybody is so short that we are letting them write on both sides of the sheet even tho they aren't supposed to because of the censor complications. Incidently I am chief censor now which is rather amusing. Would you like to make some guesses as to where I'm at despite the fact I can't confirm or deny it.

Today was rather warm for a change and not too comfortable. Usually there is a wind which blows from one direction for 6 months out of the year and another direction for the remaining time. Rain continues to fall at regular intervals. These nights by the way, are really something to behold. We can look over the ocean toward the east and somehow there always seems to be a full moon. The stars are larger than in Texas and those waving palm trees — Sounds as tho I might break into verse or something but never fear. We do have a fellow in the company that sends home poems (or as he calls them "pomes") regularly. The spelling is wonderous and the thoughts pretty corny but I suppose someone appreciates them.

I liked those articles you sent — I wonder if you read the one about that tropical storm — did you? Time out until tomorrow —

Decided to add a few lines tonight before movie time. I was duly impressed with your escort to the party you spoke of — also got a big kick out of the Colonel's remark about nudging you. I can imagine that it was well appreciated. Glad too that the interval between meetings with Cal has lengthened somewhat. Would like to hear more of that but guess that I better be discreet —

For heaven's sake don't get into the service! Guess that I told you that a few times before but I'll repeat it now. You have nothing to gain certainly (except perhaps the Nurses' Training program.) I can't emphasize that enough. I believe after the war it will make little or no difference whether a person has been in the service or not — and don't feel patriotic — enough of that.

My dad has been in the Navy about 2 years now after serving about 6 years in the last one. It was foolish but that's a long story. Nothing but his own desire for a last fling before settling down made him do it.

Sat. Jan. 20

Inspection is over and everyone is out on liberty. Sounds rather strange but there are quite a few things of interest to see and do here. Native villages and swimming for the most part. We have also set up a rifle range which affords some pastime also. Gave that clipping to [Thomas A.] Edwards who is intelligence officer so he'll probably use it in his next lecture —

Still haven't succeeded in getting into Jasco but I have hopes. You are right about what they do. It's a comparatively new setup and they come in about H + 15.

Better close now as I seem to be at the end of the page but I am still waiting for your letters every day and I'll always find time to answer them.

Love, Gene

✧

January 21, 1945
[Chicago]

Hello my darling,
     We have been sitting here listening to the Symphony and feeling quite pen-
sive. I read Night Flight by Antoine de St. Exupery yesterday, and it put me in
a pleasant wistful mood that has lasted all weekend. That man is terrific as an
author. If you have never read any of his books, you should at the first opportunity. I have one, "Flight to Arras," which I'd gladly send you. They are so
beautifully written it's like reading poetry. They express a deep courage and
conviction of the dignity of man which is really inspiring. In "Night Flight" he
speaks of "a dark sense of duty—greater than love" and says, "We behave as if
there were something of higher value than human life—but what thing?" Then
the whole story is a definition of that thing. I wish I could tell it to you.
     Gene, you will be getting tired of all these clippings I send you. This one may
not be of particular interest to you. It seemed an unusually good piece of literature for a newspaper. Sad and lovely. That name Hanffalize fascinates me. Did
you study French? I didn't, and if I hadn't heard a radio announcer pronounce
the name, it would just annoy me. Knowing how it sounds, though, I like it.
     It will be swell for you to get a promotion. By the time we ride the "El
Capitan" again, you'll probably be one. When did you get your commission?
     Having asked a question reminds me that you never answer them. I can
think of about two you have answered. For shame!
     So you have 250 nurses on the island now. I hope they are well outnum-
bered so that you have lots of competition!
     I can imagine that you must have been glad to find a reasonably current
issue of Time. I truly cannot see that they have shown any bias toward the Rep.
cause. As a matter of fact, if Luce is a Republican, he must certainly be a liberal one. As far as I'm concerned, a Republican who hates [Robert] McCormick
is OK with me. You should see the pictures of Roosevelt he put in the Trib. yesterday—one taken at each inaugural and every one of them lousy. On the last
one, he looks as if he had one foot in the grave. Makes me so mad! I wish he had
a whole staff of George DeWitts.

Write soon dear, Marian

�֍

January 24, 1945

Dear Lt. Sweetheart,

Yours of the 17th rec'd and contents thereof duly noted—see what happens to a poor business girl after taking dictation for five years! Come to think of it, it has been exactly five years this month. Funny, it doesn't seem that long. I still enjoy it, too, most of the time.

Paul came back today from Texas where he attended an R.E.A. convention. He was gone about two weeks. Seems so nice to have him back. I really learned to appreciate him this time. Mr. Ripley, to whom I have to go for information when Paul's gone, nearly drives me mad! Either he gives me no answer at all or else one which, in my opinion, is all wrong. And then I wonder why I didn't just do it myself! One incident I shall have to tell you, even if it is a long story.

We had an order for 325 turnbuckle barrels originally scheduled for delivery Dec. 20. We had to change the schedule to Jan. 15 & then inefficiency & absenteeism messed things up & we couldn't meet that date. We had a stock of thousands of the darn things out there which the Govt. had agreed to purchase at 12 cents each on a contract termination, & I suggested to Ripley that we ought to ship some of those on this order. It could easily have been done, but, no, the market price is now 11 cents so rather than lose that penny apiece ($60 on the order) we just let that aircraft plant's assembly lines wait another two weeks. Without a doubt, any practical businessman would laugh at me for being concerned about it, but that's what I don't like about business! It has no sense of responsibility unless a profit is involved.

Gene, what did you think of [Arthur] Vandenberg's[14] speech? Darn nice for a Republican, don't you think?

I was quite surprised to get a letter from my best friend Jane [Haseltine Basse], advocating a negotiated peace. She lives in Seattle and her husband, an Army Sgt., is stationed near there. This is what she says: "What do you think of this rising feeling against unconditional surrender? I have a deep-seated idea like the Army people that the Allies are now sorry they ever made that statement. I can't quite see that the thousands of casualties are worth the price of such peace terms." Where does she get that "like the Army people," I wonder. What can I say, Gene? Will you tell me why you think it's necessary? That ought to be material for quite a letter.

Which reminds me, you don't need to worry if you don't hear from me for a while. It will be the mail service, for sure! And if you worry about finding news to write to me remember that everything about you is news to me. You could think of just about anything that's happened to you in the last 24 years & it would be more interesting than you think.

I'd surely like to meet your grandfather. If you think as much of him as I do of Franklin, he must be a wonderful man. I wonder sometimes, dear, if you like to plan, as I do, all the things we might do when you come back. It's fun to dream about even the impractical plans that couldn't possibly come true.

Much love, Marian

Perhaps it would be better to restate that question thus: Do you think lasting peace is impossible without unconditional surrender?

Jan. 27, '45

Hello dear,

I hope none of your fellow Marines razz you about getting a letter on such coy stationery. I wanted to show it to you, though, because I think it's such a clever idea. Each sheet has a different design. Ruth Borge, who used to be Rev. Hjortland's secretary, gave it to me.

Wish I had a little sailboat like that off the coast of Guam now.

I knew you would mention that tropical storm. Pretty good guess? Was that the article you meant you had given the intelligence officer?

The nights must be gorgeous! I'll bring my sailboat in to shore and sit under a palm tree with you. May I?

When you say H + 15 do you mean 15 minutes? It's too soon anyway. You're a fine one to be telling me not to feel patriotic! I saw something rather interesting about medical technician jobs in the WAC & have asked for further information. You may be sure I won't join unless there is something worthwhile in that field, though. I'd like something like occupational therapy—something constructive, humanitarian, so to speak.

Have you done any investigating of the accuracy of Time's reporting on the 3rd Division?

Margie sent me this piece of Coronet, "Into the Wild Blue Yonder." Will you send it back, please? I'd sort of like to keep it. Wish I could show it to Al. He'd love it! Margie, by the way, has decided not to come to Chicago. I guess June is leaving this week, so Murph & I will probably try to get a smaller apt. in this building. In any event, we'll be here until March 1.

Sunday eve: June and I went to see Katherine Dunham's "Tropical Revue" this aft. Those negroes can really dance! Some of them are quite beautiful, too. What kind of shows do the natives give over there? You were saying they were pretty good.

See you later, Gene.
Love, Marian

❧

Jan. 22, 1945
Central Pacific [Guam]

Dearest Marian,
    Time tonight to start a letter your way. I expect Edwards and Borrowman[15] in soon to go to the movie which is our primary pastime during the evenings. Borrowman is a Mormon and has been to a church conference today. I also went to church but it was extremely crowded and so I came back. The church in this area has somewhat of a history connected with it. Built by early missionaries, it was used by the natives, Americans and Japs. The latter stored ammunition therein and so the roof today shows straffing marks that look like .50 caliber (Probably that foolish Air Corps.) Incidently there is much that I could write concerning the AAF but no. They are doing a wonderful job here which practically everyone knows.
    Can't remember if I told you about seeing "Wilson"[16] last summer in New York but I think we talked about it that last day in Chicago. However I saw it again last night here at the movie and still think it's one of the greatest of all time and know definitely that I was thrilled as never before. Good night.

Later. Jan 23
    Received your letter last night with the article from the "Sun." Thanks—it confirms my ideas. I have passed it around and you have no idea what a sensation it caused. Everybody was up in arms ready to damn "We the Mothers." It really made me angry too but I am glad that the "Sun" gave it all that publicity. Don't you think that it was the best way to be handled. Had it been put on the back page nobody would have paid much attention even if they had seen it and all their underhanded work could continue. I would suggest a treason trial—the article is posted on the intelligence bulletin board at Edwards' suggestion.
    Other news is as follows—
    Ernie Pyle[17] is here and we may expect him at our place any time now. I'll let you know what develops. Wish he'd go on the next operation with us. "Time" of Jan. 8 finally arrived but only one copy is available to the officers. Thanks to you I had read previously the most important part. I liked very much the "miscellany" of that issue. My favorite of last year was the one on Napoleon and the lie detector. You probably remember.
    The article on Anita Colby[18] was excellent though particularly interesting because I had a chance to meet her and Jennifer Jones in New York last summer. If I haven't told you about that, persuade me—
    Time for the mail to go out so I'll stop for awhile.

The only regret in receiving your letters is the fact that I probably won't get one the next day.

Love, Gene

✧

Jan. 25, 1945

My dear Marian,

Today I am O.D. and putting in my tour of duty at the officers' club, drinking beer and writing letters. It was a very uneventful day as is becoming usual here. Saw a parade however which was quite impressive. About 10 fellows were given the DSC and silver and bronze star[s] for the usual bravery. They were from the 3rd Regiment of this division and ranged from Captains to Privates. Incidently the 3rd Reg took the worst beating and lost the most men in taking this place. You know something about the division as a combat team I suppose. There are 3 regiments in a div. and 3 battalions in a regiment and 3 companies in a battalion. This might help you keep things straight when I refer to them from time to time. The regiments of this division are the 3rd and 21st and part of the 9th. They are usually referred to as the being the 9rd Marines, 21st Marines, etc.

The above looks like a lecture and I hope you are not too bored.

Edwards is back from the movie and trying to annoy me. Everybody here is betting on where we will land. It's interesting and you should be here to listen to it. Incidently where do you think? Your letters are not censored of course and you can say anything —

That Marine gunner is quite happy these days as liquor can be had — also — his girl is here (an Army nurse) — also — his wife is getting a divorce. Good Heavens! What a life. He also has someone in Shanghai who he is looking forward to seeing if we ever get there.

I have to close now and inspect the guard. We have had a few scares lately. Goodnight darling and till next time.

Much love, Gene

✧

Jan. 28, 1945
Central Pacific

My dear Marian,

Your letter of the 17th arrived yesterday and I meant to answer it immediately, however I got tangled in the movie last night and this afternoon played volley ball and slept. Also have another date with Edwards and Merle (Borrowman) to go to the movie tonight so I don't know how far I'll get.

I don't know if I told about several of our officers getting assigned to a special M.P. detail to guard a someone who has arrived here—anyway they came back tonight to "snow" us with the swell deal they fell into. Among other things there are—hot & cold running water, a beautiful B.O.Q. [bachelor's officer quarters]—Army nurses galore—soft innerspring mattresses—all the liquor they can drink and so forth. Made us wonder as we wandered back to our tents, cots, dust etc. whether some people are just born lucky. They succeeded in picking three of the worst officers of our draft for that job. I'm not complaining because I couldn't have taken the job if offered it. It will be a duration job—at least—and certainly a godsend for somebody who doesn't desire combat.

Monday 3:32

I am in an extremely ugly mood because I wanted a letter from you today and none came. I don't blame you however.

There is much scuttlebutt about concerning the Russians and their drive on Berlin. Officially thru the press they are 98 miles but a fellow in the draft heard that Germany had sued for peace. It sounds too good to be true. Also the word is circulating that MacArthur asked the President to withdraw all Marines from the Pacific in hope the Japs would find it easier to surrender. Sounds very unlikely to me and much more like some Marine propaganda to build up Morale etc!

Found the chief enemy is boredom with the Japs a poor second. If they held mail call during an air raid I'm sure no one would be missing—least of all me. Don't know how long this peace and quiet will continue tho—incidentaly, if I don't write for sometime in the future you are to interpret it as being for the best—that is, I'll be busy and _not_ that we have ended corresponding again.

Despite the fact that there are 250 nurses on the island I have seen only 10 of them at that time I mentioned several weeks ago. Still haven't talked to any white woman since I left.

The "Rains" really came lately as we have had 3 days of nothing else. The camp is a sea of mud and water. I took a working party out yesterday and we were wet all day. Today I am all alone in the tent and slept till 11:00 AM this morning. The weather has been chilly and I have seen several field jackets around. I guess that I mentioned this before—but here goes again—these nights are beautiful—don't think that I ever have experienced anything like them. Perfect weather with a full moon and the usual waving palms—truly a romantic setting in most every respect. It amazes me that something they wrote about the So Pacific is really true.

The article from Hanffalize was, as you say, very well written. I had 2 years of French in College but would hesitate about pronouncing that name.

Time to quit again but I'll be back in a day or two—till then Much Love and please write often. I look forward to your letters very much. Gene

P.S. the clippings are <u>always</u> welcome.

I have meant to ask if you had any word from Franklin but I suppose you would have told me if you had.

I am inclined to agree with you concerning the "Pinks" attitude and outlook tho I haven't read any of S.L.'s books. Made me angry today to find several officers here rejoice in the M. Ward decision in the courts. I hate to see any man tell the U.S. government where to get off at. Practically all the letters I've censored today mention the Owassa case (spelling?) which you've probably heard of. Anyway it's about the women at the canning factory who aided the German prisoners to excape and subsequently were found in bed with them. Never have read such bitter letters.

If you like it I'll say it again, so long darling till tomorrow and

Much love, Gene

⚘

February 1, 1945
[Chicago]

Dearest Gene,

It would appear from this that Anita Colby didn't enjoy Time's article as much as you did. The Editor's comment is apt, don't you think. You hadn't told me about meeting her and Jennifer Jones in New York. By all means, do. I'm very much interested!

Speaking of clippings, I feel quite flattered to be supplying an occasional one for your intelligence bulletin board.

Have you seen Ernie Pyle yet? I'm anxious to hear what you think of him. I've been wanting to read his "Brave Men" but haven't had the opportunity.

Don't ask me to guess where the 3rd Division will land next. I'm no military expert, dear. I understand, though, that Gen. [Albert] Wedemeyer says the Japs expect a landing on the China coast & will not be disappointed. Perhaps Formosa first? Incidentally, I'm glad you explained the organization of a division. I had often wondered about it. Al never bothered to tell me such details. He thinks I know just as much as he does, bless him!

That fellow who was lost over in Italy a couple of months ago & whose sister works in our office is on his way home now. How I envy them! Hope I have a chance to talk to him.

Wasn't that wonderful news today about the prisoners who were rescued in the Philippines? It's not surprising that one of them died of a heart attack from the excitement. It's terribly tragic, though.

June is leaving the end of this week, for sure now. Marge and Ed [Dervishion], the couple upstairs, have been looking for a larger apt., so Murph and I hope to be able to trade with them. Theirs is just large enough for two.

Chicago is having a small blackout to conserve fuel. They've been conserving it so darn well at the office & here at home that I had to stay home with a cold again today. It makes me disgusted to be such a sissy!

Say that Marine gunner is quite a lad! I'll bet his wife will be better off without him.

Did I ever tell you about my friend, the Trotskyite, whose interests, he said, were Politics, Poetry, and Women—in that order. It's a long story. He used to visit some people we knew in Milw., & we had many a long and heated argument. He has millions of facts at his fingertips & we were invariably outclassed. I've been wishing I could ask him about the ELAS. Churchill, you know, has accused them of being Trotskyites & I wonder if it's true or if he said that to make them appear as obnoxious to Russia as they are to him. What do you think of this article in the Sun?

Getting back to my friend, (His name is Jim Brown.) he's a labor agitator. Used to be on John L. Lewis' staff & has been thrown out of Detroit by gangsters hired by Henry Ford. His appearance is revolting & so are his manners, but it's decidedly educational to talk to him. We're going to try to get him to come over sometime when he's in Chicago.

June just brought me a hot sling. Gee, it's good! Liquor makes me feel lonesome, though, sometimes. Wish you were here. That I would anyway, darling. Remember that couple on the train? "Nice kids!" They were right about you.

Love, Marian

❧

February 4, 1945

Dearest Gene,

I hope I can write a sensible letter in half an hour. There's just that much time before we are going down to Orchestra Hall to hear Anton Rubenstein, and after that we're going up to have dinner with Marge & Ed. So there is my Sunday, all used up. That's what I get for sleeping all morning.

June & I had a lot of fun yesterday. It won't sound very exciting, but people are always nicer to each other when they know they're going away, it seems, and then even silly things are fun. I made some brownies yesterday aft. & we ate all but four of them. They really were that good! Last night we went to a show. They had a short feature called "Brought to Action" filmed by the Navy & other branches of the service & portraying the naval battles in the Philippines. It was very interesting. I don't know why they always show the comedy directly after something like that. I never feel a bit like enjoying it.

What do you think Gene, of all this about [Henry] Wallace? Personally, I'd trust him with RFC funds further than any business man I know or have heard of. I've greatly admired him ever since I heard of his remark to Sidney Hillman in Hillman's luxurious suite at the Stevens. "You common men surely live well." That's classic!

My half hour is gone, dear. I hope I can do better next time. The trouble is I sit here and think about you instead of about the things I should write.

All my love, Marian

✛

February 5, 1945

Hello my darling,

I just came home after an evening downtown with a couple of gals & found two letters from you, the latest dated Jan. 31. In one you said you were in an ugly mood (dark brown with streaks of purple, no doubt) because you didn't get a letter from me. It made me feel so penitent that I decided to write right now — even tho it's 11:30 & past my bedtime.

I was very much interested in your story of the officers detailed to special M.P. duty. Doubtless you cannot reply, but I'm wondering if their charge was Adm. [Chester] Nimitz. I read somewhere recently that he planned to transfer his hq. to Guam & then was somewhat surprised when communiqués were reported from his new hq. "somewhere" in the Pacific. Is it a secret or is it not?"

We saw "30 Seconds over Tokyo"[19] tonight. It's a marvelous picture! I was a little surprised that I didn't shed a single tear—guess it was too exciting. Those shots of the take-off & the flight over Japan are just like being there yourself.

I wish you could have been with us last night at Marge and Ed's. Beside a good dinner (roast beef), we had a very interesting time. Ed has the place all cluttered up with radio & television equipment & likes nothing better than to talk about it. His newest joys are an oscilloscope & a radar unit such as is used on naval aircraft. No doubt you know all about those things but they were quite fascinating to me. The radar unit he did not attempt to explain to us, but we really had a time with oscilloscope. He connected it to the radio & also to a microphone so we could see how our voices look. He has a recording that's just a long squeal graduated from high to low frequency. He played that (somewhat to Marge's displeasure) & varied the range, etc.—the etcetera being the stuff I have forgotten. From that we went into a question-answer series on television.

I actually acquired a fairly good understanding of the principles of its operation, although I doubt that I could make it sound logical to anyone else.

That word etcetera reminds me of a poem by Ogden Nash. It's called "Schizophrenia," I believe. Do you know it? If not, remind me to send it to you. It's not long and it's really good!

The concert we went to yesterday was Artur Rubenstein, the pianist, not Anton. I never know which is which. He played an all-Chopin recital. I love the stuff!

It's amazing, dear, how easy it is to write a letter when there's something to write about or, especially, one to answer. I do look forward to your letters so much, Gene. I hate to think of there being any long intervals when you are unable to write. Guess there's nothing we can do about that, however.

When are you going to send some snapshots?

Much love, Marian

❈

February 8, '45

Hello dear,

I read this article on Russia last night & decided I would have to send it to you today to be sure you'd have a chance to read it. It is quite profound, don't you think? There is no aspect of the world's problems that concerns me more.

I wish you could read shorthand so that, when I have to stay at the switchboard, I could write to you without worrying about people looking over my shoulder. This notebook provides a fair camouflage, though.

The mail man will be around here soon so I'll have to cut this short. I'll write you a long, long letter tonight.

Love, Marian

❈

Feb. 9, 1945

Hello Sweetheart,

This is a day later than I promised, so I hope the plane will be a little faster. Honestly, this has been such a busy week I can't believe it's Friday night already.

It seems a little silly to be sending you this advertisement, but I thought you might like to see this picture of your predecessors, the original Marines. Pretty, aren't they? Or does that make you angry?

The copy of the "Leatherneck" came today. It's an excellent magazine. I have spent more of the evening than I should have, reading it. Those illustrations of the landings on Guam are very good. I was also quite interested in the article about the Marine Barracks at Klamath Falls, Ore. I think we must have been there when I was a child & we lived in Spokane. Either that or Dad has been there often. He used to do construction work in schools during the summer for the company he worked for out there.

I think that story about MacArthur asking the Pres. to take all the Marines out of the Pacific is a riot. Not that the Japs might not find it easier to surrender, but it's just too silly an idea to take the crack troops out of the field right in the middle of a war! Either someone had a bad dream or MacArthur is crazy. Ainit? (As they say in Milwaukee.)

That Marine pride is contagious, dear. The two girls with whom I went to the show Mon. night were talking about how conceited Marines are & said they thought Marines were not as nice & certainly no better fighters than the Army & Navy. I nearly bit my tongue to keep from losing my temper. It wasn't worth arguing, though. They just can't stand to be outclassed. When Al got his commission, Betty [Beeker] said she had never seen a 2nd Lt. who wasn't arrogant! But when her brother was commissioned several months later, he was still the same sweet boy. Oh, such <u>people</u>!

I've asked Mother to send you "Flight to Arras," so you'll probably get it in a month or so. I'll be anxious to know how you like it. You don't need to return it. Just add it to the collection of mystery stories over there or something.

Thank you for answering the questions in that letter. I'm beginning to think my rebuke was probably not justified as you may not have rec'd all my letters. Did you get the one I sent from Wittenberg sometime ago with the poem about Saipan? As it was written by a Marine officer, I rather thought you'd make some comment.

Also, I wonder if you rec'd the letter in which I asked where you sailed from—or is that still unmentionable?

Here's a brand new question. Is Merle Borrowman one of the fellows you knew at Marquette? You've talked about him & Edwards, & I'm just curious. One of the not so admirable feminine traits—

I don't blame those fellows for being bitter about the Owasso incident. (I don't know how to spell it, either.) That isn't malicious conduct, though; it's just Stupidity. Don't you think so? The average factory girl just doesn't know better because she can't see any farther outside her own personal world than those damn Republicans who criticize Roosevelt for the W.M.C. controls[20] which sometimes interfere with their seeking of personal profit. That I have been wanting to say ever since Wed. night when I had dinner with a few of said Republicans, some girls from the office.

I know how you feel about the Mont. Ward[21] deal. From this article in Time, it would appear the Judge was not too happy about it, either. I would like to know whether he was truly being conscientious or whether his reluctance was purely for the purpose of keeping his bread buttered on the right side, being a Roosevelt appointee.

A rather long and vague train of thought here brings me to recalling this witticism I read recently: "The difference between a prejudice & a conviction is that you can talk about a conviction without becoming angry." Well said, isn't it? A sobering influence in a heated argument.

We had a telegram for June tonight saying her application has been accepted at Western Reserve. She's visiting her mother in Sheboygan now. We placed a call for her and are waiting now for her to call back. She'll be so pleased. I'm glad she can go. It will be a good thing for her.

This is really a long letter. I'd better say goodnight, dear.

With love, Marian

⚜

February 11, 1945

Hi, honey —

Here are some pictures of our Army-Navy E party. I hope you'll enjoy them.

Reading from left to right on the first picture are my friend, Colonel Peterka, A/C., Lt. David Ross, U.S.N., and John Brown Cook, President, R.E.Co. (Reliable Electric). Isn't the Colonel's mustache awful! You can see, too, that he doesn't take calisthenics.

On the group picture, there are not many people I know. The girl on my right (left as you look at the picture) is Greta. She doesn't like to have her picture taken; so she engaged someone behind us in urgent conversation at that point. Darn it! The rather large woman in the first row is Marion Martin, the switchboard operator whom I relieve. The woman to my left (Murph says she looks like a rabbit) went on a week-long spree after this party. She is really a very nice person & one of the most conscientious workers in the office. I felt sorry for her.

My dear little boss is not on this picture. He was on only one of all those they took and then way off on the edge of the film, scowling at the floor!

Well that's enough of that. I ought to go to bed. Last night I jokingly suggested that Murph & her Captain bring me a Martini when they came home. They did — but I'm sure there were at least six instead of one. We had a gay time. Write soon, dear.

Love, Marian

❖

February 14, 1945

Dear Lt. Sweetheart,

Will you be my Valentine? I'm glad you like this salutation because I do too. The only trouble is, when you are promoted, I'll have to change it to Capt. Sweetheart, and that sounds just like Capt. Midnight. Guess I'll have to find a funny paper and see if that is good or bad. I don't even know what kind of character he is.

Speaking of Captains, we've been having more fun with Murph's friend, Capt. Bauer. When he calls on the phone, he can't tell which one of us answers; so we play tricks on him every once in a while. It's the funniest thing! I can't understand why he can't tell which is which. Last night they took me to the show with them & also a Lt. Rossi, who works with Bauer. We saw "Our Hearts were Young and Gay". It's a cute picture. Did you read the book?

Rossi double-dates with Murph & Ed all the time. He's engaged to a girl neither of them likes. He had quarreled with her last night, so Ed invited him to come with us to cheer him up. I don't know if it helped much, but I know the rest of us had a good time.

I got a kick out of your "taking a poll" on the subject of unconditional surrender. (That phrase "a kick out of" always bothers me. I had a friend in Milw. who used to say "out from" instead of "out of" & we kidded her about it so much that it doesn't sound right to me either way now.)

Well, anyway, I wrote a long letter to Jane yesterday and scolded her for imitating "We the Mothers," even though her statements were not so rash.

Isn't this article about the eggs in Chungking a prize? I like Annalee Jacoby. Those dispatches she sends with a date line, 250 words censored, and then "Well, I tried," aren't bad either. She must have a good sense of the dramatic.

I just found the article about Vandenberg's speech, so I'll send it, too.

Goodnight, darling. See you later.

Love, Marian

P.S. It just occurred to me—I'll bet every letter you censored today started exactly like this one. Too bad I couldn't think of an original way to say it.

❖

Feb. 3, 1945
3rd Division [Guam]

My darling Marian,

Today is Sunday and supposedly a day of rest and all that. However this morning we had a rather stiff conditioning hike and I just finished taking some shots. We also had our clothes impregnated against brush lice or Tsutsugamki, a Japanese pest that is supposed to be almost deadly. It's found on several islands where the Japs have been. Don't know much about it but someone said "Time" ran an article on it lately. The doctors are generally "snowed" too.

Received your letter of about the 25th. I have read it several times but better check again to see if there are any questions.

Concerning Unconditional Surrender—Everyone here (I made a poll) is of the opinion we should stand on our original demand and get it. However exactly what it implies (or rather what a negotiated peace implies) nobody is quite sure. As I wrote to my grandfather several days ago, we out here know at first hand that there can be no compromise with the Japs. Why the government should believe that they can trust the Japanese imperials any more than we can trust the Jap soldier, is beyond me. To offer them anything more than their lives is pure folly in my estimation. That means unconditional surrender. If their future intentions are peaceful, they should be satisfied to give in to those terms. Certainly nobody here wishes to fight again in a few years. I hope that the people don't sabotage the government again like they did in 1920. Negotiated peace smells too much like a modern form of "isolationism." If the feeling exists and persists it won't be long before some congressman takes up the cry "as the will of the people" and demand that the government retract its peace conditions. That will be a sad day but not too surprising to me. My faith in individuals is still practically non-existant at least in political matters. "Wilson" proved that and made me more cynical than ever—oh well—There is something extremely fascinating about politics and yet it is a thankless job if you fight on the peoples' side.

I did not read Vandenberg's speech however I do remember that I was terribly impressed with one he made about election time.

Time to close for now but I'll write soon again. That "Dear Lt. Sweetheart" sounded on welcome ears.

Perhaps we should have known each other better—um!

Love, Gene

2

"I hope you're all right, dear . . ."

BY THE TIME *I joined the Third Marine division in early 1945 the war had moved from the South Pacific to north of the Marianas Islands. Guam had been captured by the 3rd the previous July, and from its airfield B-29 bombers could reach the Japanese homeland 1,500 miles away. For the first time in the war the United States could regularly destroy industrial plants and seaports, and firebomb buildings. Yet as our bombers made their runs, they were harassed by Japanese fighter planes based on Iwo Jima, which was halfway to Toyko and which* Time *[19 February 1945] called a "pimple in the Pacific," where there were three airfields and a radar station. In January and early February, the small island was increasingly the target of both air force bombers and naval shelling. When my letters abruptly stopped, Marian feared I was with the Marine landing force the Japanese reported on Iwo Jima.*

February 17, 1945
[Chicago]

My darling Gene,

How are you? It seems so long since I've heard from you. Your last letter was dated about Feb. 3. I've been wondering today if your Division might have made the landings the Japanese have reported on Iwo Jima. I'm saying all my prayers for you, dear—just in case.

Are you pleased with the results of the Crimea Conference?[22] Of course the Tribune says, "Roosevelt surrendered to Stalin." That dirty McCormick would probably have had Russia declaring war on us if he'd been there! I think it's marvelous they've (the Big Three) been able to work together in such harmony.

Gene, I have a weighty problem to discuss with you tonight. I shall probably have to decide what to do before you answer, but it will help to tell you about it anyway. Did I tell you about these medical lab. technician jobs in the Wac on which they've been advertising for recruits? I sent in a request for information

& last night a Sgt. & a Wac Corporal came over to explain it. The work really sounds very interesting—if I could be sure of getting into that particular field. I've always liked chemistry & math, so I think I'd enjoy a job like that. After 6 weeks basic training, they send you to school four months, after which you are assigned to a hospital. At this point, they say, you can pretty well choose the hospital you'd prefer.

There are two distinct disadvantages. First, mother and dad would have a fit! I'm going home next weekend or the one after & will see what they say. Second, and really more of a problem to my conscience, is the fact that I could no longer be free to go where I pleased when I felt like it. That really seems an awful disadvantage to me (particularly when I think of your coming home and the possibility of Franklin's coming back) and yet I know it is very selfish. What do you think?

I haven't found out yet whether or not overseas service is voluntary. If not, I just couldn't enlist because my dad would be heartbroken. In any event it would be six to eight weeks before I'd enter. I dislike intensely the idea of being in the Army, but I feel that to do a job like that of a lab. technician would be a great satisfaction.

Enough of this—it is perhaps unkind of me to trouble you with the subject at all, especially as mother and dad will very likely pronounce an emphatic "No," and that will be the end of that!

I'm so glad it's Saturday night. I don't know what we've been so busy with all week, but I feel as if time has been on a roller coaster. I even had to save all the newspapers until today to read them.

Goodnight, Lt. Sweetheart.
Love, Marian

⁂

Feb. 20, 1945

Dearest Gene,

I was very much relieved yesterday to read that the Marines invading Iwo Jima were of the 4th and 5th Divisions, although I could imagine how impatient you would be at having been left behind.

When I came home, your letter of the 10th was here, and I was glad to hear that you are watching for sailboats. If it were possible, I'd surely bring one over.—Well, it was a nice dream anyway, wasn't it?

I hope you enjoy these cartoons. The first one reminds me of Franklin. He sent me a whole suitcase full of letters to keep for him. He didn't want to send them home, as Mother would be sure to read them all. I shouldn't laugh at him, though. I hate to throw letters away myself.

Don't you think this editorial on the inter-American conference is intelligent? When I read something like that, it makes me realize how illogical my own thinking often is.

For example (in quite a different field), that idea about being a Wac medical technician. I am really sorry I wrote you about that Sunday. It wasn't a good idea at all.

I was amused at your complaint about having to censor your own mail. It must be awfully hard to write sometimes because I know that when your mind is absorbed with some very pressing or interesting situation, it is almost impossible to think of any thing else. Everything seems trivial in comparison. Franklin used to complain of that, too, when he was in Italy, & said that the one thing they lived & breathed & talked about they couldn't write a word of.

I had a letter from Peg tonight & she asked me to say hello to you. Ray, her P.F.C., has just arrived in France. I enjoy her letters so much. She takes everything in such deadly earnest. She said she was going to a meeting Sun. "designed to put the church back of the social forces moving to create world peace." When I thought of the little churches in Galesville, it just struck me so funny! I do think her qualities are excellent for a teacher, though, as high school students need to have their interest primed a good deal, and that enthusiasm of hers can't help but brush off a little at least!

Well darling, I'd better be off to do a little reading. I've had a book here for two weeks & only finished half of it. Time is so fleeting when you don't want it to be!

All my love, Marian

⚘

February 22, 1945

My darling Gene,

On the other side of this clipping of Ernie Pyle's column from the Marianas, you will see what the headlines were this morning. When we read the casualty reports last night, I told Greta I was awfully glad you were not there—and this morning, very probably, there you are! I wish I could tell you how deeply concerned I am, dear. I don't know what to say, or how, except that you mean so very much to me.

It seems almost callous to talk about anything else—other things seem trivial too,—but perhaps by the time this letter reaches you, you will be glad to think of something entirely peaceful.

That book I've been reading is very good. It is Irving Stone's historical novel, "Immortal Wife" about John Charles Fremont and his wife Jessie.

Perhaps you have read reviews of the book. Being a student of history, doubtless you will know who Fremont was. I have forgotten so much of American history, I did not know until I came to that part of the story that he was the Republican candidate for president in 1856, defeated by James Buchanan. The Democrats offered him the nomination first and he declined because it would have been necessary for him to compromise on the slavery issue & he was definitely anti-slavery. That is only one of the varied phases of his career. Besides the history and adventure, the book is a marvelous love story. Theirs was truly a love that consisted "not only in gazing at each other, but in looking outward together in the same direction." Incidentally, Fremont's career would confirm your idea that politics is a thankless job when you work for the people's interests, but it also gives encouraging evidence that the task is not wholly one in which worthwhile accomplishments are impossible.

It's getting late, so I'll have to say good-night.

With love, Marian

✤

United States Navy
Feb. 10, 1945

Dearest Marian,

Please excuse the several days' delay but it couldn't be helped. It will happen again soon and I don't know when I will get a chance to write again. Had an unexpected mail call today and a letter from you—rather I should say 3 of them. One was the "Sun" issue and the other the notification of your purchase of the "Atlantic Monthly." As with everything you send this way I appreciated it. Many thanks darling.

This letter is going to be utterly devoid of any news of <u>any kind</u> from here because of censorship regulations. We do censor our own mail but it's on the honor system so that makes it somewhat worse. Sometimes I wish I were an enlisted man—then I'd write everything I cared to and let the "horrible censors" cut it out. Also this stupid stationery is a necessity—it will only be for a limited time.

Sunday Feb. 11
Today at breakfast we received the news. It consists of a typewritten copy which has been received over the radio. Washington sends out a "Press" almost constantly in plain English, and this is copied by Navy radiomen and outposts—hence the news—understand?

Meant to write on and on but it'll have to wait. Mail is going out and I'd better get this off.

I'll answer your questions later as there are quite a few of them. Guess that you mentioned the Army nurses here once. As someone so aptly put it — Never have so many got so little from so few —

Much love, Gene

P.S. I'm watching for sailboats —

❋

Feb. 13, 1945

My dear,

Probably when you receive this there will be evidences of spring in the air back in Chicago. Haven't much hope of getting mail away for some time but I'll keep writing. Still am not sure what we are allowed to write about so I'll have to let that go until I do locate someone who knows. This censorship is a pain and certainly takes some of the glow away that is, the thrill of writing home about it. I hope that I have a good memory and can eventually tell you what goes on —

Feb. 14,

Just finished reading the Feb. 5 issue of "Time." It's most interesting to note their interpretations of events here in the Pacific. We have also received stacks of newspapers from home which are several months old but still eagerly read. Your Christmas card finally arrived which you mailed December 10. Airmail takes about 8 days and regular mail 2 months. I also received your first letter you wrote Oct. 30. If nothing else, it proves that mail finally reaches a destination if given enough time. I do agree with your definition of "Love" most whole-heartedly. Can't imagine you (or me) gazing into someone's eyes for indefinite periods of time. Having many interests in common is probably just another way of saying it. I have always had a fear of that "Post Honeymoon" period when the realization becomes suddenly evident that after all "she" is a woman and you a man.

Still haven't answered some of your questions, but your letters are on file and I'll get around to it soon. Till later then.

Much love, Gene

❋

Feb. 18, 1945
Pacific Area

Dearest Marian,

Well now it can be told officially that I am, as you might have suspected, aboard ship going into combat. It isn't as dramatic as it seems but nevertheless I am really getting a thrill out of it. Seems strange to have a ringside seat and actually play a part in the real thing. Certainly anyone's heart would skip to see all this power.

Can't say where we're going but you will know probably before this letter reaches you. Perhaps sometime in the future I can give you the real inside story but at present it'll have to wait.

There was an interruption as I looked up and found myself in the midst of Church services. There sure is good attendance the closer we get to—. Have been studying maps and intelligence reports daily for the last week—they are really complete.

This pen is terrific—not mine but one I borrowed from Ossowski. He's a fellow Lt. from my outfit and a super all-American football player. Oss has the distinction of playing in the Rose Bowl game for 2 straight years for 2 different teams—Oregon State and U.S.C. I like him a lot.

Strange things do happen. I met two fellows I graduated with from Marquette here in the 9th Regiment, 1st Bat. which I am attached to.

I think I told you that there is a radio station on the island I just left. Well anyway they present songs as requested by the people back home and oddly enough, the other day a song was requested for someone here by a girl I dated a few times back home. Strange?

We received mail before we left and included among mine were some letters from you. The last one was about your friend the "Radio man." Enjoyed the part about the oscilliscope. We fooled around with one at Monmouth quite a bit. How does he manage to get Radar equipment?

Feb. 19, 1945
0905

Suppose that you'll be reading of this operation soon back home. It's Sunday there now- we have not landed and don't know whether we will or not now.

This may all be very confusing but maybe you can untangle it. Bear in mind I am in the 3rd Division.

Feb. 20 aboard Ship

I have been trying to write a coherent letter but that seems almost impossible with the many interruptions as the latest dope arrives. The "word" changes momentarily.

Been meaning to tell you about the food since we got aboard ship. It simply has been wonderful in every respect. I am sure that nobody in the states has had any better. They are probably preparing us for a session of "K" or "C" rations. We have had fresh meat every meal and everything to go with it that could be desired. It's amazing! Movies have been extraordinarily good too and in every other respect they seem to want to give us a good sendoff.

Wish I could tell you more of what is coming in over the radio about the operation but can't. It has been thrilling altho we have played no part in it so far. *[letter ends]*

Marian read about the campaign in newspapers like the Chicago Sun *and Chicago* Tribune *and by seeing official motion picture film shown in local theatres; the film was taken and narrated by accredited newsmen who worked side by side with the assault troops. At Iwo Jima the bloody story was told by Robert Sherrod, who wrote for the Associated* Press, Time *and* Life *magazines. When Joe Rosenthal took his famous flag raising photograph on top of Mt. Suribachi, I was aboard ship getting ready to land. While I wanted to let Marian know what was happening, I didn't have time to write letters. Yet I knew this was "history" and I was there. So for the first week I made notes on any available piece of paper, including 3 by 5 inch pages from a spiral notebook, rough gray cardboard packing material, and one long entry on the back of a label for "Queen's Taste" green beans, packed by the Rush Canning Co. of Cassville, Mo. I would later send these to Marian.*

Feb. 24- 0800 landed with the 1st Bn. 9th Marines—mortar fire close—dove in shell hole with dead Jap—scared—orders to go to first airfield—shelling heavy on our location—dump afire 50 yards north—shell hit 10 yards from foxhole—worked all night.

Feb. 25. 12 hour break, still shelling beach, work on advance ammunition dump,—shelling occasionally, foxhole under Jap Zero—dud landed ten yards from where I was standing—fairly good night's sleep.

Feb. 26. 0830 back to ammo dump—still shelling beach and advance dump where we're at—*first A.A.F.;* plane lands, recon. type—brother! do they look good—seabees at work on airfield no. 1—about 200 wrecked Jap planes on airfield—

Feb. 27. almost froze to death last night—still shelling beach and ammo dump—4th Marines [division] held up on ridge for 5 days now—terrific arty barrage today—Japs still hold high ground—hot coffee this morning tasted good—getting used to it now but it's still hell—

Feb. 28. 1000—artillery still falling on dump—6 men wounded here last night—terrific arty barrage this morning—3 Jap prisoners so far in stockade—M.P.'s to prevent Marines from killing them—. Planes dive bombing & rockets galore—still unloading ammo—nice clear day—wonder how war in east is going—had a little hot food last night for first time

Mar. 1. 1100—first fighter lands—still shelling dump—got the 5th Div. dump last night—Borrowman and Edwards landed at last—will be replacements—Much ack-ack fire—cub shot down—progress still slow—Lt. Glass killed—casualties heavy in 3rd Div and 4th div—5th easy—supposed to have captured a Jap general, doubt it—

⚜

Mar 1, 1945
Iwo Jima

Dearest Marian,

So much to say but it will have to wait. I am OK (or am I?) Right now we are located on the southern shore of hell with the 3rd Div. Rec'd mail today and <u>thanks</u>. More later about that—

Will you save some news clippings on this affair and send them. I've been here 6 days and it seems longer. Could use a hot bath and sleep but like other things it will have to wait. Don't mean to sound dramatic. Till later.

My love, Gene

Mar. 2. still shelling airfield and ammo dump—took 15 of my men for replacements—Henrickson shot—

Mar. 3, 1945 I.J. shells still falling near ammo dump and airfield—several transports landed on field and a fighter—also dropping supplies by air—island should be secured soon—army started to move in—Edwards and Borrowman still back—made 1st Lt. today, not Edwards yet—flame throwers working on pillboxes in front of us—3rd div has casualties—beautiful day for dive bombing—

March 4, 1945 Iwo Jima. still shelling dump and airfield—infantry officers gone to front but not many specialists—9th day today—haven't had my clothes off yet—Discovered 3 Japs on beach still alive and had to blast them out—mail again—inspected some fox holes of Japs—8 feet deep and lined with stones and steel doors—3rd div has heavy casualties but still moving ahead—hope to secure soon and get out of this hell—

March 5, 1945 1300—fighter just landed in flames—gunner killed—just heard Lt. Pace and Lt. Ray [23] killed—tough blow—from 28th—still the shelling continues—the bastards wont give up—we're all damn tired—must be 100 dive bombers in air over north end of island—a B-29 landed and several transports—army started moving in—

March 6—The Army air corps is here! Do they look good! 15 'Black Widows' night fighters just landed and also 50 'air cobras'—What a change in this place from the first night! Am beginning to smile again—big push on today by the 3rd—should secure island soon—shaved for the 2nd time in 13 days today—had a nice beard. Marines wont forget this place.

⚘

Mar 8, 1945

My dear Marian,

Just finished your last 2 letters from the 28th and many thanks for the clippings and so forth—especially the "so forth." Been wanting to write you an intelligent and worthwhile letter for so long but things have been happening but can only refer you to "Time" of about the 23th of Feb.

Right now I am located in a Jap pill box which is made of reinforced concrete. We have our foxhole right in it, but can't dig too deep for fear of locating the 15 dead Japs and 10 dead Marines buried here. Things have been rough and there were times I would have settled for another 41 hours of "gazing." But now things have been pretty well under control the last few days. The Japs have been here since 1887 and it looks like they spent most of the time digging—their fortifications are really out of this world—literally—Tokyo Rose[24] said that after this operation "you can put the 3rd division in a telephone booth." I wonder—

Been working at the 1st airfield regularly and really felt a little jealous when the A.A.C. moved in—somehow I feel as tho it's mine. I have not been at the front since about the 7th day but those 7 days were enough. We still get a little shelling but it's nothing compared to those first days. I was really scared for the first time in my life. An artillery shell landed 10 feet from where I was standing but fortunately turned out to be a dud. I hope this doesn't all seem too dramatic, but practically everything here has an air of unrealness.

We were thankful the Navy was standing by and the Air Corps looked mighty good to us. However bombing and shelling had <u>little effect</u> on the Jap positions due to the depth of their fortifications. It does keep them punch drunk but the infantry has to move in and blast them out. One pill box has been burned out for 6 straight days and every night there are more Japs that infiltrate back and take up their positions.

I hope to go back to—after awhile and it will seem like heaven then. Had my clothes off and took a bath for the first time in 13 days. That was out of a helmet.

Must close now and get back to work. We are on for 12 hours and off 12 hours.

Your letters are a constant source of enjoyment—as are the thoughts of you. Only hope I'll be able to write as many after this thing clears up. I am planning on sending some notes which were written day by day—hope you can get something out of them. They are dated. For awhile then, Much love and please keep writing.

Gene

P.S. Hate only to say that "I like" the clippings but they usually aren't around to comment on when I'm writing a letter. I like Wallace too—can't help thinking that Wilson's enemies said he was an idealist too. The cartoon on mail lovers was good—I'm one myself.

❖

March 10, 1945
Iwo Jima
(Sulphur Island)

My darling,

I am sitting at the water's edge here on the beach and it is a perfect day. There are about 50 ships anchored off shore and about 75 planes in the air. I have moved from the ammo. dump down to the beach and it really is getting to be tolerable around here. Hot coffee for these cold nights and I even have found a mattress for my foxhole. Mail comes in regularly by air, (PB4Y's) and all in all we are beginning to appreciate the little things again that everyone always takes for granted. It's wonderful, except when I think of the casualties which are terrific. Of the 50 officers that were aboard ship with me (first bat. 9 marines) more than 10 have been killed and 30 wounded.

I am still waiting for a comm. assignment but as yet it hasn't arrived. Supplies are moving in fast and we are kept busy. The Japs have been cornered on the north end of the island and most of the progress in the last 10 days has been made by the 3rd Div. We hope to secure soon and go back to our base and let the Army take over. That can't come any too soon.

Jap prisoners say that they have been told that Japan has practically won the war except there was a flotilla of Marines at sea that were so hungry that they might land on Iwo Jima. Also they were told that if they held out here they would go back to Japan and everything would be fine. Of course they all believed it. It's no wonder they fight like madmen.

I have been getting your letters regularly including some you wrote last December and sent by regular mail. It takes about 2-3 months that way. The last letter was dated Feb. 27.

I notice that this stationery is really dirty and rugged looking. It is rare here altho they do furnish all the "V" mail we want. I don't like it and it certainly doesn't go any faster.

Food has been good and there are plenty of cigarettes which go at the rate of 2 packs a day now. Been working 12 hour shifts which accounts for it. Water is still a problem and we'd give a lot for a hot bath and some clean sheets again.

We are still located at the pillbox and have a room about 20 ft. square now. The opening is our fireplace. Sometimes the smell isn't too good as below there are some dead Japs and Marines.

Have to close now and get back to work. Mail call is still the No 1 attraction especially when there is a letter from you. So long &

Much love darling, Gene

While I was on the beach on Iwo Jima, Marian was going through Franklin's military belongings in Wittenberg. Her mother had carefully washed and pressed his uniform, and it was hanging in his bedroom ready for his return. Marian was particularly interested in the flight book in which Franklin recorded his last few flights from the Italian airfields. Although it was now eight months since he had been declared missing, she and her parents hoped he had been found safe and was being hidden by Romanian partisans.

February 24, 1945
[Chicago]

Hello Lt. Sweetheart,

Your letter of the 14th came yesterday, & I was so glad to get it that I sat & gloated over it for half an hour. I had thought there wouldn't be another one for weeks—until, as you said, there were evidences of spring in the air, which is definitely not the case at present.

I do feel almost as light-hearted as spring today, though, because I'm going to Wittenberg for the weekend. I don't know why I should be so glad—just the prospect of seeing <u>clean</u> snow and open spaces, I guess.

In your letter you said you could not imagine either of us gazing into someone's eyes for an indefinite period of time. I agree with you, and yet I have to laugh when I think of those two days on the train and how almost exclusively we did just that! Fun, wasn't it? Guess you could hardly call that an "indefinite" period of time.

I'll have to go down to the station now or I won't have that extra half hour's time you (& I) like to have to catch trains.

I hope you're all right, dear.
Much love, Marian

❖

February 27, 1945
[Chicago]

My darling Gene,

I had planned to spend the whole evening writing to you as there seems to be so much to tell you. However, Marge came down to tell us that they are all set to trade apartments with us April 1, and she stayed until just now, which is 10:30. I am surely glad that apt. deal is settled, though. As you may not be getting any mail for some time, I'll give you our new number now. It will be Apt. 1507, same building.

On the train home Saturday, I rode with a girl whose husband is also in the 3rd Division, so the Marines were the topic of enthusiastic conversation for many miles. I did not ask her husband's rating, but he and a couple of others are in charge of some sort of repair shop in the 3rd Engineers. His name is Vernon Schulz. Her name is Helen. She's a very pretty girl with dark hair and blue eyes (which I like).

It was really nice in Wittenberg. They have a lot of snow. The drifts are piled high & make the town look sort of like a Christmas card.

I was in Milw. yesterday aft. & eve. & came down here on the North Shore. A crowd of sailors got on at Kenosha. They'd been having a gay evening and were in the mood for song! After they finished "Anchors Aweigh," one of them said, "Now let's sing a civilian song," and started with "In the halls of Montezuma." I had to laugh, but at the same time I was wishing there were at least one Marine there to defend the cause!

I shall try tomorrow night to write a less hurried & more intelligent letter. Until then—

All my love, Marian

✬

February 28, 1945

Dear Lt. Sweetheart,

Do you know that today we have known each other a year & 10 days, exactly. That makes it sound quite respectable, doesn't it? Seven days out of 375 isn't a very good percentage though. It seems longer than that to me—longer than the 7 days, I mean. Postal service is a wonderful thing!

At home this weekend I spent quite a lot of time going through Franklin's things. There were so many of interest that it didn't make me feel too sad—except that to see his uniforms hanging in his closet made his absence a little harder to take than it has been.

There were copies in his files of his flight records, and he had saved clippings from "Stars and Stripes" telling of many of the missions on which he had been. It was enlightening as the only one he had ever mentioned was the big bombing of Cassino. Some of the other places he'd been were Vienna, Wiener-Neustadt, Zagreb, Belgrade, Cannes, Toulon, & Rome. I wonder if it seemed as exciting as it sounds. "Too damn exciting!" he would say. His flight record for the last two days looks something like this:

Date	Time	Type of Plane	No. of Landings	Flight
9	3:10	F-38 J	1	Foggia 3; Cannes; Foggia 3.
10	1:50	F-38 J	X	Foggia 3; Ploesti; Missing.

That X gives me an awfully empty feeling. The F-38J, though, looks good. When we were in L.A., Frankin used to talk about "the new J's" with enthusiasm. It was a great day when they'd have a chance to fly one. Apparently they flew nothing else the last two months at Foggia.

There were some pictures of the club they built and the other fellows in his squadron, which were fun to see. I found the cameos Mother thought were missing. They are lovely. There are two about the right size for rings.

I hope you don't mind my talking about all this so much, dear. It makes him seem a little less far away.

Paul has gone to Buffalo this week. It's a good thing because I am so busy as it is that if he were here, too, I'd never finish. I really enjoy it, though, even when I lose my temper and want to throw everything in the waste basket.

That reminds me—when Paul is gone & Ripley has to come over to my desk quite frequently, he invariably steps in the wastebasket & stumbles all the way back to his own. I have the worst time trying to look sympathetic.

News of the campaign on Iwo Jima is on the second page of the newspapers as the more recent advances on Cologne have the spotlight. I'm sure I have never bought & read so many newspapers as I have this last week. I've discovered the news is not so much the same in all of them as you'd expect. It probably seems that way because I am as much interested in the relatively minor incidents as in the actual progress of the battle, and, of course, each correspondent relates a different story. I'll send you a few clippings as you may be interested to know what is being reported here.

Good night darling.

Love, Marian

❧

March 2, 1945

Hello my dear,

I really haven't much to say tonight, but wanted to write to you anyway & also to send these clippings.

I wish I knew you well enough to be able to judge how you might be reacting to what you have been experiencing these last several days. When I think of how you might change, it seems I may be writing to someone who is even more a stranger than you are—although you've never seemed that. What I'm trying to say is that I want very much to write letters you will enjoy, and it is difficult to know how.

I dreamed the other night that you came home. It was wonderful. Speaking of dreams, here is a poem Franklin had which I dearly love—

"As you go dreaming,
Save a dream for me
A dream of gay, inconsequential
things,
When all we were to know was yet
to be
And young illusion colored
all our springs.
Yes, while you dream, I hope that
you recall
A moon that dipped across an
April sky . . .
That tiny inn we sought when
night would fall . . .

The candlelight . . . the wine . . .
and You and I . . .
There is an end to laughter in the
rain,
There is an end to shadowed
streets we knew
Yet as the past cries out to me
again,
It is a simple thing I ask of you.
As you go dreaming,
Save a dream for me . . .
Spun of the gossamer of
used to be!"

Tis many a dream I save for you, darling, and many a wordless prayer.

Marian

⚜

March 4, 1945

Dearest Gene,

Murph invited Capt. Bauer over for dinner this aft., & he brought along some beer. Consequently I am sleepy.

It was such a nice sunshiny day, I was going to walk down Mich. Ave. & window-shop. I had hardly gone four blocks when some old character came along & wanted to "window shop" with me. To keep from being rude & losing my good humor trying to get rid of him, I had to turn around & come back home. I maintain that when you can't walk down the street unmolested in broad day light, the male element is really degenerate! Disgusting!

Yesterday afternoon I went shopping in Evanston with one of the older women in the office. She lives with her sister, who is ill and rather irritable, & I feel sorry for her. She seemed to enjoy the aft. — I hope she did.

I found a good piece of navy blue wool to make a skirt. You should see all the stuff I have to sew. Murph and I are going to rent a sewing machine for a month & make all our spring and summer clothes. I think it's a lot of fun. It's also a great satisfaction to my thrifty nature — or what there is left of it.

The other night I read a condensation of a book called "On Education" by Sir Richard Livingstone. It was very good & I thought that since you are interested in teaching, you might like to read the book. If I can find it, I'll send it to you.

The papers said several tons of mail were delivered to Iwo this last week. I hope some of it was for you. When they told about the Marines jumping out of their foxholes to run & pick up the mail sacks, I thought of what you said about having mail call during an air raid. For a letter from you right now, I could ignore an air raid myself, dear.

Much love, Marian

☘

March 7, 1945

Dearest Gene,

I just finished baking a cherry pie. Wish you could try some with me. I don't know how good it will be—it's the first pie I've made in several years. However, we discovered this can of cherries that had been hidden away in the cupboard & decided there could be no <u>great</u> harm in trying.

Mimeographed sheets like this blue one were being handed to everyone as they left the plant tonight by union workers who are trying to get a union started at Reliable. This is the first time I've actually seen union organizers at work in a situation where I knew the facts of the case & I'm very much interested. If their methods continue to be like this, I shall also be thoroughly disgusted. I'm glad to see it's not a C.I.O. outfit.

That very first sentence [in the flyer] is infuriating to me because it so unfairly & underhandedly exploits the tension that always exists between factory & office workers when they're in the same building—and to no real purpose except to create dissension.

Then those remarks about the bonus plan & wage cuts are distortions of the facts calculated to appeal to the selfish greed of the least worthy employees. The bonus plan seems to me one of the most progressive, fair & generous systems of payment yet devised & it makes me angry to hear it criticized so stupidly.

I think unions are fine when employees have any real grievance, but this petty bickering is disgusting. I felt like asking those fellows if they couldn't find some more constructive ways to spend their time. Surely it shouldn't be difficult. That sounds like my mother. I'd better change the subject.

I thought the article by John Lardner was clever. Didn't you leave a watch or something here that you could come back for? Darling, I do worry about you very much. Most of the time it seems impossible that anything could happen to you—you know how you almost always feel that the worst things can happen to someone else but not to you—but when I remind myself how illogical that is, I am really frightened.

All my love, Marian

❖

March 9, 1945

Gene dear,

I had a funny dream about you last night. In the beginning we were on a train (very unusual), and there was a fellow in the same car who was crazy & kept climbing up on the baggage racks & stuff. Someone called the conductor to do something about it, & when he came in, he fainted! About that time, a doctor appeared — quite an elderly man, who turned out to be a very good friend of yours. With no connecting incidents, suddenly the doctor & I were off in space somewhere & he was telling me how much he thought of you & showing me a large collection of <u>red ties</u>, several exactly alike, which you had given him from time to time. He simply could not understand why you should always be sending him red ties! I have been laughing about it all day. Every time I think of it, it seems funnier.

I was just thinking it was a good thing I had that dream to tell you about because I've been so busy at work and at home (with cooking & sewing) that I haven't read anything at all except the news about the 3rd Division, & that is surely not a subject I could tell you anything about.

I had a letter from Peg tonight. She plans to come down the end of this month — just in time to help us move to the apt. upstairs. It will be good to see her.

Some of her students gave the play "Our Town" recently, and the townspeople enjoyed it so much they asked for a second performance. You can imagine that Peg was very much pleased.

I wish the newspapers would quit saying every day that the battle is in its final stages. It only makes the time seem longer.

I love you very much, dear.

Marian

❖

March 11, 1945

My darling Gene,

Today's "Sun" printed parts of a letter a Chicago family just received from their son who is with the 4th Marine Division. Now I shall be even more impatient to hear from you. Actually it has been hardly more than two weeks since your last letter arrived — but such a long fortnight, as Time would say!

Paul had some samples to send to San Francisco the other day & asked if I wouldn't like to deliver them in person. Indeed I would, particularly if I could stay to be there when the United Nations Conference takes place. I should like to be one of [Harold] Stassen's secretaries, for instance.

I should have asked Paul, though, if he didn't have something I could deliver to Iwo Jima. This afternoon I went down to the Telenews to see the first news reel films of the invasion. For a few minutes, I could almost imagine what it was like to be there. I wish I could <u>know</u>. Franklin would call that foolish, and perhaps you will, too, but I do wish it.

I forgot to tell you the other day that Bob Hope was at Camp Pendleton. He said they'd had a circus there & a gorilla got away & had worked up to sergeant & was in line for O.C.S. before they found him. Your sergeants are not <u>all</u> like that, are they?

Last night I went, all by myself, to see "None but the Lonely Heart." Have you seen it? It's a very good story about an idealistic young man in one of London's poor districts and his search for the "good life." There is a great deal of beauty in tragedy—a spiritual kind of beauty. Does it seem so to you? Probably that is not true of all tragedy.

Murph just came in so I'd better quit.

Good night, Lt. Sweetheart.

Marian

❀

March 13, 1945

Gene darling,

If there weren't another good thing about the Marine Corps, I would still like it for having such wonderful mail service. I can't resist the temptation to add that in that one respect, it excels <u>even</u> the Air Corps. Your V-mail of March 1 arrived today & to say I am pleased is a gross understatement. It is so very good to know you are all right, my dear.

I hesitated for sometime about sending you this clipping regarding Hearst's editorial, having in mind the various lectures one hears on what <u>not</u> to write to the serviceman overseas, but I decided you would be glad to know what a lot of righteous indignation it stirred up. One newspaper stated that the Marines in S. F. talked darkly of marching on San Simeon, & I'd venture to say they could do a good job of it without the Army's help, too! I'd like to put a little arsenic in his wine myself.

Murph & I have talked so much tonight that the evening is gone & I'll have to quit. Will write again tomorrow.

With love, Marian

P.S. I've been thinking how glad your grandfather must have been to hear from you, as undoubtedly he did. I wish I knew him, Gene—or have I said that before.

❀

March 16, 1945
Iwo Jima

Dearest Marian,

A few lines today to let you know I finally have been transferred into comm. work. It has been a long time but finally the 28th draft, or what's left of it, has broken up. I am attached to the Signal Co. More about that later when I find out myself. Makes me feel good to get back into what I want. Borrowman (who went to Brig. Young Univ.) went to Jasco and Edwards (Colorado Coll.) went to the 21st Marines as comm. officers.

My Sgt. was transferred with me which makes it rather nice. Am still looking forward to leaving this place but censorship regulations start again and I'll not be able to say much more.

There are still many questions you have asked that I have not answered but I have the letters and will answer them in the future. I am enjoying your letters so much that I get bitterly disappointed when there is none for me at mail time. I will try and comment more about them in the future also. [I am] still sitting out here in the sand with the dust and dirt trying to write. Not too condusive to thinking and certainly does not make for intelligent letters. Oh well—

The island is pretty well under control and we begin to move freely. Want to take a trip to Mt. Suribachi before long. Had to move to the Div. C.P. where the Sig Co is located so that meant building a new foxhole etc. My Sgt. and I were very comfortable and had enough canned food to last for a month. Rations are extremely available and everyone is eating well. Mail comes in regularly and so we have no complaints. Still it will seem nice to get back to our island paradise. Note the lack of quotation marks. So long Darling

and Much Love from
Gene

For exactly one minute I saw the March 6th "Time" and then somebody grabbed it. Would appreciate a copy from Chicago if possible?—Thanks—

❀

Iwo Jima
March 18, 1945

My dear Marian,

Today is Sunday again but unlike the others I have spent here, this one is quite peaceful. Your letter of March 4 arrived last night which made my trip to the beach successful. I still go down to the 28th Hdqs for mail despite the fact that it eventually will be transferred to the Sig Co. where I now am located. It is a rather long and dusty trip down there but mail is worth going after any time.

When I got back I was just in time to see a movie (no kidding) called Saratoga Trunk. Maybe it was just the relief or lack of movies for quite awhile, but I really enjoyed it. I think Ingrid B[ergman] combines looks and acting talent as well as any actress in Hollywood. Everyone else seemed to enjoy it too, but then at this stage of the game anything goes.

Edwards transferred to the 21st Marines as comm. officer. Reports came back that he and the captain were out getting Eddy orientated and 2 Japs charged them. The captain hit his in the head and Edwards shot the other in the stomach. By the time the two officers got there (to the Japs) about 20 other Marines had stripped them thoroughly for souvenirs and were starting to remove the teeth! Borrowman (who went to Jasco) and I were talking it over last night and before Eddy gets a chance to tell his version we are going to accuse him of shooting a Jap that was coming out to surrender. Otherwise we agree that it will be impossible to live with him. He's really a swell fellow tho and we'll just be kidding.

Last night they shot a Jap about 15 yards from our former foxhole down at the beach. He was walking in the midst of hundreds of Marines carrying a sword and pistol. He fired back but his Luger jammed and by that time he had 25 slugs in him.

It's getting to be quite a game now to take off for the front and look for Japs. There are probably several hundred left.

Finally (after waiting for 2 hours) I got a chance to see "Time's" account of the battle in the March 5 issue. Then a few hours later your copy came. Somehow I knew you would send it so ignore my request for the copy in my last letter.

The account was excellent I thought—certainly did justice to the affair. Sherrod's estimate of casualties was "slightly" low but I suppose you know the whole story now. I am glad that I was here as I was getting a little tired of hearing about Guadalcanal from the others who had been there.

We also received a can of beer last night tasted good and looked better as it had Milwaukee's name on it. Don't know if I mentioned that the weather is cold here—especially at night.

Met another Lt. from Marquette who graduated from Law school the same time I did from Liberal Arts. He was oddly enough my Lt. over 2 years ago when I was a P.F.C. at Camp Pendleton and had a little to do in getting me through pre-O.C.S. at Elliott. His name's Williamson and his wife had twins several months ago. This may or may not be important or interesting but I had to hear about it and so you will too.

I am now located among the "elite" that is in Div. hdqs. with General [Graves] Erskine etc.! I think it's going to be G.I. but the advantages back at— will be enormous socially.

Everyone's talking of a <u>beautiful</u> nurse that's supposed to be here for some reason or other. Haven't seen her tho.

I have not got a definite assignment yet and probably won't until I return to our base. Then I'll be able to tell you more about my work.

We now have a library run by the Chaplain and rather a morale builder. I did read a very cute (?) and pertaining (?) story in "Colliers" called "Return Trip" all about a train ride from somewhere to Chicago. Meant to cut it out & send it to you because of the thoughts of the young couple. Tho it happened in 1917 many of the events were duplicated back in Feb. 1944—including a breakfast in Chicago.

I have gone on and on and haven't said too much. I, too, like the poem of Franklin's which you sent or wrote in your last letter.

As far as this "changing me" (getting back to "me" which seems to be a favorite subject) I don't think it will. I have always been inclined to be cynical and more or less distrusting.

Your letters are perfect as they are so don't think of changing them. You bring back some favorite memories and I still regret the fact we have seen so little of each other tho it has been a year now. Till later

Much love, Gene

❖

March 14, 1945
[Chicago]

Hello, Lt. Sweetheart,

My Murphy has gone out tonight (looking very pretty too, in a new blue dress) so I should be able to do much better at letter writing than I did yesterday.

I was surprised & rather amused by my mother's letter tonight. I had told her I was anxious to hear from you & she said, "I hope you are writing to Gene.

He will probably be glad to have something besides Japs to think of when he gets through on Iwo." Real sweet of her, wasn't it?

Today is Franklin's birthday. I wrote to Mother Mon. eve so she would get the letter today. Funny—she must have been thinking the same thing when she wrote to me. But I have been so glad all day to hear from you—

I thought you might be as interested as we were in a letter Murph had last night from Mac Howard, a Navy officer who is a friend of hers. She said I might copy parts of it so here it is. He had made a trip to Russia and been there for the Big 3 conference. "Yalta was a quite picturesque place & Sevastopol the most ruined I have ever seen. Russian girls are husky and even formidable when armed with a tommy-gun which tends to discourage amorous advances. Vodka is powerful, especially when mixed with champagne.

"We saw Constantinople, which is now called Istanbul by the Turks, from the ship, Turkey still being neutral at that time. We could see the minarets and domes of the famous St. Sophia and Suleiman's mosques. The old seraglio & some of the more modern palaces were down at the water's edge—definitely a town I would like to see some day. (I, too.) We anchored off the city at night and it was good to see all the lights, neon signs and street cars."

Wouldn't you love to hear the parts he couldn't tell? That comment about Sevastopol reminds me of a statement in Roosevelt's report to Congress which impressed me deeply. He said, "I have heard about London, Stalingrad, (etc.) but I have <u>seen</u> Yalta and Sevastopol, and I <u>know</u> that there is not room in the same world for German militarism and Christian decency." Guess I'd better send you Time's review of the speech.

The 15th Air Force gunner who was reported missing a couple of months ago & whose sister works in our office, came home Monday night. I'd like to have a chance to talk to him. She has told me a good deal about his experience & it's very interesting. He parachuted into a corn field & a 9-yr. old boy hid with him in the woods nearby until dark & then directed him to the home of some Partisans. He stayed there a few days & then Partisan soldiers came & they marched for four days to a secret airfield. After several weeks a plane came & took him & the other Allied airmen who had been brought there to Bucharest. There they were given a banquet by the Russians & in due time transported back to Italy. He is the only one of his crew who has returned so far, & he knows the others must be alive somewhere (3 or 4 are reported prisoners) as he was the 9th to bail out & he saw the pilot leave the ship safely, too.

I must say good night, darling.

All my love, Marian

⚜

March 16, 1945

My darling Gene,

Rec'd your V-mail of Mar. 7 tonight & also the various notes. I've hardly been able to sit still all evening so this may not be very coherent, but I do want to tell you how much I appreciate your sending those notes. Murph had a real good dinner for us tonight & she says she ought to have had just any old thing because I wouldn't have known the difference. She's probably right.

These headlines in tonight's paper look pretty good. I am so glad it's over. I shall not feel quite at ease, though, until I have a letter from you dated today.

In someone else's (Mine, too, I've just noticed) newspaper today, it said 30 B-29's have made emergency landings on Iwo—involving the lives of approx. 330 airmen. I thought what a tremendous debt of gratitude the Air Corps owes to you Marines. You're wonderful, Gene—and I wish that would sound as sincere as it is meant to be.

To change the subject considerably, my mother has to have an operation on her eye next week and wants me to come home & stay with Dad while she's gone. It's nothing serious, but she will have to stay in Appleton for a day or two. Things are a little more quiet at the office just now, & Paul says I may go. If it's as much like spring there as it has been here the past few days, it will be almost like a holiday.

I'd like to have seen that beard you had, dear. Oh—and congratulations on your promotion! You mentioned it so casually I almost didn't notice.

Much love, Marian

⚘

March 20, 1945
[Iwo Jima]

Dear Marian,

Just a plain "V-Mail" as I'd like to let you know my complete address. It is above so you can start using it right away. Still haven't got any duties but expecting to go to work soon. All goes well and I now am a veteran (it says here.)

Am really appreciating the small things of life again which everyone takes for granted but which were notably lacking here. Saw another movie here last night, "Here Come the Waves" with Bing Crosby. It was rather good. Really got cleaned up after a hot shower (no fooling) and some fairly clean clothes. Succeeded in driving a rusty nail in my arm and ended up in "Sick Bay" for a day. Made me feel rather silly to go for such an insignificant thing, especially as I had to sit next to a Jap prisoner who was practically blown in half.

Much love, Gene

✣

March 22, 1945

Dearest Marian,

Your letter of March 9 arrived last night and also one from March 7.

Just finished breakfast which consisted of pork cheeseburgers, bacon, cocoa, crackers and jam. We are becoming quite handy in the kitchen but also getting sick of it and this whole place. The weather has been terrible consisting of rain plus cold dark gloomy days. Censorship regulations have clamped down again so that limits the matter I can talk about. We are still here.

Went down to the beach and talked to Borrowman last night and also picked up my mail. As yet we haven't received any letters written in reply to those we wrote from here. I think managed to get off a "V-Mail" about Feb. 27 or thereabouts and have probably written 8 or 10 more since then. I imagine you will get them all at once sometime in the future.

One of the men here blew off three fingers while fooling with a booby trap. At that he was lucky. I have not bothered to pick up much stuff but when we get down to the field the pilots and seabees will buy almost anything. One Marine has been making "Jap dog tags" and selling them since D + 4 and the favorite pastime seems to be painting large red circles on target cloth and selling them for Jap flags.

I don't know if I mentioned I was at the dedication of the 3rd Div. cemetary a few days ago. Attempted to draw a picture of the layout but it looked so horrible that I better not send it. As you might have suspected I am not an artist — hm —

Thanks for the March 12 part of "Time" in your last letter. It was the first on the island. so by now it is practically wore out. "Time" is as rare as the Japs now and for some reason everybody wants the magazine. Sherrods coverage of the operation was excellent I thought and that seems to be the consensus of opinion here. He really gave the Marines a build-up and now-a-days everybody is going around feeling very proud. I don't think the Marine Corps public relations bureau could have done a better job.

Your letters continue to be the most pleasant thing to look forward to. I just hope you get half the thrill out of these. I have been meaning to ask you if you have any snapshots etc. that I could talk you into sending me. I would appreciate them. Till later then.

Much love darling, Gene

❖

March 24, [1945]
Iwo Jima

Hello again Darling,

Will start a letter to you tonight mainly because I feel like writing to you. The sun is beginning to set tho and I don't know how much longer I'll be able to see. I.J. is not blessed with lights for Jr. officers as yet and after sunset here is nothing to do but go to bed. As a consequence we sleep about 15 hours a day. Most of the time tho I just lay there thinking how nice it would be back home and what I'll probably be doing.

Thought about that last night in Chicago and succeeded in getting very disgusted with myself because I couldn't remember more of what you looked like, what we talked about and the general air of things. As far as these things are concerned, I do have a good memory however and it often amazes me <u>why</u> we should have had such good times as that night and the one in Milwaukee. Kinda think that it was do partly to the fact that when the glamour of obvious things faded we did have much to talk about that we enjoyed in common. That all adds up to "that Post honeymoon period" that always bothered me. Things after the war are going to be generally fouled up but it is nice to day dream about. I imagine that those are the things that keep most fellows going out here when things get rough.

Which reminds me — something you said about not being able to imagine or realize that harm can come to "you" — believing it can only happen to others. How true that is and how frightful the feeling is when you realize that it is so illogical. That's exactly the way I felt before I landed and the realization came Feb. 24 — the first night ashore and I was at the ammunition dump on the airfield. The Mortar shells were flling [*sic*] all around and if you were brave enough to look, you could see the Jap rocket launchers and the red glare as they sailed in the sky — and always it seemed toward our foxhole. I actually was convinced that I never would get away alive and that, believe me, is a horrible feeling. I had read hundreds of stories about the same experience but one has to have that experience himself before it really means anything.

The movie last night was "Ship Ahoy" and rather stupid. There is none tonight. Been reading "The Hundred Years" which I personally enjoyed. Don't imagine that many people would however but I made up my mind to attempt at least to read something of an historical nature regularly as it seems I have forgotten too much about the only thing I once knew something about. It may be a little confusing through that last paragraph.

Well darling the sun has set and so I'll end this. Received your letter of March 11 today and as with all of them I liked it very much.

Goodnight dear, Gene

✤

March 18, 1945
[Chicago]

Dearest Gene,

Your letter of the 8th came yesterday. Don't be concerned about its sounding dramatic. I don't see how it could possibly be otherwise, unless you didn't write at all—and that I wouldn't like. However, I do understand that you can't always write when you'd like to. In fact, I've been surprised, and very much pleased, to have heard from you as often as I have, dear. It's rather wonderful how near you seem when there's half a world between us.

Yesterday afternoon, Cecil B. De Mille gave a speech on the radio which I had hoped would be printed in today's paper as I'd like to have sent it to you. However, I didn't find anything on it. He was speaking at some railroad union meeting, I believe, and explaining why he no longer broadcasts on Radio Theater. He belonged to the American Federation of Radio Artists. Their union board of directors, without consulting the general membership, assessed each member $1.00 to fight a measure in the Calif. legislature which opposed the "closed shop." De Mille refused to pay & was therefore suspended from the union &, automatically, from his job. He took the issue to court & a Los Angeles judge ruled that the union had the right to make the assessment because the issue was not "political," which is a dirty lie. In his speech De Mille stated that he favors unions but insists that no small group has a right to take away the freedom of the individual to support what political ideas he chooses. I thought it was truly an inspiring speech. Among other things, it made me realize more clearly than before that it is impossible to accomplish anything toward a better world without taking an active part in its organizations, regardless of whether or not you agree with their methods and purposes. It is a lesson I hope our nation has learned well regarding international cooperation & one we ought to apply to political parties, as well as to unions. Do you agree? I was talking to Capt. Bauer about it today, & he said he thought that if union leaders were required to be men who had spent many years at their trade, the racketeers who misuse those positions could be eliminated. Good idea?

Capt. Bauer & Murph's mother were both here for dinner today. My mother sent us a chicken, & we decided we ought to have someone help us eat it. Sometime when there's nothing better to write about, I'll tell you about Murph's mother. It's quite an interesting story.

I hope you will go back to Guam. If you do, tell me you're looking for sailboats again, will you? I don't like people who have codes, but I kept that secret well before & I'm sure I can again. That's a nice piece of rationalizing, isn't it? For shame!

This is an odd thing to think of right now, but I've been wondering for a long time—What does the "T" stand for in your initials? Perhaps I've asked you before.

I felt like reading poetry tonight, and there are two I'd like to share with you. This first one you've probably read in Time, but it may mean a good deal to you to reread it now.

It has to me—

Epitaph to the Heroes of Tarawa

"To you, who lie within this coral sand,
We, who remain, pay tribute of a pledge
That dying, thou shalt surely not
Have died in vain.
That when again bright morning dyes the sky
And waving fronds above shall touch the rain,
We give you this—that in those times
We will remember.
We lived and fought together, thou and we,
And sought to keep the flickering torch aglow
That all our loved ones might forever know
The blessed warmth exceeding flame,
The everlasting scourge of bondsman's chains,
Liberty and light.
When we with loving hands laid back the earth
That was for moments short to couch thy form
We did not bid a last & sad farewell,
But only 'Rest ye well'
Then with this humble, heartfelt epitaph
That pays thy many virtues sad acclaim
We marked this spot, and, murm'ring requiem,
Moved on to Westward."

—By an unknown Marine

This other is not exactly a poem, but it was written by Shelley: "I think one is always in love with something or other, the error—& I confess it is not easy for spirits cased in flesh & blood to avoid it—consists in seeking in a mortal image the likeness of what is, perhaps, eternal."

I used to agree that it was an error to search for such a thing, but now I wonder that a poet as great as Shelley should have been so blind that he could not see the likeness of eternity in any mortal image, for it is surely there.

With love, Marian

⚜

March 21, 1945

Hello my darling,

Last night I meant to write to you, but Capt. Bauer came over and we sat & talked all evening. Murph had been at home with a cold all day & they didn't want to go out. Ed is very interesting when he tells about the people he used to know in the drug business. He was a sales manager for Squibb before he joined the Army. Like most salesmen, I guess, he has quite a talent for story-telling, not the shady kind, however.

I was pleased this week to receive a decidedly unexpected letter from each of my two good friends in California—Ginny, who was my roommate, and Tip, the pilot I told you about when I was planning to come out there before you left. Tip is at a gunnery school on the desert for a couple of weeks & says, "I'm off the booze, bright lights, and gay young things while I'm up here, mainly because they aren't." I get a kick out of that. He never does write unless he's been forced to give up those more immediate pleasures.

I thought I'd be in Wittenberg today, but Mother wrote that she hadn't heard from the doctor yet as to when she should come down to Appleton & I should wait until she did. I don't know why she didn't call him up and get it settled! Sometimes I really sympathize with my Dad when he says it's enough to drive a man crazy! "No system!" he always complains, and you should hear the despair he puts into that remark.

Ed Dervishion fixed Murphie's radio today. It is certainly a pleasure to have one that works. Mine is on its good behavior mornings & sometimes in the afternoon, but evenings it's a lost cause. Isn't that silly? What could it be? Have you any ideas?

Your letter of the 10th came today & thanks, also, for the "newspaper." I was very much interested. If that story about MacArthur is true, it surely reveals an unpleasant personality & a sad lack of a sense of humor.

The number of casualties among the officers who were aboard ship with you really takes my breath away, darling. My God, how lucky we are!

It's no wonder you smoke 2 packs of cigarettes a day. I'm glad they are plentiful. I had been wondering if the water supply wouldn't be quite a problem as the maps do not show any streams & I should think any water there might be would be pretty awful with all that sulphur.

If those stories they tell the Japanese were not so disgusting, they'd really be funny. It's a low-down dirty trick their leaders play, isn't it? What a world we live in. Almost makes you feel like retiring to a cottage in the north woods somewhere, doesn't it? Shall we? Well, it would be nice for a few weeks, any way.

Do you know that sonnet of Shakespeare's—

"But if the while I think of thee, dear friend,
All losses are restored and sorrows end."

It works very well for me, dear friend.

Good night, Lt. Sweetheart.
Marian

⚘

March 22, '45

Dearest Gene,

I just want to write a note to keep this from being a dirty trick.

It's a good idea for me to send this stuff to you because it gives me some incentive to concentrate on reading it rapidly. I think this is the first time in history that I've finished so much of Time in one evening.

That food situation has been under discussion a great deal the last few weeks. There is really a meat shortage in Chicago. There's practically no meat at all in the butcher shops & it seems there must be something peculiar somewhere because it all happened so suddenly. If it is going to France and Belgium, it's a fine thing, but it would be nice to know just what the score is. I certainly hope this doesn't sound like a complaint as there is one person at the office who complains so much about her damn meat points that I wish she'd starve. Incidentally, her nearest relative in the service is a nephew who hasn't been outside of the U.S.A. in 3 yrs. in the Army. — Oh, I shouldn't be so vindictive. See you later darling.

Much love, Marian

⚘

March 23, 1945

Dear Lt. Sweetheart,

Rec'd your letter of the 16th today. I'm glad you have a comm. assignment at last. I hope your new foxhole is somewhat less gruesome. The 25 corpses in that last one were enough to give even an undertaker's daughter the creeps.

I told Murph what you said about answering all my questions "in the future," and she says, "What he means is that he'll answer them when he comes home." I hope she's wrong. However when you're working 12 hrs. a day, I feel fortunate that you write as often and comprehensively as you do, dear.

I checked the Mar. 5 Time and find that I sent the "World Battlefronts" Section at the time. Hope you have it by this time.

Mother has now definitely arranged to have that operation on her eye Wednesday, the 28th, so I'm going home Tues. morning & will probably come back on Friday as we have to move next weekend. Peg is coming down, too, I hope.

Paul told me this morning that one of those radio quiz shows called his wife. She answered the first question correctly. "What 2 U.S. Presidents served simultaneously?" Jeff. Davis & Lincoln. That was worth $5.00. For the next one—"What state erected a monument to both men?"—the prize was $500. She said either Ky. or Tenn. They said she'd have to take one or the other so she chose Tenn. & the answer is Kentucky. Paul said she was fit to be tied & I don't wonder.

Darling, I wish I could write to you every day so you'd never be disappointed at mail call. But if I did, some of those letters would be more disappointing than nothing at all I'm afraid.

All my love, Marian

⚜

March 25, 1945

My darling Gene,

There are so many people around today that I don't know whether I can make sense or not, but I wanted to write as I know I won't have time tomorrow.

Two of Murph's college friends are spending the weekend with us. They are both very nice, but I must admit that I'm a little weary of listening to reminiscences of their sororities & particularly to lengthy descriptions of the one girl's recent pregnancy.

Their talk of college days, however, makes me very curious about yours, and about those other two Marions.

Yesterday afternoon I saw the play, "Glass Menagerie." Cal suggested that I go. He had seen it sometime ago & said he was amazed at the similarity of the experiences & reactions of the principal character to his own. It was quite true. I thought it rather amusing as he is always dramatizing his troubles & then hating himself for doing it. I really feel sorry for him, though. In this story, it was chiefly the mother's fault & I think the same is true of Cal's mother. In the play, the boy runs away from his responsibilities in search of freedom & adventure but is forever haunted by the image of his crippled sister whom he dearly loves. Cal suffers the same conflict between his desire for adventure (which I do not quite understand) and his sympathy for his mother & love for his family. His only rebellion thus far has been in drinking & occasionally crying on my shoulder. Not literally. I hope that will always be the extent of it as I'm afraid he'd find "adventure" an empty shell.

It is good to think of you, dear, in contrast to the confusion of Cal's personality.

Do you understand this article about International transmitters? I can't figure it out at all.

Oh, more people are coming now & I'll have to be polite again. Until Tuesday then —

All my love, Marian

⚘

Wittenberg, Wis.
March 27 '45

Dear Lt. Sweetheart,

Yesterday would have been a gray day with streaks of purple if it had not been for the amazing & extremely welcome 7-page manuscript you wrote the 18th. That character who complains about ration points came to work last week with a dripping cold so, of course, I have one now. "That damn Virginia" is my favorite saying now.

It surely brightened things up to get your letter. I got a kick out of the story about Edwards & the two Japs. Were there any teeth left for him? Seems rather a horrible souvenir.

Lt. Williamson's twins are certainly both important & interesting, especially as I was under the impression Marines probably had little gorillas or lion cubs, maybe, instead of children. 'Course I guess you didn't specify just what variety of twins they were —

That's all right, dear. I like you anyway.

I wish you had been on the train with me this morning. It leaves Chi. at 1:50 A.M. and gets to W'berg about 10:30. It would have been so much more comfortable sleeping on your shoulder. I'd like to read that story in Colliers. Was it a recent issue?

You should have heard the conductor when we changed trains at Appleton Junction. He was really in a jovial mood. "Change for the <u>fast</u> train to Hortonville, Clintonville, New London, Wittenberg, etc. We'll stop here 20 minutes for breakfast. Have some nice fresh eggs smothered in bacon, some nice fresh coffee smothered in cream, some nice fresh toast smothered in butter on both sides! Take your time, folks. The fast train will wait for you." I like foolish people, don't you?

It's good to be up here. "It's so peaceful in the country." Especially when Mother isn't around. Isn't that mean? No kidding, though, my Dad is a changed man. I was just asking him if he liked clam chowder & he said, "I'll eat anything. Say! Do you like buckwheat cakes? Oh, boy, we can have something besides eggs for breakfast!" With that he went tearing off to the store like a little kid to get some buckwheat flour. It's really fun.

Apparently he has heard rumors of your communication training because he has a new angle to his campaign regarding the "business." I hadn't been here an hour until he began to tell me what good prospects there'd be for radio & appliance lines after the war "if only you had someone who knew how the stuff works." It amuses me greatly.

Well, I'd better start getting dinner before he puts me in mother's class.

See you tomorrow darling.
Love, Marian

❖

March 28, '45
Wittenberg

Hello, my darling,

You know, it's awfully nice when I sit down to write a letter, to know that you think my letters are perfect. It's very encouraging.

Was I a busy girl today! We had those buckwheat cakes for breakfast & then Dad went to the store to buy some material to fix his vest or rather to put a new back in it. What he really needs is a new vest, but he won't buy one & mother wouldn't fix the old one. So there they were just waiting to see who could hold out longer. I don't think Mother will appreciate my fixing it for him.

Someone died this afternoon. First time in two months & he would pick the day I'm home! Can't say that I enjoyed the job of holding instruments & stuff for Dad. However, it wasn't too bad.

I also made a new skirt. Not bad for a day's work, is it? Now I will quit being proud & talk about something else.

Have been waiting anxiously to learn whether or not the Jap reports of landings in the Ryukyus [Okinawa] will be confirmed. Some commentators say it's probable; others say it's not. Very elucidating.

The news from Germany is certainly super. I'm afraid, though, to feel too optimistic about an early surrender.

Aside from radio broadcasts, I haven't heard much news. Dad takes the Milw. Sentinel & I like that about as well as the Tribune.

Guess I'll go out & mail this & go for a walk. It's a lovely evening. If you were here, we could walk over the viaduct & look at the moon & the railroad tracks. It's really quite romantic. Believe it?

Much love, Marian

✿

March 30, 1945
The "400"

My darling Gene,
    If you find it difficult to read this, it is because the pencil is dull — & perhaps partly because the "400" is not so smooth as it might be. Seems to me we have on file a minor controversy on that subject. Well, anyway, it's more like the El Cap than is the "fast train" from Appleton Junc. to W'berg, & it makes me real lonesome for you. We'll be in Milwaukee soon & that intensifies the effect.
    I saw Mother in Appleton between trains. Apparently her eye did not heal quite as well this time, so she couldn't go home until tonight.
    Incidentally, that left me with the job of helping Dad dress that corpse this morning. That's really exercise. I know for sure now why they're called "stiffs." This old fellow really was. He'd creak so loud when you'd try to bend his arm to get a sleeve on it that you'd almost be afraid the bones would break before the joint would give. Such a business!
    Here's Juneau Park & the lagoon & Cudahy Towers & a big old coal barge just going out. It's my favorite part of Milw. & I've always been glad the train comes in this way. Would like to stop off for awhile but Peg is probably in Chicago waiting for me. I'm also anxious to get there & see if there's any mail from you.
    Well, we are almost in Waukegan now & I haven't had a sensible thought yet, so I'd better give up. See you later, dear.

All my love, Marian

Oh — no letter from you. Not even a little one. I am so sad!
    Peg isn't here, either. Won't be in until tomorrow morning. Murphie isn't even home! Guess I'll go eat worms.

✿

March 26, 1945
Iwo Jima

Dearest Marian,

'Tis a beautiful day today for a change and everything seems to be going right. No mail however and that sorta took the something (can't think of the word) out of the perfectness.

Have noticed I've forgotten how to spell and my vocabulary is really limeted now. I don't know why this has come about but it is rather annoying at times.

In the middle of a fairly good movie last night we had an air raid alert so that stopped things rather abruptly. The name of it was "Hey Rookie." For some reason the Marines get a bang out of these strictly Army pictures. A lot of wise cracks are always in the air—particularly when some doggie says very earnestly that he wants to get over and fight "those Japs." Everybody laughs rather bitterly. No particular reason outside of the fact that it was Army troops that always relieved the Marines at these various islands. Last night the hero mentioned something about Formosa and some wit sang out—"You can't go there, we haven't been there yet." It is amusing to listen to the bitter side remarks that always go during the movie.

Most of the fellows here rate rotation, (28 months) and that is the basis for many cynical remarks.

"Rotation Blues," is a song which has some questionable lyrics. I meant to get a copy of a form that somebody in D. H. wrote stating the rules and requirements for being rotated and send it to you. Part of it was in "Time" but this was very complete and drawn up as if it were a regular Naval order. One of our Lts. read it over and actually believed it! I liked the part "If a man dies it is to be interpreted that he does not want to return to the states."

There was absolutely no reason for writing this letter and all of yours are packed away so I can't answer your questions. Hope you have received some of my letters by now and have my new address. If anything is discouraging it is waiting for mail to be forwarded after a transfer.

Will end this rather abruptly now so—Goodnight Sweetheart and

Much love, Gene

P.S. The article in "Press" March 12 "Time" on the Marines and Hearst[25] was wonderful!!

This is a prize winning Iwo Jima battle song composed by a member of the Garrison. It was sung over the radio by Japanese school children as an inspiration to the troops during the early phases of the operation.

IWO JIMA GARRISON SONG

Where dark tides billow on the ocean
A wink shaped isle of mighty fame
Guards the gateway to our empire
Iwo Jima is its name

We brave men who have been chosen
To defend this island strand,
Filled with faith in certain triumph
Yea to strike for Fatherland

Thoughts of our task are ever with us,
From Dawn to Dusk we train with Zeal.
At our Emperor's command
We'll bring the enemy to heel

Oh for Emperor and homeland
There's no burden we wont bear,
Disease, hardship and foul water
These are less to us than air

In the lonely mid Pacific
Our sweat a fortress will prepare
If the enemy attacks us
Let him come we will not care

Until the hated Anglo Saxons
Lie before us in the dust
Officers and men together
Work and struggle, strive and trust

P.S. The typing is strictly Anglo-Saxon by yours' truly.

For me the Iwo Jima campaign was over, and it was now time to board our transport for the return trip to Guam. As I wrote to Marian, I had attended the dedication of the division's temporary cemetery not far from the First airfield. In their brief speeches the division and Naval leaders came back to the recurring theme of whether the cost in lives to take Iwo Jima was worth it. And of course they agreed it was. Even as a speaker was making his remarks, his words were drowned out by a pilot bringing his disabled B-29 and crew down safely in an emergency landing. Iwo Jima had to be in American hands to carry out the successful bombing of the Japanese homeland which ended the war. Nevertheless, the final statistics were staggering by any standard. In thirty-six days of fighting on eight square miles of volcanic sand, 25,851 Americans were casualties. Of these, nearly 7,000 died and now lay in neat rows beneath their religious symbols; if the dead Japanese soldiers were included, there were another 20,000.

3

"Obviously I 'care' about you, . . ."

SOMETHING HAD HAPPENED *to me on Iwo Jima. Japanese shells and sharp-shooters had missed me and I was thankful for that. Other than a small scratch on my arm from trying to put up a cot, I left unscathed. But I did not leave unchanged. When I had descended the ship's rope ladder onto a waiting landing craft on 24 February, I wanted to experience combat, but when I climbed up that ladder a month later, I was not anxious to experience combat again. However, I was changed in another way. My mother, grandfather, and a couple of cousins were very much concerned for my well-being and kept my spirits up by writing to me regularly. Yet as I trudged through the Iwo Jima black volcanic ash to the beach to get my mail, I was always hoping there would be one from the girl I had met on the train. It was not that my relatives meant less to me but that my future was with Marian. In fact, I had to admit that during those difficult weeks she was uppermost in my thoughts. I began to see this as love.*

For Marian, the spring of 1945 was one of hope and despair. Despite difficult conditions I was writing to her and had survived the Iwo Jima campaign. The war in Europe was going well and the allies were closing in on Berlin. The principle of a United Nations gave her hope that future wars like this could be avoided, although it was troubling that serious differences between the United States and Russia had arisen. Then on 12 April the free world was shocked to learn President Roosevelt had died suddenly at his winter home in Georgia, and the country was now led by a virtually unknown politician from Missouri. When I told her I had turned down a "safe duration job" as a coding officer in Pearl Harbor to stay with my friends in Guam, she was not pleased but made the best of it.

April 2, 1945
Central Pacific

Hello Darling,

Oh what a beautiful day—for some reasons I can't tell you and others I can—showers! hot good meals! cots to sleep on! good movies, cold beer! <u>clean</u> clothes news! and a lot of letters.

Got situated in a Japanese house today with electric lights if you please. Received about 25 back letters at 3:00 PM including about 10 from you. headed over to see O'Leary[26] at Jasco but finally ended up at the Div. Officers' club and found him. It was a fond meeting. However he had a date (Navy nurse) and after talking a few minutes and having "several" rum and cokes decided I might be intruding and said I'd better head back. However both insisted I should stay and as I hadn't talked to a gal for 5 mo. I did linger for several more hours. I really had a grand time. Got back to the house about half hour ago to find more letters (mostly from you which I didn't find hard to take.) Decided to go to bed tho and not read them till morning to save some of the joy. Couldn't sleep however because I was thinking of them and it ended I got up and after locating my flashlight read them theish [*sic*]. Then Britt and Fielding came in (2 other Com. off. who transferred with me to sig. co.) and found a light switch and so here I am writing at 11:00 P.M.

That includes as much of the day's activities that I can tell you, but actually all that's important. Our ex. off. just came in to see how we are doing. He's a swell fellow—Captain Kasten from Milw—also our top sgt. is from West Allis.

Darling I am going to answer your questions and I am fairly sure that I'd be able to get caught up in the next few weeks. Many thanks again for all the articles—you usually scoop the island with the news and editorials from the states. Really got quite a kick of (from) your comment of "So Soon" at one of them. Pretty much the way that I felt but by now you know "Time" has as usual given the Marines a break and don't think we don't appreciate it. Forrestal's reply to that women's letter was excellent and very true.

Concerning that officer's attitude toward the Germans—it surprised me somewhat <u>but</u> on this side of the world the attitude is <u>typical</u>. Don't think I could feel that way very readily toward the Germans but I surely have grown into the Marine spirit of regarding the Japs as being no more than animals. Their fatalistic philosophy certainly puts them so far remote from our way of living and thinking that I can feel somewhat justified. They have no regard for moral or international law and that in itself tends to make them inhuman.

When I come home remind me to tell you of an unfortunate incident that happened to some pilots there.

I must close for now darling as the other fellows want to go to sleep. The "sailboat idea" still sounds wonderful dear and I'll be watching. Goodnight and

My Love, Gene
More soon.

❧

April 5, 1945
Central Pacific

Dear Marian,

Everything is so beautiful here that I feel like I'm in some part of heaven or something—when I think how close I was to the other place it is all the more amazing. I am really quite happy sitting under the palm trees and standing in the showers for hours, clean sheets and even the occasional sight of a woman. (I assure you those last two idems are unrelated—)

Was officer messenger today and really got around and saw a good deal of the island. Made me think it wouldn't be the worst place to spend a honeymoon.

Stopped at the Red Cross canteen for a cup of coffee at the insistance of my jeep driver because there was supposed to be a very beautiful gal there. She was—Also he recommended a Fleet P.X. and so we stopped in there to stock up on stuff hard to get around division (Philip Morris, ink and handkerchiefs.)

You will be seeing some 3rd div. men around there soon—

Borrowman (Merle) and I went over to see Edwards who was just made Comm. off for the 3rd bat., 21st Marines and is really snowed by the job. He'll be able to handle it O.K. tho and I have a lot of faith in him. Incidently he found out 3 weeks ago (at an odd time!) that his "girl" is engaged to be married. I know he felt bad but we figured the best way was to kid him—which we did. Merle is expecting to be a father any day now so he keeps talking of his family. Oddly enough we are all within a hundred yards of each other, tho in three different organizations.

That train ride to Wittenberg sounds swell to me. However over here it's best not to think about those things. (I do tho)

The regimental C.O. of the 21st Marines held a formation to thank them— started a speech and suddenly broke into tears as his voice faltered—walked away. Several in the ranks were crying. He's a full Colonel so maybe the Marines aren't so tough after all.

Enjoyed your letter of March 26 about Cal etc. Been wondering what sort of man he was that you should love him. For some reason it is a thrill to hear about other people that "certain" people care about. Obviously I "care" about you, and how past that stage it has gone I never had nerve to ask myself. I will some day—about the time I start to grumble about rotation.

Speaking of radio & appliances etc—I became very interested in a plan that my best friend's cousin (Friend Reuben Snartemo & cousin Herman Madland) had when I was home last time about a partnership in selling them (in a store) after the war. It really appealed to me no end. Herman's plenty sharp—a grad of St. Olaf's college and at present in the Chemical department at Allis Chalmers. Mr. Geist the president is the backbone of our little Norwegian church and consequently a good friend of ours. Snartemo the elder is the Pastor.

Reuben is a doctor now interning at the childrens' hospital. Well anyway the idea was to buy a store and sell radios and phonograph (records) Told him I probably would want to go to school but he said that it made no difference. We never worked out the details but he seemed enthusiastic enough. Me too!

You told me once but I'll ask again. Where is Wittenberg? Have to stop now darling.

Much love, Gene

P.S. Two weeks in the north woods, on a train, here, or anywhere would be wonderful—with you

⚜

April 6, 1945
Central Pac.

Hello darling,

I was glad to receive a letter from you tonight even tho it was dated Feb. 28. Which reminds me—you have been sending them this way in great quantities but the quality remains the same so I don't agree with you. Rather hesitated about writing to you tonight because I have had 6 beers and 6 scotch & sodas and it's only 6:00 P.M. So I may seem a little garbled. A friend of O'Leary's from the Coast Guard came ashore to see him. John was busy and as I happened to be around I got the job of being a host. The club opens at 4:00 PM and we have spent the time over there.

I wish you were here tonight. Oh! in so many ways that it hurts. It's times like these that I get tired of it all. Reminds me that you said you get lonesome when you drink too so that adds up to the long list of things we have in common.

I really don't care too much for liquor however and that's actually a fact. I've had a quart of Seagrams in my locker box for 4 months and never had a drink. Sorta saving it in case my dad gets up this way. I do like beer tho. Rotation has come to us at last so you'll be seeing some of my friends from the 3rd around Chicago probably.

Are you going to send me some pictures of you??? I would like some very much. Got to close now because I promised I'd meet John again before the movie. I saw "To Have and Have Not" (H. Bogart & L. Bacall) last night. "Time" said it was a pure case of "unaltered Sex." They weren't kidding.

Good night darling and my love,
Gene

❦

April 7, 1945
Central Pacific

Hello darling—

Haven't heard from you for about 5 days now and if I wasn't so busy getting squared away here at the Signal Co, I would really have something to brood about. The way it is—is bad enough.

I had a pleasant surprise a few days ago when my dad flew in from the South. It was sure good to see him after 27 months and he is well. At present he should be near the states as he left yesterday by plane. We talked ourselves dry but I managed to get a case of beer so that helped. He said he may get out of the service which I hope, but at any rate has a 30 day leave to look forward to. I envy him but my time will come. The last 6 mo. have flown.

I felt the best news since "Pearl Harbor" came in yesterday with Russia making the break with the Japs. I <u>know</u> you feel that way too because we both have been sympathetic with that country. I haven't heard much about it yet or what the results will be—

Don't you think it would be the thrill of the lifetime to be at the conference April 26 in San Fran? Wish you could be Stassen's 1. secretary and forward your ideas to me. In general the war looks good all over. A wave of optimism is sweeping this place but I am reserving my elation till bigger developments occur. Rotation has come which is all I can say. We will be the core of the new 3rd and the only "vetrans" to speak of as most of the division is made up of fellows who took part in three campaigns. They are still "blowing smoke" (praise) at us for the last one. Envy these fellows getting back now at the height of the affair. The Ryukas (spelling?) seem to be a picnic so far. I supposed you wondered if I were there.

Today is perfect here after a rather wild night at the club. The radio is on (Ford Program) and a cool breeze makes the weather better than usual.

Last night Edwards, Merle & Steve [Mohorovich][27] were at the club and we had a rather loud reunion. Steve stayed behind in the Rear Echelon and so we kidded him unmercifully about that. Edwards told and re-told the story of the Jap he shot, and we told the version we cooked up. After many Bourbons and ginger ale, Ed almost cried at the last re-telling at 0200. He tried to make us believe that he told the truth but we insisted the Jap had stepped out of a cave (naked) waving a bed sheet as a surrender flag—and then Ed shot him in cold blood. It was so funny. I like him a lot. No news on his girl yet but he's pretty sad. We finally helped him back to his tent at the 21st Marines.

The staff nco's also had a party last night—about 20 of them managed to get 40 steaks and 40 cases of beer which they proceded to eat and drink at 1900.

The O.D. let them stay at their club till 0200 instead of the usual 2300 and by that time each man drank 2 cases of beer—which is a lot of beer for one man to drink, "ain't" it? Everybody here is very happy about rotation.

I enjoyed the remarks by Mac Howard about Russia and the descriptions. I'd like to visit those places too.

Just stopped to read your last 15 letters to see if there was any questions you had asked. I'll stay up to date from now on. The "T" in my name stands for Thor—and I am not named after the washing machine—which someone once asked me seriously.

The Tarawa Epitaph is good. Perhaps you've heard that the flag raising picture will be used in bond drives. One Marine is still alive who was in it. It was a beautiful setting—

Guess I'd better close for now again as I see I have gone through 6 pages of this not-too-thin paper. Will be back soon again darling, meanwhile I am waiting for your letters more anxiously than ever.

Much love, Gene

❧

April 10, 1945
Central

Dearest Marian,

I was glad to get your letter today dated Mar 29. Noticed you are still in Wittenberg and hope your mother has come through the operation all right. Give her my best wishes and regards to your dad. Kinda envy him having homemade buckwheat cakes. Can you really cook? I didn't ever really think you were just an ornament. Been meaning to ask you if you still have "that hat"—have you?

I have been meaning to tell you something for so long but always forget it until I had sealed the letter. It is concerning that story in the Readers' Digest that you sent me. I received it aboard ship but I never had a chance to send it back and then all my clothes including the letters from you got lost. In fact they never got off the ship and I have been running around for days trying to locate the blanket roll with my letters, clothes, and other gear in it. I hope you will forgive me for not sending it right away.

I didn't lose much considering I had left most of everything I have back here, but at Iwo I was usually without the slight comforts we could have brought.

Which reminds me I found out today we can still talk of the campaign— after I had carefully avoided it for 2 weeks. As you probably have guessed we are at our base again.

I have enjoyed "Time's" constant reference to the campaign and of course the buildup doesn't make us feel bad either. We all agree that the report of Sherrod's was accurate and true which is something in his favor. I think it's an indication of the "straight dope" that "Time" puts out.

I'll probably work in the Div. Message center for awhile at least. Not what I really wanted but it's not too bad. Was doing that kind of work before I started school in Los Angeles (at camp Elliott.)

Today completes 6 mo. overseas and I hardly can believe it. The time has flew and I still haven't any legitimate complaints. Did I tell you we have a Radio station? "Station—on—on the road to Tokyo" is the phrase they always use. Most of the programs are broadcast from the states special to the forces overseas. Usually they are worth listening to. Now they even present plays enacted here on the island by Hollywood folk in person. News is broadcast regularly for which we are all thankful and sometimes they have natives singing which is not too bad.

Today they set up a div. program which among other bad things includes chow at 0600, 1330 and 1730. Sorta stupid hours don't you think? Hope you understand Army Navy time—if not—subtract 12 if it is 1300 or more and you get PM. hours. OK?

Last night in my dreams I fought the battle of Iwo again and I think it was just about as bad as the first time. Really almost a nightmare and the shells and mortars so realistic that I didn't hear the alarm go off at 0530. The bugler finally woke me up personally so I had just enough time to get into my clothes and be present for the morning roll call. I was O.D. and really in a daze out there. Then I remembered suddenly we had to start exercises that particular morning—asked for a volunteer to come out and lead the company. No one came out so the situation became a little trying. In desperation I decided to lead them myself but then suddenly realized I did not know any of the counts of the exercises (which is an art in itself.) Without too much delay I gave them "double time" for about three minutes whereupon I became tired and had to quit. All this happened in about 7 minutes and the events were decidedly ahead of my thoughts so early in the morning. What a life!

I have covered much paper again without saying too much and don't like to do that. I should get some letters from you tomorrow written in April. Time to go to bed again. The evenings are beautiful here and of course I wish you were here (or I there) to spend them together. Goodnight sweetheart and

Much love, Gene

✤

Easter Sunday
[Chicago]

My darling Gene:

There were three letters from you yesterday, the latest dated Mar. 26, and my disappointment of Friday night was well forgotten. I feel the same way you do about them—I just hope you get half the thrill out of mine.

You asked about some snapshots. We've been wanting to take some for a long time & if we ever get around to it, I'll send you some. Perhaps your encouragement will help us get started. Sometime ago you mentioned that you might send some to me. If you can, I'd surely like to have them. It would be the next best thing to seeing you—and that! It's too good even to think about.

Peg came about 11:00 yesterday morning & we talked furiously until about 2:00. Then we had to go to work & move up here to 1507. It was a hell of a way to treat a weekend guest, but she was a good sport & even seemed to enjoy it a little. I did. Must be a little gypsy in me or something.

Last night we went to Shangri-La for dinner. We'll have to go there sometime when you come back. It's a very interesting place. The decoration is unusual and sort of makes you feel as dreamy as if you were in the real Shangri-La. Or could it have been the "Moonbeam" that did that? (Strictly a lady's drink, the menu said.)

I let Peg read the notes you sent, and she was so impressed she insists they ought to be published.

I wonder if you are "making notes" on Okinawa today. The landings were reported this morning & the announcer said three Marine divisions were taking part in the action. The only unit identified, however, is the new 10th Army. They say it's not as difficult an operation as Iwo Jima & I'm glad of that.

Well, dear, I'm the cook today, & it's time for dinner, so until tomorrow—

All my love, Marian

✢

April 3, 1945

Dear Lt. Sweetheart,

It's day after tomorrow instead of tomorrow as I promised. Ed & Marge came up yesterday to get the last of their belongings & we nearly had to bring the beds out to let them know it was time to leave. I started to write to you afterward, but couldn't make anything sound sensible.

I've surely been having trouble trying to figure out what Marine divisions are on Okinawa. One commentator said, "the same Marines who took Guam," but the newspapers say the 3rd Amphibious Corps & it is my impression that has nothing to do with the 3rd Div. Isn't the 3rd Div. a part of the 5th Amph. Corps?

It just occurred to me yesterday that one of the letters I rec'd from you Sat. had been en route less than 5 days. Isn't that amazing — & wonderful? On the other hand, your V mail of Mar. 20 arrived yesterday.

You mentioned how much you appreciate the little things in life that we usually take for granted. It may sound rather silly, but since reading your letters about those first few weeks, clean sheets & showers & clean clothes have seemed much greater pleasures to me than ever before. Apparently it is possible to learn by someone else's experience, provided you are sufficiently in sympathy with it.

Peg & I went to see Larry Adler & Paul Draper Sunday night. I didn't like Paul Draper's dancing, but Adler was very good. Have you ever heard him? I would never have believed a harmonica could sound so pleasant. He plays classics beautifully & boogie woogie — inexpressibly!

After the show we stopped at the Bismarck for a drink, & two Sgts. asked if we'd listen to their troubles. It seemed rude to say no, especially as they were Marines. Everything closes at midnight, you know, but they found a place that's open all night — obviously run by a paying "friend" of Mayor [Edward] Kelly's. We danced & drank beer until almost three. It seemed quite an adventure. The place was sort of a dive, but not rowdy as you might expect. The only difficulty was that my Sgt. kept proposing all evening — strictly legal, too. "I swear to Christ," he kept saying, "You're the type!" Horrible, isn't it? It was really funny, but at the same time embarrassing. Reminded me of the girl in Los Angeles you told me about.

I haven't done so well with this week's Time. No time. Finally finished the World Battlefront section, though, so I'll send it tonight. I liked Bob Capa's account of the paratroop landings especially.

Murph & I have been making plans most of the evening for all the things we want to do Saturday aft. to fix up the apartment. We're pretty well settled now & like it very much, except for the slight inconvenience of the beds in the wall, which it is time to bring out right now.

I <u>will</u> see you tomorrow this time, darling.

All my love, Marian

⚜

April 4, 1945

My darling,

I've missed you so much today. It can't be the Spring because it's been cold & damp, rather like November.

Last week I noticed in the Milw. Sentinel a reprint of the speech by DeMille about which I told you a short time ago. I forgot to cut it out, but Mother sent it to me today, so here it is. It has been edited somewhat & while I haven't reread the whole thing, I know they have deleted at least one part which affirmed his belief in the basic fact that unions are necessary &, if properly administered, a good thing. I distinctly remember that he finished the speech with some such statement as this: "There is, however, one union which I place above all others & that is the Union of the United States of America."

This other clipping from Time brings up a point which seems to me of greatest importance. I sincerely hope that the smug greed of the individual will not blind him to the vital importance of this food question. It seems to me it would be the height of tragedy—& ugly tragedy—if the suffering & sacrifices of the war should come to naught because people are too selfish or too ignorant to let themselves realize that they must give up a little food—be humanitarian enough to feed the starving or near-starving peoples of Europe—not only out of kindness but to preserve our way of life by proving it is worthy of preservation. This sounds rather dramatic, I'm afraid, but I do feel very deeply about it. It seems to me the most fundamental of all issues of war & peace.

This is rather peculiar for a love letter. That was what I really wanted to write, but it doesn't seem to work very well.

Goodnight, sweetheart. I like you so much.

Marian

✤

April 6, 1945

Hello, Darling,

This Friday is as bad as the last one. Haven't heard from you all week, except for that V-mail Monday. I hope it means you're on the way back to Guam.

I went to the B&G around the corner tonight for dinner & Capt. Eddie Albert, U.S.M.C., was there. It was quite a surprise. I used to think he was rather homely in the movies, but he isn't a bad looking fellow. Has a build worthy of any good Marine. I still say you're the handsomest one, though!

Which reminds me—the only thing I don't like about you is the way you fold your letters. It takes me five minutes to find where they start. I suspect you do it on purpose just to add to the suspense. Peg tells me Ray does the same thing. Are you sure you didn't see him that day?

Did I tell you I heard from Tip again this week? His students in gunnery had the highest average in their class, so he got 4 or 5 days off & a P-38 to travel in. Isn't that marvelous? (Purely a rhetorical question. No answer required.)

I was glad to hear that the Russians denounced their treaty with Japan. It's nothing very concrete, but at least it's a beginning. Do you think they will eventually declare war?

I'd better go back to my Time magazine now so I can send you some of it. One of the men in our office told me he knows the editor of "March of Time," & this fellow told him Time has writers of various political beliefs and lets them write pretty much as they please. Luce sometimes writes a series of things himself, but any time they see that a one-sided viewpoint has been running for any length of time, they put an end to it. Have I said that so it makes sense? As he told it, it more or less explained how they manage to report the news with flavor & at the same time without bias. Real smart, isn't it?

Goodnight, dear.

Much love, Marian

⚜

April 8, 1945

Dear Lt. Sweetheart,

Since there was no mail yesterday, I decided I'd just have to read some old letters over again. I told Murph about your breakfast of pork, cheeseburgers, bacon, etc., & she wants to know what you have for <u>dinner</u>.

Yesterday afternoon we went shopping for some odds & ends of household necessities, & then we cleaned the upholstery in our living room. It was so dirty we'll have to do it over at least once more before it will look ok. It's an icky job, too.

Last night we went over to Capt. Bauer's apartment. He mixed some Manhattans for us which were very good. We talked & read cartoons & stuff, & first thing we knew it was 2:30. So this morning the plumber woke us at 10:00 & wanted to fix a leaky faucet. You can imagine what a welcome he got. If we hadn't been so surprised to get the faucet fixed, we'd probably have thrown him out the window with glee.

I went to see the films at the Telenews again today. They had some on the fleet's bombardment of Okinawa, but not much on the landings. I'm still confused about that. Even Time is of no help.

Darling, one of the letters I reread today was the one you wrote Mar. 24. It's one of my favorites. I was deeply impressed by what you said about the feeling that first night on Iwo Jima that you'd never get away alive. It must be horrible. It's odd—I was always so confident nothing would happen to Franklin. I suppose the fact that illusion was so rudely shattered is the reason I worry so much more about you, dear. I'm basically an optimist, though, and usually limit my worrying to brief intervals.

On the lighter side, it pleases me to see that you use the past tense when you speak of your concern over that "post-honeymoon" period, which I hope may be more in the nature of an era than a period. An era is longer, isn't it?

Much love, Marian

✤

April 9, 1945

Gene, my darling,

I've been sitting here all evening just glowing with pleasure over your letter tonight. In the first place, I'm so glad you're back on your island paradise; and in the second place, I'm glad I can count on hearing from you regularly again for a while. I've surely no complaints on that score—just getting spoiled!

Speaking of mail, dear, if 10 of those 25 letters waiting for you were from me—where did the other 15 come from? Your grandfather? All right, I'll believe you. Or didn't you say yes?

I hope I remember to ask you about the incident of the pilots. Were they the three you mentioned in your notes, who died the day you landed? At the time, that notation seemed rather incongruous to me, as I imagined there were many more Marines than pilots dying.

Does Capt. Kasten perchance have any connection with Schwanke Kasten, the jewelers? I can think of more darn questions, can't I? You'll never catch up, Gene. It's probably a good idea to ignore more of them, as I might ask twice as many if you answered them all.

Do you remember (this one is rhetorical again) that you said that last night in Chicago you'd like to hear me talk when I was drunk? Murphy says I'm funny & she knows because those Manhattans Capt. Bauer makes are powerful. That's not what I started to say, however. Since you are even more reticent than I (Or is that my imagination? There would be a good reason if it is.) I've been thinking it would be much more fun to let you do the drinking. If the rum & coke had any influence on your letter tonight, I believe in it.

I liked the story about how you were going to save those letters for the next day. If they were from you, dear, I couldn't do it either.

Say, I hope that nurse likes O'Leary. Wouldn't want him to have too much competition.

I like you—

Goodnight, sweetheart,
Marian

✤

April 11, 1945

Gene, dear,

Last night I had two real wonderful letters from you, dated the 5th & 6th. I can hardly believe that was just Friday night. Why, think, if you had a 10-day leave & a priority, we'd have two days left over!

I shall be interested to know how you answer that question you're going to ask yourself when you start grumbling about rotation.

Rotation — 28 mos. — reminds me of that song they used to play in 1941, "I'll be back in a year." No one believed that either. Franklin nearly had kittens every time he heard it.

I was interested to hear the idea about a radio store. Two of the details were somewhat obscure, however. Is his name Herman or Kerman? And how do you spell Rueben's last name?

Speaking of Allis Chalmers, this friend of mine who used to be Rev. Hjortland's secretary at Ascension, Ruth Borge, worked for A.C. also sometime in '42, I believe. All the stuff in their dept. was being shipped to Switzerland, which at the time was surrounded by Nazi-occupied countries. We thought it peculiar, to say the least.

I wish you had asked about W'berg two weeks ago. I think we had a map of Wis. which we threw away when we moved. It's about 75 mi. north of Oshkosh, though, and about 60 mi. directly west of Green Bay.

What does the 3rd Div. insignia look like? I'll be looking for them just as I do for the 15th Air Force. It's a vain pursuit, but it's sort of fun.

About those pictures you want, a couple of months ago I sent one or two by regular mail of the group pictures taken at our Army-Navy E party. So you should be getting those one of these days if they're not completely battered by this time. Those, these, them — what a sentence! Must be I need some sleep. See you tomorrow, my darling.

Love, Marian

✤

April 12, 1945

Oh, Gene, darling,

What a sad day this is! I feel a personal loss almost as great as when my own Franklin died. I wish I could talk to you about it, dear. It's so hard to believe, & I most fervently wish I could wake up in the morning & find it isn't true.

Paul heard it from a friend he talked to on the phone just about 5:00 tonight. His comment was, "Well, it's a fine president you have now!" One of the girls in the office said, "I guess that's what they wanted." I could have thrown inkwells at them both. The Republicans, damn them, are the ones who wanted it that way!

I am concerned about Truman myself & deeply concerned by the difference it may make in our ability to deal with Stalin & Churchill. However, my greatest worry is the harm Truman's enemies can do to the future of our ideals by exploiting his Pendergast record to the detriment of his possible effectiveness as a leader.

Roosevelt's death seems to me a tragedy greater than the assassination of Lincoln. Good Lord, what a world we live in, Gene. Remember what a short time ago we were so glad he was our President?

"Here Captain! dear father!
This arm beneath your head!
It is some dream that on the deck,
You've fallen cold and dead."[28]

Security is the dream.

—

Murphie and I just took time out to relax & have a glass of wine. I really worked hard today & with this on top of it all I felt sort of like a rag doll.

I think I shall send you this letter from Peg as I think you will be interested in the talk she heard Clifton Utley[29] give in La Crosse, & I don't have the ambition to copy it. There is nothing very personal about the letter, so she would surely not mind. The offer he assumes the Japanese will make seems quite logical to me. Does it to you also?

I must write to Peg tonight and also to my mother, so goodnight, darling. I miss you more every day.

Love, Marian

❀

Margaret Borrebek to Marian:

Galesville, Wis
April 9 1945

Dearest Marian,

I am reading "The Immortal Wife," and I am completely devastated. I think it is one of the best books I have read in some time. I could hardly put it down until I had finished it. I am so glad that you have read it only I wish you were here to talk it over. At first I (you know how I always try to find flaws in the perfection) thought he insisted too much that she kept the marriage first, but through that you realized better what kind of person she was. I also like his choice of material. I would get so tired if he made her always wonderful etc. but I thought that bit about her journey to Lincoln was wonderful. I think every girl ought to read it. It makes me appreciate Ray so very much, because I never had to make a bargain to be an intellectual partner like she did, he has assumed and even demanded that I try to be. Oh, I love that man! I also liked the very fascinating picture of Fremont's life, I didn't know he had been that prominent in American history.

Two very nice things have happened this week. The best was a letter from Ray. And I was all wrong. He is in Patton's army! I can't find any mention of the 65th except a picture of two men, but they were still at Saarlautern where Ray said he crossed. All he said of that was, "I will tell you all about it someday." I wish he had Gene's verbosity. He also said that they had liberated some Russian prisoners but they were no more spectacular than G.I. Joe! I was so glad to read that John never ceased to have a physical effect on Jessie, because Ray will always have on me and I wasn't sure that was normal. Even his letters can stir me into a whole churn of emotions.

The other was a present from Mike that you would be quite interested in. There was a darling note with it to this effect—"You said you felt like an old lady, so here is something to make you look like a bobby-soxer" and it was a huge white silk scarf, about a yard square printed profusely with the Twelfth Air Force, its emblem and the names of some of the planes. It's very attractive, and made of the finest silk. He said they all wear them when they fly.

I also got some newspapers from a friend in England and I enjoyed reading them. They seem to be so much clearer about the war, its aims, and its pursuit. The front page is devoted to war news exclusively, no monkeying around like our papers do.

This week also the mayor invited me to go to La Crosse with him to hear Clifford Utley who gave a very fine speech. I wish you could have heard it. It was so interesting and his points seemed to be those of a very high-minded, sincere person. He told many interesting things about what we have done lately that looks sinister to the Russians and he emphasized that the conference at San Francisco should be upheld and cemented even if it seems there will only be a 20% or 30% of success. And he emphasized a point that I had made many times, don't plan for permanent peace, plan for 50 or 100 years and make it stick. Then you won't become disillusioned if the plans for lasting peace look like they will fall through and you will become no help as far as active participation goes. He had gone to school at Munich during the last war and so knew the terrain and the people of Germany well.

For the Germans between the ages of six and forty-five, there is no hope, as they have been too thoroughly poisoned by the Nazis. It will take 20 years to educate a generation who will not be outlaws on the earth. Japan, he said, will make an offer soon to withdraw from all captured territory and live on the Japanese Islands. Then he will order all his generals to commit suicide and tell the people that those men had betrayed them by urging them to leave the islands where they had lived for 2000 years. In this way the nation will save face. Utley believes that this should not be accepted but occupation of Japan should result in the destruction of Emperor worship if we do not want to have this again. It does seem very uncivilized doesn't it, when you think that they worship a mortal.

I am so anxious to get to Washington. It seems such a long time that I have been trying to get there.

I ordered a dress like that lime one we liked only I am going to have it in black and white, as I want a summer black. I saw it in La Crosse yesterday, and it is very nice material.

I have done nothing today except write letters, fix dinner and take a walk which ended by staying for supper at the home of a friend. I have papers to correct, but I guess I have spring fever.

Write soon. Have you or are you going to Othello etc.?

Love and kisses forever,
Peggy

❧

April 14, 1945

Dearest Gene,

I have just listened to an eulogy for the President in the form of a poetic conversation between 4 people in the woods at Hyde Park. It was beautiful. I imagine you have heard some of these things. I hope so. Each one, each newspaper article, and each flag at half mast makes my sorrow deeper. It is rather wonderful, though, to see the Allied world apparently more united in this tragedy than ever before. I hope that is not merely a passing feeling. As Pres. Truman said, "It has pleased God in his infinite wisdom — " I feel like rebelling against that "infinite wisdom" sometimes, but quickly agree to accept it when I think how far from infinite is my own.

Rec'd your letter of the 7th yesterday. It must have been a real treat to see your dad after 27 months. How did he ever have the good fortune to take that particular route home? What did he do before the war, Gene? I'd like to know more about him, and your mother, too. Just that curiosity about "other people 'certain' people care about."

My dear, it would never have occurred to me even to remember that there is such a thing as a Thor washing machine. It's a pretty good joke, though. Wasn't Thor the god of war? Or was it just thunder? I rather like the name, but I like Gene better.

I'd like to have heard all the versions of Edwards' encounter with the Jap. He must be a good sport. I'm awfully sorry about his girl. It's probably just as well for him, but it would be difficult to see that side of it.

Franklin used to have the same kind of trouble rather consistently. It was pretty much his own fault, though, as he'd never make up his mind he really liked a girl until someone took her away from him. A perverse nature, I suppose.

Guess I'd better quit & try to finish Time so I can send it to you. I'm rather late this week. Did you ever get any of your own copies of the Pacific Edition? Goodnight, darling.

Much love, Marian

⚘

11 April 1945
Central Pacific

Hello darling,

Have really put in a full day's work today. It is about 10:30 and just finished typing up the last message. Really felt strange to type again after all this work. I am assigned to the message center which is not too well to my liking. The work is interesting enough but it's still office work.

The mail situation has not been too good lately and as a result have not heard from you for about 6 days. (that is a late letter) Rec'd one today you had enclosed with that picture you sent. They were very good (tho I rather hope it would be larger.) I did like it very much Marian. We all agreed that you were the most attractive girl there. Which reminds me—you <u>are</u> attractive. Kinda been thinking all along about your personality which after all I consider No. 1 on the list of desired elements.

I am on watch tonight after working almost steady since 0730. I can hardly keep my eyes open now.

I suppose that you are back in Chicago by now. Hope your mother is all right. My dad should be near home by now and I sure wish that around Chicago-ways about now. Am getting a little restless and don't think I'd mind going into combat again—but not another Iwo. Goodnight darling.

Thurs. 11 April. Back again and it's now almost 1700. Played hooky from work today because I didn't feel too good. Kinda think I got Dengue fever but now am getting back to normal. Been sort of sick (stomach) ever since we got back. Maybe these comforts don't agree with me. Finally rec'd a letter from you dated March 31 I believe. You wrote it on the "400." Did we ever have an argument about that train? Makes me very disgusted that I can't remember more of what happened on that trip. Maybe sometime you could send a play-by-play (?) account of what you remember.

Sorry that (here occurs a break of 5 hours and I can't remember what I was sorry for)

The movie tonight was a new version of the "Dr. Kildare" type with Van Johnson and some glamorous blonde.

Met Edwards & Merle up there after I had decided to go. Got called to make a run to town with some message thus the break.

Well anyway, I just arrived back at our house to find 3 letters from you which helped matters considerably. Found out that many are sick here from eating de-hydrated food which is probably my trouble. I'm glad you are starting to get my letters again. There was a period of 4 days I couldn't write.

Concerning the Marines and your general picture of the organizations you are absolutely right. Undoubtedly some dopey announcer didn't get the word about the 3rd Div. Wish I could tell you more but it'll have to wait.

I've been sending mail to both apt. numbers because you didn't mention lately that you were moving. Wasn't quite sure of the new number either because that letter was lost with my belongings. However I see you have moved so it'll be 1507.

At present it is raining like hell and I am sitting here with all your latest letters spread out like tactical maps at G2. Will answer your questions too so—. Incidently if there is anything you want to know about my life etc! don't hesitate. I feel rather silly to write it because I suppose you are not interested in an autobiography after all.

Glad you had a good time with the Sgts despite the fact I would have given them plenty of competition had I been there. Don't know if I told you the final chapter in that gal affair in L.A. but since you mentioned it in the "proposing connection" you may be interested.

The last weekend in L.A. I decided to have a date because it looked very much like the last liberty in the states. Dropped her a card about Thursday and lo & behold on Friday received a telephone call from Martha (her) reminding me to be sure and call her that weekend. So I did that Saturday and went out to her house. Much to my surprise she was very glad to see me. (I had not wrote) We took off at "high port" for Hollywood and during the evening succeeded in getting very drunk. Prior to this she had made the not-too-startling announcement that she had been signed by MGM as a starlet which substantiates my remark that she was very beautiful. Then to my surprise this ballyhoo (again) about being in love and wanting to get married before I left. For some reason (that's another story) I was very disgusted with womenkind at that particular time and decided to play along with her. So we pledged undying love till the wee hours. It was all so funny because I think she thought "how silly it is"—and I knew how foolish it sounded. That is the only time that I have not been truthful with a girl but only because she thought that she was getting by with something. I wrote a letter the following Monday to uphold my end of the agreement but as I figured she never wrote hers and I of course never wrote again. The whole thing struck me as very unusual and inasmuch as it was all seriousness outwardly, very funny.

Darling it's way past my bed time so I guess I'd better close for now. Could really write on and on tonight to you. Goodnight sweetheart and I am <u>not</u> kidding <u>you</u>.

Much love, Gene

⚜

15 APRIL 1945

DARLING,

MY BAD HANDWRITING IS PROBABLY ONLY EXCEEDED BY MY BAD TYPING WITH THAT WARNING I'LL START THIS LETTER TONIGHT. WHILE I AM ON DUTY HERE IN THE MSG CENTER TENT JUST HAPPENED TO THINK THAT I NEVER COULD FIND ANYBODY HERE THAT CAN READ SHORTHAND AND SO TELL ME WHAT YOU SAID AT THE END OF ONE LETTER . WHAT WAS IT? DECIDED TO GO TO SICK BAY TODAY TO FIND OUT IF I HAD STOMACH ULCERS, CHINESE ROT, OR WHAT AND IT TURNED OUT TO BE VERY SUCCESSFUL AS THE MEDICINE HELPED MUCH AND I AM BEGINNING TO FEEL ALMOST HUMAN AGAIN . THE DR'S FINALLY GOT TOGETHER AND BLAMED THE EPIDEMIC ON THE COKES. SOME OF THEM WERE SUPPOSED TO BE SOUR OR SOMETHING , IRONICALLY I JUST BOUGHT $40 OF IT (WE DO THINGS IN A BIG WAY HERE.) INCIDENTLY I DON'T KNOW WHETHER I TOLD YOU ABOUT OUR FORMER MAJOR IN THE 28TH. WELL ANYWAY HE HAS A LOT OF POWER AROUND HERE FOR SOME REASON AND IS VERY INTERESTED IN THE FOOD SITUATION WHICH,IF YOU COULD SEE HIM WOULD BE QUITE OBVIOUS AND ALWAYS MANAGED TO GET US THE MOST UNUSUAL THINGS TO EAT AND DRINK. FOR INSTANCE ONCE HE SUGGESTED TO THE 28TH CLUB THAT HE WAS ABLE TO GET A VERY LARGE AMOUNT OF ICE CREAM. AS A RESULT WE HAD A

CORNER ON ALL THE ICE CREAM ON THE ISLAND AND EVERY-
BODY ELSE WAS VERY SAD WE HAD 200 CASES. ALSO WHEN
EVERYONE ELSE WAS LIMETED ALONG THE BEER LINE WE HAD
ENOUGH TO SWIM IN. IT WAS AMAZING TO SAY THE LEAST.
NOW THIS REMARKABLE MAN IS GOING BACK TO THE STATES
AND ONE OF HIS MEN FROM THE 21ST MARINES REMARKED
CASUALLY THAT THE MAJOR HAD 1000 CASES OF BEER IN HIS
OWN NAME TO GET RID OF. I IMAGINE THAT YOU REMEMBER
THAT I MENTIONED HOW GOOD THE FOOD WAS WHEN I WAS
STILL IN THE DRAFT HE WAS PERSONALLY RESPONSIBLE FOR
ALL THAT.

EVERYONE IS STILL ROTATION HAPPY THAT IS QUALIFIED
BUT MOST OF THEM HAVE ALREADY LEFT. IT SURE TAKES THE
HEART OUT OF THE DIV AND WE ARE NOW THE VETERANS AND
THE NEW BOOTS LOOK IN AWE AT US. AS I SAID BEFORE I WAS
GETTING VERY TIRED OF HEARING ABOUT GUADAL AND
EVERYONE SEEMED TO THINK THAT IF YOU WERE A MARINE
YOU SHOULD HAVE BEEN THERE.

LAST NIGHT WAS A LITTLE OUT OF THE ORDINARY AS
JASCO HAD A DANCE FOR THE ENLISTED MEN AND AS THEY
ARE RIGHT NEXT TO US WE LOOKED IN TO SEE THE UNUSUAL
SIGHT. THERE WAS FREE BEER AND 150 NATIVE GALS AND ALL
THE JASCO MEN WORE LITTLE TAGS SO THAT NO ONE ELSE
COULD CRASH THE PARTY. I HAD CALLED STEVE MOHOROVICH
AND INVITED HIM OVER TO OUR CLUB FOR THE EVENING IT
ENDED UP THAT STEVE, MERLE, AND MYSELF GOT IN A COR-
NER AND PASSED SARCASTIC REMARKS ALL EVENING, AND
STEVE GETTING VERY DRUNK TOWARD CLOSING TIME. STEVE
INVITED US OVER TO THE PIONEERS FOR SOME CANNED
CHICKEN ETC WE AGREED AND AFTER ARRIVING IN HIS AREA
HE TOLD US TO WAIT A MINUTE WHILE HE WENT IN THE NEAR-
EST TENT TO GET SOMETHING. NOT KNOWING EXACTLY WHAT
WAS GOING ON WE WERE COMPLETELY IN THE DARK AS TO HIS
ACTIONS. HE CAME OUT OF THIS TENT AND HANDED ME A BIG
BOX WITHOUT SAYING A WORD. THE BOX WAS FULL OF HARD
BOILED EGGS WHICH I SOON FOUND OUT BY MYSELF. THEN HE
MOTIONED US TO FOLLOW HIM AS HE WENT INTO ANOTHER
TENT. WHEN I GOT TO THE DOOR WITH MERLE FOLLOWING
SOMEBODY WAS STANDING IN THERE HOLDING THE DOOR
OPEN SO I FOLLOWED STEVE IN AND MERLE AND SOMEBODY
ELSE (A STRANGER) CAME IN BEHIND ME. STEVE KEPT
MOTIONING TO ME TO DO SOMETHING (I LATER FOUND OUT)

BUT ANYHOW I STEPPED ALONG SIDE HIM AND THESE TWO
OTHER FELLOWS GATHERED AROUND THE ICE BOX THAT HE
WAS NOW OPENING. THEN FOR THE FIRST TIME I NOTICED
ANOTHER MAN (BESIDE THE ONE HOLDING THEDOOR OPEN)
WHO SAID "ITS GETTING A LITTLE CROWDED ISN'T IT" ALL THIS
WHILE WE DID NOT KNOW WHAT WAS GOING ON AND NOT A
WORD WAS SPOKEN STEVE KEPT MOTIONING AND BY THIS
TIME HAD 10 BIG SLICES OF HAM IN HIS HAND WHICH HE HAD
TAKEN OUT OF THE ICE BOX. THE FELLOW WHO HAD SPOKEN
BEFORE THEN SAID "BETTER SEE IF YOU CAN ROUND UP SOME
MORE MEN." IN A VERY SARCASTIC MANNER. STILL NOT SPEAK-
ING STEVE TURNED AROUND AND WALKED OUT AND WE FOL-
LOWED. I SAID "FOR HEAVEN'S SAKE STEVE WHAT IS GOING
ON?" HE SAID "GOOD GOD, THAT WAS THE COLONEL AND HIS
ICEBOX I RAIDED." I ALMOST FAINTED AND COULD NOT HELP
BUT LET OUT A LITTLE GROAN LATER WE ALL PRACTIALLY
LAUGHED OUTSELVES SICK AS WE COULD WELL IMAGINE THAT
THE COLONEL MUST HAVE BEEN BOTH SURPRISED AND PROB-
ABLY SNOWED AND CERTAINLY NEVER DREAMT IN HIS
WILDEST MOMENTS THAT ANYONE IN HIS RIGHT MIND
WOULD STEAL HIS HAM WHILE HE WAS STANDING THERE. THE
ONLY EXPLANATION WE COULD THINK OF WAS THAT THERE
WAS A PARTY GOING ON PREVIOUSLY AND THAT THE MESS SGT
HAD USED HIS ICE BOX TO HOLD SOME OF THE FOOD AND HE
PROBABLY THOUGHT THAT WE WERE CONNECTED WITH THAT
AFFAIR. SO WE HAD SWELL HAM SANDWICHES AND HARD
BOILED EGGS
 THE RAIN HAS JUST STARTED AND IT IS COMING DOWN IN
SUCH LARGE QUANTITIES THAT I CAN HARDLY HEAR THE TYPE-
WRITER. TOMORROW I AM HDQS BN DUTY OFF AND THAT
MEANS ANOTHER NIGHT GONE. I EITHER GET CO DUTY, BN
DUTY OR CWO (CHIEF WATCH OFF) MOST OF THE TIME SO MY
TIME IS NOT MY OWN ANY MORE BUT IT DOES MAKE THE DAYS
FLY .[30]
 Later but I better get this off in the morning's mail.

Lots of love, Gene

⚜

15 April 1945 [2]

Hello darling,

Have been working for a change and really putting in some long hours. As a matter of fact I have not had any time off in a week. Today is Sunday and I am C.W.O. here in msg. center. The time passes rapidly but I think the disadvantages overshadow the benefits. It's interesting of course and as I'll probably be telling you from time to time what I am doing so no need to go into any great detail now. Your last letter took 6 days to get here which isn't bad. I'm sorry that you received no mail last week from me but you can probably reason out why that was so. It is now 1000 and I am on till 0800 tomorrow—certainly a stupid way to spend a Sunday. Would like to go to church for the memorial services for Roosevelt. The flags fly at half-mast for 30 days here.

I haven't much comment to make on his death. I felt shocked and my faith in the future greatly diminished. I have always regarded any hope we have for World peace and he as inseparable. As for Truman—I don't know. Makes me so damn angry when I think of the stupid political setup here which makes it necessary to compromise upon a man for Vice President whose only qualification is that he is harmless. We could very easily have a parallel to the Andrew Johnson days after Lincoln was killed. He too was harmless and altho a good man and desired to carry out Lincoln's wishes was too weak to stop the opposition. So the "reconstruction" period of the south became the blackest period in American history and probably made Lincoln turn in his grave.

The only course to follow now is to back Truman to the limit and pray that the intent of Congress and the American people is for peace and that the sacrifices that will have to be made be done without personal selfishness or sectional greed. The days to come will be rough and there will be need for men like Roosevelt and greater need for the American people to begin to think in terms of understanding the World problems. Unfortunately I have little faith in the common people to rise to the job in front of them. There is too much need for education and too little general interest (which accounts for my cynicism in general) It takes unusual circumstances to make people work together. One of the best things that ever happened to me was to notice how men work in combat. There is perfect teamwork and everybody is really giving forth 100%. It makes for a grand feeling to see everyone doing (and desiring to do) his job without grumbling or worrying if he is doing too much in comparison with the other fellow. When the going gets tough it actually does happen. (I wouldn't have believed it.) but—after the smoke dies away cooperation is forgotten. Oh well.

This isn't much of a love letter either but if I could write them they would be to you. More later.

Much love, Gene

✤

18 April 1945
Central Pacific

Dearest Marian,

Rec'd 3 letters from you yesterday so that made the day very nice. Really got surprised that the latest only 5 days ago—that is the record coming this way I believe. It only takes 2 days more to get here than it did to Pendleton. Kinda think that it is because we are at this particular place.

DECIDED TO TYPE THIS SO I WONT BE SO OBVIOUS AS I WAS SITTING AT THE CWO DESK. OH BOTHER—DID I HAVE MY TROUBLES TODAY. IT ALL STARTED THIS MORNING WHEN THE COLONEL OF HDQS HERE CALLED UP AND WANTED THE MAN WHO WAS O.D. LAST NIGHT. UNFORTUNATELY IT WAS ME (OR I AS THE SCHOOLTEACHERS SAY) AND SO I PRACTICALLY FLEW OVER THERE TO HIS OFFICE EXPECTING ALMOST ANYTHING AND IN THE MEANTIME LINING UP EXCUSES FOR EVERYTHING IMAGINABLE. IT HAPPENED THAT YESTERDAY WE HAD A VERY DISTINGUISHED VISITOR WHO WAS THE GUEST OF GEN. ERSKINE LAST NIGHT. WELL THIS GENTLEMAN SHAVED HIS BEARD ON THE PREVIOUS AFTERNOON AND CAREFULLY LAID HIS RAZOR ON THE WASHSTAND NEAR THE TENT HE WAS LIVING IN. WISHING TO SHAVE AGAIN THIS MORNING HE QUICKLY NOTICED THAT THE RAZOR WAS MISSING FROM WHERE HE HAD PLACED IT. THAT WAS THE SITUATION WHEN THE COLONEL CALLED ME IN. HE TOLD ME ALL THE FACTS AND ALL THE CLUES (OF WHICH THERE WAS 1- IT WAS A BLACK AND GOLD SAFETY RAZOR. NO SENTIMENTAL VALUE WHATSOEVER AND AS A MATTTER OF FACT -IF I KNOW THIS GENTLEMAN- HE PROBABLY SAID, "TO HELL WITH IT" BUT THE OLD MAN WAS VERY MUCH CONCERNED AND SO WE ALL WALKED VERY BRISKLY TO THE X PLACE OF THE CRIME (THESE LITTLE "X" ES HAVE NOTHING TO DO WITH THE STORY FOR THEY ARE MERELY MISTAKES) AND DURING THE COURSE OF AN HOUR I CRAWLED ON MY HANDS AND KNEES LOOKING FOR THAT DAMN RAZOR. NO LUCK, AND AS I WAS GETTING VERY TIRED THE WHOLE AFFAIR, AND TRIED TO TALK THE COLONEL INTO BELIEVING THAT MY MEN OF THE GUARD PROBABLY HAD NOTHING TO DO WITH IT BECAUSE WE DID NOT PATROL THAT PARTICULAR AREA. HE FINALLY AGREED AND I THOUGHT -AH I AM OUT OF IT. WHEN I WAS ABOUT TO WALK OFF HE DECIDED

THAT HE WOULD PUT ME IN CHARGE OF THE INVESTIGATION WHICH WOULD CONSIST OF GETTING THE NAMES OF ALL THE PEOPLE IN THAT VICINITY FROM 1630 TO 0600. SO THAT IS WHAT I HAVE BEEN DOING ALL DAY AND AS YET—NO SIGN OF THE BLOOMING THING. WISH THAT THIS STORY HAD A GOOD END-ING AND IF I FIND IT—IT IS VERY LIKELY THAT I'LL CUT SOME-BODY'S THROAT.

WHO IS THE MAN? CAN'T SAY THAT AT PRESENT. HE DID GIVE A VERY GOOD SPEECH AT A RECEPTION LAST EVENING AT THE OFF CLUB. QUOTE THE THIRD DIV. IS THE BEST IN THE MARINE CORPS AND THEREFORE THE BEST IN THE ARMED FORCES UNQUOTE. IT MAY HAVE JUST BEEN A LOT OF SMOKE BLOWING BUT IT SOUNDED GOOD FROM SOMEONE WHO SHOULD KNOW. YOU CAN MAKE YOUR OWN GUESSES AS TO WHO HE IS.

MANAGED TO SNEAK OFF TO THE MOVIE LAST NIGHT AND SAW "GOING MY WAY" FOR THE SECOND TIME. (FIRST TIME AT THE WISCONSIN IN MILW.) IT UNDOUBTEDLY WAS AN OUT-STANDING PICTURE BUT I DON'T THINK THAT I WOULD CALL IT THE BEST OF THE YEAR. DO YOU THINK SO? THE BAND WAS PLAYING "I'LL GET BY" THIS NOON WHICH I CONSIDER ONE OF THE OUTSTANDING SONGS OF THE WAR. HAD TO REMEMBER THE SCENE IN THE PICTURE "A GUY NAMED JOE" IN WHICH IRENE DUNNE SANG IT TO S. TRACY. IT REALLY IMPRESSED ME NO END ESPECIALLY THE PART WHERE TRACY IS LEANING ON THE TABLE WITH HIS HAND HOLDING HIS HEAD AND SIGHS, "SING IT AGAIN" I LIKED THAT.

Back home again for the night. I really feel good tonight—not because I received a letter from you but just thinking how good the mail service can be at times. Just took a shower and got all cleaned up—made a pair of house slippers out of some field shoes and oddly enough they look good.

I spent the last 45 minutes sorting your letters and reading them again. The first one was dated Nov. 5 and (still with me?) got as far as Dec. 15. Made me a little embarrassed to see all the questions I didn't answer and the clippings I didn't comment upon. It's surprising you are still writing to me.

We did come close to seeing each other in November—didn't we? Has it only been 65 hours we have been together? Kinda think it's better to say we known each other for 14 months.

We have got to know each other very well I believe through the mail sys-tem as you said we would back in November. I'll repeat that statement I've made before that you are very adept at letter writing and likewise for saying the right things at the right time.

There are some planes zooming over here at mast-top height. Those P-51's are beautiful but I still think my favorite is the P-38. They seemed so much faster and I liked the peculiar whistle they had. (Confusing?) I am all alone at home tonight sitting at a big table. Made myself a closet a few days ago which helps the clothes situation considerably. Steve gave me a blanket roll for the one I lost at Iwo. It belonged to a friend of mine who was killed there—McCreary—inside I found a whole laundry bag of clothes so am wearing them tonight—in fact all I've got on was his. Not too pleasant a thought but it doesn't bother me.

Guess I can tell you about those pilots now that were on Iwo. About the last night we were there several Japs got through to the 2nd airfield and stumbled across the fliers' tents. (Note—the Marines slept in foxholes but the pilots had tents and cots) Well to make a long story short—the Japs cut the throats of 12 of them while they slept before the word got out and they sent some Marines back to get them. It struck me as particularly sad that they should die like that but then I thought of the first one (pilot) I'd seen there and how he'd stepped out of that plane in fresh starched kahki and how we looked after not having our clothes off for a week.

Sgt. Austin just came in for a talk so there has been some delay. He was my sgt. up there and I can thank him for half the headaches I didn't have. At least I knew when I stepped out of the shell hole after the mortars he'd be right behind. As a matter-of-fact I had to convince him that I should go first because after all I was being paid more by the Marine Corps.

Talking about confusing letters—this should be the number one prise. Better close now before it becomes worse. The pictures are pretty bad but then—Goodnight sweetheart—I am thinking of you always.

Much love, Gene.

⚜

19 April 1945

Darling,

I have the morning free so I'll get off a letter now. I have been tending to my other correspondence which you have made me neglect of late. I do get a lot of mail which I'll explain by saying that the majority comes from the family. I have to write 3 letters to the family due to my dad's desire to break up house-keeping long ago whereas I should only have to write one. To my grandfather to my mother—to my dad—to my stepmother occasionally. Most of them go to my grandfather however because like you he writes the best letters and the most and I enjoy writing to him. My ambition is to be as much like him as possible. Wish I had half as much on the ball as he has at 80 years. We always have agreed 100% in everything which is indeed remarkable. Don't know whether it's because of his young outlook or my old-fashioned ideas but probably a little of each. I told him I would give him my share of Iwo as a birthday present.

I have been reading "Flight to Arras" which I received yesterday. As you said—it is a remarkable book. The questions the author asks himself—such as why go through with the flight when the results will probably never make any difference anyway—is the same one that every serviceman who does any thinking wonders about at times. "Why should we fight and die if there is to be another war eventually anyway" The only answer that I can see that this _may_ be a war to end all wars. We've got to take that chance. I'll have more comments after I finish the book.

Also through the mail yesterday I rec'd a couple boxes from home containing sheets, Milw. Journals and odds and ends. Most important was your picture which somehow or other got mixed up with my old orders and was sent home. I wrote for it right away but it just arrived. So you see all this time I have only my memory to bring back some memories of what you looked like. Never told you about that because I figured you might think—if he's so careless with my picture, he probably doesn't give a damn. Of course that is not the case darling.

Rec'd the Feb. issue of the "Atlantic Monthly" for which I was very happy. I like the articles. Would you do me a favor?—tell them my new address. I hope that it's the last change for awhile and it begins to look that way now.

Mail is going out so I'd better get this letter on the way. Much love darling and I'm looking forward to seeing you back there too much already.

Gene

⚜

20 April 1945

My dear Marian,

You are still probably tangled up in that letter I sent a few days ago. What a masterpiece of confusion and if you are disgusted with me I wont blame you a bit. I wrote a few pages to you this morning to get out in the morning's mail and this afternoon will say some more but I will finish the letter sometime tommorrow.

At present it's rainning again which is nothing unusual for this time of year they keep telling me. Our house stands on piles about six ft off the ground so there is not a chance of us being washed down the cliff out to sea. If I thought I possibly could reach the Chicago river (dirty as it is) I would take a chance and set out on my own. That reminds me—do you like Chicago? I know that you always complain of the dirt but outside of that how does it appeal to you?

Incidently <u>Where</u> would you like to live if you had your choice? I am going to fire a lot of questions your way in the future sorta to get on the offensive. Not that I resent all the questions you have been asking me in the slightest because that after all is the secret of letter writing. Men especially like to talk about themselves which you have probably found out. If we both have enough to drink when I get back, probably the conversation will last for days. I really would prefer to listen as I do most of the time. However this is not the case when I have had something to drink. Oftimes I have tried to found out the reason why this is so after I've had a few drinks. Never could find out the solution however, and above all I hate to think of having to be half tight in order to be amusing.

By the way it seems to me that we had quite a bit to drink that last night in Chicago. Didn't we? I can't remember all the details but it seems to me we were on the subject of love at one time or the other. I do remember that I thought "How I'd like to hit her over the head and take her along to LA." Would you have put up much of battle? Speaking of trains — on the way back east after my sick leave on the Columbian I sat next to a girl who in the course of the conversation turned out to be somebody I'd gone to school with way back in jr. high days. She was also "Miss Wisconsin" of 1943. She was going east to meet her ensign who is J. P. Heil's[31] nephew. We had a grand conversation of dancing, jitterbugging, her clothes, and other vital subjects. Don't imagine you know her — Charlotte Lemmer —

Edwards came over last night to invite me to his club for a party which he was giving to celebrate his making First Lt. As it didn't start till later we went to the movie at our club here at Div. Being high class we have a special movie just for officers right in the club. This is most extraordinary because all the others are out in the open and when the rain starts everybody just puts his poncho on and acts very natural. I (and Borrowman) keep reminding Edwards of that and constantly find fault with his club in contrast with quote the staff officers' wine mess unquote. He then becomes very bitter. In fact we ridicule everything about the 3rd Bat 21st Marines. Incidently that was the outstanding Bn. of the best Regiment (of the best Div at Iwo?) Last night I made out a diagram of the 3d Div so that you would be sure to know what I was talking about but I don't know whether I can send it.

To go way back to the original subject — we did go over to Edwards' club and spent the evening talking and drinking rum cokes which is about all three fellows can do out here. Merle is getting along O.K. in Jasco and is still expecting to be a happy if distant father one of these days. He says he has a feeling it is going to be twins. Wonder exactly what kind of a feeling that is —

Steve has left the 28th Draft and is now situated with the 3rd Marines. I don't know what kind of job he has over there — in fact I haven't seen him since the night he raided the Colonel's icebox.

Just time enough this morning to finish this. Saw "Meet me in St. Louis" last night at the 21st Marines. It rained and of course we got wet. He'll never live that down. Also met Dr. Weinstein who had the write-up in "Time". (Performed 7 major surgeries in an hour, etc.) He's quite a character—very young. Everybody keeps asking him, "How high was the blood Doc?" He points to his shoulder—"That high." He has taken quite a bit of kidding about that article. When they introduce him now they say "This is the Dr who performed 196 major operations in 10 minutes at Iwo."

Good-by again darling. I am looking for a letter from you today as always. I do like you very much.

Gene

⚓

My darling Marian,

Hope that you aren't getting tired of wading through all of these. The quantity should keep you busy even if the quality should be improved. The letter you wrote the 13th arrived this noon and as usual it made me very happy. That is— all of it except the comment on Roosevelt's death—which made me quite sad again. I feel exactly as you do about it and will be watching Truman very carefully to see just what he does and what the reaction to him will be—which is probably more important in the long run. We heard his address to Congress here on the island and I liked it very much. Also was very pleased with worldwise (as Time says) New York Times praise of the speech. At present he has little to do but to follow Roosevelt's wishes and to interpet what he would have done under the circumstances. However there will be a time when Truman will have to strike out on his own and there lies the trouble. I am anxious to find out what my grandfather's reaction will be. He has been so optimistic and perfectly satisfied with the way things have been going that I know that it will be a blow to him—as it was to all clear thinking people. Makes me so damn mad to see the easiness and "what's the difference" attitude that so many people took his death. I didn't make any comment until I saw Merle and then we had a long discussion. I like him a lot. We agree in politics to a very large extent not-withstanding the fact that he voted for Dewey. Said he was sorry afterwards and I never could get him to give a clear reason why he did it. Merle is a history teacher which accounts for the fact that we have something in common.

I like to listen to him talk about his college days and about his early married life. He went to Brigham Young Univer. and while working his way through his freshman year—got married. From then on things really were rugged I gather. He worked during the summer in a canning factory and managed to scrape up enough money to last them throughout the year. They paid $5.00 per week for a room and their food budget was something like $4.00 a week. He wouldn't let her work except during the last year and then only for a couple of weeks around Christmas. She spent all the money she earned to buy him a Christmas present. When he told how she had come home so happy explaining that they had saved 25 or 50 cents on the food budget some weeks, it almost had me in tears. Then they would go to a movie or to some free dance that the school was giving. Certainly when people have that much faith in one another as they did it is one of the most wonderful things in the world.

Peg's letter was very interesting—I should like to meet Ray sometime. I'll have to read the "Immortal Wife" after that buildup. I know that you mentioned it some time ago in connection with the historical background. Never knew much about Fremont—That reminds me of something else—it seems everybody here heard some wild stories about "Forever Amber" and a lot of the fellows have written home for the book. They all seemed to arrive at once so now everybody in Jasco seems to be an authority on the book. At least there is much argument as to how many persons the heroine had affairs with and all the vivid details. Merle's roommate gave it to him so now he is reading it too. It seems that there is a rather good historical background which interests him more than the seductions and on that basis I will probably read it later. I had to laugh at Peg's doubt whether she was normal too—glad that she is. Give her my best wishes and advice she quit the teaching racket as soon as it is practical. I mean this—on the presumption that she is getting married of course. Nothing is quite so repulsive to me as an old maid school teacher. I keep telling myself that it possibly can't happen to me but I really think that the profession (?) has a different affect upon the men.

Talked to John O'Leary for a few minutes at the club this noon. Don't see much of him as the result of his nursing etc, but we had a good talk then. He told me something very interesting. It seems that the Div is going to set up one of these free educational service on the island under the Armed Services Institute. You have probably heard of it before and the fact that servicemen can take correspondance courses for high school and college credit in most any field or subject they desire. Well anyway they are going to teach these subjects in a classroom here to all that are interested. Don't you think that is a wonderful idea? It impresses me no end. Would like to take Spanish, more French, physics or some more history courses. The catch is—where are the teachers coming from. Right about then John said "By the way what were you doing in civilian life?" Not to get caught in the snare we agreed that I am to become a former street sweeper or something. Right now I shouldn't doubt but that I could do better at the latter.

We heard of Ernie Pyle's dying on Okinawa this morning and it seems that it never rains but that it pours. I never read a great deal of his work but the universal praise that he received seemed to indicate that he was the outstanding correspondent of the war.

I hate to bring this up—but have you heard any more about Franklin outside of the fact that he is missing? In your letter you seem to conciled [*sic*] to the fact that he is dead. Certainly hope that this is not true and everytime I hear of the Allies releasing some prisoners of war I hope that he is among them. I remember that one of the first things I noticed about you was the fact that you were wearing the silver wings of the AAF. I thought to myself—good God, not another one. It was very much relieved that I became when I found out that they were your brother's. Only because of you—I don't scowl at our friends the airplane drivers. If not before, I was very happy to see them up at Iwo. I could have gone over and kissed all the night-fighters.

Utley's ideas about what the Japs will do seem very reasonable to me. Their great problem these days should be—not how to win the war but how to save their face. If they are able to save their face some way it certainly will be easier for them to stop the war. We should demand unconditional surrender but that doesn't necessarily mean we should destroy Emperor worship. I don't believe the emperor was greatly responsible for the war and we can't hope to instill democracy in them overnight. As far as I am concerned I don't care who is running the country so long as his purpose is peace. We can't take the word of these countries that their intentions are going to be peaceful, we must see that they are by some sort of control. We must set up peace machinery to make this the last war for a few generations but I can't see why improvements and ammendments can't be made constantly as the need becomes apparent so that in theory there will be no more wars.

Time to close again darling. If I had a wish tonight, you would be here to help spend these 24 months.

Goodnight and
Much Love,
Gene

❖

21 April 1945
Saturday

Hello again darling,

I have had the day off and spent the morning doing odd jobs around the house. The only explanation I have for all these letters is that I got far behind on Iwo and what's more closely the truth—I like to write to you. You don't mind do you? I am glad I have someone to tell my troubles to and it is amazing how much there is to write about when one likes to write—There really is always something to write about—so none of this "there's nothing new here" for me. Besides I am tired of reading that in the letters I censor.

Spent part of the morning finishing reading your old letters. Noticed that some of them I had along on the campaign still have Iwo sand in them. Would you like to see what it looks like? I send some along. The island consisted of almost all of this ash.

Two things you said in different letters struck me particularly funny. I still have to laugh about it. The first was the fact that you wanted to throw a nutcracker at those "damn Republicans" in Wittenberg. I guess it appealed to me because the time was right around Christmas and I could just picture you at home enveloped in the true Christmas spirit—and then letting a nutcracker fly—

The other was your mention of Peg's letter in which she was going to a meeting designed "to put the churches behind the social forces moving to create world peace." Like you—I also could visualize some of these small churches whose greatest problems to date probably consisted in building membership.

The acting first sgt. was just in to call me to the phone. It was Steve so I invited him to the club tonight. He's Reg. Chemical officer for the 3rd Marines. Our first sgt. is having his troubles. We are very short of men in the company (enlisted) temporarily and he hasn't enough to furnish the guard quota. We do have a lot of officers (20) so I suggested making one-sgt. of the guard and a couple of the others privates of-the-guard. As one fellow said the other day— Trouble with this company is we have too many chiefs and not enough Indians. Mail just came in but none from you—I'm not complaining tho—because I <u>know</u> I'll get one tomorrow.

So long darling and as usual I am thinking of you.

Gene

❧

22 April 1945
Sunday noon

Dearest Marian,

I've been waiting for Steve to come by and pick me up in his jeep. We were supposed to go swimming today down at the beach.

Last night we had a party at the club and I invited him over. I don't think he was in such good shape when I took him home last night. In fact we were both extremely drunk—first time that's happened out here. I remember getting a jeep from the message center and we took out for the 3rd Marines. Merle was in back and probably saying his prayers as I was driving. Nothing happened however and that's the end of the drinking for awhile.

There were about 25 nurses present I think. A group of extremely talented enlisted men put on a show that was remarkable. Most of them played in big name orchestras and some were entertainers on the stage. Our guest was there and I wondered how he is getting along without his razor. Never found out any more details about it for which I am thankful.

I have to go to work this afternoon for a few hours and tomorrow I am C.W.O. again (chief watch off) That means I'll have to sleep over in the message center tent again as it is a 24 hr. job.

Saw Rankin (the Marine gunner) at the club last night. Several days ago he gave a party after making Chief Warrant Officer. What with all the liquor and the promotion—he is in his glory. Heard too that two other fellows in the draft have died in the hospital, Lt.'s Ryan and Novak so that makes 9 in all.

Meant to tell you of the organization of these amphibian corps. The 5th Amphib. Corps includes the 3rd, 4th and 5th divisions. The 3rd Amphib. corps has the 1st, 2nd and 6th divisions. O.K.? The shoulder patch is that of the 3rd division so if you see any around Chicago you'll recognize it. I see the Marines on Okinawa have cleaned up their sector.

Monday morning.

Didn't get a chance to finish the letter yesterday so I'll start again this morning. I am C.W.O. and there will probably be too many interruptions to get far but then—

Your letter of the 15th arrived last night at about 10:00 PM. For some reason mail call was late. Of course I was glad to get it—wanted a letter from you yesterday more than anything.

I didn't know you lived in the Marq. Apts. Reuben was in the army as a P.F.C. during the time he went to Med. school. The procedure is to discharge all men after they graduate, let them do 9 mo. of interning and then snare them as 1st Lt.'s. O.K.?

He was with me that day I met you. To answer two other questions from a few letters back—his name is Reuben Snartemo—of Norwegian nationality and his cousin's name is HERMAN MADLAND (pronounced Mudland) I am answering your questions—aren't I?

Just received a letter from Reub a few days ago which I'll send along with this. Nothing unusual about it or him for that matter outside of the fact he has a terrific sense of humor (which I like) and also probably is the most brilliant fellow I've met. He's engaged to this Phyllis Rieboldt (a very nice girl) and the "Marsh" he speaks of is her brother who is getting married to some gal I don't know. (Are you still with me?) Marsh went to State Teachers for 2 years and Rueb attended S.T. for 3 years and then transferred to M.U. med school. I have known both of them practically all my life. When we started basketball in the Lutheran Federation league, Reuben & I also started dating two girls from

Wauwatosa who had come to watch their church play (Redeemer on 19th and Wisconsin) On my part this lasted for almost 3 years but meanwhile he became interested in Phyllis. The girl I went with got married and has a baby etc. and seemed fairly happy the last time I saw her. Her name was Marion. I don't know if all this is interesting or not but then it may be -

You are right in calling it the "post honeymoon era." Actually what I was refering to was that period which comes before the "era." There is such a time I believe in which you suddenly realize how you are going to spend that "era."

Better close again but I'll start another letter tonight. Wish I could tell you how much I'd like to be in Chicago tonight. But until I'm there—

Much love, Gene

❀

24 April 1945
Central Pacific

Darling,

Back again tonight for no other reason except that I might as well be writing to you as thinking about you. Everything is pretty well squared away here in the msg. center so I hope they leave me alone with my thoughts for awhile. Merle and my Sgt. from Iwo promised they would drop in later to help pass some of the time here tonight. I am on until tomorrow morning and the time until I can go to bed generally drags if we're not busy. Sgt. Austin is from N.Y. and really tops.—can be thankful that I had him up there. He is still talking about those four dead Japs that we were cuddling up to during that first shelling. I will never forget the look on his face and I imagine mine looked worse. Right now he is in the supply and repair section of the Signal Co. Actually he is a radar man. I would have liked to get the job as off. in charge of that outfit but there is a fellow here who has just about 18 mo. out and of course deserved it more than I. Will try again in earnest after he goes back.

Yesterday Merle, Eddy and I went for a jeep ride after arranging to meet Steve at the fleet off. club on the other side of the island. Steve was supposed to pick me up but got there too late and then when I got off duty met the other two fellows. This club is really terrific—is about 150 ft. long with over 25 bartenders and they serve practically anything your heart could desire. We don't belong there but there usually is so much confusion that nobody seems to care. The last time I was there was with Lt. Pace who was killed on Iwo. I can't remember if I ever told you about him. If I have this is going to be extremely boring and you can probably skip the next couple of paragraphs. Well anyway Pace was in my estimation a typical play-boy. I got along very well with him dispite his irresponsible attitude and carelessness. He obviously had had everything handed to him on a silver platter. He had gone to V-12 school at Mullenberg (SP?) and there got in some affair with a girl. Now the only thing that Pace knew for sure was his ideas on love. After many explanations to me on the subject (which was his favorite) it appeared that his idea of being in love was 100% sex. Example: Post-war plan — to live in Los Angeles with several girls while being married to no one. Well this girl at Mullenberg had a baby, and Pace was very anxious that his parents should not find out about it. It seems that they are quite wealthy and would cut him off without the necessary money he needed to carry on his post-war plans. Neither did he like to leave this girl in the lurch so they figured out a plan whereas she was supposed to be married to him and even went so far as to introduce him to her parents. She had the baby while he was at New River and through intricate plans his sister acted as the go-between. Then when he was transferred to the west coast she followed him for the purpose of getting a divorce — so she told her parents at any rate. At LA they couldn't get a divorce because it seemed they weren't married. So that left the situation very confused to Pace who didn't care too much for details anyway. He sailed and she went back to Allyntown Pa. No husband, no divorce but the baby which sadly neither of them cared too much about. He kept writing to her as Mrs. S.B. Pace and of course she sent many letters out here. What worried Sidney was the fact that she might locate his parents and put the heat on them for some money. The end of the story came about the time that we were about to leave and he decided to make out a will and leave her and the baby each $1.00 so they couldn't get any of his money. I said that I thought if he figured he would die during the campaign, he should leave her everything he had in his own name which was not too much. It seemed too much like a dirty trick on his part to me but that's the way he wanted it and I signed the will as one of the witnesses. The last thing that I heard about it was that he had made out a new will just before he went up to the front but I don't know if he took my advice or changed his plans in any way. Seems as though he knew something was going to happen. Anyways a sniper shot him before he ever reached the front lines killing him instantly. It makes me angry to see somebody go through life without any thoughts about his actions or that he might hurt someone else. In that case the parents are surely to blame to a large extent. He was an extremely handsome and good natured fellow but outside of that probably absolutely worthless. Sidney B. Pace II

I meant to ask you if I have ever met Murph — have I? I remember Peg in connection with her anxiety over her friend who was asleep in that hotel. At least that was the reason he didn't call her I think you said. One of the fellows here is singing the Arkansas state song — good God — I never heard such singing. It's about 90% hillbilly which I don't like at any rate. Reminds me — we have been kidding Merle about the new senator from Idaho who has a guitar and sings these cowboy songs. You probably heard his "give me a home by the capitol dome." Also said he was going to introduce a bill into Congress which would provide barracks for Congressmen. Seems he couldn't find a place to stay. I also am thinking about Mayor Zeidler from Milwaukee who by his singing got elected and defeated one of the most progressive and ablest men Wisconsin ever produced—D[aniel] Hoan. That election really left me bitter to think that he got elected by the women of Milwaukee who liked his blonde hair and "God Bless America" I remember him making a speech at our church which convinced those "clear thinking" Lutherans that Hoan had been absolutely worthless. As we shook hands with him after a 10 minute speech and 45 minutes of singing I remember saying I hoped Hoan would be elected again. I think it sort of stunned him.

The Republicans from Wittenberg and the Republicans from my church undoubtedly have much in common. There were many times that I would have liked to throw a nutcracker at them. They are so well satisfied and content to live in their own little world that they hardly know what is going on anywhere except that little community. For example: the first time I got home was right after I had received my commission at Quantico. So I came to church very bright and shinning in probably the true 2nd Lt. frame of mind. One of the men of the church looked at me very sympatheticly and said "no stripes yet hey?" I said "No, I expect to make P.F.C. as soon as I get back" end of conversation. It really didn't annoy me because I expected nothing better but it is typical of the non-interest of those people. Don't you think that it is sad when people have never heard of Casino, St Lo, Potesti, Iwo? I can think of nothing worst than coming home and somebody ask me, "Where is Iwo Jima?" Not that I give a damn because I was there but I get mad when I think of those thousands of Marines who died—and stayed at some place these people never heard of or have forgotten. If that attitude is typical then it seems that this war is merely the survival of the luckiest and to hell with those men who were killed. I know I will never forget or be able to thank enough those assault troops who literally paved the way in blood up there so I could sit on the beach in relative safety. Well enough of that—

Just been sitting here thinking that I probably should forget all the rest of this stuff and concentrate upon telling you how much I like you, how much I look forward to your letters, and how much I think about you. But no—I am not going to make my letters just that exclusively. I hope that you realize those things by now and I will be sure to remind you from time to time. We are going to have a perfect time when I do get home and there is no reason on my part why we shouldn't be thinking about it now. There will be much to do and certainly plenty of variety, so long as we appear to be gazing outward in the same direction there is much to look at. Goodnight sweetheart and

All my love, Gene

⚜

26 April 1945

Hello darling,

The San Francisco conference has slightly overshadowed my birthday but I don't mind. These are trying days out here. Haven't had any late letters for 5 days. I know you are writing but the mail is "snafu" [Situations Normal All Fouled Up] for some unknown reason — Probably the campaign in Okinawa.

Heard a resume of Truman's speech to the conference a few minutes ago and it sounded good. From what I have heard of the new president he sounds O.K. to me. I imagine you will send me some dope on the developments at S.F. so I need not ask. Wish you were Stassen's secretary too —

Really got a surprise today to read about one of the men in my company (in the 28th) who had stowed away in a plane and landed in Kansas City. I might add wistfully — wish he had taken me along — or at least tell me how he did it. I might have told you about him before and all the trouble I had with him aboard ship. The 1st Sgt. recommended I talk to him because his attitude was becoming terrific. After a chat I decided he was crazy because of the stupid ideas he had for example: he had a fatalistic idea that he would get killed as soon as he arrived here and decided that he might as well have as much fun as possible while he could. So he never obeyed orders or fell out for formations. Frankly I didn't know what to do with him but tried to convince him he had a better chance to live than I did (or the other officers) Merle said I made it sound so logical that he was sorry he was an officer!

Back from chow and two letters from you at last. It <u>was</u> a long stretch. The last one was dated April 18. I am in the message center again, very contented and eating an "O'Henry" bar. Managed to get a whole box of them yesterday.

To answer your questions about my dad — Before he entered the service (about 26 mo ago) he was Engineer-Janitor at Walker Jr. High school. No particular reason for getting into the service except that he could get a leave-of-absence easily — and wanted a last fling I guess. He had been in the Navy for about 5 years during the last war, got out and married my mother and a couple of years later was divorced. I had arrived in the meantime and after the divorce my grandparents wanted me so I lived with them since I was about 3 years old. My dad married again in 1931 and is undoubtedly very happy. My mother did likewise in 1932. She was from Waukesha and has lived there ever since. Both my stepparents are swell and I have always got along well with them. My dad has 2 children ages about 9 & 4 years.

After my grandmother died my grandfather & I lived together for several years. However he figured it would be better to sell his property and live with my aunt or my dad. So about 2 years before I went into the service we lived at my dad's house and I worked for him at Walker while going to school.

Both my mother and father had practically no affect upon my life—or I on theirs. Everything I've got I owe to my grandfather and of course we are very close to each other. Tho this all sounds like a letter to I. Q. Griggs[32] , I hope it is somewhat enlightening to you.

There have been many interruptions during the writing of this page. The new C.O. of Hdqs Bn who is a b—came in and I had all your letters spread out on the CWO desk. I expected the roof to fly off but he meekly asked if he could see those clippings from "Time," mumbled something about a generator and left.

Meant to tell you about one of the fellows who just left for the states. Name was Kohn and a rather brilliant radio man. Just had made 2nd Lt from technical sgt—and engaged to a girl in New Zealand. Well anyway we were talking about you and I mentioned "turnbuckles" and he knew about them. He then poured forth for 1/2 hour on what they were and where they were found etc.—even drew a picture—Whereupon if the handle is turned both ends are pulled together. Is that a good explanation? You did explain them to me that last night on the streetcar.

I think this letter is long enough and besides I have to have something to say tomorrow so goodnight again darling and

Love, Gene

P.S. Will find out for sure about the "time" difference. I think we are 16 hours.

❦

27 April 1945

Dearest Marian,

The news just said that J. W. Snyder has been confirmed by congress as F.L.A.—you mentioned him in your last letter. Also was interested in that article by Landis drawing a parallel between Lincoln's and Roosevelt's dying because I had written practically the same thing a few letters back—right?

I called Merle last night and we went to the club to see "The Brighton Strangler." Pretty moldy and a British affair. Could more logically substitute "because" for that "and." After the movie we sat in the club till closing and had a new good discussion about Roosevelt. Told him about Landis' article and also found out something that has been bothering me for some time. Couldn't think of the leader of congress who fought Johnson—it was Thaddeus Stevens. Merle said that his chief fault to find with Roosevelt was that he promised one thing and did another however after he was elected the last time Merle said he felt an "intellectual and moral" relief and decided he was the better man. I said that I couldn't agree with him as far as his opposition to Roosevelt on those grounds.

It has always appeared to me that Roosevelt had some premonition of what was coming about and did succeed in gradually turning the country from its thoroughly isolationist viewpoint into some means for preparation of the inevitable. The steps he took back in 1940 were very gradual because they had to be that way and he saw what so many people failed to see—that is, we would be in it soon.

Merle has faith in the desire of the common people to put forth effort and give sacrifices to maintain peace while I am still in doubt. Hope that he's right. Also liked Grafton's[33] "When we don't know where we're going we've got to go in a body." That's good. You might also say, "We may be gazing in the wrong direction but we are gazing in the same direction."

Have you ever told me what Capt. Bauer's job is?—beside mixing Martini's for you and Murph?

Time to close again sweetheart. I'm over to see Edwards for awhile this morning and then play volleyball this afternoon. It's my day off. Still checking on that time difference.

To answer another question—I never did get my copies of "Time"out here. Snafu.

All my Love, Gene

�֍

29 April 1945
Sunday

Dearest Marian,

There are 15 hours difference in Chicago time and our island time, That means in order to change from C.S.T. to mine you must add 15 hours. Right? At 2100 CST it would then be noon here. Now it is 7:00 PM last night back along Elm st and 10:00 AM here at _____.

Just received the unconfirmed report that Germany has surrendered to England and U.S. but not to Russia. I am not believing any reports that come in at any rate because of the bitter disappointment upon finding out it is just scuttlebutt. One of the things I'll never forget was the premature celebration on Iwo when the Army shot off everything they had. As with everyone else I hope that it is true.

The newspaper this morning mentioned something about a deadlock in the Conference between Russia and U.S. over the chairmanship. That's about all it said but I hope that by now things are squared away.

Back from chow and at long last, Mail! So it has turned out to be a perfect day after all. Glad they came today because I'll have lots of time to write to you tonight. Your letters were dated April 19 & 21. Sorta hate to get mail in bunches like that but mind you I'm not complaining. Your letters are wonderful or have I said that before. This noon I locked myself up in the code room and read to my heart's content and as a result everything in the msg. center stopped a while and as far as I was concerned all time could stop.

To answer your questions—Last year at Ft. Monmouth I happened to sit next to a fellow named Lynn Phillips, an army signal corps Lt. We developed a rather nice friendship and I liked him a lot. Well one morning I happened to see Walter Winchell's column in the "Mirror "and noted that he had quite a long (10 lines) writeup about a Lynn P. and his wife (the former somebody) and the fact she had had a baby. Showed it to Lynn and became very surprised to find out it actually was him. So he said he had been advertising manager for "Cosmopolitan" and his wife also adv. manager for "Harpar's Bazaar." After that we had many friendly arguments about Hearst but I knew that he had no sympathy with W.R.H[earst]. Phillips said that every Christmas Hearst would present all of his employees with an autographed picture of himself. Isn't that great? To get to the point—one day he insisted that I come up to New York with him that following weekend and promised me a date with Jennifer Jones. He explained that Anita Colby was a very good friend of his wife and that Jennifer, Anita, he and his wife, were going out together that Sat. night. It sounded too fantastic to me despite the fact he was very serious. I was almost convinced to accept the offer—and then backed out at the last momment. All of which makes this anti-climax but that is the way it happened. Now how in hell Shirley Temple got into all this—I don't know—do you? Lynn was a very remarkable fellow with a terrific sense of humor and told me some amazing stories of his life.

Been sitting here daydreaming during several interruptions—thinking about you and your letters mostly—wondering if this glorious feeling can last for another 18 mo. It does seem like eternity but we also have got to know each other better through letters—we weren't doing too well at Ft. Monmouth you know. That is the one consolation to this long period overseas.

Another interruption—Britt and I took off a few minutes to go over to the club. It's only about 50 yards from here (and about 300 yards from our house) I had 2 double rum cokes so I don't know if I will make too much sense until it wears off.

Glad to hear you could remember certain details about our trip that I had forgotten. For instance—the character who had "found somebody else" That had slipped my mind entirely but I remembered the people who thought we were "nice kids" and also those who insisted on looking at us constantly and the lady who got so excited in Kansas City because somebody in the troop train alongside didn't have any clothes on. Remember how we waited so long for them to turn off the lights that last night? Didn't know I had long eyelashes or "silken" hair. The sun out here has bleached it so I may be a blonde when I get back. Also recall now the discussion about the "400"—Milw. Road—I did take your advice. One of most pleasant memories was that night in the Schroeder tho. I really did have fun—and was disappointed the next day when you would-n't ride down to Chicago with me.

To change the subject again. At the last new broadcast from the states they gave short summaries of the speakers' speeches at the conference. It amused me to hear the rather lofty idealism of most of them about a world brotherhood etc. and Russia say bluntly in supreme realism "We need a military power to enforce the peace"—period. That's something like "How many divisions has he?" You know—I am getting to appreciate the Russians' realism—at least what they say is not cloaked behind great phrases and meaningless words. I like that. I know you do too.

Time to close again for today. Many thanks for the pages from "Time" again and of course for your swell letters.

All my Love, Gene

P.S. I thought you better <u>not</u> throw that hat away.

❖

30 April 1945
1830

Darling,
Hadn't planned to write to you tonight because I've promised Merle I'd stop by and pick him to go to the movie. But I just rec'd your letter of 25 April and it was so nice I figure I'd better write a few lines tonight.

Been thinking tonight there is only one bad thing about knowing you now and that is—every month seems like six and the time doesn't pass so quickly as it once did. It is passing tho but I have a deeper longing every day to get back there and see you. It has occurred to me that I did discover how much you meant up at Iwo. It was <u>your</u> letters I waited for without a doubt—which is a good sign—isn't it?

Britt & I made the off. mess run today down to town and I never cease to be amazed at the construction that is being done here. It looks more like state-side everyday. I'll tell you about it in as much detail as I can later.

It is now the next morning. Had to stop last night when Merle came in but I'll add a few more lines now. The news report said the Allies had freed 270 American airmen so I am hoping very strongly Franklin is one of them. Incidently <u>you</u> never did answer my question about him.

I'll have time to write you a real long letter tomorrow as it's my day off. Till then darling, all my love and please excuse the short letter—

Gene

❀

April 15 '45
[Chicago]

Dear Lt. Sweetheart:

In today's paper there is a picture of a beach in the Marianas. I see what you mean when you talk of how beautiful it is. How I'd love to be there. The contrast of the dull gray view from our apt. windows is depressing.

Right in the middle of our view & just a couple of blocks from here is a tall building called the Marquette apts. It would remind me of you—if I needed to be reminded. Did I ever tell you that about from Jan. to Aug. of '41 we lived in the Marquette Apts. across from the Children's Hospital in Milw.?

I was surprised when you said Reuben was an intern there. I thought he was in the Army. Or could he be both? Didn't he come downtown with you the day you met me at the Pfister?

Murph's brother took us to dinner today at the Illinois Athletic Club. It was very nice. Although he and his wife live here in Chicago, Murph hadn't seen him for nearly a year, so, of course, I had never met him. He's real cute—as much like a little boy as would be possible at 33, I think. Gale was so glad to see him. Imagine living in the same city & not seeing each other for so long! No reason for it except that he lives quite a distance from here.

I've been meaning to tell you that I think it's amazing what new movies you see. "Here Come the Waves," for instance, just came to the Chicago Theater about a week ago. I probably won't see it until it comes to one of the theaters around here a couple months from now.

This is one of those letters for which there is no excuse except that I felt like writing to you, and I'd better quit now as there's nothing more to say, either sense or nonsense, except that I miss you, which is not nonsense but all too true, darling.

With love, Marian

❀

April 17 '45

Hi, honey,

    I hope this letter will make sense. Murphie is home tonight for the first time in days & days it seems, (Ed's gone to New York.) so we have been catching up on conversation. I did want to write to you, though, as one of my last letters came back because I'd forgotten the stamp (Disgusting, isn't it?), so I'm afraid there will be sort of a long space between. If that is as hard on you as it is on me, I am truly sorry, dear.

    Did you hear Truman speak tonight? I wondered as we listened if you were listening, too. Which reminds me, I have often wondered about the difference in Time (I should have spelled that with a small "t") between here & there. When it's Tuesday the 17th here, what day is it there, and at 2100 here, what time is it there?

    Back to Truman, he's been doing fine these first few days, don't you think?

    Perhaps you heard that he has appointed one John W. Snyder of St. Louis as Federal Loan Administrator. Mr. Snyder's secretary (her name is Daphne) is Murph's chief rival for the affections of Capt. Bauer. She was offered a job as Truman's sec'y once (Daphne was, that is) and turned it down partly because Ed said he didn't think she'd like Washington. Needless to say, she's sorry now. Rather interesting don't you think?

    I had two letters from you tonight, Apr. 10 and 11, and I'm very happy about it. I might say "as usual," but it always seems better than before.

    I was much interested in hearing about Martha. Would also like to hear that "other story" about why you were disgusted with women in general at the time.

    I had forgotten about the story about the pilot I sent you. If you do find it, I'd still like to have it, but don't worry about it.

    Yesterday I bought some real pretty new pajamas, midriff variety. Have been wearing them around the house tonight & feeling very glamorous. They look as if they belonged under a palm tree—and I wish they were.

    There are many more things to say, but they'll have to wait until tomorrow. See you then, darling.

Love, Marian

❧

April 18 '45

Hello, my darling,

    Right now, before I forget again, I want to remind you that you were going to tell me about the time you saw Anita Colby, Shirley Temple & Jennifer Jones in N.Y. Shirley's recent engagement has reminded me of it, but I never seem to think of it when I'm writing to you.

Last night I dreamed you came home & I was so excited I woke up half an hour early—darn it! Would have been so much nicer to go on dreaming.

I hope you are feeling all right now, and certainly hope it was not dengue fever you were getting.

The argument we had about the "400" was occasioned by the fact that I talked you into taking the Milw. Road home from Chi. instead, as it has <u>better</u> trains and <u>faster</u> schedules. Only you had to pick the one train that was slow & ancient. Remember?

So you want to know if I can really cook. Always being practical, aren't you, dear? It happens you asked at a very opportune time as several people offered yesterday (<u>before</u> I had read your letter) to write and tell you how good I was. So there! I had baked some brownies and brought a couple for my special friends. I'm not sure whether they said that just to be appreciative or whether they really thought the cookies were that good, but I thought they were pretty good myself. Aside from one or two such shining accomplishments, my cooking is not exceptional, but I've never had any serious complaints. Is that a satisfactory recommendation?

You know, Gene, this Martha gal rather puzzles me. I don't understand why she would make all those promises, etc., and not write to you afterward. I suppose Franklin would laugh at me for that and say, as he did on one occasion, "I can see that you still have the romanticist's idea of love." Do you suppose she was one of these people who make a practice of marrying servicemen for their allotments? Or was she only vain? It's interesting to speculate on.

To change the subject radically, it seems that sadness never comes in small pieces. Ernie Pyle's death is another tragic thing. I had never read his column consistently, but to have read it only a few times would be enough to give anyone an understanding of his greatness.

I'm glad you finally got that picture. Without intending to be "catty," I might say it wouldn't take a hell of a lot to be more attractive than any of the girls at Reliable, altho there are two or three real cute ones who didn't happen to be in that picture. I'm afraid that sounds as if I didn't appreciate your compliments, and that's not true for any girl loves to be told she's attractive & I'm no exception.

Would you really like to hear, darling, some of the things I remember about that trip? Tonight I remember how nice it was to stand on the platform between the cars and watch the mountains go by; I can remember how long your eyelashes are & how they tickled my cheek & how silken your hair is (Those things I suppose will annoy you.), how you'd say, "Fine," when I asked how you were. Less solemnly, I remember that you took me to dinner the first evening because you wanted to avoid that character you'd met in the bar car who later explained that he'd found "something" else; also, what a lively interest the other passengers had in you & me. Our conversations I don't remember much about either. Odd, isn't it?

I'd like to spend another hour writing to you, dear, but it's getting late & Murph wants to go to sleep. So goodnight and

Much love, Marian

P.S. You didn't think I'd throw that hat away, did you?

⚜

April 20, 1945

Dear Lt. Sweetheart,

Rec'd your letter of "15 April 1945" today. Your typing isn't half bad, said she, magnanimously. Who am I to complain, anyway, as long as you write the letters?

I enjoyed the stories about the Major & about the Colonel's ice box. My Lord, you'll find yourself a buck pvt. one of these days at that rate! Is Steve in Jasco?

I took the afternoon off today. Paul has been out of town all week & I actually managed to get caught up enough so that I could take the time off—which I'm supposed to, anyway—without feeling guilty. I was going to have lunch with Cal, but, as usual, that didn't work. Some character came up from St. Louis & they've been conferring all day on his lousy advertising program. I'm glad you don't mind hearing about Cal because I like to complain about him every once in a while. What makes me so mad is that he never lets me know about stuff like this until three or four hours after he's supposed to have called or to have arrived at the appointed place.

Last night on the radio I heard a "newscaster" say something in regard to Ernie Pyle which impressed me a great deal. "The next time I pick up a newspaper, I'll remember how much a few cents can buy." A profound thought, isn't it?

I've been trying to figure out how you came to the conclusion you've been overseas six months. It doesn't seem that long to me because I can only count five and the twenty-three that supposedly remain seem like eternity.

Question Dept.—I know I've asked before, & you told me, too, but I've forgotten. Is your grandfather your mother's or your father's father? What is his name?

Do you hear the "March of Time" over there? They had a dramatization last night of a new book called, I think, "Am. Guerrilla in the Philippines" about one Ensign Richardson. It was very good.

I imagine you will have seen this week's Time, but if you haven't you'll probably be as anxious as I was to read what they say about Roosevelt. So I'll finish it tonight & send it to you.

I'm not sure what it was I wrote in shorthand at the end of that letter, but I think it was which means "I like you." 'Tis true, dear, and that's not all!

I'd better quit now and concentrate on Time. Goodnight, darling.

All my love, Marian

✢

April 21 '45

My darling Gene:

This was such a lovely day that even the noise & dirt of Chicago couldn't spoil it. I went for a walk along the lake this afternoon & have felt wonderful ever since. The trees are green, the sun was shining, & spring is here!

I did something else revolutionary today — bought a copy of Sumner Welles' "Guide to the Peace," and have worked out a schedule by which I <u>hope</u> to finish studying it within a month.

There was an article in the paper today saying that our armies have seized the Nazi's master files on all Allied flyers downed in German territory. I wonder if we'll hear anything now. Mother said the other day she had found some money she'd put away & forgotten, so she added it to a sum she's been saving for a watch for Franklin. It made me feel sort of sad.

I discovered today that it's possible to get to the airport by street car, so I think I'll go out & see if they have any P-38's there. Someone told me they have & I haven't seen one since I left L.A.

Reminds me — I had a letter from Ginny, who was my roommate out there. Perhaps I told you she was married last fall just about the time I had planned to go out, & I was trying to figure out how she had divorced her other husband so fast. (He was in Texas, an air cadet.) She finally admitted that by strict law she's probably a bigamist. Someone is sueing (How do you spell it?) John Carradine for bigamy & she says her case is practically identical, except that no one would bother to sue her. Optimist, isn't she? I feel sorry for her, though. She really doesn't sound particularly happy now, either. The poor kid has probably been kicked around so much she's afraid even to try to be very happy.

This is an inconsequential thought—Have you ever been in Santa Barbara, dear? Franklin & I were there a day or two in '41. The weather today reminded me of it. It's just about the most charming little city I've seen.

The story about Fort Drum in this section of Time is very interesting, don't you think? I'm a little confused on the details, but it looks like a clever job.

This is certainly a disconnected letter. There was really nothing much to write about in the first place, but I like to talk to you anyway. Goodnight, sweetheart.

Much love, Marian

Sunday—Ed came back from N.Y. today, & Murph went down to the station to meet him. Wish I could go down & meet you. Maybe if I wish long enough—

❀

April 23 '45

My darling Gene:

Three letters from you today! My mood, which had hit an all-time low of ill humor due to a battle with a stubborn mimeograph machine this aft., is now soaring through the clouds like a P-38. Incidentally, I liked what you said about the peculiar "whistle" a 38 has and about preferring it to the P-51. You knew I would, of course.

In one of these letters were the snapshots you sent. It _is_ the next best thing to seeing you in person, only I wasn't quite prepared for its being _this_ good. I like them so much I can hardly quit looking long enough to write this. I'm glad you sent the one with your grandfather. He looks so proud. Can't say that I blame him. Thank you, darling.

I'm glad you like "Flight to Arras" & shall be interested to hear your further comments. You were saying it is remarkable that you & your grandfather have always agreed on everything. I think it is, too, especially as it is usually difficult enough for father & son to agree—with a much shorter space of time to separate them. It is a rare thing for any two people to agree more or less consistently, and that, I think, is the most surprising & also the nicest thing about you & me. It's so good to think, "Gene will feel this way, too." You are so much less alone in the world—know what I mean?

I've been trying hard to guess for whose razor you were searching, but everyone I think of was reported to have been at the President's funeral & could hardly have been in the Pacific at the same time or so soon after. Tell me who it was when you can. Have you solved the mystery yet? I enjoyed the story—which is probably not a very kind thing to say since it was hardly much fun for you.

I felt quite flattered that you should take the trouble to read over my letters from way back in Nov. As to the questions you didn't answer (This is getting to be a long story, isn't it?) I ask so many, I'm surprised that you haven't told me to mind my own business.

Tues AM Was interrupted by visitors & am finishing this at work, which is practically an impossible thing to do. I'd better just put it in an envelope & see you tonight.

Love, Marian

❀

April 24, 1945

Hello, Sweetheart:

You know this letter-writing is interfering with my education as a conscientious citizen. It certainly lures me away from my study of "Guide to the Peace." That's a darned good book, though. Already I have learned how inevitably the economic condition of some of the small Balkan nations forced them into the German sphere of influence. You can't honestly say it was a choice of principles.

When I read your remarks on your lack of faith in the common people & their interest in world problems, I was glad I had started this little project & could consider myself more or less above the criticism. "Less" is the more accurate word. Murph is emphatically in agreement with your complaint on the lack of education. I think that is the cause, chiefly, of the half-hearted interest.

About the choice of a man for Vice Pres., don't you think it's the fault of the stupid voter more than the political set-up? Or don't you?

Ed is here tonight and has been telling us some interesting things about big league baseball. He's very sad because "Happy" Chandler has been appointed Comm. of Baseball to succeed the late Kenesaw M. Landis. Landis, he says, was an honest man, which can hardly be said of Chandler.

Did you hear Bob Hope tonight? He broadcast from Alameda. There's already been one casualty in San Francisco, he said. "A sailor passed a marine on Market St. & dislocated his jaw trying to smile & sneer at the same time."

I agree with your opinion of "Going My Way." Didn't think it was exceptional. I would probably have chosen something like "A Guy Named Joe." I was thinking tonight how very pleasantly like Franklin's some of your letters are & it reminded me of the way Van Johnson in that movie was always telling the girls they reminded him of his sister (who had never existed). I liked that part.

Darling, I think it's almost an exaggeration to say we've really been together 65 hours. Every time I think of it I am more sorry I didn't go to New York last year. Unfortunately, nothing can be done about it now.

Since that last sentence, I have been sitting here <u>wishing</u> for all of 15 minutes, and if I don't just stop now, I'll never finish my quota of studying for tonight.

I do love you, dear,

Marian

✤

April 25 '45

Gene, darling,

Your letters are getting better all the time — and so are my dreams. I hadn't intended to write to you tonight, but your letter of the 20th arrived & I can't leave it here unanswered.

So you want to know where I'd like to live. I wouldn't dare neglect to answer after all the complaints I've made. (You know I'm only kidding you about that most of the time, don't you.) I do <u>not</u> like Chicago — not one inch of it do I like, & if anyone ever suggested that I should spend the rest of my life here, I'd cheerfully boil them in oil.

My mother always says you will be happy in whatever place you make good friends & a comfortable living & I think she's quite right. I believe I'd like best to live in Los Angeles. No doubt the fact that Franklin & I enjoyed so much being there together has a great deal to do with that choice, but I like almost everything about the city & its climate. I'm glad you asked about it. I have often thought it would be nice if you would go to U.C.L.A. for your Master's. I could go there to work again & it would give us a chance to get acquainted. That almost sounds silly, doesn't it? I haven't mentioned it before (at least I think I haven't) because the choice ought to be yours. Also because it is hard to say what circumstances might influence our plans. I like that — "<u>our</u> plans."

About that last night in Chicago, I wouldn't have objected the least bit to being taken along to L.A. In fact, if I'd thought I might somehow get past the gateman, I'd have gone along as a stow-away. One thing I distinctly remember about our conversation is that you were saying you thought it would be easy to fall in love with me & I was wishing you would at least try.

I don't think I like your traveling with "Miss Wisconsin." Her name sounds familiar. Perhaps I've seen it in the Journal. You aren't by any chance being ironic in saying you had a grand conversation re dancing, her clothes & other "vital" subjects, are you?

Didn't you like Margaret O'Brien in "Meet Me in St. Louis."

It seems to me that most prospective fathers think they're going to have twins. No personal reflections on Merle, but I think it's plain inflated ego.

Did I tell you about going to the Art Institute Sunday to see the Encyclopedia Brittanica's collection of contemp. American art? I was delighted to discover that I could recognize the work of a few artists without having seen the particular painting before. It's fun.

We finished a chicken tonight that Mother sent this weekend. You can hardly buy them in Chicago any more. I roasted this one & it was darned good, if I do have to say so myself.

Darling, it's ten o'clock already, & if I don't quit, I'll never get <u>anything</u> done. You can't get any sympathy from me about having to neglect your other correspondence. My friends are beginning to hate me, too, & I used to be quite dependable. Oh, well, I'll get by—as long as I have you, dear.

Love, Marian

⚜

April 27, 1945

Dear Lt. Sweetheart,

I thought I would have lots of time at work today to write you a letter in shorthand & copy it later on the typewriter, thereby contriving to look busy all the while. But what a day it turned out to be! I spent the whole morning collecting information to answer letters, etc., & every time I left my desk someone put another stack of work there for me. Needless to say, it was a short day.

I also had a few minor arguments with Mr. Ripley. As I've probably mentioned before, I have to get his ok on some things when Paul is out of town (as he has been for the past two weeks). Ripley is always drooling over the girls & it is impossible to keep him on the subject of business. It's damn annoying sometimes. I think he is naturally quite affectionate, but I am also very sure he uses all this flattery under the <u>mistaken</u> impression that it makes the gals think they are appreciated & keeps them happy. The net result is, we all think he's a darn fool, which he is in that respect.

Now that I have that complaint off my mind, perhaps I can think of a more interesting subject for conversation.

Don't you like this editorial of Grafton's? He's always so calm & so sensible.

Had two letters from you last night, much to my surprise & delight. I am definitely not getting tired of reading them & I'm so glad you don't say "There's nothing new here." It's such a depressing idea. By the way, do you still censor mail? You haven't mentioned it for sometime.

I got a kick out of that remark about your co. having too many chiefs & not enough Indians. I could send you a few Indians from W'berg. They have quite a supply up there. Daddy's always lending them money on useless pieces of junk which they offer as "security," and Mother is always giving him hell for it—and I do mean hell!

I'm going to Racine this weekend to see Margie Thompson. She's the girl, you may remember, who was going to come down here & live with me & then changed her mind. It'll be fun to see her. She's almost as much fun as Peg.

Darling, I wish I knew how to tell you how I felt to know that you were so sympathetic to Merle's story about his early married life. I wouldn't have thought it would affect you that much & I like you all the more for it. I do agree to have that much faith in each other is the most wonderful thing in the world.

While I like & wholeheartedly approve of the instinct that made him refuse to let his wife work, to me it would seem very impractical. I'd rather work than be a housewife with only one room to keep, altho I'm not the least interested in a lifetime business career.

Peg will be pleased with your advice to quit teaching as soon as possible. I wonder if you'd like Ray. I didn't get to know him well enough to judge, but one incident which it would not be fair for me to tell you makes me mistrust his sincerity. Suffice it to say that he can think up the darndest reasons for postponing their marriage.

I think that educational program is a fine thing. I'd laugh if you had to teach. It would probably be excellent experience for you, though.

I'm certainly glad you are not on Okinawa. It seems they've been fighting so long, & if you were there, it would be an eternity.

I sent that clipping about the capture of the Nazi files on Allied fliers to my mother. She wrote, "It should end the suspense for a lot of people, but I hope Franklin is hiding." Bless her heart, I don't blame her for not wanting to face it. It is nice to be able to think there is a chance he'll come home. Since we first heard he was missing, though, (that's all we have heard) I haven't really believed he was alive. People talk about how wonderful it is to have faith & it doesn't seem wonderful at all to me. I'd rather be surprised by a miracle than count on one & be disappointed. The disappointment would be too great.

Don't ever hate to bring up the subject, dear. You know I like to talk about him, and it always makes me feel good to have someone say they're hoping he's all right.

I'm certainly in the mood for writing to you tonight. Guess it's time to quit, though. Good night, my darling. When I'm not writing to you, I'm thinking about you. Quite a monopoly you have—

Love, Marian

April 29 '45
[Enroute from Racine]

Hello, my darling,

This is another train-ride letter. (It's a rough ride, so I hope my writing will not be too illegible.) As I've said before, trains make me lonesome for you, & tonight it's a triple threat loneliness—the train, liquor, and reminders of California.

Since the last time I wrote, I've been nearly knocked out by one of those damn <u>blitzkrieg</u> colds. I stayed home in bed Sat. morning, being unable to do otherwise. Went to Racine in the afternoon as planned since, by that time, I felt somewhat better. Margie had a cold, too, so we've spent a good share of the weekend drinking shots to cure same. It really seemed to help & we stayed surprisingly sober. Just felt kind of good—& talkative. As I've probably told you, Margie lived in L.A. for a year or so, also, & we always have fun talking about it.

She has been going out lately with a man from Chicago who is quite wealthy—& also married. I am concerned about it, but, as you know, I'm in no position to criticize. Suppose I shouldn't worry—she is not as much a child as I was when I first went out with Cal & she well knows that if she takes it seriously it will be darn hard on her. So I guess as long as they do nothing really wrong, it's ok.

While we're on the subject, Gene, I want to tell you a little more about Cal. You know that I still see him—probably an average of once in two weeks—but I'm getting so that I feel guilty every time because I know I'm not really in love with him anymore. I actually don't care whether I see him or not, & when I do, I'm thinking about you most of the time. I wouldn't blame you a bit if you didn't believe that, but it <u>is</u> true. I wish I could explain to myself and to you why I don't break it up entirely. Partly, I must admit, it is because it's nice to have a date once in a while, and I do like him & like to talk to him.

One thing I have told him, however, is that I never want to see him when he's been drinking & I do not intend to make any exceptions to that.

I don't know, darling, maybe it would be better not to say anything to you about it, but I want to be honest with you & it doesn't seem quite honest to say nothing at all.

Shall we change the subject now? I showed Margie the little piece of Iwo Jima you sent & from then on I had to show it to everyone we saw. (If anyone ever loses a piece of it, I'll fine them, so help me!) As a result of the ensuing conversation, I heard about one of the 3rd Div. men who is at home now in Racine. Lt. Andy Rasmussen. He was in the 9th Reg., too.

Margie thinks you look like Tyrone Power on that snapshot taken at Lake Arrowhead, so you can't use that argument anymore when I tell you you're the most handsome Lt. in the Marine Corps!

We're almost in Chicago now, so I'll see you tomorrow, sweetheart.

Love, Marian

❖

April 30, 1945

Hi, darling,

I went to work this noon & untangled a stack of work that had been worrying me since Fri., but after an hour or so gave up & came back home. Makes
me so damn disgusted to get a cold like this for no apparent reason.

Had two letters from you today which I read on the way to work. It always
takes a while after that for the glow to wear off & I was thinking I probably
looked ridiculously happy for anyone supposed to be too sick to work.

Thanks for sending that Div. shoulder patch. I had just about figured out
by myself that that must be the one. Saw a sgt. downtown last night with his girl
& they looked so happy I could hardly stand it. It's encouraging, though, to see
that those days really do come.

You've probably realized by this time that you forgot to send Reuben's letter. I often do that when I'm writing to Mother & her comments on my carelessness are <u>caustic</u>. So I can't criticize you.

Is the Marion from Wauwatosa the girl you saw last time you were home
who wanted to meet you somewhere later?

To answer <u>your</u> question—you didn't meet Murph. When you were home
on sick leave, you missed her by just about an hour. You never were here long
enough! Murph has mentioned several times that she'd like to have met you.

I read her the story about Lt. Pace, and we agree that his leaving this girl
& the baby $1 apiece is about the lowest trick we've ever heard of. I hope he
changed it. Murph says it's no wonder we have wars when there are people so
small & so selfish.

I was thinking the same thing the other day when I read the recent history
of Bulgaria. As in most of the Balkans, it seemed just about the time they'd have
their problems pretty well in hand, someone would get proud & upset the whole
business over a perfectly irrelevant issue. They really had a hell of a time there.
When I think of how pessimistic my father is about everything in this country,
I just wonder what he'd do if he had to live in Bulgaria for a few years.

I really had to laugh at your telling Zeidler you hoped Hoan would be
reelected. I could just picture the fire in your eyes. I heard Zeidler at Ascension
one time & thought his speech was absolutely worthless. As far as I was concerned, he could have confined his campaign to singing. For that he had some
aptitude at least.

I was also amused by your reply to the churchman who couldn't tell a private from an officer. How can people be so stupid? Apparently it is true that the average person is not at all interested in anything unless it concerns him very directly. It's very unfortunate. (Pardon me a minute. Murphie just brought me a glass of rum & coke, and in that I am interested.) Seriously, I thought sometime ago when you said you envy those fellows coming home now at the height of the affair, you are probably getting a lot more out of your experience being where you are than you would here. It is amazing how quickly people forget. Perhaps it is not as bad a thing as we think. Truly, the names & locations would not matter if people will only remember the ideals for which they fought & learn that in a democracy, particularly, it is not only the policies of the leaders which will make or break the peace, but just as surely it is the attitude of the individual on such a simple thing, for example, as a shortage of meat. If people would realize that they are responsible for their country's policies regardless of how inactive in politics they are, they'd understand the importance of being well-informed. I wonder if I'm being carried away by the subject here. Does it all sound logical to you?

Darling, I like your saying that "so long as we appear to be gazing outward together in the same direction, there is much to look at." There is, indeed, and I'd rather talk about those things than spend too much time on the subject of love. It seems to me that is something you can't talk about a great deal without its beginning to seem insincere. And not that I don't get impatient with an exclusively mental relationship, but since the touch of your hand is something I have to wait for, it's much better to try to be intellectual in the meantime, don't you think?

Nevertheless, I love you, dear,

Marian

❀

1 May 1945
Central Pac -

Dearest Marian,

Practically every time I write your name I think of the time you reminded me that it is spelled with an "a."

Been wondering all day what kind of a book "Guide to World Peace" is that you should have study periods. It sounds good tho, but I hope it doesn't interfere with your letters to me. Perhaps I should say I would rather have you "stupid" than not writing so regularly to me. It is not the case tho. I am not connecting you up with the word "stupid" in any way darling. (Somebody just asked what I was smiling about) I did smile when I thought of the implications of that last sentence if you interpret it wrongly. Obviously (to me at least) I know of your interests and ideas so I don't class you with the Americans whom we have no patience with today. The more I write the deeper I'm getting—you are a darling—

Rec'd your letter of the 22nd this noon after getting the one 25 April last night. I'll have to do something about my "Time" one of these days and subscribe for the Pony edition. Lippman's[34] article was good and encouraging but I don't think that Truman would have been the peoples' choice for Vice Pres. if they had had anything to say about it. Not that the majority is always right— but how many people ever heard of Truman or his record? You have to admit we are "taking a chance" when we nominate someone like that. But it has been that way all through history—and some stupid Americans even take pride in saying a Vice President should be a nobody and always has been a nobody. That's the part that aggravates me to no end. I hate people! Guess I should have been a capitalist or at least a Republican!

Steve was in again today. He is recorder (prosecutor) in a Summary Courts Martial case and up to his neck in work and worry. The fellow is defended by a pvt. who in civilian life was a lawyer. Steve's in the 3rd Marines and a Chemical Warfare officer. This is just part of his extra duties and he knows as much about law as I do—which is nothing. He has a good "line" tho which I haven't.

I have never been in Santa Barbara—However my grandfather (father's side before I forget again) has never ceased to talk about the town. Said it's the prettiest town he's been in and made me very anxious to go there some day. Now you mentioned it too so I really am impressed.

The weather is <u>hot</u> today. One of the worst days we've had. I still think it's a perfect island tho. Have heard so many fellows say they would be quite content to stay if their wives were here too. Rather amazing don't you think? Of course then I always think of you and how nice it would be if you were here. Don't know about staying forever but a vacation here with you would be perfect. At our off. club we have a beautiful view overlooking the ocean. I like to go there and watch the waves etc.—it is awfully peaceful.

I think I have answered all the questions—have I not? I have a million letters to censor so I'll have to stop for now. Maybe I can get some new ideas on how to tell you I miss you—

All my love, Gene

P.S. When V-E day comes have a good time for me because I hope the next one we can celebrate together.

✢

2 May, Just managed to find my lost gear that I took up to Iwo. Among it was this letter I had written to you & the article you want back. It rather amazed me that none of my equipment was missing—even $2.00 I had in the pocket of my khaki.

Thought you might like this letter now even tho it is old—nothing lost anyway by sending it.

Merle was just over and I guess we'll play volley ball this afternoon. Nothing new to add except that I do like you very much—which isn't news any more.

Much Love, dear,
Gene

❖

3 May 1945

My dear Marian,

Didn't plan on writing to you tonight but as usual, when I received your 2 letters just now I changed my mind. I don't want that to sound like a high pressure statement to get you to write—but merely as a sincere fact.

Incidently I can't imagine you get half the thrill out of my letters as I do yours—that too, is a fact. I never have developed a "line" which I often regretted but I think I'm too old to start now. Your letters were dated 24 & 26 April.

We have been busy the last few days building a super mess hall for the officers of the Sig Co (about 20 of us now) As such it had to be constructed by officers and with what material we could bargain from the Seabees. For 6 quarts we got the cement for a deck and all the lumber to construct a house 50 x 30. More of the details from time to time but would like to mention now that I worked hard yesterday (on my only day off this week) At times I was standing knee deep in concrete.

Today the Major told Britt & I we would have to move from our house to a tent because they were going to use it for a radio school. So we packed our gear and dragged it over to an old broken down tent—undoubtedly the worst in the company. P.S. (all the other officers have screens etc.) Oh unhappy day! Not even any lights which makes me mad!

Steve just called and wanted to go down to the army hospital (and nursing) but I talked him out of that. I must be out of my mind but he is coming over here instead.

A couple of nights ago Gertrude Lawrence[35] brought a show to the island and it eventually got around to the 21st Marines.

Friday morning—

about the U.S.O show—it was probably the worst entertainment I had ever seen. Never expected that from G.L. but we all agreed on that point. With her were a man tap dancer, another man who acted as M.C. and a cute girl accordionist. After the show they came up to the Div. club and had a wild party but I was too angry to go. Can't say exactly what the show lacked but I think it was the same old story—that is, putting on an Army show for Marines. She talked about Normandy continually and even tried to get us wild about some stupid French song "that they were all singing over there" and of course nobody here gave a damn about it. The rest of it consisted for the most part of suggestive stories which implied we were all a bunch of sex maniacs and waited for that sort of stuff. In short—she missed the boat entirely.

Haven't too much time to continue this letter this morning but I am CWO again today and promise to write a long letter tonight.

I'm glad you don't like Chicago either which is another thing we agree wholeheartedly—and that is beginning to be the rule. Would pick U. of Chicago for my M.A. if possible but Merle is enthusiastic about U.C.L.A. too. It is something to think about—

I have also thought of living in Los Angeles because it has appealed to me for the same reason you like it but undoubtedly I'll stay in Milwaukee so long as my grandfather lives. After that I'll be alone—and we can probably cry on each other's shoulder.

I'll close now with that extremely pleasant thought—

All my love, Gene

※

4 May 1945

Dearest Marian,

Back at the msg center now for a 24 hr shift. It is about 0930 and traffic is slow—just finished censoring letters which usually is interesting if there aren't too many of them.

I don't know if I told you my dad has arrived in San Francisco according to his latest letter but whether he is going to get out of the service is still in doubt. I think he would like to now—

Been meaning to ask if you like the P-61 night fighter. It is very similar to the P-38 except that the whistle is missing. I have seen quite a few of them elsewhere and they are just about as evil looking a plane I've seen—except for the Varga girls[36] painted on the nose.

I told you about the G.I. show in my letter I mailed this morning. Outside of that it has just been the regular routine as far as work and recreation activities are concerned.

1330—Back again after chow. Hope you are able to follow this without too much trouble. Spent part of my noon hour watching them sort the mail which I often do if it happens to come in at that time. Then I came back here to let Britt go to chow & told him he had a letter "of the right kind," which is of course one from his wife.

The other night we saw Edwards & the movie, "The Unseen"—at least part of it. Invariably it rains when we are at the 21st Marines and before we decided to go home, got soaked. Now today I read the review of it in "Time" and was sorry we didn't stay to see the finish.

This morning the "Time" of 30 April arrived here in the msg center. Have just managed to read one article on the concentration camps of Germany. Good God! have you ever imagined anything so horrible? It is impossible to make any comment that would add or subtract from the plain accounts of the news. I do believe it can't be fully comprehended by anyone—except the victims themselves. After reading that everything seems not only insignificant but callous. It is an experience a reader will want to forget but always will be conscious of the fact that those who went through it and lived will have to contend with the memory always. That is what bothers me.

1730—Incidently that time difference is 15 hours I think I said 16 but we are that many hours ahead of you at any rate. I think you have been trying too hard to guess who the man was that lost the razor. He is the most obvious man of all and I know you know him well (at least I hope so) Anyway the case is not solved and as a matter of fact I never heard much about it as I thought I would.

I have finished "Flight to Arras" and as you said—it was filled with bits of philosophy and gives the reader (this one at any rate) more faith in Man & men. I had marked certain passages that particularly appealed to me so if you don't mind the book being messed up in that manner—I will send it back to you thus, O.K.?. Merle has it at present. I hate to mark a book but then you said I might have it so I don't feel too badly. I will claim it sometime in the future—about Nov. 1946? ?

You asked about the Radio programs in one of your last letters. We don't hear Bob Hope except as re-broadcasts occasionally but the radio setup here surely is wonderful. At 7:00 PM every night there is a 1/2 hour news broadcast from the states and the Armed Forces Rad. Ser. presents both popular and classical music most of the day. News is broadcast at regular intervals in the same manner it is at home. At 4:00 PM there is a movie review of what is playing at the 100 (?) theatres here with comments about the pictures. example: "This is the worst picture ever filmed" or "highly recommended" etc. They don't beat around the bush.

Merle just stopped in on his way to the movie after seeing Edwards. Eddy has come out all right with his girl after all after according to reports which was rather surprising after we had extended our deepest sympathy and so forth — Merle is still expecting the good news between now and the 15 if all goes well. He is still betting on twins but I always forget to ask him exactly what that feeling is like. I think that he may have some inside dope which he is holding out from us. Steve was at our club last night and we had a good session again. The trial which I told you about has not come off yet but last night Merle and I succeeded in breaking down all his arguments he was going to present as proscecuter and consequently he is extremely worried. I hope that he wins because actually it is a cut and dried case of insubordination on the part of the defendant but any small technicality is enough to get the case thrown out of court. It is a headache to be a recorder and the sad part is that any officer is eligble to be summoned for the job.

I have meant to ask you if you'd like some odds and ends that I picked up on Iwo that were formerly Japanese — if so I will send them provided I can get it okayed by G-2. It isn't much but it may be interesting . To change the subject again — I was interest in your study of "Guide to the Peace" and I hope that you keep giving your reactions to it and tell me what it is about from time to time. I have not been reading anything since I finished your book but somewhere around "The Green Years" is available. Have you read it or heard anything about it?

Time to quit again — I am afraid this is a poor excuse for a letter but I will try to do better next time. Trouble here too is that I think about you instead of writing but on the other hand I am trying rpt I am trying.

All of my love, Gene

✤

6 May 1945

Dearest Marian,

Just am finishing a hard day here and doubt if I have the thought to even write you a letter but when the heart is willing — It has been rugged all day from 7:30 until now at 1600. Hope I'm not confusing you too much by mixing Army Navy time with civilian time but I usually put down the first one that comes to my mind. Also had a tough decision to make today and to condense it — it amounted to the fact I could go to FMF headquarters Pearl Harbor for "to be" a coding officer. It probably would be duration duty. Didn't know what to do actually because obviously the advantages are great but it ended up that I figured I would stay here — something like the hero in the movies — I think that the personal satisfaction is greater and that the ultimate feeling derived from actually fighting is something I need more than to save my neck. It would amount to a desk job and of course you would only have to sweat out the duration without any fears of not getting back. It isn't the fear of not getting back that would have made me accept but merely that it would be good duty.

The next time the mortars start dropping I'll probably get somebody to kick me but on the other hand I will be able to listen to other men from other fronts talk about their experiences and still always feel that I have done my part. It is not patriotism but mostly to satisfy my own infer. complex. Understand, darling?

Well at any rate there are 5 off from the Sig Co going including Britt.

It doesn't look like there ever will be a clear cut national surrender in Germany does it? I figure at this stage that the various armies will just give in peecemeal. By the time you receive this I may have been proved wrong but at present it seems like a good guess to me.

Grafton is good and as you say very calm and collected wish that was the case all over America but I find myself often making apologies for the S.F. conference and what they will or will not do there merely for the benefit of the many people and newspapers who will possibly call it a flop. One of the greatest things Roosevelt said after Dumb[arton] Oaks was, "It is a start" and that's the way I feel about S.F. I don't expect miracles because they would be out of place. The world doesn't operate on miracles but upon changing systems of principles in keeping with the times. The analogy of the conference and to our own beginning in drafting a constitution was excellent and if people knew what a hellva mess that was and that some of the greatest leaders of the times said it couldn't work and would not support it—Patrick Henry for one I believe—then possibly a more understanding attitude would be had. As little faith as I have in Man, I do believe world organization for permanent peace can be founded—not perfect at first but gradually through changes and amendments approaching what people demand now. National honor will have to be sacrificed much like states' rights were sacrificed in this country. It was done with force in 1861 and it can be done with force in the future. Agree?? There is no perfect set of principles for insurance of peace just as there is no perfect constitution that need not be ammended. The interest in peace will have to be stronger than national honor.

Does this sound like a love letter? Actually it is—I write them to my grandfather regularly and I know how I feel about him.

Goodnight darling, Gene

4

"... security is worthless & temporary if ...
at the expense of others."

WHEN VICTORY IN *Europe arrived, it was celebrated throughout Europe and the United States. Hitler was defeated and dead, as were about 50 million others in this war that he started in 1939. Church bells rang throughout the land, and in some cities people danced in the streets. But the war was not really over: the Japanese still refused to accept our demand for unconditional surrender. On Guam I reported the only "celebration" was some hard boiled eggs with faces painted on them in the officers' club. For Marian and others with men in the Pacific the observance was also subdued. She was aware that the Third Marine Division was preparing for a final assault on the Japanese homeland. Our love seemed to strengthen with each letter, and she noted I now ended my letters with "all my love" instead of the weaker "much love." Then finally on 7 June I told her flatly, "I love you," something I had never said before. However, in late June I had to accept an unexpected transfer out of the Third Division which meant leaving my friends in Guam.*

---

8 May 1945
[Guam]

Darling,

Just finished censoring letters for the last half hour which answers your question about "Whether I do it or not." It is something that I will always have to contend with I guess.

Today was my day off and I have been busy since 7:30 this morning. Built a rather nice desk out of old lumber but it appears to be quite comfortable. Anyways I like it even if Merle and Britt laughed at it for quite a while. Your picture graces the top of it and I have a couple History books there too. You are the only girl I know whose picture I could place alongside a History book — Well you can laugh now — I am the divisional History teacher as of this afternoon. Don't know many of the details but I think Merle had something to do with it and I didn't have a legimate excuse so I'm it. It will be rather interesting and will function as a sort of planned study & question period for a couple of hours each week. All kinds of History and Civics will be among the courses and the students will assemble here in the Signal Co from all over the island to complete high school or to increase their general knowledge. While we were over to see Lt. Jenkins from Jasco (the div. Educ. off and a Ph.D. from Columbia) Merle got interested in some maps and books—to get them we had to sign up for a world History course of the Pacific. The setup here is wonderful because of the large no. of courses available and it made us practically sick to see the opportunities to increase your general knowledge—and the general lack of interest or in some cases—lack of time.

Merle suggested a course in Spanish after this Pacific affair and I am very favorable. I will eventually have to have some foreign lang. beside French if I do go on to school for any length of time: I don't have definite plans because I hate to plan and then have it fall through—sort of just think about it a little and then when the opportunity arises, go after it with all my heart. It is a rather stupid way to do things, I admit, but I hate to be disappointed in something. Girls and school always seemed incompatible but actually they don't need to be—do they? It would appear that I have met the wrong type of girls until you came along.

Last night at the movie we saw "Tonight and Every Night" Have you seen it? Our general reaction here was that the girls were beautiful, music good but the plot corny. It never ceases to amaze me that 90% of the stories about servicemen are so awful and untrue to life. In one scene they are talking about shutting down this particular theatre because of the air raids (in London) A swaby [sailor] steps up and says "Oh you can't do that. I'm on a mine-sweeper and these shows are so nice to come home to." When I heard that I laughed out loud which caused a Colonel to turn around. It is so stupid and I can't imagine in my wildest dreams some sailor making a remark like that. Maybe they aren't making these movies for the servicemen but at least they should try to portray us halfway true to life. It is no wonder that some of the fellows don't know what to write home about if the folks back there expect servicemen to be like that. My mother is one of them. I still think she believes I am afraid of sergeants because she has seen in the movies that sergeants are tough. Ah well—

Merle is still in doubt and we are all anxiously awaiting the word. That reminds me—commercial cable is in out here and sometime in the future I may use it to you merely as a something (can't think of the word.) We can send night letters or straight cables about anything to any place. Rather nice hey? Also they have these "canned msgs" which you have heard about.

I am at the bottom of the page again and it is a good place to stop. Your letters are still the most important part of the day and thoughts of you are extremely pleasant any time.

All my love, Gene

✧

10 May 1945

My dear Marian,

Vaguely I remember spelling actually as "accually" in a recent letter. Sorta think it was to you and remember also that I looked at it for quite some time thinking that it looked silly. Oh well—Neither Merle nor I can attribute this spelling lapse to anything definite but I am glad it is not only me (or I) who has that trouble.

Another day at work—due to these fellows leaving we now have no days free entirely. It is a little rough but I don't mind too much. Borrowman was just in to read the cable regulations and is planning on sending his cable address to his wife. She will be able to inform him of the "situation." These are trying days for him.

I have my first history class this afternoon at 1500 and am not prepared to lecture or anything like that. They are all taking different courses so I guess the only way to do it is to have a planned study period. In Am. Hist they just read the book until they feel they are able to pass the final exam. Other courses have worksheets to be filled out. I don't know how many students are enrolled but they will be from all over the island. I can hold the class wherever I desire so I think the Sig. Co. is the best for me.

Glad that you appreciated that "piece of Iwo." I see they are raising the Suribachi flag over the capitol today. One of the fellows was from Wisc.

Was interrupted for about 6 hours but now it is 1800 and I'll be able to finish. My class met today and it was fun for a change. One of the fellows asked the prise [*sic*] question I rather figured I would have to answer sooner or later but never bothered to plan a good straight forward answer. He pointed to "Beowulf" and said, "Why is this stuff so important? Nobody understands it and why do we have to read it?" I poured forth for 15 minutes giving him anything but a direct answer and I think he's still in doubt. It is a hard question to answer. Outside of that the course will be some fun for me. I have a couple of English Lit. students too for variety. They are studying Chaucer and the "Canterbury Tales" so I told them the "Miller's Tale," which is one of the most obscene stories of English Lit. Any resemblance to the approved method of teaching is purely co-incidental but I am trying to make it as interesting as possible to these fellows. It won't take much to get them discouraged and drop their courses and that seems to me as rather tragic.

I asked Merle about the 5th Internat. in connection with your writing of J. Brown. We don't know much about it in fact I have only heard of the 3rd International and I think they were operating after the World War. Got a kick out of the fact he figured you wanted to have an affair with him. Seems to me

that all the Communists I have known were not shy about their sex relation-
ships. As you said, "Politics, Women and Wine."—don't think I'm a good
Communist. I can understand somewhat the kind of person he is. <u>In fact</u> I do
have a fellow who <u>is the exact</u> Brown. I'll tell you about him His name is Leon
Primley—a Jew—undoubtedly one of the most brilliant fellows I've met and by
like token one of the most disagreeable. He is rather tall and has long shaggy
hair with pimples on his face. Met him first aboard ship as it happened we were
in the same stateroom together. I was impressed at first and we used to argue
and discuss everything in general. But gradually I couldn't stand him because
he would insinuate you were some stupid ass and would never really argue
friendly. You could get him to talk on any subject and even if he happened to
know something about it, his disagreeable nature soon made all the fellows disgusted with him. He was radical and a dreamer but had an exceptional background. Kicked out of U. of Virginia, N.Y.U. and Colgate, he decided he was
going to educate himself and to hell with the schools. That he did—wrote newspaper articles and poetry on the side and lived with some girl (I have great
friends) She was an artist and they were deeply in love—that is, until she met
some Ensign whom she later married. This about killed Leon but he continued
his writing of poetry etc. Then he came in the Marine Corps and for some
ungodly reason got through a special O.C.S. and was sent overseas. Then as I
said we argued politics (he loved Roosevelt, tho) philosophy and Religion but
despite his brilliance on any subject he was extremely radical and certainly did-
n't give a damn about what he said. It gradually grew that even tho I appreciated his intellect I hated him. Then at Iwo just what we always knew—he was
proved incompetent and relieved of his command up at the front. The last I
heard of him was from Ossowski who promised if he could ever get his hands
on him he'd break his neck. He is a character but I think that it is almost better
to be stupid than that obnoxious.

It is hard to write about a subject like that—wish I was there to tell you
which would be a lot easier.

I hope that you are over your cold. I usually got one every winter back
home. What you need is—to sit under one of these palm trees, look at the moon
and have somebody holding your hand—say me—

This has got to be another lengthly story and I see there are about 50 letters to censor. Reminds me—one fellow just wrote his girl that she needn't kiss
the outside of the envelopes because not he (her lover) but the censor sealed it.
It's a great life.

All my love, Gene

10 May 1945

Hello dearest,

Your letter of the 29th was here when I returned at noon. I see that you have been train riding again. Needless to say—I wish I had been there.

Merle is coming over soon and we are going to the club to get our liquor ration (1 qt. per mo) & all we can drink at the bar. Incidently it is 10 cents per drink no matter what you order (Scotch etc!) rather unusual dont you think? Reminds me for some reason of that night in Chicago at that quaint (can't say cute) bar where you paid for the drinks.

Merle is here—I'll finish later—

Back from the movie now. It was "Show Business" and we both liked it. Your letter of May 1st came just before Merle stopped in. Of course I had to read it immediately. After I finished, he said, "Does she still love you?" I said "yes"—and told him he sounded like he expected it to stop any minute. He replied very seriously, "Guess I've been reading too much about the Russians— I'm getting too realistic." It did appeal to my sense of humor and I think it was mostly the serious way he said it.

We (Merle & I) have been having some excellent talks lately about practically anything under the sun. It is enjoyable to discuss politics, Religion etc with Merle. Really wish you were here to hear us—we sound like two old men reflecting on 60 years of experience.

Was interested in Cal as usual and I'm always glad to hear anything you want to tell me about him. I think I do understand darling and at least I know have faith enough in you to believe you are doing what you think best. I am realistic enough too not take anything for granted as far as we are concerned but that doesn't prevent me from hoping if there are any difficulties between us, they can be straightened out when I do return.

Been sitting here thinking of those "difficulties" for the last 10 minutes and I am not too sure that it wouldn't be better if you would come <u>here</u> to meet me instead of me returning to the states. It is an idea—isn't it?

I was wrong about Merle and U.C.L.A., he wants to go to U.C. at San Fran. (or I guess Berkeley) Claims that either there, Harvard or Chicago has the best History schools. I keep asking about his post-war plans because his case is similar to mine and it never ceases to amaze me that his wife is behind him earnestly in all his plans. If I know Borrowman, he will succeed too. He says he is going to major in Latin American History and probably study in Mexico if possible. His plans are so concrete that I accually believe he will carry them out.

I have to finish this letter soon. Lights are going out and besides I plan to write you a really long letter tomorrow during my CWO watch.

"V-E" day has arrived at last and the only celebration here was the appearance of hard boiled eggs at the bar. They were interesting—painted characters on them—but all in all Victory in Europe was greeted in the Pacific rather bitterly and ironicly. The war here has still to be won and I hope people remember that in the midst of their celebration. Those with sons etc. out here will not have to be reminded. It will be interesting to watch the reaction back there and see if there is a let down. We are closer to that day I'll arrive in Chicago darling and anything to hasten it is worth celebrating. More tomorrow and

Love, Gene

❁

12 May 1945
1100

Hello again darling,
    Just finished censoring letters and I'll start this letter to you before chow. I have 1/2 day free which is the total amount of time for myself during the week. Should have prepared something for my history class but I'll probably get to that later in the week.
    Rec'd two more letters from you yesterday the lastest being yours of 3 May. It is always a pleasant surprise to find them on my desk when I come back from the Msg. center. Yesterday I had two off. Mess runs down to the airport so Merle went along for the ride. We don't get down there much anymore except on business but to see the buildings and living conditions of the Air Corps and Naval personel is really a treat. The 3rd Div. camp is quite far from the center of things and sometime I think they completely forget us. It is usually that way when our "allies" move in. The barracks at the airfield are wonderful and practically stateside in nature. They have three red Cross workers behind a counter serving coffee and cake. On the wall is a big sign saying "For transients only" and off to one side is a notice which states that this place is operated by the Red Cross for men returning to the states only. That of course excludes all the Marines on the island and so we are not supposed to be in there. Somebody had written very neatly on the bottom of the sign "Who supports the Red Cross??"
    My actual experience with the R.C. has been very slight, but I know they are not doing for the Marines what so many people back in the states believe. I have heard many bitter remarks about them. On the other hand—nobody here can praise the Salvation Army enough (of those fellows who were in Australia) but I have not seen any of that organization here. My dad tells me it was the same way in the last war. Well enough of that—I hope I don't sound bitter on the subject because as I've said, my experience with them is slight.
    I am at Merle's tent writing this. He is right across the road (50 yards) I wanted to get some letters written and others censored but in my own area a few

officers (who have no duties at all) are working on the off. mess and I hate to be seen sitting there writing letters when I should be out helping them. Makes me a little angry tho because they don't work on Sunday and we do in the Msg. Center.

The picture of you was cute—why-fore the pants? If you can forward one taken approximately 20 years later I would be doubly thrilled—Incidentaly here's a question—how old are you? & Franklin? You did tell me I believe at one time—When is your birthday? And thanks for the birthday greetings—I am 25.

1800—Wish I could finish a letter to you just once in one sitting. The interruptions are many in this place. I am back at my tent now. Couldn't even hope for a letter from you tonight because of the two last night. We have a party at the club tonight but I don't think I'll go. Merle should be here soon—Last night we went over to the 3rd Marines to see Steve in his new club and we both were very impressed by it, not the least unusual thing they have is a "flush" toilet for the nurses room. He insisted upon showing it to us after 10 Rum Cokes so we all went in and flushed it a couple of times just to make him happy. He is proud—and being the first one we'd seen since November it was quite a treat for us—. I didn't mean to pour forth so long upon something so insignificant but it does help you to visualize we are not living like so many people back in the states imagine. Wish you could see our camp, I know you would like it. On second thought I'm glad you are not here—the competition is terrific and I haven't the confidence. These are just stupid thoughts passing thru my mind. I hope you understand.

Merle is here again and suggested the 21st Marines movie for tonight. Told him I couldn't go until I'd finished your letter but he keeps interrupting me even tho I gave him the "Atlantic Monthly" to look at. Reminds me, I <u>am</u> getting it O.K.

Better quit for tonight sweetheart but more soon again—probably tomorrow.

All my love, Gene

P.S. That was the Marion I saw when I was home in Oct 1943—you asked about it a few letters back.—

15 May 1945

Dearest Marian,

Merle is writing to Mrs. B. along side me and has just remarked "Wonder what she'd like to hear tonight?" Makes me wonder what you'd like to hear—but if I say that I miss you and would like to be with you tonight maybe that would help. I do—

To the more trivial things—We saw "Saratoga Trunk" again tonight (the first time on Iwo) and enjoyed it as much as the first time. That seems to be the general opinion here which proves we aren't always cynical and do appreciate good entertainment.

I am writing this in Borrowman's tent because the lights go out in mine at 10:00 P.M. Today received the sad news that we will have to give about 4 lectures per week to Msg. Cent. personnel which gives me less time than ever for myself. The case is just the opposite with Merle—in fact he is going to start research on this island concerning native customs and the Jap occupation to perhaps complete a Master's thesis. Good idea—don't you think especially with the wealth of material available. Among things to do are 4 lectures on map reading and outlines of American, Modern and Ancient History to prepare. As I said before, I don't have half the time to do the things I'd like to do. In a sense it will be a relief to have another operation when we only have our regular work to do.

Your letter of the 4th came today but I don't have it with me to answer the questions. The editorial on Truman I liked but still have my doubts as to congressional action after the war. Sorta think he'll have trouble later on on some post-war technicalities. Got a laugh out of Congress deciding they would let the Army regulate the furloughs of men in Europe. Would like to know what business that is of congress anyway. Also liked Truman's reaction to the extension of the draft bill. Guess I've already told you V-E day received a cold reception in the Pacific. I don't actually believe Japan will see the "light." The way they are sacrificing men it doesn't seem that they care if anyone in Japan is alive in a few years. The Marines are on southern Okinawa—something we knew for quite a while. Seems it will be a little hard for the army to explain that but it is true that the North was lightly defended. The 6th div. is a new div most of whom have never seen combat but they seem to be doing O.K.

My dad wrote a letter which I received today. He is out of the service of course and enjoying life to the utmost. My step-mother wrote a few lines at the end of it. Someone had said to her, "I suppose Thor is sick of the water" and she answered back "I'll say, he hasn't drunk any since he's been home." I can understand that. I believe that he will be satisfied now. Edwards, Merle and I were talking about "readjustment" last night. It sort of has me worried at times and apparently Edwards feels the same. He said he'd probably marry the first girl that understood his problems and would listen to him when he returned. Probably exaggerated but I believe that it will happen in lot of cases—don't you?

I have just four minutes to finish darling—for tonight. To see you when I return makes any problems I may have much more simple. It does worry me at times but right now I do feel confident. Goodnight darling and

All My Love, Gene

❖

14 May 1945

My dearest Marian,

The thought suddenly struck me that it is rather ironic we should have become quite interested in each other just at the most inopportune time of my service life. In a sense it is the most obvious way since we are getting to know each other—probably far better than we would have had I been back there dashing through Chicago at regular intervals. Don't like to think that it sounds foolish when I say I'd like to be back with you most of all either—because that too is a plain fact. Figured I'd better just mention that—mostly because I just finished censoring a letter to a gal written by one of the men and he apparently is in the same tactical situation I am. His letters sound so insincere tho that it makes me sick to read them.

Your letter of May 6th greeted me this noon much to my delight and surprise. Didn't think it was possible to get another one so soon but when I think of all the writing I've done to one person in the last two weeks nothing along that line seems impossible.

You mentioned that cafe on North ave in your last letter which I had entirely forgotten—I do remember now however and also the "Yes dear" part of it. It gets me very angry at times when I try to remember things that happened and can't no matter how I try. I do remember telling you that I had a swell time at the Schroeder which I actually did—

"Forever Under" seems to be very appropriate from what I hear about it but Merle insists he is reading it for the historical background. Sorta agree with your mother about her viewpoint concerning sex but I do think there is need for (it)—wrong word—teaching it in the schools probably the last year of high. Can't help but feel that if I do raise a successful family I'll owe it all to the Marine Corps. Prior to that my education had been sadly neglected.

Told you about the Jasco off. recreation quonset hut I guess. Bought & built by the Seabees for 1 qt. of Seagrams and 4 cases of beer—Several nights ago they had housewarming so Merle & I stopped in about 10:00 PM. It was rather a rough scene with about 10 of them dead drunk and singing for fair. That is a devil-may-care outfit if I ever saw one—we call them the 1st Separated Nurse Chasing Company because there are at least 4 nurses there every night. I still haven't taken the trouble to get a date which makes me wonder sometimes if I'm normal (like Peg). Merle & Britt are faithful to their wives which is encouraging at a time when the married men are usually at the hospital first every night.

Thanks again for the pages from "Time" I read it today at work off and on. Liked the part you had marked on "Final thoughts of Roosevelt." and share with him the hope that the "trend" of public opinion will be such that we will regard all nations as co-equal and end the America First idealism which is still prevalent it appears.

This high tariff question is up again and can readily appreciate Wallace's stand on the question. This Knutson seems to embody everything I hate. The reciprocal trade treaties have appeared to me as being a perfect example of America's willingness to cooperate in world affairs.

Bringing back the P.O.W.'s to guard the German prisoners seems to be an excellent and realistic idea—if some of the mothers in the land don't object to the way the Germans will be handled.

Just opened a can of pinapples of which I have a case—will now take time to eat them and read "Terry and the Pirates"—With your cooking and my can opening we should get along well—

Back again at 9:50. It is now about 7:00 AM this morning back there and I suppose you are just getting up. I hope you have a pleasant day darling and meanwhile I am dreaming about you. Good Morning sweetheart and

Much Love, Gene

⚘

15 May 1945

Darling,

The work here is finally cleared up so that I'll be able to write to you. It wont be too much because I will have more time tomorrow and a better chance to concentrate. I have CWO duty tomorrow night. Will have to make a history outline also sometime in the near future as I promised my "pupils." Don't think they would approve of being called that. I had a couple lectures on Map reading yesterday but managed to get out of the other two scheduled. Merle & I discussed the Argentine Polish question and found out we both have our opinions and after an hour found that "A man convinced against his will, is of the same opinion still." At any rate he is more in sympathy with the Argentine gov. than I am. I feel that, as you said, the Polish have more right to some form of representation at San Fran than our late newly acquired allies. On the other hand Merle stresses the North American unity that is achieved by allowing them to enter the conference I don't think that unity (if there is any) should be had at the expense of world cooperation. It seems to me that Russia is being very realistic in her objection to any country who was not in sympathy with the Allies. I also believe there are too many Fascist factions in South America for our comfort. We did have a good discussion and I know we both profited by it. That way I like to argue.

The newspaper here (Daily Advance) played up the Harvard-Hollywood fight which you have probably read about. (I don't know of course what news is emphasized back there so when I say "you have probably read" I may be similar to that kid in the 6th Div. that wrote to his mother "he had landed on an island called Okinawa and if the newspapers mentioned it would they send him the clippings?")

Anyways I got a laugh out of the battle and my sympathies are definitely with the boys from Harvard. Outside of the picture "Kismet" those they picked for the "10 Worst of the year" generally satisfy me. Maria Montez as the worst discovery of the year satisfied me too.

I hope that you had a good time on V-E day. It was sorta an anti-climax don't you think? Which reminds me—acccording to the new "Time" it appears the American press is performing at its worse in regards to the conference. Made me a little disgusted to read the account of the stupid things they have done. Sometimes this freedom of the press is a pain-in-the-neck and must be embarrassing to the state department.

Merle is starting his Master's thesis in earnest now and I think he has a good idea. He has interviewed the island commissioner and the Educational governor already and is really making progress. I'd like to do the same if I had the time. I [would concentrate on] the Jap occupation of the island and the effect on the natives. There appears to be much material to be had.

I still have to make an outline of the American History course I'm teaching and rather wish I hadn't told them I'd do it now. The only contributing factor is the self satisfaction I get which often enough is sufficient.

Would like to hear what made Franklin a Republican sometime if you care to write about it. I think the fact that I sometimes hate people when I see how stupid they are—and feel sorry for them—has made me liberal. But after talking to Borrowman I am convinced that all Republicans aren't wicked. This tariff question and Big Business appear to be too closely connected for the good of the average man. "America First" still seems to be the platform of the old reactionaries.

This letter has become quite long after all and I guess I'd better quit for now.

It's getting hard to think of a new way to say that I like you and your ideas but the feeling is still the same—and it is a nice feeling, isn't it?

All my Love, Gene

P.S. Back at the tent and there were 3 letters from you—You are a darling. Concerning that Harvard-Hollywood affair, I didn't see "Winged Victory". Think they mentioned it <u>but</u> if you say it's good—darling, it is good.

❖

16 May 1945

Dearest Marian,

Just returned from the movie where "Fighting Lady" was shown. Undoubtedly it was one of the best pictures of its kind filmed (aircraft carrier) but somehow I didn't enjoy it too much. Those planes diving into those red balls of anti-aircraft fire was too much like sitting on Motoyama Airfield No. 1 watching the rockets come over. For the first time I know how fellows felt when they said they didn't appreciate war pictures.

This is letter no. II today but I have an hour till lights go out and I'd rather spend it writing to you than making up that history outline. Your 3 letters today were wonderful especially the one after the wine. If liquor affects us both that way we should have a great time at the homecoming. Would like to be in Chicago on V day or sooner if possible but I am reconciling myself to 2 years over here at least just to make sure I'm not disappointed. I think that is always a good idea—don't you? As you said—then if a miracle does happen the thrill is so much greater.

Merle and I were talking about where we'd like to go next. He wants to land on Japan [while] I'd rather go to China. Think I'd be very disappointed if I didn't get to see Hong Kong or Shanghai before I came home. China has always facinated me a great deal—more so than Japan for some reason I can't understand. Think probably it's because the former is so large and the cities have much more diversity and intrigue with the great foreign element. Japan always has been restrictive and of course never too friendly.

Feel in a sort of morbid mood tonight. I think the picture had something to do with it.

Been reading the clipping you sent on the "Trusteeship of the US. supported by Russia." The subject is a ticklish one (concerning the desire of Vandenberg to submit questions of treaty obligations to the international organization & objected to by Russia.) Both sides seem to be well taken. Whether Britain will ever let loose of her mandates is something I doubt, but it seems absolutely necessary if the spirit of Dumbarton Oaks is to be carried out. Can't see also why Russia's proposal of writing in the Right to Work and Right to Education should be objected, to. There are many situations that have sprung up but the willingness of the delagates to compromise and keep discussions open is encouraging. If one of the big 4 walks out now the whole framework will collapse as it did when the U.S. refused to join the league of nations. The big question that will always arise is whether the big 4 will be willing to trust each other and make the necessary sacrifices of honor and policy to make the international organization a real and potent body. The English will have to relinquish political and economic dictatorship of her mandates and the U.S. will be obliged to suffer the people at home industrially if necessary to make the reciprocal trade treaties work. Don't think that we are ready to sacrifice our high standard of living to help the Chinese or even it appears, the South Americans which may be necessary. These are questions which will undoubtedly come up in the future and if an immediate solution can't be found at least there should be continued attempts to work out the problems. This idea of one nation walking out should stop. If nations are unwilling to carry on prolonged discussions to find solutions to these great issues, then I believe war is inevitable. I still hate people who say wars are unavoidable because they usually are the ones who choose to argue a question rather than discuss it. It is a slow tiresome process that's true but actually the only way. Democratic governments aren't the most efficient ones in war and it stands to reason a democratic world organization isn't going to be the fastest or smoothest machinery in peace. There need be no such thing as a deadlock because what may not work today might tomorrow. For instance, India can't be freed in a moments notice but certainly she can be working toward that end continually.

To change the subject—

I liked the paragraphs from Pearl Buck on Education. Seems certainly to be essentially true—ignorance and distrust breed desire to rule. I still do not believe that the German people have always been warlike people and that there is something inside every German that craves power. I'm more inclined to feel that it was a combination of economic, political and possibly religious circumstances together with a few warped-brained radicals that made them what they are today. So many people I've talked to seem to think that all Germans are born with a war club in their hands and they are serious about it. I believe that Germany and Japan will have to be held down by force if necessary because they are the <u>potential</u> enemies of mankind due to the above reasons. They are not actual and determinately evil because they are of these particular races.

Darling, I have to go to bed—can then think about the more pleasant things—you for instance and meanwhile

All My Love, Gene

17 May 1945

Darling,

If 5 letters in two days means that you like me I am convinced dear— Somehow that sounds familiar—think possibly from you but I hope that you don't mind. I was amused to find out you were going to see "Fighting Lady" after I only mentioned it last night.

Tonight we saw the "3 Caballeros" after I talked Merle into going. We were impressed by it despite "some" obvious propaganda features. Never can quite appreciate animation and humans in the same scene but there were strokes of genius throughout undoubtedly. All in all everyone appreciated it and it was a good picture to see over here.

You mentioned something about Ray and the German 88's. Made me think that artillery is much easier to stand than Mortars or Rockets merely <u>because</u> you <u>can</u> hear artillery. Practically everyone will agree that the Mortars are the worst, I believe. Besides being able to put them practically in your back pocket, they give no warning. That "aint" good. I like to hear & see stuff. The Germans are as good with the 88's as the Japs with the Mortars which may account for some of Ray's reaction to them. Wonder how he'd like the snipers over here —

Haven't much time to write tonight. I have been busy all day. Finally moved again and am now living in the <u>best</u> tent in the compound with 2 captains. They are both nice fellows and as I'll probably be telling you about them from time to time, I wont spend time on that tonight. Capt. Styke & Capt. Murphy are their names — the former was my instructor at Philadelphia. At any rate I am very comfortable now in a swell screened-in tent.

I am glad you will have a chance to see the air show. I believe that the P-61's are larger than the Lightnings and seat 3 men Radar — Gunner — Pilot. That's about all I know about them outside of the general appearance. Seeing them is very much like meeting a policemen on a dark street — very comforting. The first thing after the air raid siren blew someone would say "Where in hell are the night fighters."

Have to close now darling. Both the captains are in bed and I better get the lights out. There is taps. Goodnight sweetheart.

Much Love, Gene

⚜

19 May 1945

My dear Marian,

Tis almost noon and I have the C.W.O. watch again. Business is slow so perhaps I can write a few lines before the first interruption. How do you like this paper? You don't have to answer that but I thought I'd mention it. We just got in about 7 packages and I am thinking of appropriating some for my own use.

Finished reading "Time" you sent this morning and Merle is coming to get it this afternoon. Always get a sort of "rosy" or "reflective" attitude when I read

"Time." So many things appeal to me and the whole thing is written in a significant tone. Right. Duly noted you underlined the reason for Germany's collapse as lack of air power or—allied air supremacy.

Personal view:—Air superiority is probably necessary to win a battle now but bombing is very often over-rated. I don't believe that Japan can be bombed out of the war or any nation for that matter. Truly tho it plays hell with their productive capacity and is ultimately one of the factors bringing defeat but it is not an end in itself. Right? Miss P-38

Thought that "Time's" review of the war was excellent as usual and I am beginning to appreciate V-E day by degrees as they said. We are still all prediced by the apparent hopelessness of a quick end to this war to share in the feeling of "At last"

The capture of Rangoon was good as you said. The Japs if nothing else, are difficult to understand at times.

I agree with you also about writing to someone every day. I'd never do that unless I really wanted to. My mother is the one seception and if I write 2 pages per week to her I am doing well. Even then it is the most stupid letter I write.

1300—after chow—Incidently the food is real good out here lately. An abundance of fresh meat and real lemonade are the most welcome. Still will never equal that food on the trip to Iwo. I'll never forget it or cease to be amazed at how they could do it. I think the thing most missed by everyone from Stateside is fresh milk. Would like a double malted right now. I have succeeded in collecting some rare things—for instance 3 qts. of Bourbon, a Zippo lighter, a .45 [revolver] and a very comfortable bed. Have been trying to swap the liquor for a radio but not much success as yet. A Jap flag is worth 2 qts. and a quart about $50 at the present rate of exchange. I have a Jap scarf which I'll try to send you very soon. It is the only important thing I picked up at Iwo—also some parts from a Jap zero. Thought of you when I hacked them off a wrecked plane.

How did you like the "Fighting Lady"? I have already told you I have seen it. It seems that the 3d Mar Div has compiled a 45 minute film on Iwo which I'd like to see next week sometime. Particularly interesting is that the whole film is concerning the 3rd Div Area as it was our camera men who took it. I'll tell you more after I see it.

Would like very much to accept your invitation but as you say—it is quite impossible. I hope you had a good time. Where is Glen Ellyn?

Incidently the man I was referring to a few letters back was Vandegrift. As I mentioned last night—I am living with two captains now. Capt Murphy and the other is Capt. Styke. The latter was stationed in Philadelphia for 2 years and is a signal quartermaster. He is quite a character. very big & fat and easy going. Has a hobby now of playing some silly instrument which I think is called a "sweet potato." He reads music while playing and has mastered "Joy to the

World" and "Jingle Bells." It sounds like hell but I smile and say, "very good captain." He said that he is going to get one for me and the three of us can play a trio arrangement he's got. Anyway he is a swell fellow and has procured much stuff for the tent which helps to make it more comfortable.

I had a dream about you last night. Seems as tho I came home and got very disgusted with everything and decided to go to Mexico City. When I got there was very much surprised and delighted to see that you were also there. Unfortunately I woke up then or something happened so I don't remember anything else. Imagine that the "3 Caballeros" had something to do with it.

Darling I have to stop now and get to work. Can hear the orchestra playing at the club and that puts me in a very good mood to think about you. Guess I have a one track mind—Goodnight Miss P-38.

All my Love, Gene

Flash! Merle just brought in a cigar. All's well and it is a boy. Seems relieved it wasn't twins but after all the talking about it—it was an anti-climax—something like V-E day.

❦

20 May 1945
1 Nov 1946 [sic]

Darling,
Wish it were that last date but the time is passing fast and it wont be too long. The Chinese have captured Foochow yesterday which is really encouraging. Sometimes wish that I was over there helping because it seems a little more adventurous to help a country that has been the underdog for so long. Then again I am glad that I am just where I am. I get some foolish notions once in a while. On Okinawa the army and marines seem to be going ahead slowly but it is slow. I have been practicing on the teletype this afternoon for awhile—it really facinates me. Have you ever operated one? Also this aft I typed up a long dispatch (about 6 pages) with out making a mistake. It really amazed me because when I type letter the mistakes are frequent—or have you noticed that? My work here is very interesting but confidential so I can't tell you much about it. We are generally in on the latest dope from all sources. I've found that the interest in seeing secret and etc. material diminishes when you can't talk it over with someone.

Last night I was over to the 12th Marines to see a friend of mine—a Capt McGuire who is comm off of that regiment (artillery) We were at Monmouth together last year. Had a pretty nice time altho I really hated to spend the time viseting friends when I have so many other things to do. I managed to paint my bureau yesterday also with some paint that Capt Styke found. Now we have almost everything white in our tent and it seems to make the place a lot more cheerful. We also fixed up some extra electric light sockets so each of the capts and myself have a bed lamp. Really amazing—don't you think. Our super mess hall is coming slowly and not too surely. Everyone seems to be too busy to spend the necessary time out there working on it. It is located right next to our tent and will be quite convenient. I hope that we can soon finish it and get some chance to enjoy it before—Jasco has been having trouble with their super-deluxe off. club. The order has been put out that they can't bring nurses in it unless it is authorized insomuch as they weren't going to use it as a mess hall. So they had an election to see if they were going to establish their own wine mess which would make the nursing angle possible or sacrifice the Navy gals and just use it as a rec room. The latter argument won and now everybody is bitter at everyone else. The advantages of the div wine mess are many which probably accounted for the final vote. It was close tho 17 to 16—

Merle has been quietly handing out cigars of which I got 3 already. Everytime he has the box out and it goes around I help myself on the grounds I stood by him during the trying weeks. His wife has got some real cute cards which I admired and hinted around that I wanted one but as yet he hasn't given me any. If he does, I'll send it to you—Darling if you forgive me for this typing I will be forever grateful. I didn't have much time to spare and now it is time to eat again so I will have to close. I am glad that you like my letters Marian because that is another thing that we have in common then. So long for awhile and—

All my love, Gene

❖

May 1, 1945
[Chicago]

Dear Lt. Sweetheart:

I'll have to make this letter brief. Still have this darn cold & ought to be in bed. Something happened tonight that I want to tell you about, though.

Have I ever mentioned my Communist friend, Jim Brown? He was a friend of the people next door when I lived on Prospect in Milw. We used to get into some interesting arguments. He's a member of the 5th Internat'l & is an active labor agitator—forever getting into trouble. He is rather obnoxious looking & used to call the working girls on Prospect Ave. "pretentious middle class." Reuben might know of him as he went to Milw State Teachers & was expelled.

I hated him at first because he would insist on being vulgar & seemed to enjoy shocking me. However, he got fairly well past that stage, & we discovered, much to our surprise, that he's also a poet & can quote pages from almost any piece of literature you might name.

A few months ago, another girl who knows him & I were discussing him & agreed it would be interesting to ask him about some of the things that have happened recently. He is extremely well informed. So I wrote one day & suggested that if he were in Chicago sometime he should come over, which he did tonight. He was here to attend a May Day meeting at which Vincent Dun (who he says is a noted labor leader) was to speak. I suppose I ought to know better, but I've been wishing for a long time that I could find out just what are his beliefs & purposes. He either thinks I am not interested or does not care to discuss it with a member of the "pretentious middle class." At any rate, when I said tonight that was why I had asked him to call, he, in a round-about way, practically accused me of wanting to have an affair with him. Horrible thought! It ended with him suggesting that he would probably be in town next week sometime & would call again. I said ok, but don't get my motives confused like that, so now I doubt that he will call. It makes me mad that I'll probably never find out what kind of monkey business he works so hard at. Do you know anything about the 5th Internat'l?

Oh—one thing he said was that there were a few Republicans who were honest about Roosevelt's death & did not lower their flags to half mast. Jim didn't. I asked him to tell me one thing wrong with what Roosevelt did & he just said it would take too much time. Aggravating, isn't it?

The air is certainly full of rumors about the peace in Europe. I have even begun to hope (very timidly) that V-E day might come this week. It would be wonderful. I heard some commentator say that if the Germans surrender, it will be that much easier for Japan to do so without losing too much of their precious "face." I wish it could happen that way.

This hasn't been so brief. I really must quit.

See you tomorrow, my darling.
Love, Marian

✤

May 2, 1945

My darling Gene:
I had a letter today from each of my two best boyfriends—you & my dad. His letters are a rare treat. They probably wouldn't be so rare if I'd write to him once in a while, but I never know what to talk about. Much as I like him, I long ago gave up trying to understand him.

You are a dirty rat for not telling me before that it was your birthday. ("Di'ty wat," Margie's 3-year old niece would say.) I hope you didn't tell me last year & I forgot. That would make me one. Anyway, happy birthday, darling. You are 25, aren't you? I'd say the San Fran. Conf. was quite a birthday gift. What I want for mine is you.

Really haven't seen much worth sending on the Conf., except, of course, what Time says. This article on Vandenberg is interesting. He certainly doesn't sound like a man of vision, though, does he?

Just heard that the war is over in Italy. I'll bet those poor guys who were stuck in the mountains so long really feel like celebrating.

Poetry dept: This is another of the verses Franklin had. That piece of Iwo Jima you sent reminded me of it:

"To see a world in a grain of sand . . .
Hold infinity in the palm of your hand,
And eternity in an hour."[37]

Like it?

You really answered that question about your dad, didn't you? Also another dozen or so I hadn't asked yet. I'm glad you did. Saves me a lot of trouble. I think it's fortunate that you like both your step parents. My dad had a step-mother who caused more trouble than any six people should. For example, when I was about five, we came back to W'berg, as my grandfather (who died in 1936) wanted dad to take over the business then. We stayed at their house, of course, & she refused to buy more than a pint of milk a day for four grown-ups & two children. Silly, isn't it? It made my mother so angry she packed up our belongings & back to Spokane we went. Franklin & I sure had fun on that trip. Maybe you'd enjoy seeing how we travelled.

Guess I ought to go back to bed again. I feel almost alive today. Paul is still out of town & I hope to go to work tomorrow & straighten things out before he returns. Just heard that Berlin has fallen & Hitler is officially dead. Things are getting exciting.

See you later, sweetheart. I wish you were here.

All my love, Marian

❖

May 3, 1945

Hello, darling,

That picture of a turnbuckle evidenced a good understanding of its principles, but it would probably take a little imagination to recognize a real one from that. To complete your education, I am sending you one of our illustrated price sheets listing, "Reliable Aircraft Turnbuckles and Parts, manufactured by a new method which results in a tremendous savings of critical materials and labor." Isn't it wonderful?

No doubt it is apparent that I went to work today. Paul didn't come back yet, either, bless him. I think I jumped every time the door opened, though. Darn him — I wish he wouldn't always be such a surprise!

I bet a soda today with Santa that tomorrow would be V-E day. (That is really her name — Santa Marzano. Probably I've mentioned her before. It was her brother who was also with the 15th Air Force & was missing for a few months.) She bet it would be Saturday & if we both lose, it will be a Dutch treat. In any case, we get the soda, which makes it rather pleasant, don't you think?

Heard a rumor today to the effect that they're soon going to remodel our offices and Paul and George Morse ("Field Engineer" on telephone equipment, who is also, theoretically, my boss) and I will have an office to ourselves. Methinks I shall like that.

Did I tell you about that title, Field Engineer? John Brown Cook bestowed it upon Paul & George about a month ago. George asked if a raise went with it & John was not amused. Paul says he doesn't know what it means, but we'll use it. I'm afraid I'll type Flight Engineer some day. I waste more time making that word come out F-i-e-l-d.

This letter is certainly a lot of nonsense, but I feel sort of nonsensical — without the aid of spirits, either.

Goodnight, sweetheart.
All my love, Marian

P.S. I am very much pleased to note that Truman intends to renominate David Lilienthal.[38] You, too?

⚘

May 5, 1945

Darling,

There were two letters from you yesterday and two today, and I feel so wealthy!

I enjoyed that article of Ernie Pyle's. That was a new experience — you sending clippings to me. On the Okinawa affair, I notice the Marines have gone down to help the Army, now that their end of the job is done. (You see what an influence you have on me!)

Can't say that I quite agree with Merle's objection to Roosevelt, either. I think he could hardly have done differently in view of the strong public opinion against "war-mongering." I sometimes wonder, though, if it might not have been within his power to change that public opinion by publishing more of what he must have known regarding the preparations & apparent intentions of our enemies. Probably there are very involved reasons why he could not—I don't like to mistrust people.

I don't suppose I ever did say much about Capt. Bauer's job. Guess I did mention that he was a sales manager for Squibb before the war. He's in charge of inspection in the midwestern area for the medical purchasing office of the Army now. Murph said he went to a stag party the other night with some business friends and discovered that their conversation, which consisted exclusively of how much money they made, had become quite distasteful to him. He has my sympathy in that.

I think it's awful that you aren't getting your Time magazine. Usually if you send them the address impression from one of your old copies, they manage to make the change quite promptly. Five months is darn slow. I hope you've told them so.

Your saying you were going to play volley ball reminded me of a remark in one of Franklin's Air Corps class books regarding his aptitude for the game. "We know he must fly better than he plays volley ball," it said, "because he's still flying." Not exactly the athletic type, you might gather. No enthusiasm for it.

Gene, the stories in Time about those Nazi prison camps have made me both heart-sick and furious.[39] I don't even think that story about the American officer who ordered the German woman & her children away from their house is sad any more. Like him, I hate the bastards, every last one of them! Really I guess they can't all be blamed—probably many of them were not aware of what was going on. But Franklin would hate them almost more for their stupidity than the Nazis for their crimes, and truly their stupidity is as much to blame, regardless of whether or not they could help being stupid.

Well, let's talk about something else now.

I'm sending you this editorial about Truman because I think that, being written by the editor of a paper that opposed Roosevelt in the last election, it is an encouraging indication of Truman's possibilities for a successful term. Agreed?

Grafton's article states (in a learned way) my own feeling about this Argentina deal. Surely any Polish govt. has more right to be there than has Argentina. I should like to know just what is so objectionable about the Lublin Poles.

Last night I went to see Paul Robeson[40] in "Othello." It was absolutely marvelous! You've probably studied the play. I had never read it & was afraid I might not understand it very well, as Shakespeare is usually a little obscure to me on the first reading. It wasn't the least bit difficult to follow, though, and I thoroughly enjoyed it. Paul Robeson's booming voice and enormous size made Othello's jealous rages so impressive, I was half scared to death by the end of the first act and was wishing I knew what to expect next so I could relax a little.

Darling, I'd better save a few things to say tomorrow. If I say I love you tonight and say it again tomorrow, though, you won't mind, will you?

Goodnight, dear.
Marian

�֍

May 6, 1945

My darling Gene,

I almost had to laugh when you said it had been a rugged week over there — only three letters from Chicago. I know how you felt, though. When there are only two days between letters, it seems like a long time. I used to think it would be not only rather silly, but impossible to write to anyone every day, but it's amazing how much there is to say, important or otherwise. It's mostly otherwise, I guess, but it's so nice to feel that you'll be glad to read it regardless.

This was a day worthy of California. I went for a long walk on the lakefront and then to a show, "Desert Song." On Sunday there is no point in trying to go to a recent movie downtown unless you like to wait in line an hour or so, and it's a rare movie that's worth it. On days like this, I really envy you the companionship of all the fellows over there. With Murph gone, as usual, there is no one at all that I know within a radius of several miles. Most of the time, though, I'm glad to be alone & be able to read and write without being interrupted.

I don't know how Shirley Temple got into that story about Anita Colby and Jennifer Jones. Maybe I imagined it, but I was sure you had mentioned her. You really should have taken advantage of the opportunity, but I don't know — Jennifer's a pretty cute gal. I should be glad you didn't.

I don't mind if the sun is bleaching your hair. I always did like blondes.

Did I ever tell you that when you took me home after our evening at the Schroeder, the elevator man said, "That certainly is a fine-looking young man." "I think so, too," I said, and we parted friends. I had a wonderful time that night. Remember that little place on North Ave. where we ate? We were having more fun just sitting there saying, "Yes, dear" to each other.

You mentioned "Forever Amber" in one of your recent letters. One of the girls at the office is reading it now. She says Paul told her he had a new name for it, "Forever Under." Is that appropriate? I haven't read it, nor have I any desire to do so. I sound like my mother now. Every time she finds some frank mention of sex in a novel, she gives a lecture on it. "Now what is to prevent some youngster in school from picking up that book in a library?" she asks. "It's a disgrace!" I am usually tempted to say that the child might get some education thereby on a subject which his parents, if they're like mine, have sadly neglected.

It's about noon on Guam now, so while you're having lunch, I think I'll have a cookie. Did I tell you I baked some yesterday? They aren't bad.

I love you today, too.

Goodnight, Lt. Sweetheart,
Marian

⚜

May 7, 1945

Hello, darling,

Two letters again today. This is really wonderful. One was the letter you had written aboard ship back in February. I'm glad you sent it. Sort of fills in some missing links in the story. Thanks for returning the Coronet story, too. I should imagine you <u>were</u> amazed to get everything back intact.

You don't need to worry about "Guide to the Peace" interfering with my letter writing. I'd much rather write to you than study, and as a result, I'm a week or so behind my original ambitious schedule already. I'll tell you how the book is organized to give you some idea what it's like. It's almost like a geography. There is a concise summary of information about each nation in the world, divided into these classifications: "The Land and its People," "National Economy," "History" (Between the two wars), and "Stake in the Peace." It's primarily a reference book, but it's also interesting reading.

This has been a day to try the patience of a saint. I imagine you have heard the many conflicting reports and all the uproar about who was holding up the official announcement of German surrender, etc. The latest report is that Truman will speak at nine tomorrow morning, E.W.T., followed by Churchill—and <u>possibly</u> Stalin. What a thing for those three to be disagreeing over—if they are.

Anyway, it looks as if I was being only a <u>few</u> days too optimistic last week. We had a lot of fun the first few hours at work this morning when it looked as if the announcement would come any minute. The joy has worn off for the present, though. I feel right now that Roosevelt was certainly right when he said there are a lot of "prima donnas" in the world. I hope they get it all straightened out tomorrow, or "squared away," as you would say.

I had to laugh at you for saying you hate people. Franklin would have appreciated that. He was a Republican—there's a long story about that. I'll tell you about it some day.

I agree that not many people knew about Truman & his record, but I think there would have been less opposition to him if more people had known about the work he did in his Senate investigating committee. I never could get anyone to believe me when I tried to tell them about that.

Reminds me of a cute story Peg told me about one of those discussion meetings she goes to at church. It seems a certain Dr. Senny (that's phonetic spelling) & a Mrs. Witherbee (I think) are always on opposite sides of every argument. At the end of one evening, Mrs. W. walked over to him and said, "Dr. Senny, I never <u>can</u> understand why everything <u>you</u> read is right, and everything I read is wrong."

I certainly do like your grandfather for being fond of Santa Barbara. When we were there, Franklin could hardly wait to show me the City Hall. Sounds silly, doesn't it? It's worth seeing, though.

Darling, I'd better say goodnight. We'll probably have the day off tomorrow, so I'll have lots of time to write. In our thoughts, at least, we'll celebrate the day together.

With love, Marian

⚜

May 9, 1945

Gene, darling,

I started twice to write to you yesterday, and just could not make it sound like Victory day, so I gave up. From the deep dark silence around Chicago, you would have thought it was a national humiliation day like the Chinese have, instead. Even the restaurants and grocery stores were closed, and Murphie and I hadn't even a bottle of wine in the kitchen to celebrate with. Ed is in Minneapolis, so we couldn't get him to mix martinis for us, either. We're going to celebrate tonight—with the Russians.

Went to see the movie version of Winged Victory last night and enjoyed it more than on the stage because, of course, they can do so much more with the scenes of the planes and the flying fields. Every time I think about the part about their graduation day, it makes me more sorry that I did not go to Williams Field when Franklin got his wings. There are so many things I could have done for him and didn't, mostly because I did not realize at the time how much it would have meant. Too often I took it for granted that he knew how I felt— Don't ever let me do that to you, dear.

I was glad Truman mentioned in his speech that he wished Roosevelt could have lived to witness the German surrender. I was hoping he would say that.

They said yesterday that the negotiations on the Polish question had really broken down. I read the section on Poland in Sumner Welles' book and learned some things about the Fascist tendencies of the pre-war Polish government represented by the London Poles which made me definitely in sympathy with the Russian attitude. In the May "Atlantic Monthly" (Incidentally, I will send them your new address today.) there is an excellent summary of the conflict between British and Russian interests there and in the Balkans and Near East. That is beginning to worry me considerably.

That damn <u>Tribune</u> published a story Monday of a statement by some character in Montreal to the effect that we would be at war with Russia "tomorrow." Wouldn't old McCormick just love that!!

I have to get back to work. Paul came back Monday, so I am no longer my own boss. Just took time out this noon while the slave drivers were at lunch.

See you later, darling, and I certainly hope we can celebrate the next V day together. I missed you so much yesterday—even more than usual, which is more than you think.

All my love, Marian

⚘

May 9, 1945 [2]

Hello, Sweetheart,

As I said this noon, we're doing our celebrating tonight. So this letter may be somewhat incoherent, but it should not be lacking in warmth. Thus far, I have had one glass of port and zinfandel for yesterday, one for today, and still have one coming for you. It has certainly done wonders for my morale, which had perversely hit an all-time low yesterday. Your letter of "3 May" also deserves a large share of credit for said improvement. Darling, you're wonderful!

I'm surely sorry they commandeered your house. Hope you don't have to live in that "broken down tent" long.

I'd like to see that super mess hall you're building. You'd better be careful about standing around in concrete, or doesn't it set that fast?

"Gale honey" (That's what one of their Southern officers calls Murph) has been putting a hem in a dress she just had dyed. 'Tis the most beautiful shade of purple.

We have also been having a lengthy discussion on education, which, I may have told you before, is her favorite crusade. We finally summed up the whole thing with these two paragraphs from a book by Pearl Buck [?], which I think are essentially true:

"Men and women must be educated out of the wish for power in any domain; and they can be, for the root of any wish for power is . . . in insecurity of some sort & in distrust of others through ignorance of them. . . .

"It is unreasonable to expect anyone to develop character without responsibility. . . ."

That second paragraph is perhaps a good explanation of such people as Lt. Pace. Right?

It was fun really to get down to work again today. I like working for Paul because he so rarely gives me time to sit around & get dull. It's good to relax when he's gone, although I usually have as much to do, but it's also good when he returns. He dictates so fast that being only three weeks out of practice, I really have to concentrate to keep up. And then I can feel so smart when I get it all done correctly—Oh, quit being so proud!

I am glad we agree regarding the merits of Los Angeles & Chicago. It's true that it's difficult to consider seriously living in California when your family is so definitely settled in Wisconsin. I feel somewhat the same about my mother & dad, particularly since Franklin has been missing. Time will tell, no doubt. That's rather an exasperating phrase, but perhaps the length of time will not be so great as we think. Now that's real optimism, don't you think?

That garrison song sounds as if the school children had also composed it. Your Anglo-Saxon typing is quite distinctive, dear.

By this time, I've finished all three glasses of wine & feel rather sleepy. Would rather fall asleep on your shoulder just now than cry. Remember how nice it was on the train, after the first hour or two we wasted thinking about it? Goodnight, darling.

All my love, Marian

❖

May 10, 1945

Dearest Gene:

A nice swift-sounding plane just flew over—it almost had a whistle. They're having an air show at the Municipal field this weekend to open the 7th War Loan drive and if they don't have at least one P-38, I shall be sadly disappointed. Haven't seen one since we left L.A. Needless to add, I haven't seen any P-61's either. The pictures of them do look as wicked as the spiders for which they're named—and to me a spider of almost any variety is about the most horrible looking thing there is. Are the 61's much larger than Lightnings?

That's enough about the Air Corps for this letter. You should know better, dear. All this was brought on by a paragraph in your letter of May 4, which arrived today.

This business about the man who lost the razor is as tantalizing as a mystery story. I give up. The easier it sounds, the more confused I am. Perhaps a light will dawn one of these days.

Gene, I hadn't intended that you should return that book—unless, of course, you want to. And I'm glad you did mark the parts you liked best. I think books ought to be used that way, don't you? It makes them that much less impersonal. There is a trilogy of the three books St. Exupery has written published in one volume. I want to buy a copy next time I see one, so don't worry about what happens to this one.

Had a letter from Peg tonight, all radiant with V-E day, which I enjoyed. Among other things she said was that she had wondered how you could tell me so much about Iwo Jima until she remembered that you censor your own letters. I can see that I'll have to give her a few lectures on that.

She also said she'd had a letter from Ray in which he tried to apply the psychology he learned in school to analyzing why he "was not afraid in combat, except of the German 88 shells, which have an unearthly whine." Does the part in quotes seem logical to you? She doesn't say what conclusions he arrived at. None, probably.

About that little brown hat, Murph is looking after your interests in the matter. It was raining this morning and I took it off the shelf to reach for another one, and she said, "I was just about to scold you for wearing that hat today." As if I would!

I hope you can send those Japanese "odds and ends." I would be very much interested.

I get a kick out of that inside dope on the twins you suspect Merle of keeping secret. Could be, though.

Darling, you don't need to apologize for your letters—ever. I like them all, long, short, confusing and otherwise. I like you, too. And if I don't stop thinking about it right now, I'll never get anything else done tonight.

Much love, Marian

❧

May 12, 1945

Gene, darling,

This will be just a short note to send with these pages of Time, and I'll write a long letter later tonight or tomorrow aft. This is rather a busy weekend. There's a picture on at the Esquire which I want to see tonight "Fighting Lady." Tomorrow, I hope to go out to the airport to see if I can find a P-38.

Would you like a date for dinner tomorrow night? Paul & his wife have invited me to their home in Glen Ellyn, a suburb west of town. I'm very much pleased, but also considerably worried. I'm glad I can count on their serving a drink or two so that I will not spend the whole evening in petrified silence. You are invited, too, but I told them I didn't think you could get back here in time. I certainly wish you could. That would really make it fun. Will tell you all about it Monday.

This story about Airman-Infantryman-Seaman Saunders capturing Rangoon single-handed amuses me no end. Bet he had a wonderful time.

See you later, dear.
Marian

❦

May 12, (2) 1945

Hello again, darling,

Just came back from the show. It was really worth seeing. Besides <u>Fighting Lady</u>, they had <u>Three Caballeros</u>. Have you seen it? It is in parts very similar to <u>Fantasia</u>, and that I like. About <u>Fighting Lady</u>, it always seems so strange to me to be watching War from a comfortable upholstered chair completely out of danger. Makes me feel somehow very inadequate.

I think I do understand why you decided against going to Pearl Harbor. It wouldn't seem right to you to take the easy way, would it? I'm sure I would have tried to talk you into it, though, if I could have—and the reason for that is both obvious and selfish. It is that important to me to know that you <u>will</u> come back.

The origin of the inferiority complex you worry about is not so easy for me to understand. I get a little impatient with that phrase sometimes. Everyone seems to have one and yet no two are alike. I suppose the fact that they are complex and difficult to analyze leads us to apply the same term to all. I used to have long arguments with myself over whether my own desire to avoid criticism was due to such a complex composed chiefly of shyness, or to conceit. I finally decided it must be both and quit worrying since there seems to be nothing I can do about it. I believe that as long as we don't belittle someone else's efforts in order to enhance our own, it's all right to be proud. Do you think that's true?

The fellow I told you about with whom Margie has been going out called me today, and I'm going to have lunch with him Tuesday. His name is Carl Morris. He seemed very nice on the phone & is surely easy to talk to. A good salesman, no doubt. I'm curious to see him. Margie told me he was going to call some day, but I really didn't think he would.

—It is now Sunday afternoon & I've given up that jaunt to the airport. Didn't even wake up until 12:30.

I enjoyed your discussion of the S. F. Conf. in your letter of May 6. Your statement that the world operates not on miracles but on changing systems of principles in keeping with the times is very true. Reminds me of an interesting idea I read somewhere quite a while ago, "The only stability attainable in world affairs is the stability of a spinning top or a bicycle." Seems a little wearisome, but it's also exciting.

I certainly agree with your comparison of the need for sacrifices of national honor with the sacrifice of states rights in this country. It is all a part of the broader idea of individual sacrifice for the long-range common benefit. People simply have to be educated to see beyond the ends of their noses and realize that their own personal gain and security is worthless & temporary if it is attained at the expense of others. And that word "educated" is all important.

Do you remember telling me one time that it would be wonderful if I could love someone else as much as I did Franklin? Sometimes I think I do. And, incidentally, I liked you for understanding that. See you tomorrow, Sweetheart.

Marian

✤

May 14 '45

Hi, Sweetheart:

As you said in your letter today (dated May 8), "Your letters are still the most important part of the day." Also they're getting to be such a pleasant habit, I hate to think of its ever being broken except by your presence—One of the incidental reasons it would have been good to know you were safely in Pearl Harbor. I won't complain, though. I know we agree that there are more important things.

I'd like to see the desk you built. Real eager, aren't you? Well, you can't be a history teacher without a desk! I am really enthusiastic about that educational program and, as I said before, I think the teaching will be good experience for you.

I've been wanting to study Spanish for some time, also. It would be fun if we could start about the same time & do a little practicing in our letters. Think so?

I think it's rather smart not to plan too definitely on anything—such as going on to school. There are always so many unforeseen events that <u>do</u> change & shape the course of men's affairs, all insurance advertising to the contrary. However, I surely hope that girls (this one at least) and school are not necessarily incompatible.

I have lots to tell you about dinner last night, so I'd better get started on that subject. Did I tell you Les Hendrickson & his wife would be there, too? Les works for Dunbar-Kapple, one of our most active distributors of turnbuckles. We discovered that his brother (he calls him "Tray") is also in the 3rd Marine Division, a scout. So we're real pals now.

I really had a grand time the whole evening. Paul is so much fun when he's not in the office, and his wife is a honey. They live in Glen Ellyn, a suburb about 40 minutes west of the loop and it's lovely out there. From that distance I could even learn to like Chicago. It seems to me they live an ideal life, but that is too long a story to try to explain in a letter. Suffice it to say that they thoroughly enjoy their friends, their family and each other.

I learned some interesting things about the turnbuckle business and about me & my job, also. For one thing, Paul is going to be out of town about half the time from now on—on orders from Mr. Cook, Sr., the great white father. "So you can have the turnbuckle business," Paul said. And I'm afraid he means it. That isn't all I can have. Our Vice-Pres. & Sales Mgr. has been spending most of his time lately in Rochester, N. Y., and will probably be there permanently before long as he is taking over the dept. store business of his father-in-law. So a good share of his work has fallen to Paul and no one else does it when he's gone unless I put myself out on the end of a nice long limb and attempt to keep it somewhat up to date. Methinks I shall have a chat with Ripley one of these days to let him know what goes on and then see if I can get Paul to go to work on him & get me a raise. I've never done anything so revolutionary before, but neither have I been a secretary to so many people before, besides being assistant switchboard operator and handler of credits. If this sounds exaggerated, please overlook it. I'm just trying to talk myself into something.

To change the subject—I haven't seen "Tonight & Every Night." I'm glad you warned me. I get a kick out of your mother thinking you might be afraid of sergeants. That made me laugh as much as the sailor saying the movies were so nice to come home to. People are crazy, aren't they?

One of the girls who used to work at our office had twins Saturday. (This has nothing to do with people being crazy.) A boy & a girl. That's what I call getting things done efficiently. Quite a savings of time & effort. I think I'd want them alike, though, both boys—and a girl later. Does Merle have any inside info. on what variety his twins will be?

I think I'd better do a little studying. Haven't even looked at that book for too long.

Goodnight, my darling. I wish you were here—

With love, Marian

✦

May 15 '45

Hello, darling,

I was just thinking how different the world would be for me if you had been sitting <u>any</u>where else on that train last February. Almost makes me believe in fate. A very kind fate it was, too.

These two clippings have to do with the other variety. They make me sad all over again about Roosevelt's death.

Truman surely did a smooth job of politicking, tho, in getting old McKellar to give up his fight against Lilienthal, didn't he? That really pleases me. I hope he will manage as well with Stalin & Churchill.

I had lunch this noon, as planned, with Margie's friend, Carl Morris. It took an hour & a half and we're supposed to have 1/2 hr. for lunch. That didn't exactly make me popular with some of the other gals in the office this aft. However — it was all very interesting. Carl seems to be really a sweet guy. I'm pretty gullible, but I do believe he's sincerely fond of Margie & all above-board. He seems to just want to see that she has a good time & do anything he can to help her out when she needs help. Which is all very noble. The only trouble is that it's so easy to become too fond of anyone who's that good to you. Maybe it's worth it. At least you learn a lot about tolerance & understanding, and that's worth a good deal.

I meant to tell you yesterday that Les Hendrickson's brother was in the 21st Reg, too.

Guess I should tell you one of the stories he & Paul told about their travels. They were down in Texas together not so long ago & were supposed to meet at a certain hotel in Dallas. When Les got settled, he called Paul and some woman answered. That seemed a bit peculiar, but when she said Paul was just taking a shower, Les began to wonder what kind of a guy he was traveling with. He left word for Paul to call back. A few minutes later, Paul came into Les' room. "What have you been doing?" asked Les, casually. "Oh, nothing," said Paul. "Well, whatcha going to do now?" asked Les. "Guess I'll go take a shower," said Paul. Well that was just too much & Les wanted to know what the hell was going on here! It turned out Paul was on the 15th floor & Les had been connected with a room on the 8th floor where another Paul Rhoads was staying. Odd?

You know those characters who take candid shots of people on the street & then hand you an envelope & a slip with a number? I got one a few weeks ago & sent it in, just for fun. The picture arrived today, but Murph says it looks like the "before" part of a "before & after" ad for some kind of pills, so you can't have it. What she says is all too true. Well, it was fun anyway.

I never did get any studying done last night, so I'd better try again. Would much rather sit here & think about you, darling.

All my love,
Marian

P.S. This is exciting! Mac Howard just called—remember the letter about Yalta, etc.? Murph isn't home tonight but he's going to be in town a day or two so she should hear some interesting tales. Good, hm? See you tomorrow sweetheart.

⚜

May 16, 1945

Darling,

Your letters of May 9 & 10 were here tonight and they're both wonderful— It seems when I have two letters the same day, there is so much to say I never know where to begin.

I had been a little worried about the letter I wrote you about Cal because it seemed such a long time before you mentioned it. Darling, you're so nice about it. You've no idea how much I appreciate your faith in me. As far as any difficulties between us are concerned, I'm sure they'd be as easy to straighten out here as if I were to go over there (although I'd love to go there).

Cal knows that when you come back, I'll probably never see him again. I think it's only being alone so much that makes it hard to give up now. Even if Peg were here, it would be easier. Know what I mean?

I laughed, too, at Merle saying he thought he was getting too realistic from reading so much about the Russians. Realism doesn't always apply when you are dealing with anyone who is as much a sentimentalist as I am.

I wish I could hear you two discussing things. To me, a nice heady argument is one of life's greatest pleasures, and friends with whom you can really talk are to be treasured. I'd like to meet Merle sometime. It would be swell if you could go to school together. I think he's wise to plan on studying Latin American history. Should give him knowledge that will make him valuable to the new "pioneers" of inter-American trade. I have a friend who, with her fiancee, spent two or three summers studying in Mexico City. It cost them next to nothing & they thoroughly enjoyed it. I should think Colombia would be a fascinating place to study, also. It's supposed to be the most cultural of all the South American countries.

Does studying at the Univ. of Chicago fit in with your desire to stay in Milw. as long as your grandfather lives? What would you do in that case—stay here & spend the weekends in Milw.? Or do you think you could persuade him to come down here, too?

On the subject of spelling, I have noticed that writing a lot, as we have been, gives me a tendency to want to spell things phonetically. I thought perhaps shorthand had something to do with it, as it's so much easier to keep up with your thoughts if you can write them in shorthand & that is based entirely on the sound of words with absolutely no regard for their spelling in longhand. Perhaps the tendency is universal, though, & not limited to stenographers. I often don't even see errors in spelling until the second or third reading. Anyway, don't let it worry you.

Did I tell you Murph & I were going to rent a sewing machine for a month? It finally came today & we are going to be some busy people. It's fun, though, & I'm anxious to get started.

Right now, Lt. Sweetheart, there is nothing I'd like better than to sit under one of those palm trees, look at the moon, and have somebody (no one but _you_) holding my hand. I don't even care if it rains!

Much love, Marian

※

May 17, 1945

Dearest Gene,

Thought I would have a lot to tell you today about Mac Howard, as Gale had dinner with him last night. I'm disappointed, though. She says she was asking him questions all evening, but about all he talked about was the girls in France, Italy & Russia & how much nicer American girls are. He's not that sort of fellow, either—at least he doesn't treat Murph that way.

His ship was a mine sweeper. Four or five of them went along to Yalta to clear mines the Russians had laid in the Bosporus, etc. He said he saw Roosevelt—could have seen them all if he'd wanted to take the trouble! Murph says she's never seen anyone with less enthusiasm than he has—over anything at all.

I just bought this stationery yesterday & I don't like it—too transparent.

Leon certainly has a great deal in common with Brown. The girl situation is parallel also. Jim lived with some gal when he was in school—thought marriage was unnecessary since people would have enough faith & respect for each other to keep a marriage contract without legal persuasion. (Not very realistic for a Communist, is it?) However, Helen (I think that was her name. No, it was Ethel) saw some guy one day who appealed to her & that was the last Jim saw of her. So he is a bitterly disillusioned lad. He gave me a copy of a poem he had written for her at one time, & I think it is surprisingly beautiful.

Tired now, and falling warm
Into the West
The wine-brimmed sun
Leans over at the waist;

Lazily the golden arms
Draw up the star-sewn quilt,
Cool blue, and rest.

Cold now, and numbing still
The rose-gold loam
Encysts; the milk
Of clouds that drowsily roam
Spills, enameling cool earth
Thus tightly curled. Clay in rose-silk
Lies wrapped in chrome.

Slip low
To sleep with me, my love,
Soft sun and placid loam,
O favored of
The night and star-chromed snow.

I agree that it is hard to tell a long story like this in a letter. Would so much rather talk to you about it. There is a lot to tell about background, which, I think, was quite different for Jim than for Leon.

Do you like the poem? It improves with repetition, I think. Cal read another one Jim had written & called it a product of the "weed." Even that would not surprise me.

It will probably seem queer to you that I should send you this copy of a letter I wrote today for Don Baxter. I had so much fun doing it, though, and thought it might give you some idea of how interesting my job is at times. Don is a very slow & deliberate person. I could hardly keep a straight face while he dictated this. He had a rough draft all written out & yet it actually took him 15 minutes to give me this one letter. No kidding, I timed it. Just try reading it over that slowly & you'll have some idea of how funny he sounded.

Forgot to mention in talking about Brown that this 5th Internat'l is still in existence. All I know of it is that they are followers of Trotsky.

That's a good story about the fellow who told his girl not to kiss the envelopes because it was the censor who sealed them. If you were the censor, darling, she'd undoubtedly be getting a better deal.

In case anyone asks you, I still love you today, too.

Goodnight, sweetheart,.
Marian

⚜

May 19, 1945

My darling Gene,
 I have had more battles since the last time I wrote you. May I tell you my troubles, dear?
 In the first place, last night I had dinner with Betty Beeker & a friend of hers, and I could hardly sit still the whole evening because it seemed such a waste of time. I think I told you the last time I saw her, which was a couple of months ago, how I was so annoyed with her for running down the Marines &, also, officers of all branches of the service. Last night there was more of it and more obnoxious, all about how her poor husband suffers in the Army. Suffers, hell! He has been sitting comfortably in Hawaii (where I wish you were) for nearly a year. Prior to that, he spent 6 mos. of "hell" on Kiska—well, maybe it was cold up there! His chief complaint, however, is that the officers are always "pulling their rank" on him—and, of course, he is far superior to any officer. Personally, I'd like to pull something a little more destructive on him.
 On the subject of Hawaii, everyone has been telling me that the govt. has been advertising for civil service employees to go over there—stenographers, etc., being greatly in demand. Does that make you as sad as it does me?
 Getting back to the Beeker family, another tale Betty told which annoyed me considerably concerned her brother, Don, who fell off his motorcycle and broke a leg at Aachen last Nov. He was in a hospital in England four months & then they sent him home on a 30-day furlough. In St. Louis, from which point he started his furlough, he immediately proceeded to get drunk. As he tells it, he lost his overseas cap & when three MP's questioned him about it, he was a trifle sarcastic, &, without just cause, they beat him up ("oh, he just came home all bloody!"), stole some of his money, left him in a gutter for an hour & then put him in the guard house. "Talk about the Gestapo in Germany, we have it right here," said Betty. Why didn't he report them, I asked. Surely they could be court-martialed for such conduct without justification. But, no, Donnie said he wouldn't dare have criticized them because it would only have made things worse for him. Now, tell me honestly, Gene, do you believe that's true? He's been in the Army four years & is still a private, due largely to frequent stays in the guard house. It just makes me so angry to hear a story like that being told to discredit authority. The trouble is that people will so readily believe that sort of thing.

On to the second battle—this one at the office this noon. That damn Virginia (I think you've heard that phrase before) has been making out the office payroll in the absence of the chief bookkeeper. By some fancy finagling she maneuvered us out of a part of the bonus which we had previously been paid & which the factory workers still get. The amt. of money involved is not large, but the way it was done was so petty that all the girls are angry with her. Virg., incidentally, is very highly paid & is not on the same basis we are. I decided we'd be darn fools to let her get away with it without at least protesting, so I told Ripley we were all damn disgusted, and he, who is supposed to be office manager, didn't even know what had been done. He said he'd talk to Mr. Cook about it, so I'm wondering what will happen next.

This is pretty awful—seven pages of complaints. I hope you don't mind too much. It certainly makes me feel better to get it off my mind.

Your letters of May 12 & 13 and the two March copies of "Leatherneck" arrived & were in very pleasant contrast to the events related above. I really enjoy the Leatherneck & your comments here & there are greatly appreciated—especially that one about the undertaker. I don't think I want him, though. I'm fussy. I'd rather have you, even if you <u>don't</u> want to be an undertaker.

I'm glad you thought that snapshot was cute. I think the pants were occasioned by the fact that travel then was a little more rugged than it is now. You should see the khaki knickers my mother wore! Sometimes in the mountains we used to get out & climb up to where the road was above, like this (That drawing is strictly symbolic. The road, of course, didn't go off into space like that. I'm not an artist, either.) Then the car would be light enough so Dad could drive it up the grade on the next hairpin curve. That was fun!

Dept. of Vital Statistics: I'm 23. Will be 24 on July 23. Franklin would have been 26 this last March. Reminds me of a story I read called "They Shall Not Grow Old." Did I tell you about it? If not, I should have.

Darling, it may be that I'm a blissfully ignorant optimist, but it has hardly occurred to me to worry about "readjustment." Of course, it is not directly my problem, but because it concerns you, it's important to me. You just come home, darling, and I'll have enough confidence for both of us.

I agree that what Edwards says about marrying the first girl who looks as if she understands him will probably happen often. In fact, it has already. I don't believe I told you that when I was in Racine, I learned some things about Margie's brother which seemed rather pathetic to me. Rudy is unusually sentimental for a fellow. He had spent about two years in Puerto Rico and Panama when he came home in the summer of '43. He had said in one of his rare letters to me that it seemed as if all the kids were getting married, and he felt as if he were sort of missing out on life. So I wasn't particularly surprised when, about three months after he came home, he married a girl in Kansas whom he'd known only a few weeks. The pathetic thing was that, as Margie told me this last time

I saw her, he asked three girls in Racine to marry him during his brief furlough at home. It was really fortunate for him that they said no. Whether the Kansas girl will be a good wife for him I don't know. Margie likes her very much. Rudy is supposed to be home from India soon & I'm hoping to see him & his wife then. Surely hope they will be happy.

I'm certainly in a writing mood tonight. If I don't quit soon, it will take you all of your

1/2 day off to read this. Better save a little for tomorrow. Until then, sweetheart —

All my love, Marian

⚘

Sunday, May 20, 1945

Hello, darling,

I really sympathize with you — having only 1/2 day off each week. I don't see how you can manage all that educating you have to do. I always plan to do so many things over the weekend & it's gone before I ever get started.

Have been sewing most of today. Almost finished one of my projects, too. If Gale will measure the hem for me tomorrow night, I can finish it. It's a dress I made over from one I had in high school. First time I ever attempted such a job, and I'm quite pleased with the outcome.

They reenacted the raising of the flag on Mt. Suribachi down at State & Madison today. I didn't know about it until it was over, or I'd like to have gone. As you know, they're using that picture in the 7th War Loan drive & it's rather nice to see it everywhere because it always reminds me of you — not that I need to be reminded.

I'm glad to hear that your dad is out of the service. Wouldn't blame him, either, for not drinking water.

These two editorials of Grafton's worry me. Hell of a possibility, isn't it? Quite a long time ago, I had the idea that it might be a good thing if Churchill were out of the picture when it was time to work on the peace, and, darn it, we had to lose Roosevelt instead.

That Trieste deal[41] is a mess. It seems to me that the Yugoslavs have every right to the city. "Guide to the Peace" says that the city itself is populated by Italians but the surrounding territory is Slavic. Probably the best thing would be to make it a free city, but, in any event, I can't see any justice in giving it to Italy.

I also think a Balkan federation such as Tito sponsors would be a fine thing. If Russia dominates it, so what? We dominate the whole Western hemisphere & are no saints, either.

In my long story about Betty Beeker's brother yesterday, I left out one lurid detail. He felt sorry for the Germans. Couldn't stand the sight of those "poor" dead Germans lying beside the road with their eyes open. "Betty, I wouldn't tell this to anyone," he said, "but I used to get off my motorcycle and close all their eyes!" Gruesome, isn't it? Really makes me feel sorry for him. I suppose he is uncommonly sensitive. Being sorry for the Germans, though, is something I can no longer tolerate.

What is Merle's wife's name? I thought it was very nice that he said he wondered what she'd like to hear — That you would like to be with me, darling, is always what I'd like to hear. Do you know that sonnet of Elizabeth Browning's, "Say yet again, I love you, love you . . . Toll the silver iterance, only minding, dear, to love me also in silence, with thy soul." Perfect, isn't it?

Goodnight, dearest,
Marian

⚜

xxx
21 May 1945
[Guam]

Dearest Marian,

Last night I called on Merle and we decided to go to the club and see the preview of that 3rd Div movie on Iwo I told you about. You will be seeing it back in the states in conjunction with some shots of the 4th & 5th division also taken up there. There was no sound but I guess that they will add that later before it's released. There were some extremely good shots but for some reason we were a little disappointed with it. Sorta think lack of sound had something to do with it. It is in technicolor and is excellent filming. There is another Navy film out called "To the Shores of Iwo Jima" which I haven't seen yet. The latter is 20 minute length and our 3rd Div film lasts 45 minutes.

After that we decided to see the picture at Hdqs Bn area called I think "And now tomorrow." Story of a Nazi youth brought to this country and the attempt to indoctrinate him with American ? ideals. We only saw the last 25 minutes of it but therein lies the basis for a long discussion between Merle and I which lasted until 10:30 last night. It is supposed to be quite controversial I guess. To make a long story short — As I said we got there late and decided to sit in the rear with the enlisted men rather than barge through all the men to the officers' section. This is usually a poor idea because the fellows are talking continually and, not being bashful, usually say out loud and to their neighbors mostly what they're thinking. In the course of the movie it is shown of course that this Nazi youth has been well trained by Hitler and has the general (?) superman theories.

He succeeds in making himself very unpopular through a series of petty acts and finally almost kills the girl in the house even tho she has been very kind to him. The interesting part of the whole thing but extremely disgusting at the same time was the current that ran through the audience such as "Kill the bastard," and, "The only thing to do is to kill all the Germans—they deserve that." When, in the picture, an attempt is made and apparantly succeeds (after the uncle almost strangles the kid) to substitute an understanding and desire to teach or mold the lad to the democratic (?) ideals instead of killing him, nobody seemed satisfied (To put it mildly).

Well that is the background and the discussion arose mainly because I became extremely bitter because I believe that that is the general solution that these men have for the problem of dealing with Germany. Merle says it is only the apparent reaction and actually they would not carry it out. But apparent or actual the part that disgusted me was the realization that these stupid people have still not learned to think and see that mass murder of a nation is not the solution for dealing with Germany. They still are not using their brains to realize that the problem goes much deeper and cannot be solved simply, as they desired in the picture, by killing the boy. If people don't have faith in the ability of this nation to re-teach the German people than there is no reason to suppose that we have gained anything in this war outside of putting down the ideals of a nation by brute force. The penalties on Germany must be hard I admit, but gradually the tendancy should be one of understanding and faith in the principle that they are after all human beings and can be taught. The problem is a big one concerning how & how much they should pay—but the reluctance of the people to realize that it is a problem makes me bitter. Probably I have been carried away with the whole thing but unless I find something that restores my faith in the ability of the people to face problems in a sensible manner—I will feel that peace and cooperation between men is impossible. N'est pas? or too confused an explanation?

Time to get back to my lectures on interior guard duty for tomorrow darling. Till later then

Much Love, Gene
P.S. If you can offer a solution for folding this letter—

24 May 1945

Darling,
Tonight I am C.W.O. and to make matters worse I am Hdq. Bn. O.D. so I spend my time running between the duty tent and msg center. It is right next door so it's not too bad.

The last few days I have been highly irritable and out of patience with almost everyone. Sorta think that it is because I have had so many duties thrust upon me in quick succession. Then I am very moody and don't talk to anyone. Outside of a few hours with Merle last night it has been that way. Have decided it can all go to hell as far as I am concerned and it really is surprising how nice that works. I feel better already. Your last 2 letters of the 13 & 14 helped matters considerably —

I have thought often of not going to the movies so much which would give me some time at night to get this work done but convinced myself that it is my only recreation and certainly offers a chance to relax. Then again Merle is usually over there at my tent at 6:45 and that helps matters. We saw "Thunderbirds" last night at Hdqs Bn. and I thought it was one of the less likely to win the academy award. Outside the fact that there were airplanes and stuff to remind me of you I might say I thought it was pretty poor. One scene was good — she, complaining of his flighty nature, said — "Remember, I came off the line as a woman and not a P-38!"

Now if I didn't like airplanes, and if I didn't like you, I might say, "Darling remember I came off the line a Marine and not a P-38!" But — I like you both quote and that isn't all unquote. I am glad you said that you don't want anything to stop our correspondence because I feel that way too.

Among other things Merle and I have been talking about is the baby. Craftily, I brought up the "twin angle" again and he finally admitted that his wife said once "darling I am awfully large" This may have been the factor that made him believe that there would be two of them. The baby weighed 9 lbs and that is a lot, isn't it? However all is well and the name chosen is Steven -I agree with you about twins (alike.) I definitely would like at least one girl. (not regard to the twins)

Last night Merle and I had a discussion about the Mormon church mainly because I kept asking him questions about their organization. Merle is probably the most tolerant person I've met and certainly would not bring up the subject on his own accord. I got interested because the news said the 8th President had just been chosen and during the course of the talk I learned much about them. It's just one of those many things Merle knows well. Of all the fellows I met in the service I think I'd like you to meet him most of all. He's so quiet and unassuming but does have a lot on the ball.

So much for post things except maybe I could mention I saw one of the best Marine pictures in a long while (propaganda?) But it was good "Hail the Conquering Hero" I thought it was best to separate "Thunderbirds" and "Hail the —" by a paragraph at least lest you would think I was predujiced. Did you see any of them?

The Spanish which appears to me to be a very good idea — if you are really going to start, I will too. Thought of it before because Merle has the course already. It will be fun. History is coming along O.K. but still haven't helped the kids much. Time lacking again. If you start Spanish I'll promise to keep up with that tho.

—Time out while I inspect the guard—

Back again to finish this up. The movie is about over with and Merle will be in soon. Steve was down the other night but I missed him. He lost the court Martial case I had told you about some time back.

Received several Milw. Sentinels from my cousin Charlotte tonight. Guess I'll read them for awhile.

Glad to hear you are doing well at work. I hope you do have success at it but so long as you enjoy it that's what counts. Will close now darling for awhile. I would like to dream about you tonight. How do you go about getting to dream of somebody? Wish I had the solution but I can do that in the daytime—and I do—

All my Love, Gene

❖

26 May 1945
Central Pacific,

Hi darling

Saturday again and the same routine as always. Steve and Edwards are coming over tonight however to go to the movie with Merle and myself. They have "Music for Millions" I think, and from what we hear, it is very much worthwhile. Last night we decided to viset Eddy and so ended up at the movie in the 21st Marines area. It was "Kitty Foyle" and very good. I always had been under the impression that I had seen it but evidently not because it seemed strange or I should say unfamilar. When I see a picture like that tho I get sort of disgusted with people again because in it she (Ginger Rogers) falls for some character whose type I don't like. Suppose that that is because we generally approve of the actions of people who are most like ourselves.

Incidently Denis Morgan or Stanley Morner is from Waukesha and I have seen him back there several times before he went to Hollywood. That is one of those things that may or may not be important.

Received your last 2 letters yesterday from the 16 and 17 May. I know that there are some questions to answer but they are back in the tent and I am here at msg cent so that will have to wait. I agree with you about those newspaper articles making Roosevelt's death very evident and consequently very unfortunate. I still am nervously optimistic concerning the conference and future policies because I believe that is the way to approach the thing but still feel down deep in my heart that it will take something just short of a miracle to set the groundwork and hold peoples interest, stupid as they are. The Tito affair in northern Italy is rather sad but there is no time like the present to stamp down on those who have strange (or are they strange?) ideas about grabbing somebody's land for no other reason than because they are the victors. Can't imagine that Italy will have much faith in the united conference if that does happen and I believe that even tho they are defeated we should attempt to play fair. That seems to be a very dangerous philosophy to hold right now but we will have to decide whether we are going to hold the former Axis people in a cage or whether we are going to set an example for them in our actions and dealings. Maybe this is all idealistic thinking but I believe that the ultimate goal in universal relations will have to be more along those lines while I think, like the Russians, the immediate problems can and should be handled in the most realistic manner. The guilty should pay for their crimes and the German people will have to work for the suffering they have wrought.

I hope you will see the fellow from Yalta and learn some more of his interesting travels. It really is amazing when you think of all the traveling some servicemen have done that they otherwise would not have had the chance to do. Also profound to contemplate whether it will have any effect on them or whether they will go back to Cupcake Gulch, Texas and carry on exactly where they left off. That seems to be the desire of most of the men whose letters I censor. "Dear Ma—if I only could be back on the farm with you and Pa again I'd never complain again. I never want to leave the farm again—only stay with you and Mary Jane and take care of all the cows."* I wonder—*Letter dated 23 May 1945. Volume 999 No. 999 of <u>Letters I have Read</u> by Lt. Censor.

This morning I had to stand inspection as plat leader of msg cent—something I haven't done for quite awhile but everything went off all right. They all needed haircuts but outside of that the C.O. (Maj. Sullivan) seemed very well pleased. He is a swell fellow.

Haven't had much time (which should be a familar line to you now) to check on that Spanish course but I will today or tomorrow as soon as I see Lt. Jenkins. Guess I told you about him—a Ph.D. from Columbia. Edwards' wire chief, a corporal, is a Ph.D. in Math. Remarkable, isn't it. The right man in the right job. That reminds me of a incident that I don't think I ever will forget. Coming fresh from Quantico, I arrived in San Diego and Camp Elliot and decided that I would get my trunk which I had sent ahead. At the railway express office I looked around for somebody to help me carry it over to the barracks. Spotted a fellow walking by and asked I asked him to give me a hand. This he did very willingly for which I thanked him. About to leave, he paused at the door and said, "Sir, I am in a rather strange position. I have applied for O.C.S. and was told that my application had been accepted but I haven't got any word from Wash. and my outfit is leaving for overseas in 2 days." He then asked me if I could do something to hurry the acceptance papers.

I told him that I would try and then asked him why he thought he should become an officer and what his qualifications were. He reached in his pocket and pulled out some papers and handed them to me. As I read them I became more and more amazed because I found that he was 1. a grad of M.I.T. 2. an outstanding electrical engineer and 3. had been in charge of a large section of the T.V.A.—and making $10,000 per year before he enlisted in the Marine Corps. I tried to help him and even got a telegram sent to Wash. concering his case but so far as I know it did not come through in time. He was a P.F.C.

I intended to write you a short and sweet letter today and find now that it is neither short nor sweet. If I tell you that I think you are swell and I do really like you very much and send all my love will that be all right for this time?

Gene

✤

27 May 1945

Darling,

Two letters from you this noon which put me in a very pleasant mood. They were very interesting and, as always, very sweet. You are a darling—

Decided that I'd start a letter this afternoon here at work if there aren't too many immediate interruptions—2 hours later—Meantime I have taken a shower and got some envelopes from the post office. Wrote you a letter yesterday and I didn't put a stamp on it so I left it on my bed—so if you receive a "free" one sometime in the future don't be alarmed because it is now gone. Think perhaps Capt. Styke picked it up. He always is doing unusual things. A couple of days ago he brought home a parachute which we used to cover the ceiling of the tent. It makes it a lot cooler and besides looks real nice. All silk & white—to go with our furniture which is also white. Reminds me—I have your picture in a leather frame now because you were starting to look rather rough. The folder had at least 10 different holes in it because of the frequent moving I had put it up—only to take it down a few days later and move it.

I have got the Spanish course now and spent a pleasant day studying the first chapter and filling out the first assignment. There are 35 assignments for the first course which is equal to 1 year of high school Spanish. Don't know how fast I'll be able to go but so far it is very interesting. I am going to concentrate on the reading angle more so than the talking. I think that is the best idea because I may need some reading knowledge of it whereas the speech part is not too important now. Merle is starting also and I hope you do too.

The movie a couple of nights ago was "Music for Millions." In my estimation a <u>very</u> good picture. Perfect music and a better than usual plot. I do like M.

O'Brien and think that Jimmy Durante's comeback is nothing less than sensational. June Allyson's portrayal of a serviceman's wife impressed me too. Have you seen it?

As I said before—yesterday proved to be very nice. I had a couple short off. mess. runs and the rest of the day just relaxed on my bed reading Spanish and listening to the Radio. It was Sunday and the first one I didn't have a full day's work in a long time. It really surprised me of the good programs they have from the states via the island radio. That of course makes it just as clear as W.G.N. I always did like Sammy Kaye and yesterday particularly I was in a very romantic mood during his program. In a sense I am glad I haven't too much time to sit and brood because I know that makes everything more intolerable. Agree? I do think about you enough anyway for my own good.

I think the Univ. of Chicago could be worked in with my desire to stay at home. Marquette would be a very simple solution—for a year anyway—but only if all these other prospects (schools) can't be worked out. Most of my plans will have to wait until the end of the war but I probably will have to make some quick decisions.

The letter from the office that you sent in your last letter reminded me of some of those in the "New Yorker" under the heading "Most fascinating Story of the week" with a caption under it of "Is that so?" I'm glad you sent it—What's a BD 97?—switchboard?—Almost time for chow again. Just returned from the club where I had a beer and talked to O'Leary. We usually get together once in awhile to talk over "old times" Mostly about the liberties we spent in L.A. on weekends when we were still P.F.C.'s. Those were wonderful days when I think back. Our favorite bar was "The Melody Lane" on Wilshire & Western.—ever been there? I think I know every inch of the ways from Western to Vermonth on Wilshire blvd. Where did you live in L.A.? Maybe our paths did cross at one time or another.

Darling I must close or I may not get anything to eat. Would hate to choose tho between eating and thinking of you because I probably would starve. That would be a pleasant way to die however—

All my Love, Gene

✤

29 May 1945
Central Pacific

Dearest,

That letter heading of "Central Pacific" sounds like I might be swimming around somewhere in the wide open ocean—It always makes me smile a little when I write it. Finished my first worksheet in Spanish now and I think that I will alternate writing to you and starting on lesson two. It says here that the stories are interesting, well chosen. and humorous. In a sense they are—at least I like to finish them so I am able to tell what the joke is supposed to be about. The text used is <u>Primer Curso De Espanol</u> by Pittaro and Green. The worksheets generally take about 45 minutes to fill out and are rather complete. I hope that you are still interested in taking it the same time I am. If you back out now, I am going to write all my letters in Spanish just to get even with you. So—Yo gusto usted muy muchas—

Back again after awhile. One of the officers was just in to tell me I had a letter back in the tent which he had meant to bring down on his way to the movies. As he forgot I went down to get it and got caught in a blinding rain the last 100 yards. It was worth it because it was yours of the 22nd. I am getting disgusted with the mail clerk because I think he is slipping on the job. They just made him a P.F.C. and now he thinks he is really on the top. We are going to tangle one of these days and would have before except for the fact that I think the major is looking for a mail officer and a good excuse to get one. We have got in some new replacements who are pretty low because they haven't received any mail for about 3 weeks.

One fellow said that what this company needed was a "Moral officer" meaning morale of course—at least I hope. They are pretty salty men because most of them are on their second trip across and still live and breathe Guadal and Tarawa from the 1st and 2d Divs. I have met three men who were with me at Camp Elliott in Jan '43 just before I transferred to stand by for OCS. I later found out that the company I was with went to Samoa for 12 mo and then came back to the states. It sounded like a good deal but now they are out again and that's what would have happened to me too. I want to stay in the states whenever I do get back and sorta think that the war will be in its final stages by the time that my tour of duty is over with out here. None of us are looking forward to the next operation like we did on the other one. We have decided we have all the "glory" that is necessary in one lifetime. I have never heard from Britt in Pearl Harbor so I don't know what the setup is at that place. Undoubtedly he is enjoying himself from what we hear of duty there but I still am not sorry that I did not go.

That poem of Brown's was good, and as you say improves with reading. Never have heard any more about [Leon] P but I don't think that he is here in the Division any more. He was in the 21st Marines and would have gone back there if they decided to keep him over here. He was writing poetry much of the time too and usually had a glassy wild look in his eye. Certainly a strange character if I ever saw one—

It is getting late so I think that I had better finish this letter tomorrow when I have company duty. That means I will have to stay in the company area and miss the movie again. I will have a chance to get caught up on my work tho so it's all right. We fire the range the day after tommorow. I will let you know how that comes out. I doubt I could hit the target let alone the bull's eye. Good night again darling. It is 7:00 AM back there now so I should say good morning—

On second thought I will send this and start anew tomorrow

All my Love, Gene

❀

29 May 1945 [2]

Dearest Marian,

Had to laugh a little at the story of Don & the MP's which may indicate we are getting cynical over here. In my mind there is no doubt of it. As far as the story being true or not—nobody can say for sure. There have been cases undoubtedly where MP's have handled the men a little "rough" particularly if the man is drunk and has a chip on his shoulder. They do not have absolute powers of course so the police can't be compared with the Gestapo. For obvious reasons (I think) there can be no democracy in the service but unfortunately the civilians for the most part can't understand that. They ask "Why do officers get liquor overseas and the men don't? Why do officers have screens on their tents [and] others don't? Why do officers have their own heads?" You know what a "head" is of course! These things are hard to explain and if you don't approach the question with an open mind, no arguments in the world are going to convince you. If you are in doubt, Marian, maybe I can convince you so don't hesitate to ask me.

Reminds me of a party I was to the last time I was home. My mother and a cousin were there too. Suddenly my cousin made the statement that "You know of course, that there are literally hundreds of basket cases since the war—whole hospitals are filled with them!" When I asked her where she had heard all that she vaguely said all her girl friends were talking about it and some of them had even <u>seen</u> the men. It got me so damn mad because the government's chief doctor had just made the statement that there were no basket cases on record. My mother undoubtedly believed my cousin and therefore took some civilian's view to that of the government. Why do people do such stupid things? It is disgusting—I can well sympathize with the Army and Navy having to deal with the people and congressional leaders. People expect generals to win battles but they are totally ignorant of service system.

1330—Back again after lunch. I am C.W.O. again today so will spend the night here at the msg center. I never did tell you much of what I have been doing. Mainly it consists of routing msgs. out and into the division. They come to us via radio, teletype, guard mail and Off. Mess. It is a full time job for 6 officers and about 80 men (working in shifts) All the officers take turns doing all the jobs. As there has to be an officer on duty here all the time, we usually catch the night watch the day we are chief Watch Off. Thus once every six days we have a 24 hour job. All in all it isn't bad but I feel sometimes that I'd rather be either a bat. com. off as Edwards or in Jasco like Merle. If it wasn't for handling highly classified material, any P.F.C. probably could do just as well. We are in hdqrs bn. which has advantages both in combat and here.

I liked your long letter of the 19th and of course I don't mind hearing your troubles. You sure hear enough of mine. I think that the only way to carry on a successful correspondence is to write about everything that happens. If I waited for something important or unusual to occur I'd probably write every 6 mo. I am glad that we have written so much because like you, I like to tell somebody my troubles. Capt. Styke got a cablegram that he is a father so last night we celebrated with a small party. Both of the Majors (C.O. & Ex) were there for awhile. I drank 6 whiskey & cokes and then stepped lightly over to see Merle. The evening ended up at the Jasco club, name ("passion point") and Merle and myself playing records. However the 2 letters from you, the 6 drinks and "Tales from the Vienna Woods" made me exceptionally lonesome—it is an awful feeling, isn't it? I confided to Merle that I'd rather be in Chicago right then than anywhere else. Strangely (?) enough I feel the same today after no letters, no music and a coke.

Much love, Darling,
Gene

14 June—
Embarrassing moments—forgot to mail this my love—which seems to be a man's right—
One reason for the anxious days of the first week in June. Forgiven?

31 May 1945

Dearest Marian,
Just three years ago today I graduated from M. U. Seems quite a bit longer than that at present. Another unimportant fact that on July 23 I celebrate 3 years in the Marine Corps. It is also your birthday so we can do our celebrating together even tho we are a half the earth apart. This is going to be a very short letter as I only have one half an hour to write it. That seems like a long time but I usually sit here and think too much and the time passes quickly. Wish there

were ways to record thought sometimes so that you didn't have to put them in words. Usually the same thing doesn't come out that you are thinking about.

Today we were down at the range most of the morning firing our carbines. Had to get up at 0430 in the pouring rain but we were lucky to have transportation. The whole thing was rather disappointing because the weather was terrific while we were on the firing line and just plain bad the rest of the time. I stood up on the final 5 rounds and attempted to shoot offhand (which is just standing with no support for the weapon) and had a hard time keeping it on the target let alone the bull's eye. The other positions were a little better—prone, kneeling, and sitting but all in all most the fellows made a poor showing. After we finished, Demmy and I hitch-hiked back to the area. He is a fellow that works here in msg. center too.

Have been busy the last few days putting a box together which Capt. Styke gave to me. I think that it is going to be large enough so that we all will be able to put our field equipment in it. I am finding it very profitable to know the quartermaster and to have him in the same tent is wonderful. Incidently his baby is named Steven. I asked him how he happened to arrive at that name and he said his wife submitted a name in almost every letter and he vetoed all of them up to Steven and was just thinking about that name when the event occurred. I haven't seen much of Borrowman in the last few days because of having CWO and CO. duty last night.

Been reading some of the articles in the Atlantic—there is a good one on Tarawa in the April issue. One of those really true stories about life there, in contrast to Life's pictures on the island of several months back. I had to laugh because I saw the pictures in that edition and they all were apparently taken in or near the high ranking officers' quarters. The Atlantic author comments on this and tells of some of the letters the fellows stationed there received from their loved ones who accused them of having a soft life on an island paradise, according to Life. I can well imagine that it is nothing like that on Tarawa.

I think that I told you that Edwards and Steve were over to see us a few nights ago. Edwards is getting increasingly impatient with overseas duty which I think is due in part to his luckless love affairs. He says that is glad that he doesn't have anyone to worry about and seems really disillusioned with most everything. We kid him along but I think that he has changed since the 28th draft days. He was going with a Wave from Wash. while at Quantico and came very close to marrying her. She was 5 years older than he which I guess caused the breakup, and after he got home to the girl back there, figured he had done the right thing. So 3 weeks before he got the news of the Colorado gal's impending marriage, he had told the Wave they had better stop writing. Consequently he is out in the cold all the way around now. My time is just about up now so I will finish this afternoon.

Back again—I have finished assignment sheet #2 in my Spanish course and I am finding it taking much more time than I had bargained for. It doesn't make much difference because we are only required to hand in one assignment per month which will be no undue strain. The news from here sounds encouraging—doesn't it. The B-29's are raising hell with Japan. Wonder how much they are willing to take. Remember—people used to say—just send a few hundred bombers over Tokyo and the war will be over. Thanks for the clippings in your last letter. Grafton and Mower say what I have sensed the last few weeks. That is the conference is setting up territorials of influence of the various nations. Nothing could be more opposite to what they should be striving for. I liked Edgar Mower's 4 principles concerning the course of Truman's action. It is consoling to know that some of the people are willing to cooperate with Russia and to include her when the talk is of nations of peaceful intent. Seems to me at times that our real sympathies should tend toward Russia instead of the traditional British policies. I was happy to see that the Republicans will be well represented in San Fran. but I wonder if their ideals are in harmony with those of Roosevelt (and mine.) It appears that Roosevelt is dead.

Aside from the disillusioning clippings (even <u>Time</u>!) I liked your letter. It was from the 22nd. I have seen a little of <u>Barnaby</u> from time to time. Just noticed that his statements are rather profound but at the same time should interest the kids. In one way I don't like supposedly harmless cartoons that pack a big wallop. Thus I don't like <u>Orphan Annie</u> which has become a tool sometimes for that rat Repbulican [sic] Herald Gray. <u>Terry</u> still appeals to me—the humor I guess is responsible for the most part.

Hope that you aren't too serious about studying Russian. Are you? The thought of it scares me but if anyone could talk me into it, it would be you.

People are sitting here staring at me because I am obviously typing a letter so I think that it is time to stop for today. I miss you very much dear and I am glad that it is mutual. The time is passing—altho when I think of all the things I want to talk to you about and how much I want to carry on where we left off— it seems a little hopeless. The day will come however.

Much love, Gene

Do you like gum? Can you get it? If "yes and no" respectfully I will send—1 stick per letter—

❧

May 21, 1945
[Chicago]

Gene, darling,

I like you better every day, truly. On Sunday, I think I couldn't possibly like you more—on Monday, there is a letter from you, and I do. I suppose it's some sort of optical illusion—well, illusion anyway—but it's certainly a pleasant one. As a "tactical situation," I agree, it is rather ironic. That is my fault. I should have gone to New York.

I always have to laugh at you for trying to convince me of your sincerity. Your reticence makes it so obvious that what you do say you really mean. Of course, I want to believe you, and I suppose that helps, too. I only hope my letters seem equally sincere to you. They are, dear.

Merle has been reading "Forever Under" for an awfully long time, hasn't he? What's he doing? Reading the history between the lines?

Your idea of a need for sex in schools is very amusing. Seriously, though, it seems to me too personal a subject to be taught in school. I think they might make more easily available good literature on the subj., but parents ought to assume the real responsibility.

Incidentally, I can picture you telling your children they owe their existence to the Marine Corps!

They were just playing Tchaikovsky's "Concerto in B Flat Minor" on the radio, so I had to take time out to listen. That's absolutely my favorite piece of music.

Gene, will you tell me the things you remember about that night we went to the Schroeder? It seems strange that I should have forgotten much of what you remember most clearly, and vice versa.

Coming down to earth, my friend Ripley came over to my desk this noon to "explain" that little deal about the bonus which made us all so angry Saturday. As I had expected, he gave me what you'd probably call a snow job. A lot of talk which amounted to, "It's too bad, but there's nothing we can do about it." He invariably agrees with whomever he happens to be talking with and never does anything about anything. I told him, (as if he didn't know) that it is just such stuff that makes people go around saying, "What we need is a union." As a matter of fact, I feel a bit like a union organizer today myself. We decided that hereafter the thing for us to do is to get together when any one of us has a complaint to make and send a committee of two or three, well fortified with facts, to see John Brown Cook. I think it might give him a shock which would do him no harm. As it is, I don't believe he gives more than a fleeting thought to his employee relations, and the result is somewhat chaotic.

It must be late. Murph just came in. See you tomorrow, darling.

All my love, Marian

❖

May 22 '45

Dear Lt. Sweetheart,

Thought you might enjoy Gracie Allen's[42] bit of humor at the expense of the Japs. I like the part about the tanks harvesting their crops.

On the subject of humor, have you ever read "Barnaby"[43] ? It's in the Chicago Sun. You can have "Terry & the "Pirates" any day. Barnaby & his fairy godfather, Mr. O'Malley, are unexcelled.

Another of life's little pleasures I've been meaning to tell you about is a commentator for WIND named Herb Graffis. I think he has been a foreign corres. for the Chicago Times, but I had never heard or read anything of him until recently. He sounds on the radio as if he were carrying on an informal conversation. Not very smooth, but unusually sincere. Gale likes him, too, and I think you would. He reminds me of a fellow I worked with in L.A. named Bill Kennedy. Bill always said everything backwards (For example, "In Bed we Cry" was "We Cry in our Sleep") but there was never any doubt about how he felt, and he's just a swell guy. He & his wife were always befriending service men, etc.

Just read a review of the autobiography of Geo. W. Norris,[44] "Fighting Liberal." It sounds like a book we ought to read. There are so many interesting & exciting things going on — I wish I could read six times as much as I do.

Didn't even get started on this week's Time until yesterday. I'll send you a piece of it tonight.

Grafton today almost makes me wish I were Russian. Let's learn Russian instead of Spanish. Shall we? — That was meant to be more or less a joke, but the more I think of it, the better it sounds. What do you think?

Darling, I've been trying to think of a good way to say it, but all I can do is dream — I miss you very much, dear.

All my love, Marian

❖

May 24, 1945

Gene, darling,

I meant to write to you last night & certainly should have as I had three letters from you. However, I had been promising to write to Peg every day since Sunday so decided I'd better get it done. Just figured out that I must have written about 20 letters to you since the last time I wrote to Peg; so you probably will not mind. Just in case you are still wondering, it does have something to do with how much I like you, dear.

This will have to be brief as I am writing at the switchboard. Wanted to send you those pages from Time today, tho. What do you think of Hutchins'[45] remarks on the peace? That part about vengeance being the Lord's really made me stop & think. I forget about it at times—perhaps too often. The question is—is it possible without being vengeful to make it impossible for the aggressor nations to wage war?

The article on Japan & Hirohito is enlightening, isn't it? More tonight, sweetheart.

Much love, Marian

�֍

May 24, 1945 [2]

Hello, again, darling,

I ought to spend a couple of hours reading tonight so that I could find out what's going on & have something intelligent to talk to you about. However, I don't feel much like being intelligent tonight, besides which Murph & I have already spent most of the evening in a long discussion of life & stuff. The rest of the time I'd like to just sit & look at your picture and dream. Wish I could make a good letter of that, darling.

Our long talk tonight started with a letter I had from Margie. She no longer feels at home in her own home, due to a complicated series of family troubles, and was feeling very blue about it. (Incidentally, she thinks her brother, Rudy, about whom I was telling you a few days ago, is in the Marianas now.) It's too long a story to tell, but I wish I could do something for her.

Gale has had a lot of trouble with her family, also, as I may have told you. Her mother & dad were divorced, and her mother lost a fortune & had to depend on Gale for her support until recently. All this, tonight, led to a discussion of the desire for security which is so important a factor in the major decisions of one's life. We agreed that neither of us has any desire for wealth and that money is not an end in itself. "Work for the work's sake" is an ideal we would follow in preference to the acquisition of material gain.

It seems I've made this a long story & failed to give it much of a point. Perhaps you will be able to read between the lines & understand. I think you will. We say the same things to each other so often, dear, I'm beginning to believe we could mention a subject, say "I know just how you feel," and that would cover it completely. Wouldn't be nearly so much fun, though, would it?

I didn't pay much attention to the Hollywood-Harvard affair. When I saw "Winged Victory" on the list, I decided the Harvard kids were a bunch of brats trying to be sophisticated, and forgot about it. A snap judgment, of course, which is never wise, whether is [*sic*] happens to be right or wrong. I don't like to be critical of movies, though, unless they're really awful, like cowboy shows or something. I'd rather enjoy them & not bother to analyze too much.

Quite a coincidence that we should have seen both "Fighting Lady" & "Three Caballeros" at so nearly the same time, isn't it? Also that we're both living with Murphys. You go from one extreme to another in living quarters, don't you? This one sounds ok, darling, & I'm glad you are more comfortable. I refuse to be satisfied, though, and wish you were here instead—it's all right to wish, isn't it?

Goodnight, dearest.
Marian

⚜

May 25, 1945

My darling Gene:
Rec'd your letter of May 19 today and I think that cartoon is a prize. Good thing you mentioned the hat would have to be changed, or I'd think you were kidding when you said you liked mine.

I thought I could rouse a little "righteous indignation" by underlining von Rundstedt's[46] admission of the effect of Allied air power. Note the quotation marks above. I like you anyway, dear. Seriously, I do agree with you that air power alone can't win a war. It can only contribute to making the job a little easier on the ground. And if anything that does that, I know we're both in favor of it.

Of course that other clipping you returned which seemed contradictory concerned strategic bombing only, which is only one phase of air power. Tactical missions the Russians apparently consider highly effective. I should hate to have to agree with them that strategic bombing is useless, however, particularly as the bombing of Ploesti could hardly be considered tactical. How difficult it is to keep your viewpoint objective when a subject has been of such personal importance. I think, too, that some enthusiasts over-rate the effectiveness of bombing, but I'm glad we agree it is of some value.

Was pleased to hear that Merle's son has arrived safely. It must be awfully hard to be a father at such a long distance. I should think it would take a lot of self-discipline to resign yourself to not being able to see your son until he was a year or two old.

Did I tell you the rest of the story about the twins this girl I know had? They were about 6 wks. premature. She has gone home now, but the babies have to stay at the hospital for another 5 weeks—at $20 per <u>day</u>. That's certainly a blow to a budget, isn't it?

It may sound rather disloyal, but this news article from today's paper pleases me no end. It's time a few "I am an American's" discover they're going to have to catch up with the world. Right?

Would like to see that film re. the 3rd Div. on Iwo. They had a premier at the Chicago Theater last night, (I found out today) of a picture called, "To the Shores of Iwo Jima." Sorry I missed it.

I did think of Vandegrift[47] as possibly the man who lost the razor, but it didn't seem logical that the commander of the Corps would be a "guest." He was in Chicago the other day & I was wishing I could ask him if he'd lost a razor recently. Silly, isn't it —

I believe an "ocharina" is the correct term for Capt. Styke's "sweet potato." That doesn't look quite right to me, but it sounds right. The Volga Boatman is quite an effective tune on that instrument. (Maybe it's "ocarina.")

I am continually amazed at all the things there are to write about, for which I never seem to have enough time. Will try again tomorrow.

There are also many things, darling, for which I don't seem to have the words. Perhaps they're not necessary.

All my love, Marian

❧

May 26, 1945

Hello, Lt. Sweetheart,

I've been thinking—again—about those two days on the train & about the women across the aisle who were so curious about us. Have come to the conclusion that you really can't blame them because, looking at it from "across the aisle," our conduct must have seemed almost shocking. To me it has been surprising—amazing, even—but much too pleasant to criticize.

Do you remember the time you couldn't open the door between the cars? Wasn't it some Army man who came along & opened it for us? Or have you been trying to forget?—Darling! I like you so much.

Murph & I decided tonight that we both enjoy eating someone else's cooking (each other's, for instance) better than our own. So I'm glad you have a talent for can opening. I'll let you cook for me sometimes.

Food around here has not been very good lately & I was glad to hear you're not having the same difficulty. We haven't had fresh meat for two weeks. It's partly our own fault for not being aggressive enough to pester the butcher for it, but neither of us likes to do that. I had to laugh at Murph last night. I had pike, for the 2nd time this week, and she said, "I'm really not complaining now—but do you actually think this fish is good?" The answer was, "Well—".

I've been sewing again tonight. Wish I hadn't taken home all the scraps of material so I could send you a sample. It's the prettiest stuff. Yellow & green.

I particularly enjoyed your comments on world organization in your letter of May 16. As usual, I agree with you. I'm afraid, too, that we're not going to sacrifice much to help the poorer nations. As Wilson said, according to the encl. clipping, the American people will have to believe in it before it will work & they lack either the intelligence or the spirit to believe in it now. However, as you say, there should be continued attempts to solve these problems & the willingness of the nations to make these attempts is encouraging. You will like this article in Time about Van Kleffens, "Dutchman on the Dike." It's a good lesson on a fine combination of idealism and practical action. "In his country, they build the dikes of dirt, not of dreams."

Incidentally, I disagree with Time's assumption that this statement of Wilson's proves he was not heartbroken about U. S. refusal to join the League. It seems to me there is not much difference between disappointment in an act of the U. S. Senate & disappointment in the ideals of the American people, unless the latter would be more profound.

I think your point about the German & Japanese craving for power being due to a combination of circumstances rather than inherent evil, is easily proved by the fact that descendants of those nationals in the U.S. do not necessarily retain any such traits. The point is an important one in favor of Pres. Hutchins arguments last week. Don't you think so?

That remark in Time about the Argentine delegate reminds me of a letter I had recently from Ruth Senjem, my former roommate, who was Rev. Hjortland's secretary at Ascension. She sent me several clippings from PM & in commenting on them, said she thought their style of interview was sometimes overdone. "For instance, in a report of a Town Meeting of the Air Broadcast, the reporter told which of the speakers dived into the washroom before going on the air. Well, really." I get a kick from that, "Well really." Incidentally, Ruth's husband, who is a Med. Corpsman in England or France now, is also a prospective history teacher.

Miss P-38 says that today's headlines read, "Tokyo in Ruins, Japs say.— The Japanese admitted Sat. that the latest B-29 raid had 'practically laid waste' to Tokyo." If that could mean you'd never have to go into combat again, darling, I'd be one happy little gal.

I do pretty well at writing on Sat. nights, don't you think? For quantity, at least. No curfew, that's why.

Goodnight, dearest.

All my love, Marian

✦

May 27 '45

Hi, darling,

I just read the story called "Hogan's Goat" in one of the copies of Leatherneck you sent. It's the cutest story. I like the part about those 30 mos. overseas shooting by like glue dripping from a tube. Too true.

Marge & Ed Dervishion came up for a few minutes this aft. He's the radio man I told you about sometime ago. Reminds me, you asked where he managed to get the radar equipment. He inspects it for the Navy. Today he told us they are working on a new kind of weapon for counteracting Jap suicide plane attacks. Good, hm?

There is an article in the June Reader's Digest about Lee DeForest's invention of the audion tube. DeForest is a pretty good friend of Ed's. After the war, he's going to work at DeForest's Hollywood plant. They had lunch together one day recently & DeF. asked Ed what he thought of the future of radar. Next day the newspapers published his reply as DeForest's view. Ed is obviously very proud of all this & it's amusing to see the eagerness with which he tells it. Surely can't blame him, tho.

Do you have the May "Atlantic Monthly" yet? There were two things I liked especially well. One was an open letter to 12 college presidents written by a young Captain. It's a very well stated argument.

The other is a poem by an Air Force Sgt. — "Death of a Bomber." Tell me if you like it, too.

Guess I'll send you some more poetry tonight. This "Of Scenery — And, One Acre" is one of the things Ruth sent me from PM. Makes me want to travel. I like the idea of the pattern. Somewhat like Time's article on Van Kleffens.

Paul, the lucky guy, is starting on a trip south tonight. He'll be gone all month. He's been so nice lately I sort of hate to see him go. Saturday morning he told me his daughter, who is about 18 or 19, had won an art scholarship. They were, he said, "the happiest people in Glen Ellyn." Don't blame them. Incidentally, Glen Ellyn is about the 8th suburb west of Chicago. Half an hour's ride on an express.

I liked that dream about Mexico City, darling. The location would be unimportant, though, if we could be together.

All my love, Marian

❀

May 28, 1945

Hello, Sweetheart,

There were 72 hours between letters from you this time, & I watched the clock all day being so anxious to look in the mail box tonight. There were two letters, for which I am grateful, dear. You see how spoiled I am. Have no desire to be disciplined, either.

Incidentally, I don't care <u>how</u> you type those letters as long as I can decipher them. If you can type a 6-page dispatch without an error, you can have my job. It's always easier to make mistakes when you're typing a letter because you're thinking about what comes next, & to type accurately you have to concentrate on the <u>typing</u>. Feel better now?

I've never even seen the sending end of a teletype machine & have been very curious about them. What do they look like?

Hope Merle gives you one of those cards. I'm amazed that you are interested in them. Didn't think confirmed bachelors would be. That's what you told me you were going to be, remember?

I think the show about which you wrote a 6-page letter (I like you, honey.) was "Tomorrow the World" instead of "And Now Tomorrow." The latter I have seen, & it's a nice love story, if a bit too obviously from Hollywood. Was Frederic March in the one you saw?

Merle is probably right that they'd never carry out such wild schemes—at least, I hope he is! However, I agree with you that they obviously lack any deep perception of the complexity of the problem—chiefly, I believe, because they don't want to take the trouble to think it out. It would make life too confusing. But relax, dear. You take it all too seriously. Really, I admire you for it, but there isn't much you can do to change human nature—certainly not overnight—and banging your head against a stone wall accomplishes nothing, except to make <u>you</u> suffer. Not that I think it's a hopeless case. I truly believe cooperation between men is possible, but it's an extremely slow process because there are so many circumstances & emotions in the way. Patience is a virtue, darling, also a necessity. We may as well learn it willingly because it's forced upon us anyway.—In more matters than one. Nov. 1, 1946.

I wish that date were here, too, needless to say. When I used to say things like that at home, mother would say, "You're wishing your life away!" And I would think maybe there were some parts of it I could do without. You never can tell, tho.—That sounds almost disgustingly philosophic, doesn't it?

I'd better quit. See you later, darling.

Much love, Marian

❖

May 30, 1945

My darling Gene:

I miss you so much tonight that those 18 months seem like infinity. Truly, dear.

This Memorial Day business is darn hard on me. We had the day off, which gave me more than enough time to think about it. Was going to go to church tonight, but decided I felt sad enough already, so I went to a show instead. Saw "Under Two Flags" with Ronald Coleman. It turned out to be a story about the French Foreign Legion, & there were soldiers dying all over the place. Oh, hell!

Gen. Mark Clark flew into Chicago today directly from Paris with some 50 of his men. They came in three Army transports and three squadrons of P-40's met them outside the city & escorted them in. I saw them fly over. It was quite a thrill.

Darling, about those P-38's, you know I wouldn't give a darn about airplanes if I weren't so fond of my brother. And I'd rather have a Marine any day (a certain Marine, I should say) than a whole squadron of P-38's.

Had a card from Peg yesterday saying she may be in town for a few hours tomorrow on her way to Washington, D. C. Her kid sister has been there for sometime, & Peg plans to work there for the summer. I wish she were going to be here, instead. She says Ray is now asst. div. interpreter and has gone to all the Russian-American banquets. I hope to hear more about that tomorrow. Sounds good, doesn't it?

I like the name they chose for Merle's baby. Think it's funny that he was expecting twins because his wife said she was awfully large. I should think any girl having her first baby would feel that way. Nine lbs. is a lot, tho. The twins this friend of mine had weighed 3 lbs. 10 oz. apiece, so I guess you can't tell that way.

I'm glad you'd like a girl. I feel as if I'd want a boy, first, so badly that I'd probably not have one. Say, what is this anyway? Maybe we ought to talk about getting married first, hm?

Greta was scolding me the other day for being so anxious to hear from you. "Is _he_ that much in love with _you_?" she asked.

"Well—I hope so."

"Well, you'd better be careful!" Sounds sort of like Merle, doesn't she?

I haven't seen either "Thunderbirds" or "Hail the Conquering Hero." Wasn't Eddie Bracken in the latter picture? I don't like him very well & think that's why I didn't go to see it. Didn't know it was about Marines or I would have. Honestly.

Listen, you doubting Thomas, I am serious about studying Spanish—or Russian. I'd like to start about September. OK? Maybe you wont be so busy then, either, I hope. Also hope I can finish the "Guide to the Peace" by that time. My schedule has been in ruins for sometime, but I'm still trying.

Wish I knew & could tell you a good way to go about dreaming of someone. I tried so hard last night to dream about you that I didn't get much sleep. Thought up some real nice dreams, though, sweetheart.

All my love, Marian

5

*". . . what I think about you now is quite different than
what I thought . . . last summer. . . ."*

OUR HOPE FOR *lasting peace rested with the United Nations, but the organizational meeting of the world body revealed a deepening split between the Soviet Union and her
allies. Marian's mother's complaint about ration points, particularly for meat, also pointed to the split between the international beliefs of her daughter and Midwestern suspicion of
world cooperation. "Just because they have to eat potato soup in Yugoslavia is no reason why
we should have to," Marian's mother said. I was concerned with the discharge point system
as well as potential problems with reconversion to civilian life. But the end of the war still
seemed far off and Marian even considered an overseas job. However, by the end of the month
my world was greatly upset by an unexpected transfer to another division.*

---

5 June 1945
[Guam]

Hello darling,

Seems a while since I have written to you but actually it has only been two
days. We have been continuing the usual work here in the msg center. Mail has
finally arrived for the new replacements and they have snowed the censors
under by answering the letters all at once. Yesterday I had nearly 100 letters to
wade through. That's when it changes from fun to work.

Last night Edwards came over so Merle, he, and I went to the party here at
the club. Some of the fellows had brought nurses and red cross workers who as
usual had a field day as somebody kept cutting in at about 1 minute intervals.
When I looked at some of them I couldn't help feel that they had better "make
hay while the sun shines," because back stateside nobody would give them a second glance. I finally decided after several rum cokes that I would cut in: So I
had my first dance (1- 1/2 minutes) since I left the states. It was an experience
but I still am convinced it is not worth the trouble to get a date (which makes
me wonder if I am normal).

Edwards is still confused concerning his romance affairs. It is rather involved but I understood it last night for the first time. The girl he had been going with (Claire) is probably playing the field and also probably only keeping in contact with Edwards to have as many irons in the fire as possible. He knows this but still loves her. The other girl (Gert) has been telling him some of the actions of Claire and seems to me to be rather sincere. At his tent later on he let us read the last two letters from the girls and we were supposed to advise him. The whole thing is rather stupid and I suppose commonplace but I hate to see a swell fellow like him go to pieces whatever the cause. He is doing a good job as bat. communications officer.

Merle may get sent down to the Pioneers on temporary duty which I would hate to see. It's a good deal however because of the practical experience but I know I'd miss him. Forgot to ask what his wife's name is—but I'll find out.

Will have to close now and go to chow. More this afternoon or evening.

All my love, Gene

Thought you might like this letter from a good friend of mine who was at Monmouth. Spent 27 months over here on Guadal and now in Germany.

The writeup on the 106th is good. Don't you think?

❖

3 June 1945 [2]

My darling Marian,

Today I am CWO again and a rather sad way to spend a Sunday afternoon and evening. Don't you think? I will write a letter to you which will compensate partly for it—at least then I can imagine what I would be saying to you if I were around Chicago.

Your letters of the 25 and 26th came this noon and of course were very much appreciated—or should I put it in a stronger way?

I have just returned from the club wherein I had 2 cans of beer and spent a little thoughtful concentration concerning your discussion on "security." Somewhere once I read that women are much more concerned with the question of security than men (are). I suppose that is right for a lot of involved reasons and some more obvious ones. I don't like to read between the lines generally because I don't want to place the wrong interpretation on the thing the person is talking about. If you were here I would make you squirm until you told me exactly what you meant—then I'd kiss you and for awhile we could forget all about everything that bothers us. Agree and willing? The girl I went with back home while I was going to school was also concerned with the question for a different reason maybe—but she gave me the alternative of marrying her or saying good-bye. It happened to be good-bye and about 2 months later she was married to some other fellow. Rather unusual maybe but it does happen. Darling, I want us to go on just like we have been until I get home at least. I don't want to be vague or have you think on the other hand that I grown to like you so much merely because I am overseas. We have got to know each other very well in most respects and that is probably due to the fact that I did leave the States. As you say—if it has been fate—it was a very nice kind. I hope that you are not too concerned with security and stuff so much at least that it will affect us. You are the only person outside of my grandfather that I care anything about and it does make me feel very good to believe in someone and to know that someone cares about me. You are wonderful—

Censored a letter yesterday which consisted of a page and a half and included 7 "I love you's" 8 "darlings" and 2 "sweethearts" He then concluded by saying that nothing had happened and that censorship rules were so strict that he couldn't write much. Wonder what kind of a girl she is—

It is now about 1730 and I just have finished dinner. We are going to try out a new schedule next week which should give us more time off. I am going to take CWO for the first couple of days which will mean being here almost continually but then I will have a couple of full days off. Sounds OK to me. If you only were here so we could pick out a nice shady grove overlooking the ocean gaze into each other's eyes (for awhile anyway) and at night look at the moon and the stars together. Wish that it could come true but the mere thought of it helps some—don't you think? Reminds me that I liked that poem of E. B. Browning. Can't remember the exact words but it was something about loving her with something inside besides saying the words. Wonder if it was from her "Sonnets from the Portugese"—do you know?

I do like poetry—especially Shakespeare. Last time that I was home I stopped in at the library in downtown Milw. Have you ever been in the literature room? I spent at least two and a half hours a day there all the time I was going to school. Got to know the librarians quite well but still felt a little flattered when they remembered me after over 2 years. It is a thrill to see those old familar places again because they do bring back memories. Nobody could understand why I went to the library tho and it is one of those things I didn't take the trouble to explain. I wonder if I could get back in the swing of things again if I started school after I get home or would I be thinking about what has happened in the last years. Just been thinking that it would be something if it were possible we both could go to school together. Probably a fantastic idea but one of those things that it is nice to think about at times. We would be great in a political science class with our liberal ideas and a "little left of center" philosophy. It is nice to dream darling even about the remote things that can't happen.

Personally I liked Hutchins'(sp) ideas about the peace and how to treat the Germans. About a week ago I told you about the picture which I think is called "The World Tommorrow" so you should have a general idea of what I think should be done about them. As I said — it is a dangerous philosophy to hold at this particular time when so many people are saying that the Germans should be exterminated. I don't doubt that some time in the future we will have the German nation in the council of nations after they earn their way back they should have a place. What do you think is the solution?

2 nights ago we saw "Hotel Berlin" which I liked. It was much different from the usual run of Nazi pictures of the last 5 years and certainly very timely at this time.

Darling, I really had to laugh about your reaction to "Winged Victory" and the fact that it was on the Harvard list. I never told you but Merle and I saw it about a week ago right after I wrote that letter. Never figured that I would be telling you this — I had told Borrowman that you had said you liked it very much and then added Harvard's reaction. Well we approached the movie in a very impartial mood saying that we would judge it solely on its merits and not be influenced by you or Harvard. After it was over with he turned to me and said, "Harvard was right." I agreed — but said that I thought that it was one of those pictures that would go over big in the states but would be a flop out here. I hope that you don't mind — Marian. Still think that "A Guy Named Joe" is tops. And I still like you —

This letter has taken me as long to write as any I have ever written. Not that there have been interruptions but mainly because I have been sitting here thinking after every sentence.

I am glad that the conference passed the "full employment question" over the United States' objections (or is it our Rep. congressmen's objections) Out here everyone seems to think that Russia is fuddling up the conference but that I think is stupid. I have heard so many say that our "next war will be with Russia" gets me so damn mad — one of the officers here in the msg cent pulled a prize tho. Said that we should "go easy on Japan because undoubtedly they would be our allies against Russia." (in the next war) How about that? I almost threw him out of the tent because it made me so angry. It is things like that make a person doubt all people.

I'm afraid that this letter is a little fouled up and as usual I have a hard time saying exactly what I mean. Concerning us — we do have a lot of faith in each other which is something necessary at this time. I don't want anything ever to destroy that faith. You do believe me when I say that — don't you? Even when it's

All my love, Gene

❧

4 June 1945

Dearest Marian,

I really do think you are wonderful—Received the May 28th Time today with your very nice letter. I enjoyed both but of course the letter most of all—you do have the ability to give me a thrill by merely what you say and the way it's said. Something like when I read an article from Time which particularly appeals to me. Just happened to think that if they knew of that, they could establish another section entitled "Romance."

Your comment on Argentina and the "dandruff" is probably true altho I laughed about it. I generally like to be sarcastic—altho it is a good way to lose friends. Probably Time's remark did not appear to be funny to the South Americans at a time when friendly relations should be established but on the other hand it is a pleasant relief from the usual press' desire to "carry a message." Also liked Van Klippen's manner and his obvious sincerity. He expresses my belief that the world expects too much from San Francisco—and that the US is too much concerned with "Regionalism." I told Merle the other day that if we are going to live up to the spirit of peace we should throw the Monroe Doctrine away or at least file it among the pages from "The Life and Times of George Washington." To me it is obviously outdated for the same reason isolationism is outdated. But I can well imagine the congressmen raising their hands in horror and screaming "idealism" (meaning stupidity.) But the principle of the peace is idealistic because we are attempting something that has never been tried before—we can work out the enforcement realisticly.

An interruption came up so in the meantime I finished reading the pages you sent. Merle will be in tonight and then he can have it. He always enjoys your comment in the margins.

It seems that the carrier "Franklin" took a beating what? We knew some of the details on it quite a while ago. One of those things it's hard but necessary to keep under our hats. Also the Joffey—Rather strange, but also in another way quite obvious that the Navy is losing so many men killed in action whereas up to now there losses in personnel were not too great. They are doing a good job but I still don't like the Navy in general. It is rather amusing to see how well the "Seabees" and Marines get along whereas neither of us will have anything to do with the common (as the Seabees say) Navy. I wish that they (CB's) would get more publicity because they are wonderful and wonderous.

There is an electric fan right behind me which keep blowing the paper up against my pen making strange marks on the paper which looks too much like my handwriting.

I'm glad you liked that cartoon which I considered a prize. They could use it somewhere to demonstrate that there <u>need not be</u> a man shortage. And a good caption under it would be—"Notice—<u>she</u> is sitting in the gutter with <u>him</u>."

Guess I told you about a new schedule here. I am CWO again today so should have 2 whole days free now except for some lectures and odds and ends. Would like to go out in the hills somewheres and think of you.

Rather funny that the soldier would get off his motorcycle and close those poor German's eyes. He should have been on Iwo—he'd had a field day. I guess I told you about that "hand" sticking out of the sand that somebody had placed a cigarette butt between the fingers. It didn't bother me to see dead Japs—but Marines I hated to look at. Reminds me—Merle and I had a long discussion about killing them and found out we both disagree. Actually think I convinced him of my side but it is a long story.

We finally found out that the president's name (of the Mormon church) is Smith (odd name) I heard the announcement of his succession but that isn't the name they gave. Told Merle about the event and he kept naming names for a week and I kept saying —"No that's not it"—They didn't say Smith because I would have remembered.

I have the "Atlantic" to read and also my Spanish to study so goodnight darling again and pleasant dreams.

Much Love, Gene

✧

4 June 1945 (2)
Central Pacific

Darling,
The time is about 9:30 tonight which is something I should mention I think because these letters are coming out of here like sausage out of a grinder. Hope that the quality is not impaired too much and your eyes can take it. It is the 4th letter in two days which is due to the fact that I have a lot of time and mostly because I received 5 from you in the last 2 days. Never expected that I would get 2 tonight and consequently didn't wait to see if I had any mail. Just now one of the fellows remarked that there was a mail call and after a trip to the tent I actually did have mail. It is always good to see mail on the top of my pillow especially when I don't espect it.

You were right about the name of that Nazi picture being "Tomorrow the World" Think that Merle gave me some bum dope. Incidently he feels the same way about my reaction that you do—that is—I take it too seriously and I suppose that you are both right. Always will remember my grandmother saying to my grandfather, "Now Pa don't get so excited." I guess that I never told you that I have always called him "Marty" and never grandfather. His name is Martin. He was always a devote socialist until 1932 when he decided to back Roosevelt who he accepted as the lesser of two evils. Since that time tho he is one of FDR's avid supporters. I always gave him a lot of credit for changing his views at that old age but liking him as much as I do I am probably prejudiced.

Another surprise today was a letter from my uncle [Aage] who it appears is permanently located in L.A. I would like you to meet him sometime and see what you think about him. I could tell you some amazing tales concerning him as he is quite a character. I have only seen him off and on all my life but I think that he is one of the most brilliant men I ever met. Formerly used to be west coast AF of L organizer under Green and now associated with somebody else. He got his start by working in the shipyards as a longshoreman and gradually got to the top of the union. Outside of these facts we don't know much about him. When I stayed in LA and he came there from Salt Lake City that Christmas I had a chance to talk to him but even then he didn't give me much satisfaction. Because he is a steady drinker we did go out one night to a lot of these dives on State street which you have probably noticed. Everybody knew him including the barmaids and it wasn't long before I had one of them around my neck, which amused Aage a great deal. Finally he said, "Well you have seen these places and now we'll go out and see the man who owns them." So much to my surprise we headed for Beverly Hills and one of the most beautiful houses I have ever seen in my life. Some man opened the door and when he recognized Aage practically threw his arms around him etc.

So we went in and he introduced me to everyone present including a star reporter for the LA <u>Times</u>. I never did find out what the score was or what he had been doing all these years but was always under the impression that he could make a million dollars if he wanted to. His first wife was practically useless but he refused to divorce her because she had cancer. Finally did after 15 years of married life and got married again to this other woman whom I think is very nice but undoubtedly has her hands full with him. Well enough of the family—

I can't remember telling you that I was a confirmed bachelor—did I? I do remember saying that it would be very easy to fall in love with you tho which is true enough.

Tues 5 June,

Ah—a day off and I have really enjoyed it. Stopped at the club to drink some beer there this noon after sleeping all morning. Merle and I are probably going to the movie tonight and will have a chance to talk some things over concerning the "Tito affair" so I'll say more about that later in the week.

The poem you sent I liked—"Of Scenery and one Acre" The conclusion is well taken that American ideals are just scenery—I think thats the way most people regard the study of history for instance.

More later sweetheart
All my love, Gene

❧

7 June 1945

Hello Darling,

Your letter of the 31st arrived tonight. I just finished writing home and now I can concentrate on you for awhile at least. Read your letter again right now and am in the mood for writing. I like to answer letters from you immediately after receiving them. Later on I will have to start preparing a lecture that is supposed to last 2 hours tomorrow. It is on comm. in the div and altho there is a lot to talk about I have to have some form of outline at least. Merle will stop in after the movie to see me as I am CWO again for the 3rd time this week. Will have it again Sat. but next Sun I will be free and would like to plan to do something.

So much for the tactical situation at present. Greta's advice is probably well taken and in general a good course to follow. Reference: "Is he in love with you etc." It has suddenly occurred to me that I never had said anything definite to you but merely implied certain things.

The Russians are keeping quiet too—probably for a reason and it appears that many people have lost faith in them. Certainly it would be much easier for them to follow a certain course of action but it may result in losing their objectives, one of which is probably security. Another may be their wish to work out their problems in their own particular manner which may or may not be the same way United States would advocate. They are honest and what they say they mean—and they mean what they say. Well enough of all that.

You are probalby [*sic*] confused enough already. I know that when you first said you loved me (March 4th I think) it made me feel wonderful and the feeling is just as strong today. I believe you and undoubtedly I am in love with you. How things will be after I get back, we don't know of course. You know so much about me in some ways and in others you don't know anything. Not that I am hiding anything that you should know but unfortunately I have certain traits that you would only realize after seeing me in person for a while. I have messed this up pretty awful and I hope that you have not lost any ambition to see me because I do love you darling. It is easy enough to say the words but I have never had any practice.

Last night at the movie we saw "The Picture of Dorian Gray." After the writeup in "Time" and the pictures in "Life" I felt as tho I knew everything about it except the details. It was very good—especially the cynicism of Geo. Saunders. Have you seen it? As usual Merle and I had a long discussion after it about various intricate subjects which are interesting to fool around with. One of them was—whether it is worse to study very ambiously [*sic*]—be intelligent—and then reach a "wrong" conclusion or—to follow the crowd—never use your brains and eventually die as most people do—in "ignorance". The picture seemed to justify the latter in one sense. It is interesting to talk about those things if nothing else but we generally reach a conclusion. I don't think that there are many subjects that we have missed. Reminds me about you and Murph talking about security—and <u>we</u> are convinced that women are more concerned about the subject than men and probably have the right to be.

The international situation seems to be rather disappointing at times isn't it? The still prevalent hatred against Russia and the attitude of some of the American papers in supporting that ill feeling makes me discouraged. We have heard that the "Chicago Tribune" ran a headline saying that Russia is the only aggressor in the world. I wonder how they would have felt if Russia hadn't won most of the war in Europe for us as well as them selves. It seems sometime that people would happily see at war with the Soviet. As I told Merle—that's the time I would head for the hills and stay there. Also would be tempted to join the Russian army if they would let me in. With as little patriotism that I hold, I do believe at times that I am fighting for something.

Reminds me of something else we were talking about the other night. Both of us feel that the United States conference representatives are slightly fouled up at times. Now Merle thinks that the deviation from the Roosevelt principles (as there has been) is due to the fact that Truman has some ideas of his own which he is now putting forward to our delegates whereas I believe that the President means well but is just too weak a man to control the desires of the delegates (especially Vandenberg) which are for the most part strictly "Republican" ideals and as such incompatible with world peace. We may both be off the beam but certainly there have been instances where the U.S. has been in the wrong. The "right to work" clause is the most glaring example for instance. Right?

It is almost 8:30 and time to get back to my lecture studying. Will write more tomorrow. You had better be studying because I'm going to start writing all my letters in Spanish as soon as I learn a few more verbs. Right now all I know is Yo hablo which means "I talk" which is probably too true already.

All my love, Gene

The enclosed letter from Marquette [means] apparently I am eligible for 4 years—or the maximum next month—[on the G.I. Bill][48] Sounds good, hey?

✢

June 1, 1945
[Chicago]

Hello, darling,

Don't you think the flags on this stationery are refined? They have been added just recently.

This letter is apt to be somewhat incoherent, as I wrote it in shorthand sort of between flashes at the switchboard. Will try to improve it a bit as I type.

Peg came in about 10:00 last night and left at 11:15, so we really had to talk fast. She had been visiting Ray's family in Plymouth, Wisconsin. His dad was educated in Germany and seems to have rather more than enough sympathy for the "old Germans." He has a theory, however, that men who preach violence die by violence, and vice versa. This applies only to the leaders, though. He also believes that there is going to be another war of "harvest" within the next few years, but after that there will be a thousand years of peace. Just what kind of "harvest" this war is supposed to reap is a bit vague, to say the least. The San Francisco Conference[49] he has already condemned as a failure, and I had quite an argument with Peg, trying to counteract somewhat his influence on her opinions. Needless to say, I don't think I like him.

Of you, dear, Peg said that you are practically the only person she knows who lives by thought alone (which she admires) and who is never emotional about anything. That seemed to me rather amusing, since her own thoughts are so easily influenced by her emotions or her loyalties to individuals. It makes her very lovable, but, as Ray is apparently even less practical, I am often concerned about their future.

Incidentally, her conclusions as to your character were arrived at by some method entirely mysterious to me. I <u>think</u> they are reasonably accurate, if perhaps a little too positive.

This interpreting Ray has been doing must be interesting. He is asst. div. interpreter and also personal bodyguard to the general, presumably the commanding general of his division. Peg makes the story of Ray "protecting" the general sound very amusing.

The fact that he had been going to these Russian-American banquets gave me the impression that it was Russian he was interpreting, but it is German. One sequence I should like to hear about when he gets back was an interview between a Colonel and the burgomaster of some occupied town, regarding "civilian complaints."

Shall have to finish this at home as it is 5:00.

It seems there isn't much to finish. I thought there would surely be a letter from you tonight as there wasn't yesterday <u>or</u> the day before, but I am sadly disappointed. Guess I'll have to practice that stuff about patience I was writing the other day.

See you tomorrow, darling. I love you very much.

Marian

�֍

June 2, 1945

Dear Lt. Sweetheart:

No letter today, either. I am really concerned now & shall be very anxious to learn what has happened —

Sun., June 3: Didn't get very far with this last night, did I? Capt. Bauer came over & they talked me into coming down to his apt. We spent a very relaxed evening talking & drinking gin & reading the funnies.

Today we have been doing nothing, also, due chiefly to lack of energy. Maybe it's the weather. It has been damp & gloomy for weeks.

I dreamed last night that I had a letter from you saying you had gone off into the wilderness for some reason having to do with the guard and had been lost from Tuesday until Friday. It seemed so real I half expect to have such a letter tomorrow.

How do you like this stuff of [Norman] Corwin's? Surely wish I had heard that broadcast.

Have been thinking about the line on brotherhood & am almost convinced that, with a few rare exceptions, everyone really does believe in the brotherhood of man — the great difficulty being the differences in our ideas on how to attain it a& also a factor which might best be expressed by "the spirit is willing but the flesh is weak."

I heard a very interesting conversation on the L [Chicago's elevated railway] yesterday between two men probably in the late 50's. The one was telling about a speaker he had heard who said, "An old world is dying and the new world is, perhaps, not yet ready to be born." He had been deeply impressed by the statement & by the speaker, and he said it had been his own observation that when one was learning about any given subject, he had a great deal to say about it up to a certain point, & as his knowledge progressed beyond that point, the amount of talk decreased until he was finally able to sum up the whole thing in a simple statement such as this speaker had made. Quite an idea, isn't it? I was really sorry when I had to get off the car.

Mother sent us a chicken again this weekend. She said she didn't know how old it was so we decided it would be best to stew it. Unfortunately, it had to be cut up for that. Woe is me! What a poor little hacked-up chicken it is now. Guess it will taste just as good, though. (It does.)

Darling, I wish I could think you might be coming home. Ed was trying to tell me last night that you might, but I told him you'd been overseas 7 mos., & he said, "Oh," and that was the end of that. I miss you, darling.

All my love, Marian

⚜

June 4, 1945

Darling,

At last there is some mail from you! Obviously nothing happened, except to the service. I feel a little silly now for having been so concerned. It <u>was</u> unusual, though.

I'm glad the Spanish looks interesting to you. No doubt you thought, when you rec'd the letter in which I said I'd like to start studying about Sept. (wish that letter could have evaporated), that you'd been right all the time about my not being able to make up mind about <u>anything</u>. I suppose there's nothing left for me to do but admit that you are right—to a certain extent. Since you have started, though, I will, too, as soon as possible. This time I really mean it!

You wouldn't be hinting at anything, would you, by telling me that picture had to be put in a leather frame to conserve it. I shall have to confess that Cal has had my camera since last fall. I have seen him only once in six weeks, & he can't remember to bring it down. I'm using threats now, so it may not take much longer.

That talk about weekends in L.A. makes me lonesome—but I like it. Franklin and I went to the Melody Lane about twice, I think. It was always so crowded we'd get impatient & go somewhere else—to Lindy's or to our favorite Sunday night bar a couple of blocks north on Western Ave. I never can remember the name—begins with an "R." On Sun. nights, they had a fellow who played the piano continuously from 9 to 12. He'd just ramble on from one thing to another & we loved to watch him. I lived at 635 N. Kenmore. Kenmore, as you probably recall, is the street that runs into the Ambassador, about two or three blocks west of Vermont. 635 N. is half a block from Melrose. You lived somewhere near there, too, didn't you?

My friend Margie from Racine worked for Douglas in the Wiltern Theater bldg. The dr. who took out my tonsils had his office there, too. "Not-too-vital statistics."

It seems surprising, and definitely annoying, that we didn't meet much sooner, don't you think?

I haven't seen "Music for Millions." You see about 6 times as many as I do. About "Kitty Foyle," I don't remember much about the kind of guy she fell for, but I do remember that we enjoyed the picture very much. Particularly the part about the gal reading in the bathtub while Kitty entertained in the living room — & the scene where they just threw the blankets on the couch & went to sleep after her boyfriend <u>finally</u> left. It was so much like the more amusing aspects of our apartment life at that time. Murph & I have learned to be a little more dignified. I'm not really sure whether that's good or bad.

I'm sure you will like this article from Harpers. It seems to confirm your ideas on the subject. I was very much interested in the traits of Japanese character which he points out & also in his plan regarding what to do with the Emperor. It sounds like a sensible plan, don't you think?

Darling, it seems I've had so little time to write lately, it's good tonight to be able to think about you as long as I like between paragraphs. It's probably a good thing I was busy or I'd have been more worried about not hearing from you. As you say, having too much time to think makes everything more intolerable.

It will probably sound contradictory to say I've been so busy when yesterday I said we were doing nothing. We were, but we both were so tired it seemed as if we had nowhere near enough time for anything. Understand?

See you tomorrow, Sweetheart.

All my love, Marian

❦

June 5 '45

Hi, Lt. Sweetheart:

We have been a couple of busy little bees tonight. Murph has been sewing, and I've been cooking. Made some dumplings to go with the chicken tonight & later I baked a coffee cake & made rhubarb sauce for breakfast. Murph thinks we ought to get up early to enjoy it, but right now I believe in sleeping!

I enjoyed your comments on Mr. Baxter's letter. A BD-97 is part of a switchboard. (You is a smart guy, honey.) I had been under the impression it was a main distributing frame, but decided I'd better find out for sure before making any incriminating statements. It is, I found, a panel on which discharge blocks, carbons and fuses are mounted. The panel, in turn, is mounted on a main frame, sometimes. Chiefly, I understand, it is used for portable switchboards, such as I imagine they might use in Jasco.

That clipping I sent the other day on Clare Luce has made me suspicious of Time's attitude toward Russia. I'm not sure I appreciate the paragraph under Trusteeships in this week's Internat'l section. What do you think of it?

In the National section, which I have just started to read, they make some remark about Samuel Grafton "wrinkling his emotional nose." It rather amused me because, as you know, I've always thought him very sensible, & I think you have, too. Could be that we are more "emotional" than we think we are.

Darling, there are dozens of things I'd like to write about tonight, but I just can't do it. Not least among them is you — & how much I wish you were here. Goodnight, dear.

Much love, Marian

✻

June 6, 1945

Hello, darling,

Rec'd your letter of May 31 today & it was a great improvement on an otherwise dull day. I told Murph "That was a good letter I had tonight." She says I always say that. It's always true, but it seems like a brand new idea every time, happily.

The answer to your question about gum is that I'm rather indifferent about it. I do enjoy it once in a while, though, & will appreciate it if you send a piece now & then. Thank you, dear, for this one. It was good. No one can get it here, except some peculiar brands which are sort of awful-tasting.

I'm glad you mentioned that half an hour is not much time in which to write a letter. It always takes me at least an hour & I've often wondered if you had the same difficulty.

Time is the most unmanageable thing, isn't it?

Did you ever read "Grandma Called it Carnal"? There was a very good comment in that book on "time," not money, being the stuff one buys life with. Knowing how to save & how to spend time, it said, was the great secret of living. It certainly has a lot to do with it, anyway.

While we're having quotations, I'd like to tell you about a poem Julia [Boe] gave me today. I'll copy it for you first (Her sister wrote it.) and then tell you the rest of the story.

"The Golden Gate"

"We stand before the Gate,
Weary & spent
With the ravages of war and hate;
Our feeble efforts bend
toward the unlatching of this Golden Gate.

In vain, each tries in turn
To lift the bar.

Our sadly flickering hopes more dimly burn —
Have we come thus far
Only to fail because we cannot lift the bar?

Before the Gate we stand
And humbly pray,
"Teach us the Password to the Promised Land,
Show us, Lord, Thy way
To work united, & to love & understand."
and lo! the Golden Gate swings open wide,
to show a world where Brotherhood and Peace abide."

Rather good for an amateur, don't you think? Julia has worked for Reliable for some 15 years, but aside from being so typically an old maid, she is the most intelligent & interesting of all the girls there. She had taught school for several years before coming to Chicago, & her sister, who wrote the verse, teaches history in a Chi. grade school. Julia was telling me today about some book she intends to buy, & the author happened to be a favorite of mine. She said, "It's really a pleasure to have someone here I can talk to about books, etc. With these other girls, when you mention books, all you get is a blank stare." Julia is inclined to exaggerate things; nevertheless, it made me feel good to have her say that. I feel somewhat the same about her.

I've been saving "Barnaby" for you since his current adventure began. He's so cute; he just cheers me up every day. I agree with you about "Orphan Annie." It's revolting. "Barnaby's" double-meanings are not malicious, though, and they're so much more subtle. I guess you could leave out that "much more." "Orphan Annie" is not subtle <u>at all</u>. It's practically insulting to the intelligence of any literate person—I sound like Julia now.

Murphie is in bed already & I must quit, darling. I'll see you in my dreams, I hope.

With love, Marian

❀

9 June 1945
[Guam]

Hello Sweetheart,
  Saturday again after a sorta hectic week. We had some days free but the remainder worked hard as usual. It is a minor strain to have the duty as CWO

for 24 hours in a stretch and even in the following day off there is so much to do that the time goes somewhere. The time is passing and June is here again. Sorta crept up on us here.

Received some bad news last night as Merle is definitely going to the Pioneers on detached duty for about 6 weeks. I hate to see him go as our frequent talks will probably be interrupted to a large extent now. He has promised to return often and he is not too far away so I'll be able to get up there too.

Last night Steve came up and we saw "The Corn is Green" at the club here. I liked it and would have enjoyed seeing E. Barrymore in the stage play. As it was, B[ette]. Davis did the role justice.

Tonight I'll be on duty here in the msg center so will miss the party at the club. Only important factor in that respect is that it will be Merle's last day here practically. Tomorrow I am going on a tour of the island with him and would really like to tell you what we see. Some scuttlebutt about that we can soon say where we are located —

Got through my lectures all right this week but to talk for 2 hours straight is really something. I was thankful I had prepared a good outline. It helps when you know exactly what you are going to say. I still am convinced I would rather teach college than anything lower despite —"The Corn is Green"—As I said before—Merle has the plan he wants to influence the kids before their ideas are formed too strongly. It is a "noble" thought but I feel that a high school teachers is too much limited and concerned with incidentals that are just plain work. Such as—correcting papers—spelling, punctuation etc and a lot of other foolishness that some stupid school board member has thought up.

1900 another interruption and it is now after 7:00 P.M. Can hear the band playing over at the off. club which makes me feel sorry for myself inasmuch as I have to stay here. Oh—how I wish this were over with—the war I mean. Most of the time it's not too bad but then there are other times like tonight. Are you going to meet me at the train in Chicago? It would be the first time that anyone was there to greet me. Wish it would come soon but as you say—patience is also a necessity. I think Merle and I will have a good time tomorrow—would like to go down to the officers' beach sometime. Guess he is going to go to church in the morning so I will too. Now he has a personal jeep too so he will be able to get around and over to see me often. Yesterday I talked for awhile to O'Leary and he claims Borrowman is the best communication officer in Jasco— Incidently they are not "Jasco" anymore but "Asco" because they are now part of the division whereas they formerly were Corps troops. Thus—just assault Signal Co.

Think I'll knock off the writing and concentrate on dreaming which is more in keeping with my mood tonight. Goodnight sweetheart and pleasant dreams— for both of us.

Very Much Love, Gene

❖

10 June
Sunday night

Dearest,
Your letter of the 1st was here when we returned from our afternoon of riding. I was <u>very</u> glad to get it as it has been 3 days since I heard from you. I have been writing regularly so I hope you are getting all mine too.

We had a very enjoyable afternoon and I wish I could tell you all about it. I know you particularly would like to hear about some of the things we have seen. We toured the entire island. Censorship is really a pain especially at a time like this but I can say that I do miss you which probably takes form in the desire for your letters and the feeling I get when I do get them. If this feeling between us can be half as great when I return, I shall know for sure I am actually in love with you—and that is an entirely new experience as far as I am concerned. It is grand tho—

Are you of the opinion I am not emotional? Remember you once said I was passionate which should have some connection with emotionalism somewhere along the line. I think probably that the answer lies in the fact that they are extremes (sensibility and passionism—word?) and at times I am both.

Glad that Peg was able to see you for awhile. If we three got together sometime after the war we probably could get a lot of talking done and at least a few things decided for sure. Wonder what kind of a fellow Ray is actually—I think it is sad when both of them are inclined to be impractible (is that the word) I don't think that you are an "ornament" as somebody once told you, I believe.

Merle and Eddy are just about due over here. I had to break away from them to see if there was mail.

Monday morning—almost time to go to work. If the above seems slightly incoherent it is because I had several rum Cokes during the afternoon. More tonight darling (that is, another letter) and so till then—

Much Love, Gene

❖

10 June 1945 [2]

Hello dear,
Just a note this Sunday morning to convince you I <u>do</u> think about you most of the time. I am waiting for my relief to come up here to the msg. center. His name is Eggmeyer—don't think I have mentioned him before. A very nice fellow—but

last night he stopped in here at 11:00 PM and really was <u>drunk</u>. So I called up the Sig. co. to tell him to take his time about getting to work. I hope that he eventually makes it —

Eddy and Merle were in last night and we talked till almost 12:00 PM. Mostly about school after the war. Edwards has tentatively decided to go back to Colorado College and possibly study teaching. The old argument of High school vs. College teaching came up again but Merle is still convinced he is going to "mold the ideas" of our young people. Well maybe — We agree on one thing however — that we would like to go home. I see that the army has quite a few men who are going to be released under the point system. No word from the Navy yet so I guess all of us are stuck. Under the Army system, if employed by the Marines — over half the men could be discharged. Oh well — I can wait if you can —

Eggmeyer is here and I'll go back — Good morning darling and

All my Love, Gene

⚜

10 June 1945 [3]
1800

Darling,

Your letter of June 1st arrived today. I am sorry that you have been waiting for mail from me for several days. I don't know what the reason is as I have been writing. I also don't know how much I have written because I don't keep any kind of an accurate count. Mostly my writing depends upon some sort of mood I am in. I hate to think of <u>having</u> to write to a person so many times a week or something like that. Don't you? I think you will find that you will get several letters all at once as I do often. I <u>am</u> glad that you are concerned which is just the way I want you to be. It has been perfect in every respect darling —

Thanks for the pages from "Time" again and again it was the first I had seen of the June 4th issue. The article on China — I liked. Their feature articles always have a certain something which is usually not to be found elsewhere. Probably due to the many excellent correspondents they employ — Wonder sometimes who the brains behind the magazine is — Luce — do you think?

We have eaten in our new mess hall for the first time today — More tomorrow —

⚜

11 June 1945 1000

Hello Darling,

Am typing this on an old Underwood which is probably the first one ever made. So there will be some excuse for the mistakes that I undoubtedly will make. It is better to sit here typing tho than writing a letter as it at least looks as tho I am working. Seems that you have that trouble at times too.

Just came back from the Off Mess. run down to town and elsewhere. It is quite a change from the scenery around the division area. I feel so much like I am back in the states because of the buildings and really civilized atmosphere some day I will be able to tell you more details about it. Merle and I saw the movie "Molly and Me" last night which turned out to be fairly good but nothing to compare with other Monty Woolley's such as "The Man who Came to Dinner," or "Tonight at 8:30" Those I really enjoyed.

Been reading in the morning's news bulletin about the policy that the Army has adopted in Europe which amounts to "non-fraternalization with the Germans." Seems rather amusing in regard to some of the ways the soldiers get around the rule. Example: "I hope that my Polish gal doesn't talk German in front of the MP's tonight." I am inclined to think that the troops in Europe are having a very enjoyable time these days and will have much to talk about when they return—even tho it is not about fighting. Some of them probably reached the conclusion war is not entirely hell as Grant thought. Today's paper also carried a very realistic speech by Joe Stillwell[50] [*sic*] about the Pacific war and what to expect from the Japs. I liked it mainly because he voiced my opinions. I still think that he is a good soldier despite the fact that he couldn't get along with Chiang ___ (wouldn't dare try to spell that name) I see also that the man has also resigned as premier of China. Wish that somebody would find out exactly what is going on over there and tell us. It is a vague situation and nobody seems to know. I think I heard or read about a book dealing with "Red China" which was supposed to throw some light on the subject.

Am also glad that Stillwell predicted another 2 years before the end of the war here. That should knock off some of this unfounded wild optimism here and in the states.

Seems like I never will finish this letter—but I'll have to end it now. It is almost 6:00 PM and time to eat again which rates pretty high here—

Worked most of the afternoon on some furniture for our mess. More of a detailed explanation tomorrow or soon on what our club looks like. Til then darling—

All my love, Gene

�֎

11 June 1945
Central Pacific

Dearest Marian,

Just back from the club after a couple cold cans of beer and the news broadcast. Sounded particulary good today—mainly because of the possibility of the Japanese Diet objecting to the premier's desire for unlimited powers to conduct the war. The possibility for an early peace is of course still remote but it is encouraging to see some people in Japan wanting some little democracy at a time like this. They are difficult to understand and therein lies the foolishness of the many beliefs that an early end to the war is coming.

The news today told the story of the P-51 fighter who got in with the wrong group of B-29's and found himself over Nagoya as the only fighter among several hundred bombers. The bomber leader told him to get below one of the B-29's wings and therefore protected him from the large numbers of enemy fighters. It was rather interesting I thought.

Merle is supposed to leave for the Pioneers some time today for about 6 weeks. Sure sorry to see him go now that we know each other so well. I hope that he keeps his promise to come down and see me often. Edwards is doing well over at the 21st Marines. I think I told you about his writing to a girl he hadn't seen in 10 years. Well anyway—last night he received a letter from her and she had just been married. We kidded him of course but I still feel sorry for him. He hates it here and is usually very bitter in a serious way.

Merle's baby weighs 10 lbs. and has got his first haircut. One of those things that only parents appreciate but I thought I'd mention it—

Don't know how I am going to spend my evenings now but I still have you and that after all will affect me ultimately—I like that "ultimately" I hope that there is a letter from you today but just the thought that they <u>are</u> on the way is encouraging and I'll provide the patience if you write the letters—

I'm sorry for your sake that Peg did not stay in Chicago instead of going on to Washington. Think I know how you feel. Was rather surprised to see that she classed me as a person "who lives by thoughts alone." That could be—Borrowman does also then but the difference is that he <u>wants to change</u> the <u>world</u> while I am <u>impatiently</u> criticizing people to myself at least in the fact that they aren't learning something. Maybe I'm like that girl in "Going My Way" with whom Bing Crosby talked. He said, "You know when I was 18, I found my father to be very stupid but after I reached 21 years of age I was amazed at how much he had learned." I think that is a minor classic statement.

Time to eat lunch darling. Wish we were having it together round about Michigan ave. But I can say "all my love" which distance doesn't diminish.

Gene

❀

13 June 1945

Hello again darling,

Tis just before chow and I will start another letter. Yours of 5th received today and as usual I was very happy to hear from you again. Can understand your feelings about not getting mail for a few days. Oddly enough in the same circumstance—I feel the same way. I believe it is called love.

Anyway I am happy you finally started receiving some of my later letters. I believe that certain situations out here hamper mail delivery somewhat and all we can do is wait—that is not something new either—is it darling?

The leather frame and your picture was not meant to be a subtle hint for a new picture—insomuch as you took it that way I wont have to be blunt "again" and ask for a picture of you. Love does not sharpen my memory of what you look like unfortunately. If you expect me to recognize you in some Chicago station, I will have to know exactly what you look like. Enough of that but I hope I have convinced you—

Back from chow and will add a few more lines now before Merle arrives. He is coming down again tonight and probably take me back with him to the pioneers. Last night we saw "A Tree Grows in Brooklyn" which I thought was very good. Rather depressing because of the old story of practibility vs impractibility because when the two occur—one in a woman and one in a man—it is particularly sad especially when they are in love. It is hard to say which is right but I think I'd agree more with Kathie—

The article on Japan by Lamott seems rather true—I haven't read it carefully yet but I will tomorrow and give you my reactions.

I had to laugh at you wishing that the letter saying you'd start studying Spanish in Sept would vanish. I hope that you do start soon tho. I do not think that you never make up your mind as you are afraid. I am that way to a large extent too and I think most people are. I am so impressed with the many things about you that I like—you are pretty, intelligent and have a very nice personality which are the things I like in a girl. Not necessarily in that order but certainly some of each.

Time passes again—it is now 14 June and I'd better end this letter tonight. Made up my mind that I am <u>not</u> going to the movie tonight—have several letters to write and also a long special one to you. So I'll say so long for awhile until I get some of these "must" letters out of the way.

Much Love, Gene

✤

June 8, 1945
[Chicago]

Dearest Gene,

I hope I can finish this without someone reading over my shoulder. I always feel guilty writing letters at work, although I really should not on a quiet day like this.

I went to the show last night, "To Have and Have Not." The only thing of Ernest Hemingway's I have read was "Farewell to Arms." That was good, but if this plot is a representative example of his later work, then I agree with whoever it was who said he should have quit writing after "Farewell to Arms." In spite of that, I enjoyed the picture. Didn't expect to like Lauren Bacall, but I think she is rather fascinating—almost sweet, in a way.

I was telling Julia about our language project, and she says one of our toolmakers, who gives her a ride home occasionally, can speak Russian. She has been trying to persuade him to give her a few lessons.

Cal told me he finally remembered to bring my camera down, so perhaps I can get it tonight. He has been trying to get a new job with an agency in the Palmolive Building—Sherman Marquette, who handle General Motors' account. It is one of the five best art director's jobs in the city, he says. I have been absolutely amazed at how badly he wants the job. I accused him of being too eager to make money, but he says it is more the idea of being able to do things his own way and accomplish some of the objectives he has been unable to attain under someone else's supervision. It is rather hard for me to understand, but it is obviously of paramount importance to him. Does it make sense to you?

I suppose I ought to know better than to send you a clipping like this one about Luke field. You have to admit, though, that those Air Corps boys are courageous when they are willing to attempt a mission like that.

Darling, I hope this letter doesn't sound as bad to you as it does to me. I never can write a good letter at work. Punishment, perhaps.

See you later, dear.

All my love, Marian

✤

June 9 '45

Hi, darling,

It looks now as if Barnaby's latest adventure will be as good as his last, so here you are, dear. They're all in order—one or two missing. Hope you like the witch's "slightly soggy" house.

We've had more fun tonight over Murph's sewing efforts. She's making a dress that has a bow at the neck. She spent a good half hour carefully sewing the skirt to the top & then when she tried it on, discovered she had stitched the end of the tie right into the seam. It sort of pulled the neckline way down & one side of the skirt way up. It looked so foolish we could hardly stop laughing.

Rec'd your letter of the 29th yesterday and have been trying ever since to find someone who could translate that Spanish phrase. It appears that I'll just have to learn how myself—you slave driver! You know, really, this is a very wise thing for me to do, as later I can learn Spanish shorthand, also, and there are excellent opportunities for secretaries with that knowledge.

I had to laugh at you for saying you'd have to miss the movie again. I don't see how you find time to go as often as you do.

Even aside from Barnaby, this is quite a collection of clippings, don't you think? The explanation is that I had to save all the week's newspapers & read them tonight. As usual, I like Grafton's especially.

Sumner Welles article and also your comments on the same subject in a recent letter have made me rather ashamed of my own hasty conclusions. I have to be reminded every once in a while to practice that clear thinking I so often accuse other people of neglecting.

Darling, this letter ought to be longer for Sat. night, but when Murph is home (Ed has been in St. Louis all week.) it's hard to concentrate. I promise to do better tomorrow.

See you then, sweetheart.

Much love, Marian

✣

June 10, 1945

My darling Gene:

Remember that song, "I dim all the lights & I sink in my chair . . . Deep in a dream of you." that's what I'd like to do right now.

I read an excellent letter on Iwo Jima today in the June Atlantic. I think you will like the comparisons with previous campaigns. One part reminded me of what Franklin said about how to find out what it's really like: "See one of the better picture magazines and imagine a <u>stench</u> to go with it."

It has been just a year today since his last flight. Also, the radio announcers reminded us, it is the third anniversary of the massacre of Lidice. A good day for despising war—if we needed any special day for it.

I think I shall go home next weekend.

Had the sweetest letter from my dad the other day. I guess I'll send it to you. Hope you can read it. We have a lot of fun over his spelling. I believe he only finished the 6th grade in school, though, & for that I think he does very well. The card he mentions was a belated birthday card I sent. I was glad he didn't think I had forgotten, because I hadn't really. Incidentally, he never calls me "daughter" except in a letter. He calls me "Toots," like in an auto horn.

The name of that place in L.A. I was trying to think of the other day is Randini's. Have you ever been there? Except on Sunday nights, their shows were rather coarse. Since it's Sunday, I'd like to be there tonight.

I've been wanting to ask you, darling, would you like it if I were there—in L.A., that is—when you come back? It might not be possible. But when I think of spending even as few as two days knowing you were anyplace where I could be—perhaps I shouldn't say that—I miss you enough now. It seems as if that would be too much.

We took a few pictures today, believe it or not. I'll take some more at home next weekend and finish the roll. I hope there will be a few good ones. It always takes me half the day to figure out how to set the camera.

I certainly hope there will be some mail from you tomorrow. Four letters in two weeks is not so good. I know you've written more often. Wish I could find a mail clerk to pick on.

Guess I ought to study for awhile. I'd rather think about you—and probably will. Until tomorrow—

All my love, Marian

❖

June 11, 1945

Dear Lt. Sweetheart,

There were three letters from you tonight, and, darling, they were worth waiting for, especially the one you wrote Sunday afternoon, "3 June." I think it will take me a day or two to come down to earth.

I can't remember exactly what I said about "security," but I will try to explain in some detail what it means to me. What Murph & I were talking about in the beginning was financial security, of which she has none, at present, except insofar as she is capable of earning her day-to-day living. I have as much of that kind of security as anyone, not being wealthy, could hope for, chiefly because my parents are prudent & thrifty. From that we progressed to the kind of security, more important & less tangible, gained from the knowledge that someone cares for you enough so that you never feel completely alone. When you combine the two you have, I imagine, what is the chief value of marriage to women, aside from the opportunity it offers them to give freely of their efforts and their love to those who are dear to them. This latter seems more important to me. I wish you had asked me more specifically about the things you wondered about. If you misinterpreted my ideas, it would be my fault for expressing them poorly, rather than yours. I agree that we should go on as we have until you come home—there isn't much else we can do that wouldn't be very unwise. You need not be afraid I might think you have learned to like me because you are overseas. I don't want to & I won't. I do think our feelings may be intensified by the fact there is nothing we can do about it, but we both know that the foundation is good. To sum it all up, there are many things more important to me than security, and you are one of them, darling.

May I collect that kiss now? 'Twas a lovely idea. You know, sometimes I wonder, too, if you're normal, but I feel reassured now.

Those two cans of beer you were talking about sounded so good I decided to get some, too. We hadn't had any for a long time.

Ed is back today, so Murph is out. I'm glad because I can think about you without interruption.

That poem of Browning's, "Only minding, dear, to love me also in silence, with thy soul," is, as you suspected, from her "Sonnets from the Portuguese." One of my classmates in high school gave me a copy of those sonnets for graduation, & I really treasure it. I like Shakespeare, too.

That reminds me of an amazing thing I learned about my mother recently. She taught grade school for 12 years, and I just discovered, when telling her about seeing "Othello" last month, that she has never read Shakespeare! Botany & physiology, I believe she said, were her strong subjects.

Yes, we used to go to the main library in Milw. quite often. In fact, the first year I was there, we used to walk over once or twice a week from Juneau & Astor, where we lived. We must have seen each other somewhere, Gene. The literature room is on the 3rd floor, isn't it?

I thought once that it would be fun if we could go to school together, too. But we could never take the same classes. I couldn't take anything I wanted to because my interests have progressed far beyond my credits. I'd rather study with you unofficially. Had to laugh at your idea about the political science class. If we could get Peg & Ray in the same class, we'd look like a couple of stuffy reactionaries.

It makes me just as damn mad as it does you to have people talk about our next war being with Russia. These pages from Time don't please me, either, although there is some compensation in the last paragraphs on the subject. What the hell — it just sounds as if some people are sitting around <u>trying</u> to pick a fight with Russia.

Darling, it's time to say goodnight already, and there's so much more to say. Tomorrow — but I love you tonight, dear. You know that, but I like to tell you as much as I like to hear it.

Marian

⁓

June 12, 1945

Hi, darling,

Another letter today — this is more like it used to be. Needless to add, I like it.

I really enjoyed the letter from your friend in the 106 Inf. Div., especially the paragraph that begins, "Why you big commando, of all things, Message Center work." He must be a lot of fun, & probably a good officer. Incidentally, I'm glad you censored the letter.

Poor Edwards — sure has his troubles, doesn't he? If it would make him feel any better, you might remind him that you can hardly blame a girl for "keeping as many irons in the fire as possible." These days, she could never tell when the hell she might lose one of them — or all of them. I don't mean to suggest that's a very good excuse for the girls, but it does indicate that their being apparently fickle is not necessarily evidence of their true feelings. It doesn't seem quite fair to me for the other girl to be telling him what Claire does. I wouldn't put <u>too</u> much faith in the truth of those tales, under the circumstances.

What you said about the Monroe doctrine reminded me of a headline I saw in the Tribune several weeks ago, something like "U.S. Delegates Abandon Monroe Doctrine." I don't remember the occasion, but I thought at the time I wished it were true.

I was interested in your comments on the Seabees. Had noticed that the "Leatherneck" gave them a lot of favorable publicity. I had a date with a Seabee once in L.A. We went to that very pretty little theatre on Vermont where that old melodrama has been playing for so many years. Know the place I mean? He was an odd fellow, very quiet. I was a little afraid to go because I didn't know what to expect of him. You'll kill yourself laughing at this — it seems awfully funny to me now — but at the time it was a great comfort. Ginny's husband had bought a little pistol for her when he left & she let me take it along that night. Franklin always kidded her about the gun. "Popgun," he called it, & said if she ever pulled the trigger, the thing would explode & hurt no one but her. She maintained she had frightened away some sinister character who followed her home one night, merely by showing the gun, so she was very fond of it. Well, as it turned out, the Seabee was quite a gentleman, thank God.

I don't think I quite follow your idea about using that cartoon to demonstrate that there need not be a man shortage. Just what kind of a man shortage do you mean? I'm not trying to be facetious, but I do think you ought to qualify that somewhat.

I'm curious about your discussion with Merle on killing Japs. What was your side, or would you rather not tell me?

Another thought on the Monroe Doctrine theme—those who would make the biggest fuss over abandoning it are the same ones who criticize Russia for setting up spheres of influence. Incidentally, in one of the copies of PM Ruth sent me, there was a story of a reporter who heard a woman (a colored woman, I think) ask some people who were talking about Roosevelt's death, "What means 'spears of influence?'" Rather an accurate misstatement, wasn't it?

Darling, I feel the same way you do about our faith in each other. I don't want anything <u>ever</u> to destroy it. We shall have to expect misunderstandings, but I'm sure we have enough love & respect for each other to be able to work them out. I promise always to do anything I can to make it so.

Goodnight, dearest,

Marian

☙

June 14, 1945

Hello, darling,

I don't know as it is worth mentioning, but I saw "Here Come the Waves" last night. It was not bad, but I can think of much better ways to have spent the evening.

Tuesday night, I read an article in the June Atlantic called "Russia and Ourselves" by Raymond Swing. I shall be anxious to hear your comments on it as I thought it was exceptionally good. In fact, I wish it could be <u>required</u> reading for all citizens of the two nations. I believe that Time, in the International section I sent to you a day or two ago, made rather a disparaging remark about the article, and now I am even more annoyed with their "Repressible Conflict?"

I brought the Atlantic down today for Julia to read this. We got to talking about Russia, naturally, and I told her what you said about the fellow who thought we should go easy on Japan because they might be our allies against Russia. She practically exploded. It almost isn't safe to discuss controversial subjects with her because she gets so excited. I was laughing at her for it today, and she said she has a friend who tells her he appreciates that particular thing about her. "You never bore me," he says. "I don't always get the reaction I want, but I certainly never fail to get some reaction, and that is much better than apathy."

I agree with him, and that brings me to the next news item. Mac Howard was in town again the other day, and we were both mad at him—chiefly because he is about the most unconcerned person we have ever seen. When Murph came in, we talked about it for quite a while, trying to figure him out. He doesn't seem to care about anything or anyone (never has, she says) and sort of makes you feel as if he is sneering at you a little bit most of the time. I don't know—maybe he is just disillusioned about women!

Coming back to this article of Swing's, there was one sentence which struck me as being particularly appropriate for you and me, as well as for "Russia and Ourselves." It said that for a partnership to work, you must have a sense of its value. That I believe we have, dear, and I am very glad of it.

I was just thinking about the time you told me you were stubborn—and what was the rest of it? If it was the girl you did not marry who told you that, it is easy to see why she would have thought so. I'm glad you were, darling. I just can't see how she had the courage to insist on either alternative in the first place.

I'd better go back to work, Lt. Sweetheart. See you later—

Much love, Marian

⚜

14 June 1945
1900 [Guam]

My dearest Marian,

I should apologize again for that letter I forgot to mail—would you like to "bash my brains out"? I hope that these three tonight make you feel better about June 22nd.

Things are going on here very much as usual. Not that there is nothing to write about tonight because I always feel like writing to you—especially right now when Bing Crosby is singing—Decided after a few minutes delerberation [*sic*] I'd like best to be with you with my head in your lap and have you tell me all those little things you say in your letters.

Somebody is saying that our sharp mail clerk has finally sorted the mail and is bringing it over—Ah! 2 from you and one from my grandfather. That is wonderful.

Later—I just got halfway through your first letter when Merle came in and also another captain to see Murphy. It happened I knew this Captain—name's Glaze and we were at Monmouth together. He was very angry at me just before we left Monmouth because of a slight misunderstanding with his girl. It is one of those long stories and not at all my fault. He was going with this gal who lived in Asbury Park. I had noticed her several times at the office but insomuch as he was interested in her, I never bothered to ask her for a date. Then suddenly one night somebody called me up and it happened to be her—she asked why I had not kept "our date" for that night. I of course knew nothing about it but it ended up by me inviting her up to the club that evening. Don't know who gave her the impression that we had a date, but at any rate—Glaze became awfully angry at me for no reason. All this is unimportant but I thought of it the moment I saw him tonight. Incidently I found out later that he has a wife a baby somewhere in Calif, and this girl at the last report was looking for him because she was going to have a baby. Almost asked him about that but thought better of it—

All of it makes me wish again that you had come to N. Y. last summer. I did have a good time in New Jersey but I think we could have enjoyed each other's company. Right?

Your letters tonight were very nice (which I always think too) They were from the 6th and 7th. I haven't thought much about "Time's" outlook on Russia altho what you say may very well be possible. My sympathies have always been with the Soviet because of all nations they alone most time seem to know exactly what they are doing. If I felt more inclined to have faith in the American people, I probably would be more patriotic and thus very easily to be more or less anti-Russia. It is hard to see what "Time" implies—that we have more right to keep our island bases than Russia has to demand her neighboring states to be friendly. It seems to me that to Russia—the importance of a Soviet-influenced Poland is just as necessary as a American Hawaii to the U.S. I believe you are right to ask the question whether Russia is more self-contained than U.S. Certainly they don't think so—and probably are right—

I <u>knew</u> you would remark about the Grafton "nose wrinkling" Have always considered him sensible—we may be fooling ourselves in thinking we are sensible as oposite of emotional. It's one of those things to think about—

I see the BD97 is up again—We use a lot of BD71's (6 drops) & also BD72's (12 drops) A BD97 is the <u>panel</u> right—I'm not so smart—Captain Styke is here coaching me. He's the quartermaster—besides I know very little about wire and any of its components. A little more about Radio—Remember you explaining turnbuckles to me on the street car. If I could see you tonight I'd talk about <u>anything</u>—even turnbuckles.

The poem on the "Golden Gate" <u>was</u> good. The matter of getting "the password to the promised land" is something we will search for—wonder if it comes in degrees—and how close they have come in San Francisco this last 7 weeks.

Time for bed darling but more again soon. This is the 3rd letter I am mailing to you tonight—which should prove something—even to the extreme sceptics—

All my Love, Gene

⚜

15 June 1945

Darling,

They are playing "For the First Time—" which strikes me as very appropriate as I am sitting here thinking about you—More appropriate than you probably think—

Wont get far on this now cause Merle called up and will be over soon but I'll finish later on, I hope. Tonight I have been gathering up all your letters again which is usually a bimonthly affair. Went back however all the way to November and they make quite a stack now—all tied up with a field scarf—no blue ribbons. Do you know what a field scarf is?

Rather wish Merle wasn't coming tonight but I am always glad to see him— and he is keeping his promise which makes me very happy too. Getting back to your letters—I have been thinking of adopting a sort of filing system for future reference so I will be able to check on what you think on certain subjects. "Winged Victory" was a little embarrassing and being 8 days apart via mail is too far to quickly cover up.

1030 Back again after the movie and a viset with Steve. We brought him back down to Division from the 3rd Marines to see the movie "The Great Patrick" or something. Not bad or good—only unusual thing was that the song "For the First Time—" which I mentioned above was played throughout— which of course made me think of you. At present I am seated or rather in a reclined position here in bed which does not help the handwriting situation at all. Murph and Styke are practically asleep except for some sarcastic remarks off and on. Styke just asked if I was writing a "progress report." It's one of those perfect evenings with a full moon and a usual cool breeze. Think perhaps it will rain tho as it often does at night.

I've been thinking that it will be rather strange when we see each other again. We know so much about each other and on the other hand we don't know anything. I hope it can be exactly like our letters and that is something which would not be impossible. Every day that goes by is a day closer to "the" day. I am glad we both are waiting for it.

It is almost 11:00 PM sweetheart and I haven't accomplished much tonight along the lines of writing a sweet letter which should necessarily characterize a short one such as this. But however—

All My Love, Gene

⚜

16 June 1945

Dearest Marian,

Corwin's poems are good. Been reading over that clipping you sent from the last "Time." I wonder tho—who does profit by war? I don't think actually that anyone does—but the causes for a war are more likely a warped philosophy attempted to be justified by some extremists. I don't believe that certain people in the world today are born fighters and are only really happy when they are fighting. That idea seems to be making the rounds at present.

I have never thought that brotherhood is just a wild dream but I wish I had more faith that we achieving it. Would like to hear some of Corwin's broadcasts.

Capt. Styke has just brought in about 100 pictures (photos 8 x 10) of Iwo and they are wonderful. I'd give a lot to own a set of them but they are official photographs and not available to us.

The time is 12:30 AM and I have had an easy day. Spent a good part of the morning looking over your letters and stapling the pages together. Now I have a rather large volume—something like "Gone with the Wind" but much more interesting—Vital Statistics—you have written 106 letters starting with Oct 30 to June 8. Interesting? Also I have all of them—

5:00 PM—Time has passed and I have had a busy afternoon in comparison with the morning. Just finished taking a shower and have really got dressed up—one of my last Stateside starched shirts and my palm beach trousers. No particular reason except it's easier to visualize a date with you tonight—Would that it were so. Oh well. Think I'll go to the club for awhile and drink some rum cokes and <u>look</u> at the nurses.

Your letter of June 8th came this afternoon and I am happy to see you have your camera back—practically. If you can get the film, there should be no excuses. Meant to tell you that some men from "Life" have been here taking pictures of the division and which should prove interesting—other facts—Tyrone Power is around here with a handlebar mustache—He is a 1st Lt. in the M.A.C. and in the opinion of many—the most handsome man in the Marine Corps—

Almost time to eat again so I'd better close for now.

Think we are going down to the beach tomorrow. They have "Colorado Day" and Edward wants to go. More about that later. I miss you very much darling

All My Love, Gene

❀

17 June
Sunday Morning

Darling,

Time for a few lines this morning at the msg. center. I am going to take the afternoon off and probably go swimming down at the officers' beach. Edwards has the duty so he can't go but Merle should be over early this afternoon.

We had a good time at the club last night and succeeded in downing plenty rum cokes. As a result I had a bad hangover this morning didn't get up till 8:30—also that familiar burnt-out taste in my mouth. Arrived here to work just in time to go to church—so took off some time for that. I heard the best sermon today since I came overseas. The general theme was that we still should have hope and faith in the future even tho the San Fran. conference seems to be fuddled up with individual greed. Best of all was the analogy of the attempts in the early part of American History to set up a constitution and the same situation today at San Fran. That I liked—and have been thinking along those lines myself. Couldn't help but feel that he was talking directly to me when he said, "We must be convinced that Right will prevail eventually despite ourselves." The minister is very young—about 28 I imagine—and new here. Think I'll go next Sunday again—

I was very happy to get your letter of June 11 yesterday—5 days—but felt bad that you have only had 4 letters in 2 weeks from me. I know I have written more than that and hope by now you will have received some of the others. Incidently you are doing wonderful—but badly spoiling me.

Glanced through some of your early letters again and really was amazed to see how many questions you had asked that I never answered. So I took some notes and will attempt to answer them in the future whenever I can find time to write a long intelligent letter. "In the future" does not mean in 18 mo. Marquette sent a questionaire a few weeks ago and after filling it out, asked them how I stood in the G.I. Bill of rights. Will enclose their answer.

I liked your dad's letter. He sounds sincere which he must be if he is your father. The tomatoes sound good. I'd like some right about now. Maybe I'll start a garden out here.

I'll have to close for now sweetheart maybe more tonight after our afternoon at the beach—You are wonderful—

All my Love, Gene

June 15, 1945
[Chicago]

My darling Gene,

I think this letter is going to be <u>long</u>, as I'm home alone with nothing else to do, except for a little planning for the weekend, and there is much to say.

Your letter of June 7 arrived last night. I'd like to have answered it right away, but I was too busy sympathizing with Murph. More about that in a paragraph or two. Your letter was wonderful, dear—like you. I shall probably remember that date as well as you remembered March 4. (Incidentally, I was surprised & flattered that you did remember.) I thought the other day when you told me you really cared for no one else, excepting your grandfather, that it was the nicest thing you could possibly have said—but there is something about, "I love you," that is unsurpassed. Funny how it revolutionizes the world—

I was amused at your comparison with the Russians "keeping quiet . . . for a reason." This is not intended as criticism for you or to carry on the comparison, but sometimes I think the Russians overdo it.

I am quite excited about going home this weekend, although I had a letter from Mother tonight which reminded me that it is never utopian. When you read the enclosed rough draft of her letter to her Congressman, you will see what I mean. My lord! Where does she get such stuff? I'm really ashamed of her. Can't decide whether to argue with her about it or just skip the whole thing. It makes me so angry. I'd probably say something I shouldn't & hurt her feelings.

Margie called me last night from Racine & said she'd like to come along to W'berg. Perhaps I've told you her father, stepmother, & brother used to live across the street from us. Her father died about 7 years ago, & I don't believe Margie has been up there since. It will be fun. Nice to have someone to ride with, too. You know who I'd rather be with, though.

I heard a cute joke today about a princess who found a talking toad. The toad said he had been a prince & some evil spirit had turned him into a toad. To become a prince again, he would have to be placed on a princess' pillow. The princess thought that was the least she could do for him, so she took him home, put him on her pillow, & sure enough, next morning there was a handsome young prince, And do you know—to this day her mother won't believe her!

I like this little piece about Gertrude Stein[51]. It's sort of funny, but it has an optimistic air that makes me feel good.

Picked up a small thread of knowledge the other day from Mr. Ripley, who is more frequently a source of what is generally known as "hot air." He was telling me he had turned down a chance to bid on a turnbuckle job through the Smaller War Plants Corp., as it's a no-good outfit. Being curious, I asked what was wrong with it, as in theory it seemed like a good thing. He said there are certain items which are naturally produced more efficiently by small plants &

can be purchased more economically through them. Those items will inevitably continue to be so produced, and any effort to perpetuate small businesses simply because they are small puts a premium, in a way, on inefficiency. He was mad at the govt., of course, for attempting it, but I told him maybe they had because so many small businesses had complained about being discriminated against. I know that is one of my father's favorite tales of woe —"Everything is for the big outfits." Any arguments?

I think I agree with both you and Merle regarding Truman's influence at S.F. I think he does have some ideas of his own, but it seemed as if it took him a long time to get started at using his influence.

I was very much interested, Gene, in hearing about your uncle. He sounds quite intriguing. Would certainly like to meet him some day. Those "dives on State Street" you were talking about—did you mean Main Street? I can't think where State Street is in L.A. It's a true democrat who can be at home there & also in Beverly Hills. I'd really appreciate a man who, being capable of making a million dollars, would think it not worth the trouble.

I think I interpreted "Of Scenery & One Acre" somewhat differently than you did. I thought of the ideals as scenery, insomuch as they are inspiration. It probably indicates that you are more of a realist, darling.

Time out for some of that planning—

Now to tell you about Murph's troubles. Some old friend of Ed's, a girl from San Francisco, is spending a 30-day vacation in his apartment, it seems, & he's staying with one of the other officers. He claims she invited herself and he's not at all pleased about it. However, Murph hadn't seen him since the other girl arrived early this week & was naturally quite hurt. Something must have been done about it today, because she's apparently out with him tonight. I really felt sorry for her, though. Ed has a girl in St. Louis & another one in New York, but he says neither of them means anything to him. At the same time, while he talks about how happy Gale could make him, he says there is some reason or other (connected with his childhood) why she wouldn't marry him. I don't know why he doesn't tell her what it is & let her make up her own mind, instead of leaving her in such a state of confusion. Makes me mad, too.

On the subject of high school vs. college teaching again, I should think the one you would prefer—& be best suited for—would depend much on what it is you want to accomplish. I suspect that Merle is much more patient than you are, dear, and would probably be satisfied with less obvious results than you would like to see. I had a teacher in high school who was very much like you. That is something I had thought about a year ago & almost forgotten until now. He name is David Dykstra. He's a Navy officer now. I wish you could meet him sometime, altho I shall be very much surprised if I ever see him again myself. He even writes like you do—that is, his penmanship is similar. He used to like me because I was practically the only idealist in the class, and he was one, too.

Franklin Smith, although he never met Gene, brought his sister Marian and Gene together. This picture of him was taken in 1942.

A P-38 like Franklin was flying when shot down over Ploesti, Romania in 1944.
National Archives (208 AA 112A-2).

Mr. and Mrs. Albert Smith in 1944.

SMITHS

FURNITURE AND UNDERTAKING

WITTENBERG, WIS. 6-22 194 4

Marian's mother's letter saying Franklin was missing in action.

Dear Marian,

We just had a telegram saying Franklin has been missing since the 10th. I shall write and have the Red Cross check all camps in Roumania to see if he has been taken prisoner. I hope to hear more sooner that way.

Love,
Mother.

P.S. Received your letter this morning will try to come down Sunday. Hope to see you there Could you get Tuesday morning off to go shopping with me?

Gene's mother.

Gene and his dad, Thor, in San Diego in 1943.

Martin Petersen,
Gene's grandfather, in 1944.

Gail Murphy at the 14 West Elm
apartment building in 1945.

Marian at her father's furniture store in Wittenberg, Wis. in 1945.

Marian, second from left, middle row, at Army-Navy E award ceremony in Chicago, 1945.

*Gene's notes from Iwo Jima written on the back of a label for
"Queen's Taste Green Beans."*

Gene on the left with some of his Jasco men, Hawaii, 1945.

Gene's letter from Iwo Jima, March 11, 1945. Lt. Thomas Edwards signed the censor's stamp.

Marines on Iwo Jima unload supplies despite heavy Japanese gun fire raking the beach.
National Archives (127 GW 346).

With all their gear on their backs, 3rd Division Marines move up to the front.
National Archives (127 GW 306).

The first mail on Iwo Jima on D plus 6 is sorted in a shell hole.
National Archives (127 GW 329).

With a prisoner-of war stockade in the background Marines read mail from home.
National Archives (127 GW 329).

Using his all-purpose helmet, a Marine shaves on Iwo Jima.
National Archives (127 GW 338-1).

While their buddies keep watch Marines clean off some of the Iwo Jima dirt.
National Archives (127 GW 338).

Korean prisoners-of-war taken on Iwo Jima, bury dead Japanese behind the front lines.
National Archives (127 GW 313).

*A Japanese scarf Gene
found on Iwo Jima.*

Navy planes bomb Mt. Suribachi before the famous flag raising.
National Archives (127 GW 306).

Marines in biuvouac alongside Airfield No. 1.
National Archives (127 GW 344).

3rd Marine Division dead on Iwo Jima.
National Archives (127 GW 312).

The 3rd Marine Division cemetery on Iwo Jima, March 22, 1945.
National Archives (127 GW 305).

Mr. and Mrs. Eugene T. Petersen
on their wedding day, February 2, 1946.

"I think I'd want . . . two boys and a girl later."

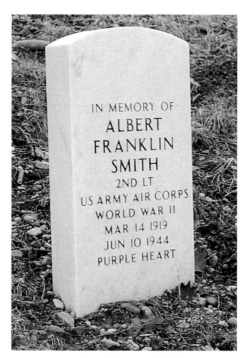

Franklin's marker at Arlington
National Cemetery, Washington D. C.

Gene and Marian at the Washington D. C. Iwo Jima Memorial in 1996.

He was also a perfectionist. He'd look so dejected when we weren't very bright that we thought he'd surely burst into tears some day. One day he lost his temper & banged his fist on the desk so hard that I jumped a foot out of my chair & burst into tears myself, as did one of the other girls. Poor Dave was so sorry he didn't know what to do. I was really quite fond of him in a strictly platonic way. We used to write to each other now & then until he got married a couple of years after I was out of school. He was the one who first talked me into reading Time. The point of this long story is that I always thought Dave would have been happier, & his students would, too, if he had been teaching at a university. He taught history & Latin. I think the same would apply to you. Just to confuse the issue, though, I'm glad Dave was teaching h.s. when I was there.

Oh, darling, there is so much to talk to you about that it seems I never have enough time. There are lots of tomorrows, of course, but I am impatient & want everything now.

It was nice to have you say that while Merle is gone, you'll still have me. I like that "ultimate" effect, too, and if, as you say, it is half as good as the effect of your letters, it is a new and wonderful thing to me, also. I told you I had been in love with Cal, & I was, but always it was confused by disappointments and reservations, which is not true of my love for you. I want it to last forever, darling.

Marian

⚜

June 17 '45
[Wittenberg]

Hello, Darling,

I haven't much time right now, as we've just finished dinner & one of the gals Margie & I used to know will be over in about 20 minutes to take us out— where to I don't know.

Really enjoyed the trip up here yesterday—especially reading the three letters from you I picked up just before going to catch the train. Margie had a little difficulty making her way through six coaches to find me, but aside from that we had no trouble.

We took a lot of pictures this afternoon, and I hope they will turn out OK.

Speaking of pictures, I brought along the snapshots you sent me sometime ago, and Mother likes them better than the other picture of you.

Have been thinking of what you said about emotionalism & about my telling you that you were passionate. Darling, that couldn't have been the day we went through Kansas because I don't see how I could have said it if I were sober. I do remember that I nearly choked on the words. It was nice, tho. I think you are right about the extremes—I don't really believe you are unemotional. It's just that you sort of keep it to yourself, which I like—to a certain extent. I love you, dear. Honestly!

Had to laugh at your asking if I'd meet you at the train, when just the other day I was offering practically to meet you at the ship! Anywhere you like, sir.

Have to quit now. I'll see you tomorrow.

All my love, Marian

⚜

June 18 '45
[Chicago]

Sweetheart,

It seems I have had so little time this weekend to be alone with my thoughts of you that I was actually getting lonesome this afternoon. Sounds funny, doesn't it?

It's already 10:00 tonight, and I've just arrived & managed to put a few things away. I bought a paper down at the station to read while I waited for the baggage to come in and was very much depressed to read of Gen. Buckner's death[52]. Somehow it seems that when you arrive at the point where victory is in sight, as in this campaign, death seems even more tragic—& sort of unnecessary.

Just to cheer myself up—did you read that poem in last week's Time called "Death, be not Proud," by John Donne, I believe. He wrote, as they said, without fear. Made me feel much better about the whole thing.

Margie gave me this poem, "The Japs Theme Song." It's real silly. I thought you might get a kick out of it.

There were two letters here waiting for me. It was almost too good to be true, as I hadn't expected any. I'll have to apologize to that imaginary mail clerk I'd been complaining about a couple of weeks ago. I agree, darling, that it's no fun to think you have to write any certain number of letters. I hope nothing I ever say will make you feel that way. Spontaneous letters are always much better anyway, don't you think?

This girl I mentioned last night (Her name is Marcella [Bloecher].) took Margie & me to a night club near Antigo,[53] which is about 25 mi. north of W'berg. It's a place where we used to go to dance on special occasions when someone had a car back in high school. Last time I was there was with Franklin, one of the last weekends I was home before he went into the Army. It brought back pleasant memories.

Also, while we were there, a corporal from your Division & his girl came in. He was all dressed up in his "pretty blue panties with red stripes down the seams," and looked at least <u>half</u> as handsome as you, dear. They only stayed a few minutes, but for the rest of the evening I wasn't exactly conscious of what was going on. Entirely too often Margie would snap her fingers in front of my eyes & bring me back to earth.

I gather that you have been going quite deeply into the argument of high school vs. college teaching. My very unprofessional opinion would be that you are right about a high school teacher being too much hampered by form & detail. I know that Peg would agree with you. While she has enjoyed teaching this year, she has often complained about the tedium of correcting grammatical errors, for instance. In fact, I think she said once that she had practically abandoned it as a hopeless task. More about that later. I'd better go to bed, darn it!

Goodnight, my darling,

Marian

&

June 19 '45

Hi, Darling,

This is the best part of the day, when I can just sit & talk to you—even tho you're not here & it's all done by airmail.

I listened to a speech Eisenhower gave tonight at a banquet in New York. You would have liked it, I think. His sincerity is endearing. He reminded everyone, as Stillwell also has, that it's a long war in the Pacific yet. Another thing he said which I liked was that practicality and idealism are not necessarily antagonistic. We can be both, he said, and I am glad some of our leaders believe it.

Which reminds me of that awful letter my mother wrote about the ration points. I'd hardly stepped into the house Sat. night before she beamed and said, "Well, what did you think of my letter?" So I told her. "Just because they have to eat potato soup in Yugoslavia is no reason why we should have to," was her response. I said no one had asked us to & it <u>was</u> a good reason why we shouldn't complain about the minor shortages we have. By that time Margie was laughing at me for being so angry, so we changed the subject.

My dad says you have to be a Democrat to get anything from the ration boards. No doubt there is some truth in that, but it is so beside the point. It condemns abuse of the system but not the system itself. That's the trouble with the local views on politics. They are so concerned with petty grievances that they can't see the broad purposes & the long-time benefits. I seem to be somewhat the opposite of the character in "Going My Way." When I was 18, I thought my parents were very wise. Perhaps I shouldn't say that. I really appreciate more now the things they've done for me & mean to me, but I am continually more amazed at how small their world is. But then it takes a great deal of time to read & learn a larger viewpoint & my dad, at least, has never had much time to spare, I suppose.

Have been reading over your letter—for about the 6th time. That "In replying refer to No." at the top of the pages always makes me laugh. It's so incongruous.

I haven't seen "Dorian Gray." It hasn't been at any of the Chicago theaters yet. Have been curious about it, though. The story is interesting, what little I know of it.

Have been thinking about those unfortunate traits you say you have that I don't know anything about. Darling, you'd never make a good salesman, but then I'm not particularly fond of salesmen, except that, in a way, they are entertaining. I suspect that I know a lot more about you than you think I do & I hope that doesn't sound conceited. It usually takes me a long time to realize what people are like, but what I think about you now is quite different than what I thought, for instance, last summer, so perhaps it's right. I know that you are stubborn & moody & perhaps a number of other things, & I love you as much because of it as in spite of it. You are also wonderful.

'Night, Sweetheart—

Marian

✤

June 21, 1945

Dear Lt. Sweetheart,

I thought I'd have lots of time to write to you at work today, but Paul came in—I never know what to expect of him. I just called his wife yesterday to tell her he would be in New Orleans today! He said Chicago was 200 miles closer to where he was yesterday, so he decided to come home instead.

Thought I'd start a letter anyway while I have a few minutes at the switchboard as I'm going to a "free trial" Spanish lesson tonight. Will tell you all about it later.

Does this article on China partially answer your desire for information on the subject? It is a good article, I think, but it sort of makes me feel, as we used to believe, that wars are always fought for "interests" rather than ideals. Why should it have to be counter to our interests to have a strong central Asia dominated by Russia? Not because they have a political system different from ours, but, as I see it, because it would give them the power to get more wealth than we could, a power which they ought not to abuse, but which we would ourselves abuse if we had it and therefore assume (with good reason) that they would, also—Is this just a crazy idea, or do you have the same reaction?

I am very curious about these arrests the FBI has made. There is a book on China by Mark Gayn which I've been wanting to read, & I am all the more interested now. Wish it were possible to know what & whom to believe.

Just had a little conversation with Julia on h.s. teaching. She has a nephew who taught math for a yr. or two & he says you have to "mold" their ideas with a <u>club</u>. Merle's Marine Corps training will be a big help. Maybe he wouldn't appreciate that, hm?

I took that roll of film to the drug store last night & it will take a week or ten days to have it developed. I just hope there is something on it. I had forgotten that you have to wind the film back to the other side of the camera before you take it out; so I had to rewind it afterward. Fortunately I was doing all this in the closet. The big question is: Was it dark enough there? Franklin explained all that stuff to me in detail the night before he left. He said he didn't know why he bothered because I could probably figure it out for myself. I must have been thinking the same thing, darn it, because I forgot most of what he told me & have been finding out for myself—the hard way!

Mother told me in a letter last night that she had a notice from the War Dept. Sat. that they presume Franklin is dead. She didn't tell me about it when I was home because she didn't want to spoil the weekend for us! And here the main reason I went was because I thought they'd probably have some such report & I might be able to cheer them up a little. Well, perhaps it had the same effect even tho we didn't talk about it. I like the phrase, "presumed dead." As long as it is merely a presumption, (sp?) regardless of what happened, he has a sort of immortality—like "I'll be seeing you, in every lovely summer's day." He has that, of course, no matter what you say, but saying it that way makes it a little more real. I guess that's awfully sentimental.

Back there where the color of the ink changes, I was interrupted & am now finishing this at home—after the Spanish, which was delightful, and three letters from you, which were even better, darling.

That Spanish is going to be so much fun! Or so it seemed tonight. Allen-Gomez is the name of the school & it is just a block north of the Blackhawk on Wabash. We walked past it that night. They use the conversational method of teaching, which I really believe is best. The only disadvantage is that I won't be able to read for two months & can't write for four or five. Beginning the first Thurs. in July, I'll have class each Thurs. from 6 to 8 & Fri. from 8 to 9. Also on Friday they have a social hour at 9 with singing & dancing & gaiety. I'm going tomorrow night & will tell you all about it. It sounds wonderful. Wish you could come with me.

The letters tonight were the three you mailed June 15, including that one from May 29. You said you hoped they'd make me feel better about June 22. Since this is the 21st, it was a pretty good guess. They made me very happy, darling, and all is forgiven—as if there were anything to forgive.

It seemed another coincidence that you should mention "A Tree Grows in Brooklyn" in one of your letters tonight. I went to see it last night, & I loved it. Did you ever go to a movie like that alone & walk home afterward in a mood that made you feel as if the sky was so near you could touch it? I felt like that last night, so I walked for about half an hour along a quiet street, just dreaming. I knew you would sympathize with Kathie. I did, in a way, too, but Johnny — In spite of his poverty, he was wealthy in the things that are important, & although he broke their hearts, he gave to those who loved him things to be treasured more than pennies. It made me think that to possess anything, you don't need to hold it in the palm of your hand. In fact, you are apt to lose it that way, as Kathie almost lost Francie. Reminds me of a related quotation from Dorothy Parker which I copied a long time ago: "Love is like quicksilver in the hand. Leave the fingers open & it stays in the palm. Clutch it & it darts away."

That's enough of a sermon for tonight.

This clipping about Eleanor Roosevelt reminds me of Jim Brown again. He claims to have met her at a tea she gave for some "youth congress" or something. He says that she remarked, "I just can't believe that all you nice young men are Communists!" That, of course, convinced him that she was hopelessly beyond the pale.

You mentioned in your letter of May 29 the story of Don & the M.P. Don used to work for Cal when he had his own studio. I told the story to Cal & he said Don was always a "wrong guy" before & didn't see why he should expect things to be different in the Army.

I think I have a fair conception of why military life cannot be democratic, but go ahead & explain it to me. I'd like to hear your ideas on why the officers have special privileges. And what is a "head?" Or are you talking about the ordinary kind?

Darling, I wish you were here, as you wanted to be, with your head in my lap. I'd tell you anything you'd like to hear. I'd _even_ be quiet if you wanted me to. Remember on the train how you scolded me for not going to sleep when I said I was going to? It was much more fun to stay awake. Gene, why didn't you just hit me over the head & take me with you to New Jersey & back to California, too? We've wasted so much time & I love you so much.

Goodnight, dearest,

Marian

❖

June 22 '45

My darling Gene:

This is going to be very brief, as I have only a few minutes before it's time to go to school. Just want to tell you that I wish I could write a long, long letter —

as long as my thoughts of you. But that might take forever, so I'd better be careful about making such statements.

Had three letters from you tonight, the latest dated June 17. That makes a total of 11 this week, & a beautiful total it is! Darling, I'm not much of a sceptic, & I am convinced that you are in love. I hope, too, that when you come home it will be the same as our letters. It ought to be easy, don't you think?

That is good news about your opportunity to go to school under the GI Bill of Rights. Four years seems like a long time, but it would be well worth while. It will be real wonderful to call you Dr. Sweetheart. How does it sound to you, dear?

I'd better go. Until tomorrow, then —

All my love, Marian

✧

June 23 '45

My darling Gene:

I hope this letter will make sense. I'm so tired today I hardly know what I'm doing. It's worth it, though, as I had a very interesting time last night at the Spanish school "social gathering." There were many unusual people there. I met only a few, of course, but one in particular I want to tell you about. He is an exotic-looking young lawyer [Alfred Castro Lee] from Central America with whom I danced most of the evening. He looks rather more Oriental than Latin, but he says many Latin American Indians look that way. He's a marvelous dancer. With that and the several Spanish phrases I learned, it seemed just like being a guest in another country for the evening. I wish I could have shared it with you, darling.

Have been reading over some of your last letters. It seemed as if the week went so fast that I hardly had time to read them at leisure — much less answer them all. And they are so nice, Gene.

That was an interesting story about the P-51 flying below a bomber's wing for protection.

I really do feel sorry for Edwards. Reminds me of what Franklin wrote when he found that one of his last girl friends had been married. "Well, sis, you'd better start looking around for some cute little 12 yr. old for me." He also said it was a good thing he was in love with an airplane, which makes me particularly sorry that Edwards hates it so over there on Guam.

Seems funny to have you talk about Murph being there. Maybe I ought to start calling my Murph by her first name, Gale. I really like Gale better, but got in the habit of saying Murph because the other kids always did.

I get a kick out of your "filing system" for my letters. I have all of yours, too, but in no semblance of order, unfortunately. What is a field scarf?

Please don't feel embarrassed about "Winged Victory," dear. There is no reason why you should I would not have expected that you'd feel as sentimental about it as I did, and while I hate to admit it, I can see that it was not exactly a "great" picture.

I'd better go out & get something to eat. It's after 9:00 and I haven't had dinner yet. Might as well mail this and start another letter later.

This is one of the phrases I learned last night. I don't know how to write it. This is phonetic spelling, to be pronounced as in Latin, which I believe is the same as Spanish. Astra verte otra ves — It sounds pretty. Can you translate it?

All my love, dearest,

Marian

❀

June 24 '45

Gene, darling,

This has been the first really warm day we've had this "summer." Tonight there is a cool breeze & it's very nice. There is nothing I would like so much as to be sitting somewhere along the lakefront looking at the moon, with you holding my hand, darling.

I am glad you liked Corwin. I disagree with you that no one profits by war. Not spiritually, of course, which is the only important thing, but materially. I know of many people who have suffered no personal loss, have been in no way directly affected by the war, and have profited much financially. Most of those I know would have preferred peace, but there are a few selfish ones who are happy about it. One worthless character from W'berg actually said to my mother that he would not care if the war lasted another seven years because he was "doing all right." Damn him! I wish I had been there. He would have heard a verbal barrage the like of which I've never even thought up before. Apparently the stories you hear about such incidents are not pure fiction. These are little people, of course, but perhaps among those who have power there are the same types.

I do not believe, either, that there are born fighters. Undoubtedly there are many cruel men in Germany & Japan, but I cannot believe they were born so. Something has made them that way — quite possibly the very system they fought to extend. It is much too complicated to understand.

I wish you could have heard the philosophy of that Costa Rican lawyer I told you about yesterday. The fact that his ideals were like ours gave me a stronger belief in the brotherhood of man, transcending race. "I will give you two words to remember," he said, "Courage and Faith." From the very little I learned about him, it was obvious that he had remembered them well.

I hope I'll see those pictures the "Life" photographers took over there. Saw one not long ago of Tyrone Power. Don't try to tell me that he's the most handsome man in the Marine Corps. I know better!

I'm glad you enjoyed my dad's letter. It's fun to be able to send you things like that and know that you will be interested.

Have been reading what you said about the sermon you heard last Sunday & thinking how similar it was to those two words, "Courage & Faith." What is the minister's name?

Guess I'll see if I can finish a piece of "Time" tonight to send you.

I love you, dear.

Marian

❁

19 June 1945
[Guam]

Darling,

Really have some news today for you. It has been a bitter day in a few respects. Wish I'd received a letter from you but somehow there hasn't been any for 4 days now. Hope you have received mine because I have been writing — and I know you have been too.

I am probably going to be transferred to the 4th or 5th Divisions with 5 others from the company. It is pretty certain tonight and I am rather sad about it. I do hate to leave mainly because all my friends are here — Merle most of all. But it is just one of those things that you can expect in the service. I dont know exactly what kind of duty I'll have yet but sorta hope for the Signal Company but not message center.

20 June I applied for the 5th Division and guess I've got it. Will not leave for a few days and wish you'd keep writing here. I'll get my new address to you as soon as possible.

Much Love, darling

Gene
Please excuse the dirty stationery.

❁

21 June 1945

Dearest Marian,

If I say that I have been busy packing and getting ready to move, I hope you realize that these circumstances prevented me from writing regularly the last few days. Just when I felt the worst about leaving the 3d division, I received your extra nice letter of June 9. You are a darling—but specifically—you do have the ability or something to say the <u>right</u> things at the right time when I want to hear them most. Your essay on security was <u>wonderful</u> and as clear probably, as putting the feeling of love into words can be. I decided I'd let Merle read that letter because I have been talking quite a bit about you and I am also leaving. He was much impressed too and came to the conclusion that perhaps we are suited for each other. He will never hardly make any definite statement so it actually surprised me. Leaving him undoubtedly will be the hardest thing as far as this transfer is concerned.

The Signal officer called us in yesterday and said he was sorry to see us go but nothing could be done as far as he was concerned. We had all done good work but the 4th and 5th needed batallion comm. officers and we were the newest in the company (except for a fellow named Callens) We then picked the division we would rather go to and I chose the 5th. I believe they did a better job on Iwo and I think I know several fellows there in the Signal company. I am quite sure I will not go to the Signal Co. however. Will probably get a batallion comm. platoon but that suits me O.K. More later when I get there. We are going to a beautiful island—

I received 3 letters from you yesterday after a bad 2 weeks but they did come at an opportune time. There are questions to answer that I cant answer at present but I <u>will</u> soon. The reference I made to the cartoon was merely the fact that she has found the way to his heart by doing the things he wants to do. As an unofficial observer it has struck me that all girls have it in their power to get a man to fall in love with them.

Several hours have elapsed and I better end this now. I will write the first chance I get.

I love you,

Gene

June 25 '45
[Chicago]

Darling,

I <u>am</u> sorry you have to transfer. Can surely understand how you feel about it, especially about Merle. I hope you will have an assignment you like better than Msg. Center & that will compensate somewhat. Of course, you always find interesting people wherever you go, but really <u>good</u> friends are rare & it is hard to leave them. Will you be on the same island?

As you see, I had a letter from Peg at last. I think it is rather interesting, to put it mildly, that a letter from Washington dated June 21 and a letter from Guam dated June 20 should arrive the same day. I am sending her letter to you as much to encourage you about your typing as because I think you might enjoy it. See how good you are, darling?

Her job sounds interesting, don't you think? I am amused at her saying the UNRRA is young & vital & fast-moving. That is definitely not what the reporters, etc., call it. I hope she is more right than they, however.

All this delight in Wash. as a city makes me wish she'd stay there long enough so that I might visit her sometime. Have you ever been there, Gene?

Gale left today for New York and Connecticut on her vacation. She is going to visit some relatives there. It will be rather lonesome without her. She will be back about July 5, I think. Ed & I persuaded her to take the Pathfinder, which, as you probably know, is similar to "our" train.

One of the girls at work had lunch today with a P-38 pilot who had been lost over Germany & reported killed about Xmas time. That was the last she had heard until he called her this morning. Wouldn't that be wonderful?

I must write that "long letter" to Peg now. See you tomorrow, Sweetheart.

All my love, Marian

P.S. The maid threw away our paper today before I had a chance to cut out Barnaby. Are you enjoying him, dear?

⚜

Margaret Borrebek to Marian:

June 21, 1945

Dearest Marian,

I am rapidly acquiring your habit of typing a letter when there is nothing to do. By that you can guess that I am working in an office. My present position is as a typist with UNRRA the new international organization which is trying to relieve the problems of peace after a war. It will change in a few days to that of a teletypist with the same organization. It is a marvelous place to work. It has only been in operation about a year so it is young and vital and everything moves fast. Also there is a very fine feeling of non-racial prejudice, internationalism, liberalism, and you can imagine how I bask in that. In fact I am very happy here, and I like Washington as much as I detested Chicago. There is such a difference. Here if anyone pushes on a bus (and they are just as crowded as Chicago), they are looked at with disfavor. Most of the people seem to be much more cultured than in the MW. And the city has so many beautiful buildings and it is planned with an eye to the beauty and comfort of a place to live in. There are trees on the streets of even the busiest and every few blocks there is a little park with a statue to some famous man. The eating places are crowded but they have marvelous food, and it is much cheaper than in Chi. The average price of the three-course meal is rarely above $1 and more often about .55 to .85.

We had a fine trip. It didn't take long at all, I suppose because we were so interested in the scenery. We met some very nice people on the bus also. One man that Edna sat with owns the Schroeder Hotels in Wisconsin. We were very dirty but not too tired.

The best piece of good luck we have had is Karl, Ray's brother. He is wonderful. . . he got us a room in the same private house he lives in and it is lovely. It has twin beds, a comfortable chair, an uncomfortable chair, a dressing table, a fireplace, two chests of drawers and five windows and two doors. It is papered in blue and has white and pink accessories. And for the price of $5 apiece. Karl has a phonograph and about a five foot stack of records and two shelves of books. He works from 4-12 these last two weeks so he lets us use his records and books while he is gone. And he takes us everywhere and loans us money. What we would do without him I don't know. We also have very good discussions. I wish you weren't so taken with Gene and I would suggest you as a wife for him. Karl, Ray and I are all looking for a good one for him (Karl least of all!)

Tonight I am going to a modern dance class sponsored by UNRRA. Sunday night we went to a Watergate concert. This is a band shell out in the water. You can guess how unbelievably lovely it is. There is a concert almost every night here. On Fridays we go up to the Capitol steps where we can sit and listen to an Army Air Corps band which is very good.

Ray is still in Germany and very unhappy. Conditions must be terrible. He says there is no end to stealing, prostitution, anger, bad conditions, etc. He drives around a Gerneal [sic] who takes a nurse out every night. Everyone of the soldiers gets drunk on the slightest provocation. Such atmosphere is not good for him.

I had a letter from Mike yesterday and he is in Brazil and is going to get me some <u>silk</u> stockings!

Well, this little bit that I have written was most refreshing relief from boredom and now I see that there are some cables for me to record so I must desist for the moment.

You can see I am not too hot a typist.

Edna is assistant manager of a cafeteria in the Munitions Building & supervises negro girls. She has no trouble with them & says they are cute.

I have met some very interesting people. One was an American girl who was in a German concentration camp for 1-1/2 yrs. She is very interesting. Another is an Austrian girl who came here 2-1/2 yrs. ago. She works in my office & I like her very much.

I am learning German from Karl. It doesn't seem very difficult so far.

Well, it is getting late. I shall expect a long letter soon & I will be getting into regular habits soon.

Love, Peggy

Is Murph still single. I'm listening to some lovely Ballet Music Karl has. It is the music in many of the Ballet Russe nos.

❖

June 27, 1945
[Chicago]

Gene, darling,

I shall have to begin this with a very deeply felt, "I love you," because all the rest seems relatively unimportant. However, it does make a letter: so—

Your letter of the 21st came today & also one from Merle, which pleased me much more than he would believe. Obviously he is just as fond of you as you are of him. Knowing that, I feel that his writing as he did is one of the nicest compliments I've ever had.

Incidentally, you have now irrevocably lost all arguments on the subject of who is the handsomest officer in the Marine Corps. Merle agrees with me that you are, Lt. Sweetheart, and please note that <u>he</u> says "officer," which includes a wider field than the previous term, "Lt." Give up?

Merle also told me that you are presumably in Hawaii. Darling, <u>tomorrow</u> I am going to inquire about those civil service jobs. If we were there together only two days, it would be worth it. Would you agree?

I had two tickets for the play "Dear Ruth" tonight. Gale's mother went with me. It was the cleverest story! Perhaps you've read about it—or even seen it in New York. The kid sister reminded me of Peg, & also somewhat of you & me, because she was always crusading for her very liberal ideals. It was funny.

I started writing this at a quarter past twelve midnight & am almost afraid to look at the clock now. Better go to bed.

Goodnight, darling,

Marian

❖

June 28, 1945

Dear Lt. Sweetheart,

As I promised last night, I did inquire today about civil service (Surprised?) and found out where to go to learn all the details. So I am going down Saturday afternoon. I keep reminding myself that this is all a wild, fantastic dream, but it's such a nice one—

Had a letter tonight from my friend Jane in Seattle. Her husband is on his way to someplace in the Pacific & she is coming home in a week or two. Eddie is in some Army construction unit, working in the message center. Odd, isn't it?

I'm glad you liked my "essay" on security, darling.

Had to laugh at your saying you think all girls have the ability to make a man fall in love with them. Don't you think it depends somewhat on which man and which girl? I have observed that it often works very well the other way, too.

Fri., the 29th—

I got those pictures tonight. They are all millimeter size, of course, so I'll have to send the film back again to get some larger prints. Some of them look fairly good. If I can get them to block out parts of the film, it will improve the composition considerably. That camera is sort of hard to aim with. I'll send you a sample of one of the worst prints, which will convince you. Gale took this one.

Did I ever tell you about the snapshot of Franklin that Cal was going to have enlarged & retouched for me? It's finally finished & he mailed the two prints to me the other day. I'm very much pleased with them. When I send you these other pictures, I'll send one of the smaller prints of this. Perhaps you won't be much interested, but I just *have* to show it to you.

Cal addressed the envelope to "Miss Marion Smith"—with an "o." Five years I've known him & he still doesn't remember. Darling, I really appreciate you!

The headlines in tonight's paper said something about GI's hanging 3 Nazis & being convicted of murder. That is Something, isn't it? It seems a little ridiculous to convict them for doing exactly what they have been trained to do for so long, but undoubtedly it is the only way to keep the situation in hand.

There's an interesting article in the new Time about Guam. I won't send it to you because by the time it catches up with you, you'll probably have seen it.

It seems to me that there isn't much sense in this letter. Better quit. I've been going around in a daze entitled, "Gene is in Hawaii."

I <u>am</u> in love with you, darling.

Marian

⚜

June 30, 1945

My darling Gene,

As you will assume from the address, I have your letter of the 25th. Imagine you are pleased about being in Asco, aren't you?

I wish I could have been with you that night & let you cry on my shoulder. I know it is always hard the first few days. Hope you are feeling better about it now.

I imagine this letter may reach you sooner than the last few I have written, so perhaps I should repeat some of the news.

Merle wrote to me, as he told you he would, and his letter was <u>very</u> nice. He must be a wonderful person, Gene.

He told me he understood you would be in Hawaii now. Needless to say, I am delighted about that & have been trying to find out about civil service there. I learned where to go to apply & intended to go down this aft., but did not have the chance. I'll take my aft. off as soon as Paul goes out of town again & see about it then. As I said in a previous letter, if we were there together only two days, it would be worth it.

My dad sent me some of his strawberries today. They are slightly squashed, but look very good. I'm sorry Murph is not here to have some, too. (She's in N. Y. on her vacation.)

More news you may not have heard is that I have started to study Spanish, the conversational way. It's fun. At a social hour they had last Fri., I met a young lawyer from Costa Rica who is very interesting. I wish you could meet him, also. He came over last night & took me to dinner & I learned quite a bit more about him. Works for a law firm on LaSalle St. & is in charge of all matters re. international law. I had read what Sumner Welles' book said about Costa Rica (It is the most democratic & cultured of all Central Am. nations.) & was telling him about it—so he wanted to read it also. Two of the country's former presidents (both liberals) are friends of his. Amazing? All this extra education I had not expected from my Spanish course.

Gene, I hope all this does not worry you. It shouldn't, believe me, dear. In a way I feel as guilty about enjoying it as I do about seeing Cal occasionally. Sometimes I really wish you would insist that I should never have dates with anyone else, & then I wouldn't. It would simplify life considerably. I like people, though, and I like to listen to their ideas & their ambitions. Unfortunately, most interesting, thinking people are men. Except where you are concerned, that makes me sorry to be a woman because it complicates matters so.

Do you understand, darling? I'm sure you do understand my interest in people because you have the same interest. I hope the rest is equally clear.

I miss you, dear, and I love you very much.

Marian

&

Third Marine Division
22 June, 1945

Dear Marian,

This, I know will come very much as a surprise and, I assure you, it is not a favorite practice of mine to write to those I do not know. Still I can't honestly say that I consider you a stranger. With Gene I talked of your cross country train ride—smiled at your irritation toward "Time" and, probably because you have in Gene a very able and enthusiastic sponsor, learned to have a great deal of admiration and feeling of friendship for you.

As you know Gene and I are no longer together. Though he has been gone only a short time, things for me are much less pleasant because of his leaving.

It is unfortunate that in a unit of this size there are few who combine the proper amount of clear, serious minded thinking with a well balanced sense of humor. However, I strongly suspect, unless I've seriously misinterpreted you, that we could easily form a sort of "mutual admiration league" for him which is hardly my intention. I do want you to know that you and your letters mean a great deal more to him than possibly you realize. He is having considerable trouble fighting off a certain amount of cynicism and pessimism, and your sensible approach to political difficulties is encouraging. Also, forgive me if this sounds sticky or presumptuous, your loyalty-sweetness-and all those other feminine intangibles, are very necessary and gratifying to him.

The real purpose of my writing is that I thought you would be interested in knowing that we are no longer together. He is now, I understand, in Hawaii. He knows of my intention to write and when I last saw him I assured him that I concur with his (or was it your?) opinion that he is "undoubtedly the handsomest officer in the Marine Corps" and intended to tell you as much.

Sincerely, your friend,
Merle

6

"How soon can you come home?"

WITH CENSORSHIP STILL *on, there were few specifics of my transfer to the Fifth Marine Division that I could tell Marian. I had flown out of North Field on Guam on a military transport that landed on Oahu in the Hawaiian Islands. After a short stay I boarded another plane for the trip to the big island of Hawaii, where the Fifth Division was based. As my letters make plain, I hated new assignments. I said I would not grumble, but did plenty of it in those first few days. As the summer wore on, we speculated on whether the Russians would enter the war with Japan. By the end of August the United States had dropped the atomic bomb and Japan had surrendered. Now for the first time Marian and I could count on my return.*

25 June
[Hawaii]

Darling,
Gosh I'm lonesome and tired tonight. Oh, I could cry—It's always that way at a new organization and it will pass. My new address is on the envelope. I probably will like this better after awhile but I hated to leave the 3rd.

Lights are practically out so I'd better close—More tomorrow—I love you that I do

Gene

Later I am in Asco. Would like a nice sweet letter from you about now. More tonight

27 June

Hello darling,

Guess I can't look for mail for a week yet. They will eventually forward my letters from the 3rd but that will take time. The mail here sometimes comes through in 4 days which is rather remarkable.

The light is beginning to shine thru as I am almost situated and getting to know the ropes. I repeat tho that I hate to move and go through the business of getting into a new outfit and meeting new people. In fact, after all these new, practically stateside experiences, it feels much like coming overseas all over again. The biggest advantage is a private jeep system because there are several places to go. Greatest disadvantage is the moldy camp and poor living conditions—Oh well—remind me not to complain anymore—

There is talk of an 18 or 21 mo. rotation for comm. officers but I doubt it very much. The only thing to actually look forward to now is the end of the war or 27 mo. I have 19 men with me, mostly N.C.O's because Jasco (or Asco now) was designed to be a crack outfit. Can't say much about what we do of course but it is the same organization Merle was in back in the 3rd Division. I wish now that I had tried to get into 3rd Asco and I'd at least be with my friends. Incidently I saw Britt, a friend of mine from the 3rd.

28 June,

Had better finish this before the mail goes out this noon. We are carrying out a training program and supposed to be present at all the lectures given for the men. That usually takes up a great deal of our time.

I hope I start receiving some of your letters soon. It seems that patience is a prime necessity these days, I miss you very much darling but that isn't news any longer.

All my Love, Gene

⚜

28 June 1945

Dearest Marian.

They say things look blackest just before the dawn. If so, dawn must be at hand. Oh brother, take me back to the 3rd Div! This camp is really terrific—to the three of us it looks more like a concentration affair. We have finally got squared away a little and are able to see what is going on—if you can see through the dust. It is cold and dusty and I hate every inch of it but I guess there are some advantages.

We did make some nice stops enroute and I have had a banana split—saw some women (white), went to a dance, had a <u>hot</u> shower—and saw some drug stores. (All of which was strange to me there) The other 2 fellows are Lt.'s Demmy & Callens.

Things have happened so fast in the last 4 days that I doubt if I could have kept you informed even if I had been able to write everything that occurred. Hope you can see the light shinning thru some of my recent activities even tho censorship prevents me from saying practically anything. At any rate I am now in the 5th Marine Div. and specifically in Jasco or as it has been changed— Asco—assault signal co. and the same work Merle is doing in the 3rd. I undoubtedly will like the whole affair better after awhile because it can't be as bad as it seems at present. I have my own private Jeep and there are places to go. The food is decidedly better—fresh milk for instance, and plenty of fresh meat.

I will be far more busy than I was in the signal company but I won't neglect <u>you</u>. Methinks I will feel much better after I receive your letters again. Well enough grumbling—

Haven't accomplished much in the line of intellectual thinking or the likes in the last few days. Did get a 25 June "Time" several days ago and read it through and last night somehow got into a discussion of Liberal Arts vs. Engineering. Demmy is an engineer and met a fellow from Huchens' [*sic*] Chicago who is rather sharp. Demmy said the little piece about our "future alliance with Japan" so I think he probably is a good engineer. I don't care much for him.

After a few days and we get settled I'll be able to concentrate a little more on these letters. I sadly miss Merle Borrowman so it will be up to you to keep me out of the rut I otherwise will probably be in. Meanwhile darling,

All My Love, Gene

⚜

29 June 1945

Hello darling,

Time this noon for a short letter before chow. Mail only goes out once a day here but I believe that we will find the mail service in general much better than the last place I was stationed. Various events have occurred to make this place not only tolerable but I believe in time I will like it better than the 3rd.

Last night George (Callens) Demmy and I made a "speed run" to a nearby town on a liberty. Tho we didn't do anything very exciting the mere fact of a change did us all good. We had a steak which was wonderful and some changes from camp routine which we appreciated even more. I do not mean to be purposely vague but censorship is more of a problem. I have always meant to tell you that Peg was right in what she said about officer censorship.

The weather has been a little better lately because the wind has died down. We are in probably the worst location as far as this island is concerned because on the whole there are many parts which are beautiful. Surprisingly we use 3 blankets at night and during the day it is quite warm. There is so much to tell you that I am forbidden to write about but perhaps after the war I will remember some of it. Wish as usual that the end would come soon and I could stop working for the Marine Corps. But at least I can thank the service for the fact that I met you so it hasn't all been in vain. More tomorrow sweetheart and meanwhile

All My Love, Gene

✣

30 June 1945
Central Pacific

Darling,

Just finished censoring and in the process waded through some pretty passionate affairs. In contrast, mine seem somewhat similar to Report of the Nation (or is it "on") as far as sentimentality is concerned. This censorship is really worthwhile now because I do it for my own team and of course I am getting to know the fellows. In general it seems that the ability to write decent letters is somewhat a measure of their usefulness as communication men. Don't know why exactly—

Was rather sorry to see Stettinius go out as Sec. of State according to last evening's paper but I don't know enough about [James] Byrnes to realize if any drastic changes will be made in our foreign policy. I wish that Hull was 20 years younger or Roosevelt still alive. Either one would be good. What do you think of Byrnes?

Perhaps you have heard of this series of movies they are showing the men in the service entitled "Why We Fight" Well anyway one of the best parts is the "Battle of Russia" I saw it today for the third time. I think you would enjoy it very much—couldn't help but think of you all through it. Two of the other seven parts are the "Battle of Britain," and "The Japanese People." Each part lasts for almost two hours.

To change the subject again—I heard a rather interesting story from George the other day. There is a fellow named Bill Herwig in the 3rd Engineers who I met once long ago. This Lt. went to U.S.C. and for his senior thesis made a study of the life of Charles II of England. When he left for overseas his wife became interested in Charles II also and told him she was going to write a book on that particular period of English history. The story goes that he didn't pay much attention to this, but suddenly one day the book comes through the mail. It was the rough copy dedicated to him—the book "Forever Amber." Needless to say he is having a hard time living that down as there are at least a 100 copies making the rounds in the 3rd Division. Forever Under <u>was</u> very clever.

Saturday Morning.
   Last night we saw "Gaslight" for the 3rd time but it is a good picture. This morning we had an inspection by the C.O—Lt Col. Power who was a classmate of mine at Ft. Monmouth. He is leaving and the Ex. off will be the C.O. He was also at New Jersey the same time—This afternoon and tomorrow Callens, Demmy & are going on a tour of the island. This civilization still impresses us after the lack of it for 8 mo. Actually it only makes me realize how much I'd like to see home—and you in particular.

All of my Love, Gene

❀

July 1, 1945
[Chicago]

Hello, my darling,
   Here is quite a collection of clippings for you. I've been spending the afternoon reading. I read about the same way I write letters—reading perhaps one-eighth of the time, thinking or dreaming the rest.
   I feel very optimistic about the world today (definitely unlike my father) and that feeling has been added to by some of these articles; for instance, the review of the book "The Anatomy of Peace" and Grafton's "Charter Creates a New Orbit of Human Activity." I like particularly what he says about living an international life. Sounds fascinating, doesn't it? These are really exciting times we live in, Gene. I think that people everywhere are aware of the need & the importance of freedom & justice as they have not been for a long time. It reminds me that several years ago, at the beginning of the war, Dr. Finnie, a Presbyterian minister I used to like to hear in Milw., said that he believed this greatest conflict in the world's history would necessarily result in the greatest effort ever made to assure future peace. It may not succeed, of course, but the greater the effort, the better the chance for success. I'm glad that in the "Anatomy of Peace," Mr. Reves says that the world state <u>could</u> come by voluntary union of the peoples of the world themselves. I do not believe it is possible in our lifetime, but that is not important.

Perhaps this would be an appropriate place to tell you about another lesson I learned from this Costa Rican. "I am very ambitious," he said, "but if I do not succeed, I will not be disappointed. I must be realistic." I think that is an excellent philosophy. The Russians, apparently, do not have a monopoly on realism.

Guess I'd better go out & find some food. I think I'll go to Grant Park tonight & listen to the symphony. I wish you could come along, darling, and hold my hand. That would make it perfect.

All my love,

Marian

❖

July 2, 1945

My darling Gene:

The letter I wrote Saturday, which was the first to your new address, came back tonight for another postage stamp. It made me quite disgusted with myself as I had particularly wanted to expedite that letter, assuming it might be the first you would have rec'd for sometime, and it might have been there tomorrow if I hadn't been so careless.

I hope that when you do get some mail, you'll feel better. Your letters of the 26th & 27th came today.

It seems that we are alike in still another way. There is nothing I dread so much as being in an entirely new situation & having to meet new people—particularly when I've been quite happy in the last one. It's really sort of a foolish way to be because new situations & new friends mean broader experience & a richer life—whether it's good or bad, we do profit by it. It's a good thing that feeling of strangeness is temporary.

Are Demmy & Callens in Asco also?

I had been wondering if Merle was right about your being in Hawaii as it seemed strange that you couldn't say so. However, your mention of Britt confirms what he said. Britt went to Pearl Harbor before, didn't he?—on that "duration" assignment you decided you didn't want?

I don't see how you could possibly be much busier than you were in the Signal Co. I was always amazed that you could get so much work done & see so many movies besides. I'm willing to believe almost anything now about the proficiency of Marines, especially that stuff about giving the moon "permission to turn on its beams."

Darling, I miss you tonight, if it's possible, even more than usual. "How do I love thee? Let me count the ways." I shall count them & tell you all about them some day.

Goodnight, sweetheart,

Marian

✧

2 July 1945
Central Pacific [Hawaii]

Hello darling,

As I said before in my other letter, I received 2 letters from you today which made me feel very good. I don't care much for the long break between letters such as when I transferred here to the 5th but of course nothing can be done about it. As usual your letters were delightful and succeeded in setting me off with a "glow" that takes a little time to wear off.

I'm glad that you appreciated me remembering Mar 4th and it is one of those things I like to remember. I am constantly sorry that I seem to remember less and less about you which has been in direct proportion to my liking you more and more. I am glad that "Love" does not respect distance. The analogy of the Russians was merely mentioned to show that it is not always necessary to make a lot of wild (?) statements in order to prove they are in sympathy with a particular thing. Likewise even tho I hesitated to say, "I love you" it didn't necessarily mean that I didn't.

Also along the same line—some people today feel that if Russia would only declare war upon Japan, everything would be fine and all our problems with Russia would be over. Actually it goes deeper than that I believe, and even tho the Soviet doesn't enter the Pacific war I shall continue to regard them with an open mind and respect them. As this anti-Russian feeling comes out in the open among Americans, I sympathize with almost everything the Russians do—or don't do—Our policy toward them when Roosevelt lived was fair and just and probably will continue while Truman is in but how will it be after the next presidential election? Stalin is probably wondering too.

Had to laugh at your mother and the "red points"—at least it shows she is thinking. Some people you know—just grumble. I agree with you about the system and the abuse of the system. My feelings too, are sometime strained when I think of the folks back home and their little petty things which bother them. My mother is much that way and as a result I can't write to her or hold a decent conversation with them while I am home. Unfortunately, dear, we have to live with these people and the way you feel about them is only partially the way most(?) servicemen will find it when they return. (Personal opinion.)

I found out that I couldn't talk to the folks back home about the broad aspects of the war which I'd rather have but my mother was more interested in what I had to eat, how I slept, what movies I'd seen and other stupid things which most people take for granted. The point of it is—that some people live in different worlds.

Gertrude Stein is interesting but apparently difficult to understand. You probably saw some letters to the editor in Time after her little speech to the servicemen in Paris. Nobody seemed to appreciate her a great deal.

I hope that Murph weathers the storm all right with the captain. It sounds intriguing (that is, the other gal's coming) but it was rather stupid to tell her that for some mysterious reason she wouldn't marry him. Seems it would have been better to not to say anything under the circumstances.

Time for lights out and I haven't said half the things I meant to. But as you say — there will be many "tomorrows" and we will have an opportunity to speak our minds before I get back. So, so long for awhile and

All my Love, Gene

❁

2 July 1945 [2]

My dearest Marian,

I promised myself that I'd write to you a long letter after we returned from our trip of the island. But then when I got back I started to read the new "Time" (2 July) and after I'd finished it was too late. This morning at breakfast I was very much surprised & happy to finally receive a lot of my back mail. Your letters from the 16 & 20 of June were among those I got and of course and my morale rose by leaps and bounds. Will really write a long letter tonight. At present it is about 1300 and just about time for the afternoon session.

Saturday the three of us took off for a nice quiet spot down on the beach. It was fun for a change and the amount of civilization continues to interest us. Actually there is not much to do except if we want to go through a lot of strain — getting a date specifically. George is married and true, Demmy is single but stupid and I don't give a damn. Methinks we will spend most of our time eating steaks (6 last weekend) and banana splits. The scenery is beautiful and probably an ideal place to spend a honeymoon.

Sunday morning we set out again to see something of the town which is in a different direction and some distance. We tried to get reservations at the hotel but they are booked up for a month. That too is a beautiful place. We also saw a friend of Demmy's who took us to some officers' clubs.

Time for class but I'll see you again tonight. This has been short but I figure you might be interested in the fact that I love you —

Gene

❁

3 July 1945

Dearest,
Time for a few lines tonight. Our C.O. Lt. Col. Powers is leaving tomorrow and the Ex off. ordered us to stay at the club tonight to make sure he has a good time and plenty to drink. I have finally got away for a few minutes after 7 Tom Collins' in 1-1/2 hours. Feel slightly wobbly etc—Rather sorry to see him go in a way but the other officers are more or less happy. The Major (Winstead) will take over and he seems O.K. I knew him slightly at Ft. Monmouth.

Received a letter from a friend—Joe Snartemo and find that he has been drafted and at Camp Livingston—and waiting to go overseas.

Received all my baggage yesterday and so spent most of the day building a cabinet and desk. Think that I have more clothes than the quartermaster. They searched it at one of the stops but I don't know exactly what they were looking for. I had 3 quarts of liquor and a carbine and a lot of classified material. Only thing missing was a qt. of liquor. The lock was broken for which I was sorry but everything else was intact.

Wrote to Merle during noon today so I should hear from him soon. I really miss him above everything else but these fellows here are swell. So long for tonight darling. I hope too that this feeling between us can last—forever.

All My Love, Gene

⚜

4 July 1945

Hello darling,
Happy 4th of July if there is such a thing. Today we are on a holiday routine for which everyone is very thankful after the party last night. It turned out to be quite an affair and everybody had enough to drink. I secured about 10:45 and it still was in full swing. Woke up at 1:00 AM because of all the noise but after that all was quiet.

Today we are planning to go down to the beach for a swimming party. Probably will not go till later this afternoon. The colonel has left and the Major took over today. The senior first Lt. will act as ex officer. His name is A. J. Christ and a swell fellow. A.J., myself and another Marine Lt. live together in the same tent. The other Lt is Glenn Gardner—plans and training officer. There is much more cooperation between the officers of this Asco than there was in the 3rd. We even get along well with the Naval men who also comprise a section of Asco.

To answer some back questions—I have been in Randini's several times but I never cared much for that place for some reason. Think perhaps it was the crowd. Seems to me that they had 4 negroes who were pretty good the Sat. night I was there—When I do return to the states, I will not be sure where I will come in—San Fran, San Diego or possibly New York. The ideal solution of course would be—you working in Milwaukee but right now it seems too far in the future to make any definite plans. Don't you think so?

1800 Back from swimming and happily 2 more letters from you forwarded to the 5th. One of them you dated the 17th and Wittenberg postmarked it the 13th. Maybe Wittenberg is a little fouled up. Anyway, regardless of the date I was glad to get them. In a few days they should start coming direct to Asco.

Will enclose a letter from Aage, his wife and Mother-in-law all of whom I spoke of some time back. His wife's mother is an extremely interesting person. The "deal" he speaks of was merely the promise to use his influence to get me a job in Southern Cal. Aage has always facinated me to a great extent.

Seems you said I was passionate (to bring that up again) that night at the Lake front and I thought that you had a very good reason for saying it.

I'm glad you had a good time in Wittenberg—and envy the Corporal even tho he has probably put in his 24 months out here. Will send a 5th Div. patch as soon as I get one but don't look for anyone of those for 12 months yet—but meantime you can transfer all your allegiance from the 3rd to the 5th.

Time to eat again but I'll see you tomorrow and meanwhile as always

All My Love, Gene

⚜

5 July 1945

Darling,

Today I am down at the beach in charge of a non-swimmers swimming party. An effort is being made to teach the men how to swim if they are unable to. Planned to write a long letter while waiting but already some time has passed and nothing done. Also brought all yours from May 26 in order to answer any questions. I am proud of my filing system and perhaps sometime in the future I'll have to send them back for you to hold till I return.

Speaking of returning—the air liaison sections of the Asco officers are going home soon as they have a fairly strict <u>14</u> <u>mo.</u> <u>rotation</u> policy. They are grounded aviators who have been put in communications—but still attached to the M.A.C.

The article of Grafton's finding the Russians human too—I enjoyed. Think perhaps I'll send it to my grandfather, like me he always enjoys blasts at C. B. Luce. Unfortunately her close domestic relationship with the owner of "Time" has blinded him to the usefulness of that magazine. He has never said much about it but I don't imagine he reads "Time." I almost had him convinced once. I remember when I was a kid he hated the Milw. Journal and of course the Sentinel & Wis. News and as a result we always took the Milw. Leader and in later years—the Post. Lately tho he likes the Journal's editorial policy. If for no other reason, I am glad for him that the elections turned out the way they did last November.

Those blank parts of the page are there because I have no place to rest my hand O.K.? Incidently how do you get along with my handwriting? Reuben's father frankly admits he can't read it—My grandfather often complains (when I am home) that it is terrible but that is rather amusing because his is practically unreadable. Will send you a sample letter sometime. He has a comparatively good vocabulary but the spelling—I guess I am not anyone to criticize tho—

It's remarkable we were probably so near to each other in L.A. Kenmore ave is very familiar. I lived on Hoover & Beverly. I am glad you were on the same train tho rather than have met you some other place. It was a swell 42 hours and we must have made a lasting impression on each other. I waited a long time for your head to fall on my shoulder so I'd had a good excuse to put my arm around you. I remember you said that you didn't think I was too bold, but on the other hand our conduct must have appeared rather unusual to the other people.

Ever since I started this letter I have been watching the swimming instructor. A platoon sgt. is in charge and is quite a character—all tattooed and a tremendous voice flavored with profanity and obscenity. He is teaching them the side stroke and looks similar to that statue of Hercules—no one dares to even smile. It is strange that so many men can't swim tho I suppose I was lucky to be born in Wisc. as there are many lakes there.

—Back to camp again darling so maybe I can concentrate enough to add an intelligent page—

We had a swell dinner tonight—steak, but frankly I am about getting my fill of it for awhile—also cake and ice cream and avocadoes (spelling) which I never acquired a taste for like the native Californians. Speaking of spelling again—it appears "fascinted" is spelt along those lines rather than "facin-" as of my last letter. Think I'd better have you as my stenog. around term paper time. You'd probably be more distracting than Webster however darling—but certainly a pleasant relief and inspiration. Not to seriously compare you with a dictionary.

I, too, was sorry to hear of Buckner's death and also Curtin's from Australia. The big shakeup in the Marine Corps was (Gieger to 5th Corps—H. M. Smith to San Diego—and the former C.O. of this div Rochery to 3rd Corps). Our new general's name is Buorke (sp?) and seems all right as generals go—

Had a letter from Carleton today and he may come over here. I believe that he is in the 1st Army. I told him I was no longer a msg. center commando—he has the job I wanted, Radio off. in the div. sig co. Asco will be all right tho if the beach isn't too hot—It was rough at Iwo.

So long again darling—I'll see you soon again—wish it were tonight.

All My love, Gene

✣

6 July 1945

Dearest Marian,

Your letters for July 1 & 2 came today which means 4 days—good hey? Needless to say (but I will) it was good to hear from you again. There is something about a letter that makes it distinct from any other form of mental enjoyment. Undoubtedly many people are finding that out these days. Letters from home are always welcome of course but a love letter—ah, that is different. So much for letters—

First of all I <u>am</u> glad you did find somebody that you enjoy talking to and I don't care particularly that it happens to be a man. Not that I am not jealous but I do figure <u>you</u> know what you are doing. If you don't, there is nothing I can do about it being over here. If I thought less of your intelligence and ability to do what I expected you to do, I shouldn't be in love with you, and if I were, by some odd coincidence, I would probably ask you not to see any men—which is quite stupid I think. I don't mention this necessarily to reserve any "action" for myself but merely to put your mind at ease. O.K.??

In a like manner I figure that I know what I am doing. There appears to me to be only one solution—and that is, we trust each other. I have one man on my team that ends his letters to 3 different girls with a "I love you"—If they all believe him, I feel sorry for them. I have never imagined that I'd come home and find you unlike your letters and I don't think that I ever will.

I am very glad you have considered the civil service job angle—but . . . I can't help but think that we might be making a mistake for several reasons. Two days are not very long darling and then you might be stuck under a 2 year contract or something. Location is another important factor—and there are other reasons which I shouldn't mention for various reasons. What confusion! but unfortunately that is the way it is. Needless to say all the reasons are because I <u>am</u> in the service and of course not for personal concern. Hope that you understand. At least I'd like to hear what you think about it.

Also was happy to hear Merle had written. When I asked him, it was more or less in a joking manner but he said he'd be glad to so you probably have a better idea of what he is like than I have informed you from time to time. I do like him very much.

This weekend we are going down to a town here so perhaps I'll have more interesting news for you Sunday. It will feel wonderful to get away for awhile. I wish I had a date with you but the time will come darling and we can wait.

I love you very much,

Gene

�֍

9 July 1945

Dearest Marian,

Was glad to get your letter today from July 5th. We spent the afternoon out in the field and besides that—was O.D. so have been kept on the move all day. Saturday Demmy & I went down to town and managed to get a room in a very nice hotel there. Attended a dance at a Naval station and more or less enjoyed ourselves the entire weekend. Managed to do some shopping and stopped at one of those places to have our pictures taken. So here they are. I am still waiting, darling!

We slept Sunday morning until almost 1100 which felt good for a change, got up, took a shower and had a swell dinner. The afternoon was spent on a tour of that part of the island after Demmy talked a couple of gals into coming along. Don't know exactly how he did it because needless to say competition is keen and I never could talk anyone into anything back in the States—so there is no reason to feel that I could over here. Consequently I don't try—At any rate we all enjoyed ourselves and that too was unusual. That is, having some female companionship. Sometimes I think, however, I was happier back in the 3rd. I heard so often somebody say—"If you have to be overseas then damn it <u>be</u> overseas and not in one of those—camps." I think they are right sometimes. I wish the war would end.

Before I forget again I mean to give you my home address my father's house and probably permanent. You have my Aunt's on Cleveland ave. but she evidently is moving as they have purchased a farm now. At any rate his is

3137 S. 31 Street
Milwaukee, Wisconsin

Also I have a request—I wonder if you could possibly (seeing you live in Chicago) buy for me a shoulder holster for a .45 cal. army type automatic. I would certainly appreciate it but you may have trouble getting one—and very possibly not have any luck at all. If that is the case <u>don't</u> trouble yourself too much. Okay? Also, if you can get the harness without the holster that is O.K. too.

I think that I like Grafton about as much as you do—also Barnaby—Looks too, like the P-38 is making a comeback. Hope so cause I like to hear them whistle—I am terribly sorry again Marian—about Franklin. There is not much I can say but I hope that there still is some remote chance of he being safe. It certainly makes one realize tho that what we are doing is so insignificant compared to what so many have done already.

Goodnight darling and,

All my Love, Gene

⚜

July 4, 1945
[Chicago]

Hello, darling,

Another holiday—with not much to do but read, and wish you were here. I'm also getting rather anxious for Gale to come back. Guess I'll call Ed tomorrow & see if he knows when she's coming.

How do you like this new P-38? I was very much pleased to see it. The trade journals on aviation we get at the office had said the P-38 would be out of production by the end of the year. I'm glad they have a modified version now which will compare favorably with other new planes. Silly, isn't it?

As usual, I like this editorial of Grafton's. He's wrinkling his emotional nose again. It seems to me more imaginative than emotional, however, and the effect is good.

Don't you enjoy Landis' historical anecdotes? I like the one about Disraeli especially. I read an inspiring biography of Disraeli several years ago. It was written by Andre Maurois. Have you read it?

Mother says one of the fellows from W'berg whom Franklin had seen in Italy is home. He told her he had tried to contact some of the members of Franklin's squadron & had also gone to the Red Cross over there but with no success. It's good to know that he tried anyway.

I should answer Merle's letter.

Will see you tomorrow, darling.

All my love, Marian

⚜

July 5, 1945

Dear Lt. Sweetheart:

I've just come home from Spanish class & was very happy to find here two letters from you. My class on Thurs. starts at six, which doesn't give me time to come home first & look in the mail box.

This Spanish is certainly fun, though. They speak Spanish all the time in class, & it's amazing how easy it is to understand what they mean. La professora es Mexicana (Beautiful, too.) El professor es Paraguayio. I do wish you were studying with me—here!

I wonder if we are talking about the same thing re. Peg's remarks on officer censorship. I know she's right about your censoring your own mail. What I disagreed with was the inference that you would therefore be able to or take the liberty of telling more than an enlisted man could. That is not true, is it?

That was indeed an interesting story about "Forever Amber." I guess I'll have to read it now.

I'm glad the general outlook has improved. You should be doing all right with an ex-schoolmate as C.O.

I don't know much about Byrnes, either. The new "Time" tonight says he may be expected to give us a more "consistent" foreign policy. If that is an accurate prediction, I think it will be a good thing. My own impression of the two men—and it is merely an impression—is that Byrnes would be a stronger executive, a better maker of policy, while Stettinius is essentially a good salesman, a quality which should make him very well suited to his new job on the Security Council.

I don't suppose anyone will particularly mourn Sec. [Henry] Morgenthau's resignation. I think he has received a lot of criticism that was not deserved, however.

I was very much amused at your saying your letters sounded like "Report on the Nation" in contrast to those "passionate affairs." This letter sounds rather like a Report, too, doesn't it? Darling, there is no less love behind it. I know you will agree that a love which combines passion with dispassionate interest and respect has a better chance to last.

I was rather shocked one day to hear one of the married women in our office admit to Julia (who tries very hard to be a man-hater) that, after some 18 years of married life, "any man would be the same." "I must be too young for this," I said, & walked away. Isn't that awful? I suppose they would accuse me of being a romanticist, but I would much rather be that than so coldly indiscriminating.

'Tis getting late. Until later, darling,

Much love, Marian

✛

July 7, 1945

Hello, darling,

I thought I'd have those pictures to send you today, but they won't be ready until Mon. now. After all this suspense, I'm afraid they'll be rather anti-climax.

Your letters of July 2 came today. That quiet spot on the beach sounds wonderful. I wish, since I couldn't be there with you, I could find a quiet spot on the beach here. There's too damn much "civilization" here, and it doesn't interest me at all today.

Had to laugh at your saying Demmy is "single but stupid." I never thought that had much to do with getting dates.

I went to school again last night, but did not stay for the social hour. We had class from 8 to 9. My other class has been changed from Thurs. to Tues. 8-10. The girl who instructed us last night is from Panama, I think. Her diction does not seem to be so clear as the others; and it was a little harder to understand what she was talking about. We learned various salutations, though, & how to introduce people & acknowledge introductions. This girl does not speak much English. She asked one of the students for his name (which was Sutherland) and had to look at her list in order to figure out how to say it. It was very funny, as we are not supposed to ask how any of the Spanish words are spelled or what they mean.

Julia let me read a letter today which she had rec'd from her nephew. He is now stationed in Czechoslovakia, near Pilsen. His comments on the attitude of the people were very interesting. The Yanks have really been "knocked out," he said, by the strict morality of the Czech girls, which contrasts vividly with the German girls. The Czechs are willing, he said, if the fellows are looking for true love. Some 21 of them left with the last unit stationed there—as wives. Any Yank caught fraternizing with a German is likely to be shot at by the Czechs & is definitely ostracized. The people as a whole welcomed our troops gladly and, as the area will presumably be under Russian control, they are not eager to see the Americans leave—such is his assumption, at least. I wonder how right he is, and why. Seems to me I have read that Czechoslovakia is in the peculiar position of being oriented to the East economically & to the West ideologically.

Incidentally, why do you think the Russians have not entered the war against Japan? I don't understand why not, but it has occurred to me that they might have to take over certain areas of China, for military expediency, and that might worry our anti-Communists more than their present neutrality. Could be it has something to do with something?

I'd better quit, darling. See you tomorrow.

All my love, Marian

✦

July 8, 1945

My darling Gene:
I've been having an awful time today trying to keep from feeling depressed. Guess I've been alone too long. Gale came back this morning. Ed went down to meet her & they came up here for about half an hour & then went out again.

Ed Dervishion just called to announce that they have a baby daughter. Guess I hadn't told you about that before. Marge was talking about having twins with such confidence that she even confused her doctor. He finally took X-rays to find out. The baby was born Friday.

What do you think of this article on the State Department? Do you remember Time's review of the book [Joseph] Grew wrote on Japan? It gave me the impression that he had been so busy enjoying the social life when he was ambassador there that he didn't care much about the basic problems or rather that he had a one-sided viewpoint. Would like to read Lt. Roth's book. I hope it will be published.

Our friend Grafton has written an article on food in which he points out that it was less fairly distributed in peacetime than it is now, due to the fact that many people could not afford to buy what they needed. He concludes with this statement: "Rationing tends to bog down, not only because of administrative difficulties, but also because an attempted equitable distribution of food exposes the fact that the country as a whole is underfed. . . . As for those who look to the end of the war as the end of shortages, they ought to realize that we will merely be substituting silent shortages, in the bodies of underfed children, for the noisy shortages cried out against by the man with money in his hand."

I shall send that to my mother.

Darling, especially on days like today, I wish, too, that I could remember more about you. It makes me wonder if we might have fallen in love with what we imagine each other to be. But then I think we are probably more ourselves in these letters than we were much of the time we were together.

Imagination or not — I love you very much, dear.

Marian

✦

July 9, 1945

Dear Lt. Sweetheart:
I hesitate to make any further comment on these pictures. They look worse than the miniatures did. I hope they won't disillusion you, darling.

I found that book called "Report on Red China" at the rental library last night. It was written by Harrison Foreman, not Mark Gayn. He must have written the review I read. It is a very interesting book—not exactly in keeping with that recent article in Time. Will tell you more when I finish the book.

Tonight I'm going to the Ballet with Julia. As you've undoubtedly heard before, that's my favorite variety of entertainment. It will be especially nice to go with Julia as we can have an argument or two afterward.

Rec'd your letter of July 3 today. I'm glad you escaped from the Colonel's party long enough to write it. The day is never quite complete without one, darling.

All my love, Marian

⚜

11 July 1945
[Hawaii]

Dearest Marian,

Mail really came in today and among it all was five letters from you. The latest dated July 6.

I'm glad you are enjoying the Spanish sessions and I too, wish I could be there with you—At least to provide the romantic interest. The Spanish fellow sounds awfully interesting but of course I hope that he has no romantic ideas. In that sense I suppose I am like most fellows over here—more or less jealous.

We've been having field problems all week and it is getting a little tiresome. My Master Tech. broke his leg or something so I'll lose him for several months. I will go up to the hospital tomorrow to see him. I actually rate a lot of N.C.O.'s but somehow the rates have been slow in coming through and as a result I have mostly P.F.C.s or Pvt.'s. or as they are called here "peons." My radio sgt. chief was an instructor in the school I attended back in '42 as a pvt. In that respect the service is strange—Of the 19 men, I believe 17 are from different states. I have an index file on their "lives, loves etc" in order to get better acquainted and I guess they appreciate it. As one Colonel said—"You are expected to be brother, sister, Mother and father to them." I guess it's true.

You are right about the Peg and censorship question—but those notes from Iwo were a little rough—on your argument. Understand?

You seem to be convinced that Wars are fought "for interests." I suppose that actually is the liberal view and possibly closer to the truth than the more conservative viewpoint I hold. Seems to me that the question of practical philosophy as it pertains to the great factors that start wars is more the cause of it all. Appears to me this was the case with Germany—but maybe not Japan. Hitler did have some philosophical ideas that were there to start with irregardless of any economic gain to be had. Unfortunately certain "interests" do profit but they often blind us to the factors of human ideals that were there at the beginning. This is rather envolved—maybe because I have taken as much philosophy as History at school. In that respect I am not realistic—economics always fascinated me but the more I studied it the more I realized that it was not what it appeared to be to so many "economic thinking" people. Remarkable statement—what? but too difficult to explain in a letter.

Regardless of anyone else—I am fighting for ideals.

"What and Who" to believe is always a question but all education is—in it's truest sense is to read, listen etc. and then form your own opinions. They say that when we are able to do that, we are educated—I agree—It is not easy however—

I have often felt like you said you did after seeing, "A Tree Grows—" Very often after receiving your letters. I guess the explanation of "being able to touch the sky" explains it as well as anything. Don't think that we have wasted so much time darling. You have convinced me that I love you—and if nothing else we've got that far.

Goodnight Sweetheart,

Gene

✣

13 July 1945
Signal Co.
5th Mar Div etc

Sweetheart—

As I promised this afternoon I am writing again tonight. This has been a great week. I imagine I received 10 letters from you and I have at least that many to answer.

First the transfer. It appears that a man has been transferred out of the msg center and they needed a new one—the C.O. is a Captain Only—I worked for about 18 mo. ago before going to L.A. When he heard that I was here—he requested me and that's the story. Actually it made no difference to me—there are definite advantages, (ex. instead of H + 10 it becomes D + ?) and also disadvantages (ex. no private jeep which I had learned to like.) I'll not have any men to worry about which is neither good nor bad. Living conditions will be decidedly better and I'll have more time to write to you (which I like) So it ends up that I am a msg. center commando again. I like Capt. Only very much. Incidently he married a Bam who worked in his office for him back in Elliott. Also incidently according to "Time" about a year ago—a BAM is a "broad axle (approximately) marine." That appealed to my sense of humor—

Your letters were so nice (as usual) that I can't quite express some phrase that would cover them in entirety (question that last word) I believe you should have been a writer. Can also understand when you say that your interests progressed beyond college credits. Too frequently it seems—college credits progress beyond interests. It has also occurred to me at times that we may have fallen in love with what we imagine each other to be—

I honestly don't think so Marian. I should have to be very much mistaken. What I am more afraid of than anything is—the practical aspects of being in love—when I come home and not whether we are in love. To have faith in each other now is probably the most important bond we have.

Darling—it is getting late & I have to finish packing for my moving tomorrow. As I said before—I will have more time to write to you from now on. Feel sorta that I have been neglecting you especially after receiving one of your super-long letters.

Goodnight Miss Sweetheart and

All my Love, Gene

❧

15 July 1945

Darling,

I <u>would</u> <u>love</u> to get in an argument with you—but—not along spelling or grammer lines. Really had to blush after reading your last letter on split infinitives. I plead guilty so there is no argument there. Haven't any excuse either except that the only thing I've had in "English" since the eighth grade has been literature. That's no excuse—so you win—

Say! I received your letter in <u>three</u> <u>days</u>! Isn't that wonderful? Wonders never cease!

This is the second letter I've started (to you) tonight. The first one—I could not pass as a censor so after blotting out portions it seemed easier to start over again.

Demmy just was in and wants to go to the movie to see "Endearing Young Charms" so I probably will later. As I said yesterday—I will have quite a bit more time to write in the future. Also have questions to answer from the 10 odd letters from you last week. Be patient dear. I hope you don't ever feel that the movies are seriously in competition with you but it seems to be our only "get away from it all" time and it does help. Merle and I always agreed that it was a waste of time but then about show time we usually went anyways. You are doing grand sweetheart and of course I appreciate it. All in all I suppose I am as happy as I can be over here. At least there are no complaints at present.

Thanks for the pictures. I like them very much but perhaps in the future could you have a large one made? Would appreciate that very much. I hope that you don't get tired of these requests but if necessary I'd go back to one of your letters about 6 mo ago and quote you upon saying that if there was anything I ever wanted etc! —

Am also surprised in a way of my grandather's (or Marty) faith in the world situation. It is strange because usually he was very pessimistic particularly after a Republican landslide at some election. He doesn't like the fact that the cabinet resigned but finds no fault with the new men. I am waiting for the outcome of the "Big 3" conference but don't think anything concerning the pacific war will be definitely decided upon. Mainly I don't blame Russia for not getting in — because they probably have not the faith that everything is so Pro-Russian as it appears in our state department and also they are aware of the feeling of certain "Americans" and their anti Russian attitude. While I believe they will live up to the S. F. conference — at present they are not carried away with the brotherhood feeling. They'll watch & wait —

Goodnight darling. I'll see you soon.

All My Love, Gene

✢

16 July 1945

Darling,

Just time enough tonight for a letter to you. Nothing much doing all day so I slept most of the afternoon. Also didn't expect any mail from you after that 3 day letter which still amazes me. Had to give up my jeep which made me somewhat sad — I planned to call it "Marian" since all the others have names painted upon theirs. Oh well —

Just returned from the club after 4 "Southern Comforts" before chow and I still am in a daze somewhat. Seems S.C. is the only whiskey that I can see any pleasant taste in so I figured I'd go hog wild tonight. We used to drink S.C. collins at the Melody Lane in LA. and they have a particular sentimental value to me —

Wish you were here tonight — wouldn't be too difficult to talk me into that job but I think we'd be making a mistake — 2 days (as a symbol) could possibility be enough but nevertheless I don't think that we'd be wise. Perhaps I am too conservative —

The fleet pounding Honshu sounds good but I wish I'd have more faith that the end was near. It looks like a year more at least to me. I hope that I am wrong.

Still haven't gone over to the Signal Co. but expect orders tomorrow. Will write then so goodnight sweetheart and I too love you very much.

Gene

✢

17 July 1945
Signal Co.

Hello darling,

Have sorta neglected you for a couple of days but will have a little time now. Haven't been incorporated in the Code Room watch schedule yet so I can't write on Marine Corps time (which I will later on no doubt.) Then there has been the matter of moving, orders etc—I hope I am excused. O.K.?

Capt. Only is very nice as I knew he would be—and I think I will like it very well over here. I must have a curse on me inasmuch as I don't stay in one outfit over a couple of months. It has not been my fault however—but I do want to stay here for awhile. Think I will too—

There is the matter of the "Atlantic Monthly" again darling—hope they (and you) don't become too disgusted. Oh—how I hate this moving and getting acquainted time after time. Everytime I do get transferred it is worse than the last.

We have a swell situation here because of the fact we are with the "Staff" again. Food leaves nothing to be desired and at the bar we have every kind of mixed drink there is—The mess is rather silly because it is sort of "formal." Negroes stand at every table (4 per) and there are always 3 courses at least. Hot & cold running water too which is a novelty to me—also stateside toilets which everyone appreciates. Best of all there is a fellow in the code room named O'Grady someone whom I know I will like very much. He is from Chicago and a graduate of Huchins' [Robert Hutchins] school. He's very quiet and reminds me of Merle very much. Plans to go back to get a M.A. & Ph.D. after the war at Chicago. The other fellows are fresh from the states (I am salty) and I don't know them too well yet.

Asco is planning a minor split up so I am not sorry I had to leave. Found out that Only had asked for me as I suspected last week so that explains the transfer.

Was rather surprised in a way to find that your favorite entertainment was the ballet—is it? That is interesting because I have never seen one—only in "Mission to Moscow" they had a few scenes. We will attend a ballet and argue about it later. By the way what does one argue about concerning a ballet?

Hope Marge & the baby are O.K. Incidentally, everybody (practically) in Asco has had a baby girl in the last 6 mo. I still want a girl—

Time for the mail to arrive in Asco so I think I'll take a shower & walk over there. I hope there is a letter from you today but I have no complaints. You are a darling—

I love you very much—

Gene

❖

19 July 1945

Dearest Marian,

First of all I guess I'd better congradulate [*sic*] you upon your birthday. Sorta think that this will be a day or so late but anyways on July 23 I will be thinking of you a little more than usual—if that is possible. And I hope that we will be able to spend the next anniversity together. As I said a few weeks ago— I am also celebrating 3 years in the M. C. on that particular day.

We are having a party (or rather Asco is) this Saturday to which I'd like to take you to but seeing that is impossible we will have to go on dreaming as per usual. It is a little tiresome at times to "dream up" various things but without that we have nothing. The time <u>will</u> come darling.

O'Grady says that he knows this Father Dunne very well and is an excellent and intelligent speaker. I had given him those clippings that you had sent which the Jesuit had written. Also told O'Grady about you after he had remarked that he knew where "W. Elm St" was. Don't know how Don (O'G) stands on the various political issues yet but undoubtedly I'll find out soon.

We were out on the field today on a short problem but will not have much of that in the future where Ill be concerned. The weather was dusty as usual and very disagreeable. I definitely liked the 3rd Div area better.

Last night I was over to Asco to pick up my mail and ended up playing bridge till 12:30 Also had enough to drink again for no apparent reason but have decided to knock that off for awhile at least after Saturday. The main form of amusement overseas is to think of women and/or to get drunk. There are better things to do however.

Now that I am situated I must get on with my Spanish so I feel I am not wasting all my time. Also want to do some reading. Don has a good collection— "Time for Decision"—S. [Sumner] Welles and a lot of St. Thomas Aiquinus (sp) stuff which will bring back some familiar scenes from M.U. in philosophy classes. Once I brush up, I undoubtedly will be able to get in some argument with you on that subject. Also mean to send you that torn scarf from Iwo as soon as it's o'kayed by the G-2 section. I <u>have</u> good intentions and I hope you don't get too discouraged waiting for me to carry them out.

I have been thinking for over an hour now—post-war plans etc—Methinks I will have to make some rapid decisions whenever I do get back. As you say— we should confide in each other as much as possible. So many of mine depend (as they say in the Marine Corps) "upon the situation and the terrain." Have decided definitely that I am going back to school come hell or high water. Anything incompatible (I like that word) with that will have to go. I have managed to save enough money so it will be no strain financially and with the G.I. bill so much the better. Despite the fact that 3 families are clamoring for me (to stay with them) I will probably be on my own. At least I am expecting that at any rate. Once Marty dies—I will have no family ties which is bad in a way but good in others. Being in love with you can be either a blessing & inspiration or a decided handicap—depending to a large extent upon you. I hope darling, that this does not seem too cold and realistic to you but unfortunately that's the way I am oftentimes—perhaps I should say most times.

There is no reason, from my side at least, why we can't make some arrangement that will be agreeable to both of us. I'm glad you "trust me implicitly" because that always helps. I figure I know what I am doing in the same way you understand your actions. Guess that all comes under "faith in each other."

Rather wish that you wouldn't see Cal when he is drunk but I won't say "don't see him at all." I am sorry to hear that is is "tangled up." What do you think the reason is?

Darling I must quit now and go to bed. It is late and I'm afraid I have spent too much time thinking and not enough writing as has become usual. Goodnight sweetheart and I hope you have a happy birthday.

All My Love, Gene

⚜

July 10 '45
[Chicago]

Hello, darling,

Rec'd your letter of July 4 tonight & have just now 10:30 had time to read it at leisure. Gale's mother was here for dinner. She brought us three pork chops—a rare treat. (You & your six steaks!)

Then I went to school, which, of course, was fun. As "el professor" said, however, it was a hard lesson—on pronouns, chiefly, & their use with various forms of the verb "es." If we'd use the wrong gender, he would say, "If you do 'wear the pants' in the family at home, don't admit it at school." One man who laughed loudly at that remark said, very shortly thereafter, "Yo sui Norte Americana."

I got a big bang out of that letter dated June 17 & postmarked the 13th. It was really the 17th when I was there. I'd better not mention it to my folks or they'll remind me that the Democrats appointed the postmistress.

I enjoyed the letter from your uncle, etc., very much. His mother-in-law sounds like a sweet person. Was amused at his comment on Marty's faith. (May I call him that?) And the fact that he himself is becoming more realistic. Merle would probably say that was a bad influence for you, dear. The realism, I mean.

I shall think about that idea of working in Milw. again. I agree that it seems too far in the future to make definite plans, but I think it's good to exchange our ideas on possible plans as that would make it easier, for me at least, to make a decision alone if it should be necessary in some situation. Right?

I should like to write a long, long letter tonight, darling, but it's getting so late. I hope to have more time tomorrow evening as my only duty is to go to the hospital for a little while to see Marge & her new baby.

In case it should concern you, my allegiance has been transferred, as per instructions, from the 3rd to the 5th Marine Division.

I love you, dear —

Marian

❖

July 11, 1945

Dearest Gene:

It's about 7:30 and I have the whole lovely evening to think about you and to read & reread your letters of the 5th & 6th which came today. I agree with everything you say about letters, especially a love letter being different. 'Tis wonderful, darling.

I didn't go to see Marge tonight as I caught a cold about 4:30 this afternoon. Saw Ed in the elevator & he proudly displayed a War Bond he has already purchased for his daughter. Deanna Mary is her name. They thought Deanna Dervishion would be cute. It's not bad, but I can't understand why people like alliteration in names.

I'm not kidding about that 4:30 business. I never heard of anyone catching colds as suddenly as I do. I went over to relieve Marion at the switchboard feeling fine, if slightly harassed by an unexpected deluge of work, and came back ten minutes later hardly able to see. Marion told Paul if he didn't quit making me cry she'd take him outside & beat him up—which wouldn't be too implausible as she is nearly twice his size.

To answer one of your questions, I have very little difficulty with your handwriting. There used to be an occasional word I couldn't decipher, but very rarely now. I'd like to be your stenographer around term paper time. I hope that by that time it will not be such a novelty for us to be together that I'll be <u>much</u> more distracting than a dictionary. Since you practically asked for it, incidentally, I'll unsplit your infinitives for you, too.

I understand there are two schools of thought on that subject. The liberal (in favor of an occasional split) was ably presented in a book which I'd like very much to have if I could ever remember the name of it. Paul always says, "We ask you to please return" or "to please advise." I've finally convinced myself that's one of the permissible splits as it sounds rather awkward with the "please" anywhere else. Perhaps that's only because repetition has made this sound most natural to me. Want to argue, honey?

About the civil service, undoubtedly it is impractical, and I do understand your attitude. I had assumed, without giving the matter much thought, that the 5th Div. was in somewhat the same circumstance at present as the 3rd & might, therefore, not go into combat again for several months. That is an unreliable conclusion, even in the case of the 3rd, but as you say there will probably not be many 5th Div. men in the States for 12 mos. or so, the situation is much less certain there. However, I do think it worth while to find out what the possibilities are for civil service. I have written to the commission & will let you know what information they give me. The 2 yr. contract would be bad, altho I know of a case where such a contract was broken with no apparent difficulty. I wouldn't think it would be wise, tho. One thing I always come back to, as you will recall from our discussions about New York, is the feeling that I ought to be near my mother & dad. We shall see —

I disagree with you about those two days, darling. I heard it said one time, "Our happiness is not measured by time — and if our time is measured by our happiness, we shall have centuries." It seems to me that has been true for us before, and I'm sure it would be then. The problem is not the length of those two days but whether or not we'd have them. Agree, darling? We shall have them some day, and they are worth waiting for.

Goodnight, sweetheart.

Marian

❀

July 13 '45

Hello, darling,

As you see, I've been reading newspapers today. I particularly like these articles by Father Dunne. Glad to see a Catholic giving the Russians a kind word.

Have been at home yesterday & today trying to get rid of this darn cold. It makes me so disgusted. For two weeks I had very little to do at work, & just the day I get a nice stack of it that should be done immediately, I have to stay home in bed!

Well, that's enough complaining. I think I found the cure this time anyway.

Have also had a chance to read more of "Report on Red China." It is very good. Think I will see if I can get a copy to send you, if you'd like to have it. The part I read today told about how the "Communists" have become self-sufficient since the Kuomintang blockade. Even the Army produces for itself an amazingly large percentage of its requirements of food, clothing & all other supplies. Some parts are rather funny, as the efforts made to "reform" loafers. It all sounds more like ideal democracy than communism.

I've been reading over your letter of the 6th & the part about dates with other men. Darling, you are wonderful! I would trust you implicitly & am glad you have the same confidence in me. I'm also very glad to be able to tell you about these things without making you angry.

This, I am sure, will not make you the least bit angry—I think I am not going to see Cal anymore. It's rather a long story. He was supposed to come over a week ago Mon. & then postponed it until Tues. I talked to him at 5:00 & he said he'd be here by 7:00. At 7:30 he called, very drunk, and said he wasn't coming . . . That is not at all an unusual procedure for him. . . he is basically a very fine person and, I believe, could be a great artist if he could only get himself untangled.

I guess that's about enough for one letter. I'd better go back to bed. Goodnight, sweetheart.

All my love, Marian

✦

July 14 '45

My darling Gene:

I wish you were here to share the festivities tonight. We're having a sort of surprise party for Murph. Ed & I are, that is. I call it "sort of" a party as there are only the three of us. Her birthday was Thurs., but Ed was out of town so we had to postpone it until tonight. I ordered a real fancy cake & Ed promised to bring some "tanglefoot," so it should be fun.

I hope that "tanglefoot" gives me a little pep. I've been in bed again most of the day & still feel rather shaky.

The day was very much improved by your letter of the 9th & the pictures you sent. I don't think the pictures flatter you, but I am certainly glad to have them.

I'm glad you had fun over the weekend. Had to laugh at your saying you could never talk anyone into anything. I shouldn't think you'd have to talk much, darling. Did you ever really try? I don't want to be giving you any such suggestions, though.

I'll see what I can do about getting a shoulder holster for you. Perhaps Ed will have some suggestion.

Thanks for sending your dad's address. I'm glad to have it.

Ed should be here any minute so I'd better quit.

See you tomorrow, sweetheart.

All my love, Marian

✥

July 15 '45

Hello, darling,

I have been in an unpleasant, impatient mood all day. Decided it would help to write to you, although that may not be such a good idea. It will probably be a very bad letter.

Have been meaning to tell you that the girl at the office who handles all our war bond stuff gave me one of the new posters she had with the picture of the flag raising on Mt. Suribachi. I thought you might like to have it, so I'll save it for you. I suppose you have heard about the postage stamp. Good, isn't it?

We did have fun last night. Ed made some very refined martinis which, as usual, made me lonesome. When we went out to dinner, there was a girl across the room from us speaking Spanish in a loud voice. We decided she had a poor accent (all of us being authorities, of course) and was merely trying to attract attention. It was sort of aggravating—oh, there I go! Let's change the subject.

Ed was giving me advice about my colds last night. He really knows quite a bit about medicine. He thinks it must be an allergy—or a sensitivity, as Squibb instructs their salesmen to call it. So he said I should take cod liver oil. (horrible thought!) The vitamin A it contains is supposed to be very effective. I suppose it would be a good idea, anyway.

I like these pictures better every time I look at them, dear—which is quite often. I wish they hadn't put so many trees in the background, though. It's confusing.

'Tis getting late—I wish I could fall asleep tonight with my head on your shoulder & your arm around me. Oh, how nice that would be!

All my love, darling,

Marian

❀

July 16 '45

Dear Lt. Sweetheart:

I went back to work today & do, therefore, feel much more cheerful tonight.

Also, Murph & Ed called about six (just when I was feeling sort of sad about the absence of mail tonight) and asked if I'd like to come down to Ed's apt. for some fish. One of the officers had gone fishing over the weekend & given Ed part of his catch. We had more fun! Ed had to go to the store three times before we could start eating because he'd forget something every time. He took a lot of punishment for that. We never did get any butter & that was rather important, too, as all we had was fish & bread & salad, plus some of Gale's birthday cake & coffee. It was all very good, however.

They've gone over to Ruth & Geo. Barr's now. Guess I ought to tell you about the Barr's sometime. Or have I? I haven't met them, but they're good friends of Ed's & quite interesting to hear about. George has an artificial leg. He has built up sort of a cosmetic business, which has made him a millionaire, or close to it, and he employs only people who are handicapped in some way. There have been articles in various magazines, incl. Readers Digest, about him, and he's been on the air a couple of times recently. They are Jewish. Murph likes them both, altho Ruth is sometimes <u>extremely</u> vulgar.

The kids were telling me today that Paul had an awful time while I was gone. We got some new price sheets Wed. which had to be mailed out. Friday Paul went to work on them. Marion said he was sighing every five minutes until she finally took pity on him & offered to help. I'll bet he could have killed me! I really hate to be gone when I know there's some such thing to be done.

He said there was a convention Fri. night at the Boulevard Room & he had planned to take me along. They had lots of fun. Darn it! I'd like to have gone.

While I'm on the subject of Paul, here is his picture on a page from a booklet entitled "Reliable at War." Aside from disliking the title & the dedication, I think it's a very good piece of advertising.

I'd better take my cod liver oil & go to bed. I was right in the middle of the nicest dream about you this morning when the alarm went off. Sure did make me mad!

Goodnight, darling. I love you very much,

Marian

❀

July 18 '45

Hi, Darling,
I've been sitting here for half an hour thinking about writing to you & haven't accomplished anything yet, except some pleasant day dreaming.

Rec'd your letter of the 11th tonight—the first since Saturday, which seemed like a long time ago.

I was amused at your index file on the lives & loves of your men. You are certainly orderly, dear. My dad would appreciate that. One of his favorite complaints is about people (Mother included) who have "no system." I usually agree with him.

Your comments on the relative influence of economics & philosophy were very interesting. Wish we could have a long discussion on the subject. I am not really "convinced" of anything, except that, regardless of what wars are fought for, it's damn difficult for ideals to consolidate the victory. Know what I mean?

This book on Red China has given me the impression that the Chinese Communists are truly fighting for good ideals & have achieved them within their "Occupied China." The fact that the Kuomintang blocks the extension of these ideals and is backed by the U.S. does not build up my confidence in the democratic aims of our foreign policy. I shall have to send you this book, Gene. I'm anxious to know if it will impress you as much. Incidentally, the achievements of those Chinese "Communists" are the best reason I've found in a long while for faith in humanity.

You were telling me that I have convinced you that you are in love with me. I don't know if I like that, darling. It really should have been your idea—but I suppose what you say is true to some extent. I guess it doesn't matter as long as you are convinced.

Goodnight, sweetheart.

All my love, Marian

❖

20 July 1945
[Hawaii]

Hello darling,
Time for a short note to go with these articles—hope that you find them interesting. It looks like the "mothers" are back with us again. My grandfather sent them some time ago and I have been meaning to send them on to you. That one paragraph really appealed to my sense of humor. I approve of the publicity that they are getting because it gets a lot of those lies out in the open so that they can more easily be laughed off.

I will start the regular schedule on Monday I believe—so far I have just been observing and asking questions. They do things quite a bit different here than they did in the 3d. The fellows all seem very nice to work with and I shouldn't have any trouble. Will also stay here indefinitely—I believe.

George Callens received a letter from one of the fellows that was transferred with Britt and he said a new order came out from Marine Hdqrs stating that all comm. off's will follow a strict rotation policy of 21 months from now on. It appears quite authentic and really is good news for a change. Now at least we will have a goal in sight which is better than the vague 24 mo idea. That means that I will have less than a year to go. Think that you can last it out?

Received a letter from Joe Snartemo and I guess he is having his troubles in an infantry training replacement command. Can well imagine what he is going through but it probably will do him some good. That is rather a cold and bitter thing to say and I didn't mean it exactly like it sounds. He is a good fellow. Reuben is also in and stationed in Penna. somewhere. I haven't heard from him as yet. Tonight I am really tired so I believe that I will close for now and go to bed. Goodnight dearest and

All my love, Gene

❀

22 July 1945

Good afternoon darling,

This afternoon is getting sort of quiet after a busy morning so I will have some time for awhile at least to write you a letter.

The party last [night] over at Asco was a success and everybody I imagine had a good time. At least the drinks were flowing rather steadily from 1700 until midnight. I had enough of course too but am just about convinced that I don't care enough about the stuff so my wife and children have to worry. What a thought that is—

The major had rounded up about 12 of the elligible [*sic*] and elite girls of the island so we who didn't have dates could at least look at them. They weren't too bad, in fact most of them were rather nice looking—or maybe I have been out here too long. As I said above, the drinks were really available in large quantities. Champagne a plenty also Southern Comfort and Harwoods. Also had good food in the form of about 10 different salads hot rolls and large quantities of meat. Some band from the 13th Marines provided dancing music which was very good. They aren't as good as the "Merry men of the Marines" who were originally from the 3d and are now snowing the whole Pacific area with their swell show. I think perhaps that after the war we will hear more about them.

Guess they are part of Bob Crosby's outfit at present. He is a Lt. also in the M.C. and really not bad looking. Some people probably think he is the most handsome Lt. in the USMC. You really don't know what to believe nowadays. That's all right darling — I have to keep kidding about that or you will think that I really believe it. Wouldn't want that to happen.

Your letter of the 14 was here for me when I returned last night and I appreciated it especially after thinking about you all evening as I said I would. I am sorry to hear that you are not feeling well. Hope by this time that your cold has disappeared. Isn't it warm back there now? I realize that it is possible to catch a cold in the summer however as I have had them. Always seem to be worse too.

I have been feeling pretty bad today but I think it is just the aftermath of the party.

Sometime soon we have to start fixing our tent which is in bad shape. When we get some lumber I am going to build a door on the front. It is necessary to keep the sides down because of the cold and dust which makes a very dreary looking affair. I hate to think of the swell set-up we had back in the 3d when I was living with Styke and Murph. Incidentally I had a letter from Merle a few days ago. Don't think that I mentioned it before. All goes well with him — mentioned the fact he had written to you and received your letter. Edwards is getting more bitter and has developed a "to hell with it" attitude which makes me feel bad. He is a good fellow — one of the few I would like to see after the war. Steve is the same as always — a friend of ours named Vatter who you may know, got 10 days hack [confined to quarters] but Merle didn't say what it was for.

There is a fellow who works here in the code room who went to the U. of Wis. His name is Boyle and if I remember right, was an outstanding football player. We just finished a lenghty [*sic*] conversation about going to school after the war. I think he said he is going to Mich. to take law.

To answer your question about talking people into things — no, I never have — wish that I had the ability however because I surely envy some of the fellows that are able to do that. I have a fear of "being told off" so that is probably the reason. I think that I will quit for now and sleep the rest of the afternoon. Maybe then I can get rid of this burnt out taste in my mouth and also the accompaning dull headache. So long sweetheart and I will see you soon.

All my love, Gene

Peg and I have something in common — we both can't type!

❖

23 July 1945

Hello Darling,

Hope your cold is better (or gone) by now and you feel back to normal. Tonight I have been getting the tent squared away and also stealing lumber from all over camp. It really is hard to get and I have decided to build myself a bed — if at all possible. Think that I'll start on it tomorrow because I have an off day. This schedule is wonderful — so much free time that I think I will become either lazy or bored. Perhaps I will do better with my desire to write to you every day. I notice you are doing that — which I appreciate and like very much. It isn't the idea of me wanting you to write every day but just that I want to get a letter from you daily. Hope you see the distinction. O.K.?

I have come to the conclusion O'Grady is a swell fellow but blinded somewhat by his extreme Catholic viewpoint upon almost every subject. Arguing with him is similar to the days at M.U — interesting but rather futile. At any rate I am going to like it up here in Hdqrs again. In general much less worry and more time to do the things I want to do.

I enjoyed <u>very much</u> that page of the Reliable booklet you sent and the comments (especially) on the side. I think I'll send it back to the "Great White Father" and have you do some explaining. Paul looks different than I had pictured him — Rodormer <u>is</u> handsome and Donald appears the type of a man who could pour forth on telephone panels. Is G. W. Rodormer E. W.'s father? That Volt Ammeter in the scene where the gentleman is testing fuses looks good. Would like one of those after the war.

The Barr's sound like interesting people. I don't like vulgarity either despite the fact that the service abounds with it. It becomes a rather stupid habit — and has no place in civilian life.

I see that you are taking cod liver oil — I suppose you don't care for the taste — as most people. I really don't mind it myself. Marty has taken the capsules for quite a few years.

Capt. Only is back and wants to go to bed — so I'll have to quit for now.

I am writing this in the message center because of the lack of light and cold at the tent. Goodnight sweetheart & I love you tonight.

Gene

❀

25 July 1945

Dearest Marian,

I have had a rather busy couple of days <u>sleeping</u> and building a bed. This is a lazy life — The bed I finally finished this afternoon and I am really proud of it.

Yesterday in the building process practically every officer in Hdqs Bn was in to ask "What is it?" Even the C.O—Colonel Sheppard. They all laughed but now I am sleeping in comfort and most of them are still on cots (which I find are too short for me) The consensus of opinion in the words of Johnson who sleeps here in the tent is that it looks like a morgue slab. (is that the right phrase, Miss Undertaker?) I had to laugh because he is right about the look especially when I had a sheet over it. I don't care however. Getting wood is the problem and I could find only short 4' pieces which made a million braces necessary. All in all it is a remarkable job. Almost forgot to add I had to take time off to go to sick bay for treatment of (1) a blood blister, (2) nail partially thru my finger, (3) scratch on my arm. This was at the Colonel's "request" because he believes strongly in medical care. So much for that—

This schedule we have at the code room is really terrific—amounts to working about 30 hours per week and the rest is of the time we are free. Lack of transportation is a problem we didn't have in Asco but there are a million advantages notwithstanding. The food is perfect in every respect. I doubt if I have eaten better anywhere at anytime.

Johnson has a radio which really makes it homelike—especially since it is a Zenith portable exactly like the one I have which was my pride & joy back in civilian days. Only sad part is the news broadcasts which imply that the war will be over any day now. It's no wonder the civilians are so optimistic.

I have noticed two things about this division that have impressed me. First of all—the morale is <u>very</u> <u>high</u> which may be due to the fact that they only have been out a year and also to the large amount of publicity they received at Iwo. The other is the unusual large display of pin-up pictures which never ceases to amaze me. This is unusual only in the quantity—Good heavens—they're <u>everywhere</u>. The signal officers' quonset hut has a map stuck in one corner (very inconspicuous) and the remainder of the walls, doors and even ceiling are covered with pin-up pictures. Even the G-3 officer, (full Colonel) has them everywhere. Quite a change from the conservative 3d.

Last night they had a movie at the club which was one of the funniest and most entertaining I have seen in many a year. It is called "Murder, He Says" with Fred Mac (Mc) Murray etc. The rest of the cast was excellent but I can't remember their names off hand. Wish they'd produce more like that one. I'd heartily recommend it to anyone. "The Corn is Green" and "Valley of Decision" were also very good.

Darling I haven't had a letter from you in 3 whole days now which seeing it's <u>you</u> makes it more like 3 weeks. Unfortunately the postmasters do not consider the fact that we're in love—Oh well—

Gene

P.S. Meant to comment on some of the articles in the new "Time" but will tomorrow—Just heard Churchill is out. Rather surprised.

❁

26 July 1945

My dearest Marian,

Only one letter in about 5 days now which isn't so good on the morale and dreams. Something is snafu but I know that you are not to blame. For some reason I have much faith in you which is rather different from some of the other girls I have known. Course I wasn't in love with them so that may have had something to do with it.

First of all I should explain about that "You convinced me that I am in love with you" business. I can see where there was room for a little confusion but actually if anything it is a compliment to you. I was not set to fall in love at the drop of a hat and in fact I had carefully avoided it for a long time. Then you started writing such wonderful letters to add to the memories that I had of you and before I knew it I had decided that it was love. Now I know that is not the most romantic way to put it <u>but</u> it convinces me and from my standpoint that is the most important thing If you had not written or had only written once a month, I certainly could not have got to know you so well as I think I do—could I? And also would not have fallen in love with you. Isn't that logical?

Something inside tells me that you were pleased with the general election in England. Isn't that right? I think that I was too—my only fear of the Laborites winning was the fact that they may foul up the war effort and let the U.S. holding the bag. That seems rather silly now and I do like their domestic ideals a great deal. Seems to me that they were decidedly against the government in the Greek confusion which was also a good stand to take. Their policy toward India should be a great improvement over the vagueness of the Conservatives. It was rather surprising that W.C. [hurchill] had plenty of opposition against him for his own seat in commons. My interpretation of the general election is that the people of Britain never had too much faith in the Conservatives but decided that the best to do would be to string along with the coalition gov. as the best means to win the war. That sorta debunks the theory of the past several years that W. C. was a national hero or something. In that way Roosevelt was different in my estimation. The Labor party has made a slow but steady climb since 1900 and I believe that they will succeed in making some permanent improvements as far as the domestic policy is concerned. Also it seems very probable that not only will Russia be more inclined to cooperate with them but also the United States. Our foreign policy has been more "democratic" than theirs. I put that democratic in quotation marks so that you don't have to say that ours is not democ—I know that you are thinking that—

We are getting somewhere but unfortunately it is a slow process. At least that what they keep telling me and I am beginning to believe it.

Forgot to bring my "Time" with me tonight to the code room so I can't comment on some of the articles. Did however get the June "Atlantic" and read the letter on Iwo. As you said it <u>was</u> good—he is right about the stench. I could look at Japs all day (the dead ones I mean) so don't agree with that statement he made. I hated to look at dead Marines because they always look like some fellows I knew. Always thought that but for the grace of God—one of them would be me. <u>and</u> good heavens! when are these correspondents going to learn that the 4th Division is not the 4th Marines. That is inexcusable. Sherrod has learned but these other characters who claim that they know the Marine Corps inside and out and still make such an obvious mistake.

According to tonight's news it sounds like Japan is weakening slightly. At least the so called peace feelers indicate that they may not be contemplating fighting to the last man. I still believe that our terms should be unconditional surrender, and the interpetations by the State Department of UCS. are O.K. I suspect that some of the "understanding Americans" who are so concerned with our hardships over here will attempt to soften the State Department's stand. Oddly enough it is those same people who were so considerate back in 1940 and didn't want any American boys taking military training because there was going to be no war. And for like reasons they don't want compulsary [*sic*] M.T. after the war because it would foster evil ideas (as one lady put it) and waste a year of Johnny's life. Oh brother—

I like the way that the 3d Flt is pounding Japan but this idea that "we can land anywhere now" is not too pleasant a thought. Sounds like some more Marines are expendable. Would like to do duty with MacArthur for a few seasons because it seems that he can pick the more pleasant beaches.

Time to get back to work darling so I will quit for tonight. There is a very beautiful moon and if you were here I could probably think of some romantic and illogical ideas why I am in love with you. But nevertheless.

All my Love

Gene

Thanks for the Barnaby's—always forget to mention it but I like him—also the little girl who is very realistic

❧

28 July 1945

Darling,

It has been a rugged week inasmuch as I have only received 2 letters from you since last Sunday. Now I am convinced that the mail situation is fouled up somewhere along the line. Oh well better days are coming. Wish that the war would end so that we wouldn't have to bother with letters.

Today George and I took a little trip where we managed to eat $1.60 worth of ice cream. We did really get our fill for a change—at least of banana splits and sodas of all sorts. It means a lot to be able to get away for a little while to relieve the monotony of camp life. Think that is probaby the reason that the morale is so high in this division. We kept remarking "Wonder what the boys in the 3d would say if they could see us now."

Tomorrow is Sunday and I have to work all day—should be able to write you a long letter then if we are not too busy. If we are, then I will come over at night and write it. I have been having trouble getting to sleep lately. Don't know what the reason is except that possibility I am not getting enough exercise. For the past 3 nights it has been after 0300 since I have managed to doze off. Perhaps I should try to get a survey—Do you know what that means? Incidentally—am I answering all your questions? I hope so—

The sort of "suspense" of expecting the war to end any minute has passed and everyone here is more or less convinced that it will drag on for another year at least. That is rather a depressing thought but one that I have held for a long time. Think that it is a matter of imagining the worst and then when the unexpected occurs—be very happy. Will close for now sweetheart but more tommorrow I love you.

All my love, Gene

⚜

29 July Sunday morning

Dearest Marian,

There is not much to do this morning so I should be able to get a letter off to you. Received one from my Dad and Gwen a couple of days ago which is rather unusual insomuch as neither of them write any great amount. If I think of it before I seal this one, I will send theirs along. You should be able to gain some sort of understanding of what they are like from the letter.

The paper this morning said the the Senate has ratified the charter almost unaimously which is good indeed. Makes me a little angry tho to think that they had to debate for several days upon something that contains all our hopes for the future and then 2 jokers voted against it. Inasmuch as it was apparently that or nothing I don't know what they were thinking about when they said "no." Something like the old Marine Corps saying that, "There is always 10% who don't get the word." Old Hiram Johnson of Cal. is a little hard to figure out. I think that he still is bitter from the NRA days. Significant is the fact from one of Roosevelt's speeches, if correct, is that H.J. would have been Sec of State under the man from New York. Wonder then what the situation would have been. I wonder just how strong feeling of the isolationism is in the hearts of men. Sometimes I think that many are not convinced that it is now a foolish policy but are too afraid to speak their views. Often times you hear fellows say that after the war we should have nothing to do with any foreign nation—which, whether they know it or not—probably not—is the old form of isolation feeling.

The cream of the opposition is thin indeed—

In looking over the latest "Time" I noticed that somebody here has put a notation after the one letter to the editor from the lady who didn't raise her boy etc.. It reads "Don't get excited lady." What a remarkable letter that is—good heavens. She isn't going to have her two boys sent to fight somewhere "at the whim of the Army and the Navy." I wonder if she thinks we are out here now at the whim of the Navy. Some people are trying at times. Why people sacrifice so much in war and then after it is all over with, go back in their little selfish world to rot, never ceases to amaze me. Unfortunately my mother is one of them—it gets me damn mad.

The mail just in and happily there was a letter from you. It was the one you had written July 23th—the day—I hope that we can celebrate that day next year—with me as a civilian again and the two of us together. At any rate I am glad that you had a good time. I had celebrated the Sat. night before at the Asco party so had rather a quiet Monday night just thinking.

The Southern Comfort Collins were practically the first mixed drinks I had to any great extent (to answer your question) also the first real liberty as a Marine. I did meet a girl—which you were probably thinking about when I said "sentimental" but that runs a poor 3d to the other two reasons why I like and remember SC. I hate to explain this (or these) girl angles when I am overseas. Would much rather be sitting there holding your hand but I imagine you feel pretty much the same when you mention Cal. But it's all the more reason that we should have faith in each other. Don't you think that is right?

Today I censored a letter from a fellow who enclosed one that he had received from his gal who had in turn decided that she was going to marry some other fellow. He wanted his mother to file it with his diploma etc. I should have felt sorry for him I suppose because he seemed very sad about the whole thing. But it rather appealed to my sense of humor in a cynical way. More tonight darling but I have to get back to work now.

All my love, Gene

✣

30 July 1945

Dearest Marian,

Just finished a letter to Merle so will write a few lines to you tonight before going to bed. It is bitter cold tonight as has been usual lately. Feels good to sleep under 3 blankets most of the time. The days are fairly nice but I don't like this area after having been with the 3rd which in my estimation is the most beautiful camp I have ever seen. Up here in hdqs bn the dust isn't so bad as the Jasco area. It really was terrific there most of the time.

I saw George today for a few minutes today—just time enough to pay him back the $6 I owed. When we were shopping the other day, I ran out of money and had to borrow from him. Something I don't like to do very much. Also the other night we rolled for drinks all evening and I managed to lose most of the time so I figured it was time that I got paid again. We just wait until we run out of money and then go over to the Paymaster and draw as much as we want. It's very convenient. As I said sometime ago, the money I am able to save is one of the consoling factors in being overseas. The post-war will be lean enough I figure, inasmuch as I don't want to work if I can possibly help it.

Your letter from the 25th arrived tonight and now it is getting more like sometime ago when I could expect one every day. You see—I am spoiled. Concerning the ballet—you said that you probable would go to see it that night with Julia but would probably argue later. Hence I figured you would argue about the ballet. Apparently not however, but that at least explains my mentioning the ballet and arguing in the same breath. Understand? It is very seldom that I don't understand what you mean.

Thanks for the assurance that you will do anything possible to enable me to go back to school. Nevertheless I am sorta worried and will remain so despite the fact that I do believe you.

I am getting a kick out of the party Mr O'Malley is arranging for Aunt Minerva—Also the way Aunt Minerva is playing along with Barnaby when the rest of them are trying to humor him.

Tonight I am going to start reading "St Thomas Acquinas" O'Grady left it here at the coding room.

We have a half of a quonset hut for our coding office. There is plenty of room to move around and a total of 6 desks. Also have a phonograph machine and about 100 records of popular and classical selections. Of course there are the usual amount of pin-ups on the walls etc. It is a swell place to work and write letters. The night shifts are no strain because business is usually slow and we have the time to write letters or read. Consequently I come up here most of the time even when I am not on duty. The schedule is very easy and we get a 72

hour leave every month beside the rest of the time off we are not actually working. I am going to try and get 5 days sometime next month in order to viset some
friends of mine. Franklin and Britt. They were in the 3d division before they got
transferred.

Demmy is getting along all right in Asco tho I think that he felt rather bitter because I got this job. I know that he wanted it very bad. I manage to get
along all right with him but I do not like him too much. To me he represents a
typical Eastern fellow with a good line. George Callens is not too satisfied here
and said that he would go back to the 3d at a minute's notice. Asco may split up
soon to live with the various battalions so now I am not sorry I had to leave.

Well darling—this has not been much of a letter tonight but at least you
know that I have been thinking about you and that is something. Goodnight
darling and I love you very much—

Gene

Please excuse the typing—

⚘

July 20 '45
[Chicago]

Hello, my darling,

Guess I'll start a letter to you while I'm waiting to hear from Murph. I just
came home from work & don't know what the plans are for dinner tonight. The
elevator boy told me my roommate went out with a man. He's a cute little kid.

A friend of Murph's from Beloit, where they both went to college, is here
for a few days. I suppose Ed will take them out tonight. Guess I'll go & eat.

Later—I can think better now.

Have to go to school tonight. It's Mr. Allengomez' birthday, so he said there
would be gallons of cuba libres there. Don't know whether I'll stay or not.

Your letters of the 13th came last night. I'm really glad you are a message
center commando again, darling. I never did like that H+10 idea.

Wish there were some object in attempting to discuss with you the possibilities of the next invasion. Seems to me the talk of invading Japan is a bit optimistic. I don't see how it could be remotely possible before September—but
who am I to know? September is not so far off either.

Had to laugh at your saying you thought I should be a writer. Peg has been
trying to talk me into it. I would rather like to be if I had anything worth writing about, but my knowledge & patience are too limited. I'd be much better as
an editor of someone else's ideas, I think.

It's almost time to go to school.

See you tomorrow, dear. I love you very much — & the practical aspects of it don't worry me a bit. Perhaps I'm just not very practical, or perhaps I've learned (I hope) not to worry about things until it's necessary.

Goodnight, Sweetheart,

Marian

✤

July 21 '45

Dear Lt. Sweetheart:

You should see our apartment tonight! It looks as if a tornado had struck, which is not far from true, the way Gale & her guest, Ruth, have been tearing in & out. A friend of Ed's is in town also & the four of them have been celebrating for three days now. Gale came in at 3:00 this morning — & Ruth at 2:30 this afternoon. She looked like a little kid expecting to be spanked — which perhaps she should have been. Needless to say, they've been having a wonderful time.

I had rather an interesting time last night, too. Guess I told you it was Mr. Allengomez' birthday & they were having a big party. Al was there & had brought with him several fellows who live at the Int.[ernational] House on the U. of Chi. campus. Among them was a Chinese student of economics. He's been in the U.S. about 6 mo., I believe, and was at Harvard until three weeks ago. He looked sort of like those caricatures of the Japs — all teeth. But he was certainly interesting to talk to. It impresses me that none of these fellows seem to have any race consciousness — particularly Al, whose poise & social grace are positively amazing. I rather envy them. I am definitely conscious of the fact that, whenever I go anywhere with Al, people are wondering about his origins. It makes me angry with myself. Hope I can learn to overcome it.

I'm glad you like the pictures. I'll have a large one made for you if you wish, darling. Your requests have certainly not been very numerous & I am glad to be able to do things for you.

I am surprised that you've never had any grammar since the 8th grade. In Milwaukee, of all places, it ought to be required in high school if not in college also. Don't you think so?

I saw "Music for Millions" this aft. Did you tell me you had seen it sometime ago? I didn't think the plot was so good, but Margaret O'Brien & Jimmy Durante were. Also the music.

It's really warm here today — practically for the first time. I can't remember ever seeing such a cool summer. Probably it will be scorching in September.

That's a silly thing to talk about. I must be tired. Better quit & go to bed. I love you, dear.

Marian

❧

July 23 '45

Hello, darling,

Are you celebrating? I hope you are having as much fun as I am. The only thing that would improve this evening would be to have you here.

Murph's friend Ruth is still here, so we three went out to dinner at Ballantine's, a very nice place around the corner. Had two martinis before dinner & have been feeling very gay ever since. Ruthie bought a bottle of Four Roses with which we are to spend the rest of the evening. I decided I'd write to you before giving into that, as this will be sufficiently incoherent as it is.

Rec'd your letter of the 16th & the invitation tonight. That's the cleverest card. Surely wish I could have accepted.

Getting back to the subject of liquor, you were saying that S. C. collins have a particular sentimental value to you. What kind of sentiment? You can't say things like that without qualifying them, dear!

Julia was telling me today that she has a watch which one of her nephews took from the corpse of a relative of Himmler's. He happened to arrive at Himmler's HQ just after these two characters committed suicide. Gruesome, isn't it?

I had dinner last night with Al & went to the concert at Grant Park—only in the reverse order. He was playing tennis so enthusiastically all aft. that he didn't realize what time it was & was two hours late. So we didn't have time to eat until after the concert. Needless to say, we were hungry by that time. It was sort of fun, though.

The paper reports that Gen. Doolittle believes it may not be necessary to invade Japan as they may surrender first. I wish I were that optimistic. Certainly hope he is right, though.

Darling, I should quit & be sociable. See you tomorrow.

All my love, Marian

❧

July 25 '45

Dearest Gene:

The way I have neglected you the last few days, I surely can't make any complaints about your letters, which have been very nice. However, it is not only you I have neglected—I just haven't done anything. I have spells every once in a while of feeling absolutely dull. St. Exupery says the life of the spirit is intermittent & only the life of the mind is constant. I think my mind is definitely intermittent, also.

Was glad to hear about O'Grady. I hope he proves as interesting as you expect.

I am also glad you are willing to go to a ballet. You probably will not like it at first. Don't ask me how to argue about one—I prefer to enjoy it and make no attempt at analyzing.

Ruth (Murph's friend) left today. Incidentally, she said I should ask if you know a Jack Gavin who is in the Marine Corps.

We were talking about Kathleen Windsor & her husband, & Ruth said someone she knows who evidently is a friend of theirs said they are supposed to be getting a divorce. I always hate to hear things like that.

Darling, I'm glad you are planning to go back to school. I know that I am as anxious for you to go as you are—& am perfectly willing to do anything I can to help make it possible. Now will you quit worrying about it?

Murphie is in bed already, so I'm afraid I must quit. I promise to do better next time.

Goodnight, sweetheart. I love you.

Marian

❦

July 26 '45

Dearest Gene:

I have been arguing with Julia all day about Churchill's defeat. It was a decided pleasure to come home & find that Murph is as pleased about it as I am. I had not expected he would lose—guess he didn't think so either. Julia has been arguing that he did such a wonderful job of bringing his country through the war victoriously that he deserves to be in for a few more years. I agree that he did a fine job, but, as I've said before, do not trust his imperialist ideas in the conduct of the peace.

Murph said the best reason she was glad Labor won is because she believed the Conservative party had forced Edward to abdicate because of his sympathy for the working classes. I had never heard much about that, but it seems quite logical. Any ideas on the subject? Would be a good enough reason for disliking the Conservatives, methinks.

Rec'd your letter tonight with the clippings on "We, the Mothers." They are horrible, aren't they? Murph enjoyed them almost more than I did. "I'm so glad he sent these," she said, "I haven't read anything so funny in ages."

There was a letter published in the Sun yesterday which Sen. Bilbo[54] had written to a woman in Chicago in reply to her protest to his opposition to FEPC. It was actually worse than "We, the Mothers." When a Senator is like that, it's really bad!

To change the subject—I'm definitely not going to see Cal again—even when he's sober! It would be too long a story to explain why I think it is that he's so unstable. However, I think the basic reason is that his father died when he was about three, & his mother did a very poor job of bringing up her children, spoiling them one minute & demanding too much of them the next.

Well, that is the end of that.

That 21 mo. rotation policy sounds good, darling. Another year doesn't seem so long—that is, most of the time it doesn't. I can wait—it's worth waiting for. In the meantime,

All my love, Marian

⚜

July 28 '45

Hello, Darling,

Does it seem good to get a letter written on <u>stationery</u> again? Or don't you mind the shorthand pages?

Your letter of the 23rd came today. I'm glad you enjoyed the pictures from "Reliable at War." Don't you dare send it to Mr. Cook! Yes, G. W. is E. W.'s father. Also, Wallace Cook is J. B.'s father. The Rodormers are of secondary importance in the firm, but nicer people by far.

I went to school last night, but did not stay for the social part.

Went to a show tonight. It was sort of an old one —"Forever and a Day." Pretty good.

That was certainly a dramatic thing that happened in New York this morning.[55] Plane accidents always seem very real to me—perhaps because I recall so clearly two crashes Franklin told me about that happened while I was in L.A., and also the effect they had on him. A very good friend of his was killed in one of them.

Did I ever tell you about "Dear Dollink" in the Herald-American? It's a weekly letter from a Jewish mother to her son in the service—all very foolish.

Ed brings it over every once in a while, & he and Murph get me to read it to them in imitation of the dialect. Something is always going wrong for "Uncle Pincus" & at the climax of the story, Momma's invariable comment is, "Noo, noo, dunt esk!"

Ed went to N. Y. this week & took with him a bottle of Manhattans. So, on the train he dropped his bag & broke the bottle. "Noo, noo, dunt esk!" Murph & I had more fun laughing at his letter.

Also, I had lunch today at a Jewish delicatessen around the corner, where they have wonderful corned beef sandwiches. I had ordered some coffee, & several minutes later the lady walked past & said to me, "I'm bringink you some fresh coffee in a minute, dollink." I nearly split!

I wish you were here tonight, "dollink." Wouldn't you like to celebrate with me the ratification of the Charter? Guess I'd better go to bed & dream up a celebration.

See you tomorrow, sweetheart.

All my love, Marian

❀

July 29 '45

Dearest Gene:

Don't you like this editorial? I really feel quite elated over the change, and much more hopeful for the future.

It's a lovely day today. I walked along the lakefront a couple of miles this afternoon. There are such crowds of people all over the place that it wasn't very conducive to serenity, but I did enjoy it.

Did I tell you that Jane is home from Seattle? I'm anxious now to take my vacation & go home, too. It will be so nice to see her again.

I'm going to have dinner with Al again tonight. When he called yesterday, I started to suggest that he should have dinner with us here at the apt. & then decided it wouldn't be so good as all we had was hamburger. However, he liked the idea & said he'd try to get some meat. This noon he called & said he had been looking everywhere & it was "very difficult" to find. I had to laugh because he sounded so puzzled. Anyway, we're eating out. Next time Mother sends us a chicken, though, he's going to fix it for us, native style. He calls it something like "roscompaio." I'm very curious.

I got that book for you yesterday, "Report on Red China," and will send it very soon.

Will also write to the Atlantic tomorrow. I wondered if you wanted me to, but thought I'd better wait until you asked.

Darling, it's about time for me to get ready to go out. Wish I had a date with you instead. It's times like this when a year seems like eternity.

I love you, dear—

Marian

✤

July 31 '45

My darling Gene:

I meant to write to you last night, but couldn't stay awake. In fact, I could hardly stay awake all day. Maybe it was the weather, as several others complained of the same difficulty.

So now I have two of your letters to answer—the 22nd & 25th—both of which I liked very much.

Was surprised to hear that Bob Crosby is a Marine now. Did I ever tell you I saw one of his radio shows in Hollywood? I think he's good, and, as you say, not bad looking. <u>Not</u> what I'd call handsome, however. No competition at all for you, darling.

You are certainly ambitious at carpentering, also. Can't imagine a bed looking like a morgue slab (preparation table, we call them) as the modern ones are enamel or porcelain. However, I vaguely remember some ancient varieties my grandfather had that might be similar. He used them for the Indians, of which, incidentally, there are quite a few.

I can't exactly figure out how you'd make a wooden bed that would be much good without springs. Or do you use slats instead of springs?

Did you read that article in the new Time about the "Japanese Peoples Liberation Alliance." That really made me mad! As much because I don't know what to believe, though, as because I am annoyed with their Red-baiting. That little pat on the back for Claire Luce[56] too! I'll have to start reading Newsweek pretty soon. "Report from Red China" puts an entirely different construction on their Japanese Peoples League.

Well—there's still the Chicago Sun. I liked this idea of Grafton's. Hope he is right.

Murph saw "Murder, He Says" a couple weeks ago & was as enthusiastic as you are. Hope I have a chance to go.

Darling, it's getting late—As usual, I've been thinking about you more than writing. I miss you so very much—

Goodnight, Sweetheart, Marian

✣

30 August [31 July]
[Hawaii]

Dearest Marian,

Just returned from the movie "Endearing Young Charms" so feel sorta romantic — I liked it very much for various reasons. Perhaps most of all because the hero was pretty much like me e.i. cynical and supposedly "woman wise" and very typical of the average serviceman. Unfortunately all doesn't happen as it did in this movie but it <u>can</u> happen and that is important. As in our cases — there is so much that we don't know about each other — but for the first time in my life I am willing to believe and trust in the future — and you. If it all seems too logical and sensible at times, I hope you won't mind.

Your last few letters have indicated slightly that you are depressed or something. I hope not and if you are I hope it is not anything I have said or not said. I feel that way myself at times but it passes — just like the time. I <u>am</u> in the 10th month now and the war looks brighter every day so I hope it is not too much longer. And we can thank the war and my going overseas for everything, practically so —

Your letter of the 26th came today. Glad you liked the article on Mrs Waters etc. It appealed to my sense of humor. Marty sent it. Also I see I was right about you being pleased over Churchill's defeat. It seems that there was some talk about the conservatives getting rid of Edward VI [*sic*] but I didn't pay too much attention to it at the time — seems very plausible tho. Senator Bilbo is a character who I would be in favor of shooting at sunrise. Concerning that — there are some good "letters to the editor" in "Time" this week.

I'd like to hear the story on Cal and your connection with him but that is up to you.

Goodnight darling and all my Love,

Gene

✣

1 August 1945

Dearest Marian,

Before I forget — that last letter should have been dated 31 July instead of 30 August. Oh brother that wasn't even close. . . . Guess that I had romance on my mind a little more than usual.

Today I spent sleeping for the most part. Have acquired the habit of listening to the radio too in all my spare time. Wish I could talk about that. Bought a new "Time" also—finally, and have managed to read quite a bit of it. I'd appreciate it if you would send some of the pages like you were doing after I am unable to get again. Right now I have no trouble. Tonight I have written a letter to Aage and also the Pres of Marq. I think that I told you that I received one from him a few days ago. It was very nice and I was flattered—insomuch as it wasn't a form letter. One thing about going back to Marq. is that it would be no strain educationally for me. Think maybe I will the first year. I wish that I would make up my mind—don't you?

Did you see that picture of the recoil-less 75mm how? I don't think that they made an overstatement when they said it was one of the most revolutionary weapons of the war. From some of the inside dope that we get (but no guns) I am quite impressed. I liked the feature article on Jeffers too—he sure must be some character but probably the type that we needed to run the war. The travel situation must be strained to the limet. I hate to think of some dopey characters sitting in "our" seats on the El Capitan. Tonight at dinner I heard a couple of Lt. Cols talking about that article which appeared concerning the 2 marines from the 28th Reg. and the Jap attacks on Iwo. They were quite concerned about the fact the article mentioned several times that their Garand jammed. Felt that the people would sell the M1 short whereas it is really a good rifle perhaps there will be a "letter to the editor" about that.

There has been a long interruption here because O'Grady came in and we started talking. Mostly it was about meeting his girl and meeting you. Told him in great lenght about our ride on the train and he in turn about meeting "Mary" at a library in Wash. DC.

Aug. 2nd Found out about 10:30 last night that I have the next 5 days free (some working schedule) so today applied for an official 5 day leave. If it goes through, I'll leave tomorrow and come back Wednesday. Now I wish I could spend it with you—or at least tell you about it.

There is much optimism about the war ending soon—probably more than there should be but I hope it's true. So long darling and I love you very much—

Gene

❧

3 August 1945 V-Mail

Darling,

I am on a 5 day leave and so far have been enjoying myself as much as possible under the circumstances. As usual I was hoping I might spend the time with you.[57] I have met an old friend who left the 3rd Div just before I did. Britt—He has been swell about getting me a place to stay in his barracks and in general has done all he could to show me a good time. There is much that is worthwhile to see here.

Have not even had the chance to write but I'll make up for it when I get back. Transportation has been quite a problem however. I have practically worn out my shoes. So long and more later.

All my Love, Gene

❧

7 August 1945

Dearest Marian,

Just returned to camp a few hours ago after my 5 day vacation to find a lot of letters I'd better answer. So tonight I'll start with you.

The "leave" was a success in most every respect and I really enjoyed myself. Now it's almost like starting overseas again but I think it has done me some good. I can't tell you much of course—stayed in the same barracks as Britt and he did all he could to show me a good time. Transportation is really rugged over there but by hitchhiking and walking I managed to see quite a bit of the island and it is very beautiful—More so than I thought and nicer than this one—I was fortunate to have several dates with this girl I had met sometime ago. We went to several dances and even to a night club. Sunday and Monday was spent swimming and as a result of that I have an uncomfortable sunburn. As far as the general situation is concerned—it can be summed in the old phrase, "There are different ways to fight a war."

It feels good to be back home at any rate. I have so much to do that I am going to be busy for the next 10 days. Bought a lot of pictures of the Battle of Iwo and have to get them in my album—

Here everyone is talking about the new atomic bomb. It sounds good to me and I hope it's true. I see where the Vatican newspaper expressed "regret that the inventors did not destroy the bomb in the interests of humanity." What foolishness is justified in the name of humanity—

All my Love, Gene

❧

8 August 1945

Dearest Marian,

Between the Russians and the atomic bomb I haven't had much chance to think about anything else today. Both those facts make the end seem nearer and I am almost as optimistic as most people around here. I can't hardly imagine what it would be like to know I'm coming home for sure and nothing to worry about except when. Suppose that everyone feels that way however—some take it for granted.

Getting back to the Russians, again—I'll be interested in what progress they make in Manchuria etc—the radio commentator said tonight they had already attacked. Hope that the Japs figure the way we want them to but they have a habit of doing just the opposite.

The "bomb" has created much speculation here as everywhere I suppose. It seems almost inhuman but all types of warfare are and it appears to me to differ only in degree. The first thing I thought about when I read the details was that the world had better be sincere in their desire to stop all future wars. If there is another it will be bad on everyone everywhere. If the late Senator Johnson[58] is observing from somewhere, I wonder if he still believes in isolationism. If I thought that there was going to be another war, I think I'd pick out some uninhabited South Sea island and stay there. Would you like to come along?

Time to go to bed—it is late mainly because I went to the movie tonight to get away from thinking the war would soon be over—and then be disappointed—Goodnight Darling.

All my Love, Gene

✣

August 1 '45
[Chicago]

Hello, darling,

Your letter today in which you mention having rec'd only one letter in about 5 days really makes me feel guilty for not having written quite so often the last couple of weeks. The postman does have something to do with it, however, as I haven't been that bad.

Your explanation of my convincing you that you are in love was very nice, dear. I'm glad you consider the fact complimentary. It all sort of amazes me, as I knew you really didn't want to fall in love—and I have never had much talent for talking people into things, either. I'm glad you did, though, and only hope you will never be sorry.

I knew you would be pleased about the election in England. I was trying to get Al to talk about it the other day, but could get nothing out of him except that he thought it was the best thing that could possibly have happened. He always talks in such broad generalities! I know he is basically in sympathy with our ideas, however, as he talks of his great ambition to do something for the common men. I have the feeling that he is actually more sincere in his love for humanity than I am. I am enough of a snob to want to avoid "humanity" if it is dirty or ugly—but Al would be different, I'm sure.

Incidentally, he told me a good deal about his life in Costa Rica—including the fact that he is married. I must have a peculiar attraction for married men. Al's wife was here with him for a while, but went back to Costa Rica. They fight all the time, as she has a Latin temper and they have nothing in common. However, he says he has sort of a "protective" love for her and always hopes that he may make a better person of her. I was rather glad to hear about it, as the fact that we are each in love with someone else should keep our friendship uncomplicated.

I'm glad you like <u>Barnaby</u>. He hasn't been quite as good lately as in the story about O'Malley's Enterprises, which ended just before I started sending him to you. I think he's exceptional today, though.

Was quite surprised to get a letter this week from Ginny, the girl I lived with in L.A. I liked her so much, and the poor kid has had such a hell of a life. If I haven't told you about it, I should, altho it's rather a long story to write. I must have told you that she was married, for the third time, just about the time you left last fall. As she put it, she's still "not exactly going around with stars in my eyes." Guess it would hardly be possible to be starry-eyed about anything, though, after all the trouble she's had.

Darling, that thought about some more Marines being expendable is certainly not pleasant. Gen. Erskine says he doesn't believe there can be anything as bad as Iwo again, however, which is some small consolation. Well—let's think about the moon instead.

I love you, dear.

Marian

✤

August 2 '45

Dear Lt. Sweetheart:

Rec'd your letter of the 28th today. In contrast to "2 letters in one week," the mail situation here has been wonderful—thanks to <u>you</u> and an exceptionally smooth bit of postal service, I've had a letter every day for quite a while. I am certainly in accord, though, with your wish that the war would end so we wouldn't have to bother with letters.

I don't see how you could ever get to sleep after eating all those sodas & banana splits. You really do things in a big way. What I like is hot fudge sundaes—especially with mint ice cream. But I'm sure I could never eat $1.60 worth, in spite of the fact that they are extremely scarce now. They used to have real wonderful ones at Heinemann's in Milwaukee. Did you ever go to that place across the bridge from Gimbel's?

I don't know what trying to get a "survey" means. Please explain—

You know, I think I must have spring fever in the summer. I don't get anything done lately. Don't even <u>think</u> coherently. Perhaps if I take my vacation soon, the situation will improve. I would like just to sit (Have to unsplit my own infinitives, also.) in, on and beside a lake with Jane all week. Since it can't be with you. See you later, darling.

All my love, Marian

☙

August 4, 1945
[Milwaukee]

Dearest Gene,

Talking about those hot fudge sundaes the other day started me thinking about Milw. so I decided to come up for the weekend. After I got here I discovered that Jo, my friend at the Shorecrest, has been in New York for three months. However, I found a hotel room and have been enjoying myself. Plan to call Martha [Dinauer] today and perhaps go out to see Lloyd [Sauer] & Kay tomorrow.

I was very much pleased to find that "Wilson" is playing at the Palace—so of course I went to see it. It is marvelous. I thought that scene with Clemenceau especially good. Incidentally, Wilson had a charming sense of humor, didn't he? I wonder what happened to his second wife. Do you know? She appeared to be considerably younger than he, and I wondered if she might still be living.

—Much later:

Decided to call Martha—it must have been an hour ago, maybe even an hour and a half—and we've been talking ever since. Mostly, I should say, she has been talking. Aside from getting a slightly stiff arm, I certainly enjoyed it. We always talk about Color Print & Lloyd & all the people we worked with. She quit about in March, I guess, because the creditors were driving her crazy. They were bad enough when I was there, but I never had to fight with them as much as Martha, being the bookkeeper, did.

Guess I'll go down & see if I can get one of those hot fudge sundaes now. Darling, I wish so much that you were here. Would like to go to the Schroeder & dream—but I don't like to go there alone. Maybe next summer?

All my love, Marian

❖

August 5 '45
[Milwaukee]

Hello, darling,

I haven't done a thing since I wrote to you yesterday, except read & sleep & think about you—none of which offers much material for letter-writing.

Thought you might be interested in this article on Japanese surrender. Being written by a Japanese, it ought to be more accurate than most of the stuff that's in print these days. I wish they would direct their sentiment in a more sensible direction and get it over with.

I called Lloyd & Kay this afternoon & am going out there tonight. They have the prettiest little house. I really enjoy seeing that almost as much as visiting with them.

Ran into Jim Brown, unfortunately, today. He is the most uncouth person. His wife was with him, & he explained that he had met her at some rally or something in Detroit & they were married within a week—the poor girl!

There are about 17 sailors in a room across the hall. Judging from the singing, etc., they've been having a good time.

Darling, I guess I'd better go. See you tomorrow.

I love you very much.

Marian

❖

Aug. 7, 1945
[Chicago]

My darling Gene,

Somehow I miss you much more than usual today. Perhaps the movie I saw last night has something to do with it. It was "The Clock." Have you seen it? I didn't really like it so much—thought they were a little childish—but for other reasons, of course, it reminded me of you.

Shall return these pictures of your dad & Marty. I enjoyed them very much—and also the letter from your dad & Gwen. Your comments & map were fun. Really had to laugh at your saying your dad's optimism is due to his being a civilian again. It hasn't seemed to me that civilians are so optimistic, but maybe I talk to the wrong ones.

Also have to laugh because you were angry about the several days debate & 2 neg. notes on the charter. Take it easy, darling! Of course I agree that it should have been unanimous, but considering the apparent mentality of some of our Senators, they did amazingly well. I get just as angry as you do, though, at people who are already planning to go back to their "selfish little world to rot." How <u>can</u> they be so blind!

What do you think of the atomic bomb? I was amazed & horrified (though not to the extent the good Vatican was). If it scared the Japs as it did me, they will surrender in a hurry. Surely wish they would. It is certainly another excellent reason why people & nations <u>must</u> learn to live together peaceably. Right?

I'd better go and get some food. More later. Another letter, I mean.

Goodnight, Lt. Sweetheart.

I love you —

Marian

❖

August 8, 1945

Hi, darling —

Wonderful news today, isn't it? Murph says, "They would! Now that it's practically in the bag." True enough — but we certainly took our time about getting into their war, and have no right to complain about the Russians exercising the same privilege. I know you agree.

Gene, it's wonderful being in love with you — & knowing that you are almost always enjoying the same things I am. It makes everything twice as good, dear.

Guess I haven't told you yet about Sun. eve. at Lloyd and Kay's. I had a very nice time. There were a few other people there, too, & we played poker & drank beer. I won $3.50, which I thought was not bad for a beginner. I gave back to Lloyd 1.50 with which to pay a traffic fine he incurred in coming to pick me up at the end of the car line. He has a genius for collecting tickets, especially for speeding. This one, however, was for honking his horn unnecessarily(!!), making a "U" turn in the middle of a block, and slowing down instead of stopping for an arterial. He claims the police think all drivers of sport roadsters (His is a gorgeous blue Buick.) need to be brought down a peg. I'm afraid it doesn't work on Lloyd.

Speaking of money, I really envy your ability to save it. The only way I can save is by having War Bonds deducted from my salary — and even those I have to cash occasionally. I don't <u>think</u> I am exactly extravagant, either.

Murph says she is going to be released from govt. service soon. I think perhaps she & Ed will be married. If not, she may transfer to a civil service job in New York, which they (her C.O. rather) have suggested. In either case, I'll lose my roommate. Have been thinking I might go home then until you come back. No doubt my dad would be pleased.

Ed finally told Murph why it was he thought she wouldn't marry him. I didn't ask her any details, but it's something about his mother and doesn't worry her at all. I'm glad he told her.

Darling, it's time to say goodnight, again.

All my love, Marian

✿

August 9, 1945

Hello, darling,

Our Uncle Joe [Stalin] isn't wasting any time putting into effect that declaration of war, is he? Guess that & the statement of our Air Forces in China that they had known for some time about the impending declaration, ought to keep quiet those characters who said the atomic bomb scared Russia into it. "Time" was being real smart this week, too, & saying that Russia "was not ready—if she ever would be—to go to war with Japan. Events in the Pacific & Asia, rather than a conference decision, would be likely to dictate Russian action." I hope they choked on that!

Since you liked "Those Endearing Young Charms," I decided to go & see it tonight. I liked it, too—the Air Corps, you know. But seriously, dear, the hero didn't seem very much like you. His cynicism, perhaps, but his decidedly unendearing insistence on having his own way was certainly not like you. I can imagine you shaking your head now & saying, "She doesn't know me very well." I do know you that well, though! I don't doubt that you can insist on having your own way about things that are really important—and that is not a bad way to be—but also I know that you are not essentially very stubborn. Certainly not spoiled as this fellow was.

You didn't tell me about the letter from the Pres. of Marquette, except that it was very nice. What did he say? I'm curious. Was it about going back there to school?

I couldn't find that picture of the 75MM howitzer. Wonder if it might have been in the Pacific edition only?

Hope you were able to get that 5-day leave—and how I'd love to be there with you!

Goodnight, sweetheart—

Marian

✤

11 August 1945
[Hawaii]

Dearest Marian,

As with everyone else we are waiting for the "word" from Japan as to what they are going to do with our counter-proposal. Most people seem to think that they will accept and I do too. There doesn't seem much else that they can do now with the atomic bomb and the Russians plowing through Manchuria and Korea. Their desire seems fair enough on the surface but I believe that the Allies did the right thing in making it clear to them that the Emperor will have to come under the jurisdiction of the COMINCH of the occupation forces. There seems to be the general run of some stupid people who will give them anything now just in order to get the war over.

All the premature celebrations are sort of a laugh in an ironic way if the deal doesn't go thru now. Especially the one on Okinawa in which 6 men were killed was rather sad. Reminds me of the Iwo affair in which it wasn't safe to wander out without a helmet for fear of getting killed with falling shrapnel.

Well—we should see soon and then will begin the "sweating it out" period At present I have a good idea what we are going to do—

I have sorta been neglecting letter-writing these last few days because it seems unusual to talk of anything else in the light of all this excitement. As I said in the last letter—it will be grand just to know that I am coming home even tho we probably will do occupation duty. These last few days we have been sticking close to the radio when not on duty here in the code room—when working we have been unusually busy due to the developments. Have managed to read the latest "Time" all the way thru now—Senator Bilbo got a lot of publicity in the last issue which he should have—it is not so funny tho when you think that it represents the view of most of the southerners even tho they don't put it in such a ignorant way. He must be stupid—

Time to go back to work now—Cheer up—the sun is beginning to shine—
I love you very much—

Gene

✤

14 August V-J DAY

Dearest Marian,

Just finished listening to a broadcast from the Blvd. Room of the Stevens Hotel and Frankie Masters. It sounded swell and I wished often that I were there to celebrate this day with you. It is wonderful—isn't it? Now for the first time I can figure on coming home for sure. Don't know of course when that will be because it is my opinion that we will do occupation duty of some sort. Insomuch as MacArthur is Supreme COMINCH of Occ. forces I am doubtful of getting home at any early date. But it is coming and that is all that is important. Truman says that 5 and one half million will be released this year and I hope that the Marines are among that number. Chances are however that we will either get a good deal or a bad deal out of the postwar duty—that is a rather vague statement but about all I can say at this time. Don't know whether censorship will be lifted and we can say what we want after V-J day

I have been to the club during the late afternoon after the "word" came through and still feel a little uncertain at this time. Practically all the off. are under the influence of alcohol in one way or another. We have heard over the radio all the various celebration from the different capitols of the world including as I said—one from the loop of Chicago. I would like to be in the States tonight.

The Emperor's speech was good—I thought but it failed to mention that Japan was beaten even before the atomic bomb and Russia's entry into the war. One character in Time's Square said that "He knew Japan was beat as soon as Germany surrendered," something the fellows that have been fighting out here for almost 4 years will undoubtedly "appreciate." Oh well, the wind will blow and the—will fly from now on I suppose. I am happy and don't care much what happens from now on so long as I can see civilian life looming up sometime in the future.

In between listening to the radio and trying to sleep this afternoon, I read the latest "Time." Am convinced that one of their best sections is the one on "Press" Usually they have a blast at Hearst or the "Daily News"—something which I like. Also in that one article on [Curtis] LeMay and B29's, they said something about living conditions were bad "according to Air Force standards." That really hit the spot with me and probably with all Marines out here. We know—and apparently "Time" does too.

Was rather surprised to see that they abolished the W[ar] L[abor] B[oard] at this time. I always figured that that agency would be of great use in the postwar days—The situation in China will probably reach a climax in the next week insomuch as it seems that the Communists and Chunking are racing to see how much of China each can occupy before the other. Unless Russia steps in it looks very much like Civil war unfortunately. Would like to see China occupy Hong Kong and the other British ports and keep them. Can't see where England has any business in China anyway. If we go to Tokyo, I probably will be able to make these letters a little more interesting and at least get a first hand knowledge of what is going on. Would not mind that too much but getting home comes first of course.

Meanwhile darling I am going to close for now and after a coke to quench this fire in my mouth—go to bed.

Good night sweetheart and happy V-J day.

All my love, Gene

P.S. Just noticed before sealing this that our location is mentioned on the back—hence the cutting—

⚜

16 August 1945

Dearest Marian,

Well the time moves on and every day that passes is a day less I'll spend in the Marine Corps and away from home. Everyone continues to be extremely happy and of course the morale is high.

Some character who reads the future in the stars down in the 13th Marines' area has had a good reading lately—we will be in Pendleton by Oct. 26 of 1945. Up here the stars look entirely different and I can very easily see us out here for 6 more months. This character was supposed to have correctly predicted Russia's entry (to the day) also V-E day (to the day) and V-J day (likewise)

Demmy's mother told him a year ago that the war would end the 15th of August—thus in various ways all learning and progress of a legitimate nature not only stops but is set back a couple hundred years. If <u>anything</u> makes my blood boil it is these people who not only are stupid enough to believe that foolishness—but try to convince me.

Meanwhile the war continues according to all reports—the Japs <u>may</u> be trying to pull a fast one inasmuch as they appear to be stalling. Frankly I doubt it because their purpose is, I believe, to make sure the Emperor's position is insured before the Allies walk in. This need not be bad because I think that the best way to control the people is thru Hirohito—and he can be controled.

Churchill's blast at the Soviet makes me very happy that he was defeated in the election last month. It was stupid altho probably true to color but the reactionaries are on the way out and apparently they don't like it. What was considered radical 20 years ago is definitely the order of the day and will be more evident after the post-war world starts rolling.

Apparently I had some "bum dope" about the W.L.B. a few days ago because I see it still is operating. Am glad of that.

The immediate international problem is the Chinese Nationals vs. the "Communists." I hate to see that but perhaps China will have to learn that the liberals are demanding (and going to get undoubtedly) some form of labor government more in sympathy with their views than the arbitrary Chungking confusion.

Time to close again darling. We are putting in some long days at work. Goodnight and

All my Love, Gene

⚜

18 August 1945

Dearest Marian,

Saturday night and on duty again but this finishes up a pretty exciting week. The war is over and we can look into the future again and make some plans. Before this all that seemed not only foolish but futile. It is 10:00 PM and I just have come on duty after going to the movie over at the mess hall. I enjoyed it quite a bit altho the plot was rather unrealistic—don't think that that is the right word but it will do. On the other hand the dancing, color and dialouge were extremely good most of the way thru. Name was "Salome (sp) Where She Danced." Think that it should be an "e" there at the end of her name but I am not sure. The other might be the stuff that goes on sandwiches. I think that you would appreciate it if only to see the ballet scenes.

I worked all this morning and most of the afternoon here in the Comm. office. We are extremely busy most of the time but the work is interesting and the time passes quickly. As usual the scuttlebutt is flying as to where we're going but now I have a good idea.

The Japs seem to be getting the word in the various parts of China but I wish that the surrender procedure would look a little more like surrender and less like Japanese entrenchment. Once we take over however in the strategic parts of the homeland we should be able to dictate their policy for many years to come and probably get the idea over to them that they actually have lost the war. It is always sad to see that men have to die after the armistice terms have been arranged and the only procedure left is the formal signing of the surrender. It was fortunate tho that we weren't carrying on any large scale land operation. The situation in China looks more encouraging tonight than ever before insomuch as the 2 factions seem willing to discuss terms. Would like to see the Chinese occupy Hongkong and the other British possessions in China.

Sunday 19 August

There were too many interruptions last night to finish. The general threw a party last night which was really remarkable to all indications—at least all the staff seem to be feeling rugged this morning. Johnson, my tent mate, was there because he was formerly General Burke's aid when the general had 5th Corps Artillery.

We have received a letter from Mar Corps asking us whether we want a regular commission and have to submit a form letter answering that question and also how many points we have according to the Army system. It appears that officers have to resign their commissions in order to get out. This I will do with great haste altho I still will be an officer in the Reserve. As far as points are concerned I stand probably a little better than average—so far as I can see—with about 54. Lack of [more] combat—and children—slowed me down somewhat but I imagine I will come near the middle when the discharge system starts in earnest. The reluctance they have shown to let Marines out makes me think the discharge will be rapid once it starts. Eventually the army of occupation will be army—I think, altho some Marines will go in first probably. All these "I thinks" and "probably" are due to the fact that we have little definite information.

This morning they announced that the peace representatives have met MacArthur in Manila so it shouldn't be long before it is officially over.

I haven't been able to get a "Time" this week as yet and I really wanted that issue. This afternoon I have to pack some of my clothes and send them home. In 3 years I have acquired much stuff that is a burden to carry around—The "Army Hour" is on the radio now. He (announcer) said, "This is the Army hour of 19 August 1945." Does this give you a hint of why my letters are dated "17 August" "18 August" "1 July" etc??

Will close for now dearest. I love you very much and that more than the Japs' surrender makes the future bright.

Gene

❀

18 August 1945 [2]

Hello darling,

I feel pretty rugged tonight inasmuch as I caught a cold sometime between noon and supper. Something similar to your case of a few weeks ago if I remember right. Methinks that it was because I stayed up last night until 0300 to play poker. Haven't played cards hardly at all since we came over on the ship. Suddenly got the urge tho last night but would have rather played bridge.

We have been extremely busy here in the comm office the last few days and I think that it will be much worse as time goes on. Wish that this censorship would be lifted here soon but I doubt if that will come about for several months.

The war still rages on several fronts according to the latest news reports from the radio and I suppose that we will have to resign ourselves to the fact that it will be some time yet before the war will be over—practically. Reconversion back in the states apparently is in full swing with gas rationing off and most of the bans on recreation lifted. Also now the last of Roosevelt's cabinet is gone (I think) when Grew and several assistant Sec's of State resigned. Was sorry to see Grew go because I think that he would have been invaluble in our post-war dealings with the Nips. Perhaps tho he will be given a responsible job under the great MacArthur. I love that man!!

Did you know that there has never been any love between the M.C. and the General? Guess that it dates back to the time that Mac wanted to abolish the Marine Corps. I see where that question of a "one service" is up again. I would hate to see that come about and I guess that all Marines feel that way. The Army men have nothing to lose because there is practically no Army spirit (if I except the Air Corps—do you still want to argue?) At any rate I hope that the Navy wins the fight. It seems to me that the question is—whether it is better to save some money and have a mass of people of "Army" caliber, or to forget the money and have at least a few good divisions and a real Navy which has pride in itself. This sounds like a foolish schoolboy argument but actually there is much to consider along those lines before the change be made—Even if people think that 6 ordinary Army divisions could have done the same job the 6 Marine outfits have done.

Back again after an hour's interruption. Don't care to write here in the tent. The light is poor and it's <u>cold</u>—Think perhaps that it will be colder.

Received your letters of Aug. 9th today. Thanks for sending the pictures back so promptly. Your letters of the 11th-12th came yesterday. As far as me influencing you quitting your job in Chicago—I don't really expect to be back for 6 mo. unless a miracle should happen—so—As I said before the best solution would be if you were working in Milwaukee—that is, as far as <u>I</u> am concerned. But wherever you are in the vicinity would be all right. I think I'll plan to go to M. U. for the first year.

Time for bed again to make up for the lack of sleep last night. Goodnight sweetheart and Much Love tonight.

Gene

❖

August 11 '45
[Chicago]

Darling,

I wanted so much to write to you yesterday, but there was so much to do I just couldn't get a chance. Would give anything to talk to you for just five minutes about this Japanese peace offer and know how you feel about it. Almost everyone I've talked to is all excited about it, but I don't believe I'll be really excited until it's definitely over. Somehow it doesn't seem real. Too good to be true, I guess.

I think the Allied reply is wise, and am especially glad they insist that the Emperor's future status shall depend upon a general election.

The reason I had no time to write last night was that, first, I had dinner with Al, and, second, Murph's friend, Ruth, came down for the weekend again. Her husband is coming today or tomorrow from Texas.

Had a most enlightening conversation with Al. I was trying to find out what he knows & thinks of the two factions in China, & he finally told me his parents were from China. He has never been there himself, but has worked for the Chinese Embassy in Costa Rica and wants to establish an export-import firm in China in about two years. About the political situation there, he says he prefers the Communists (Hurrah!) They are better organized, he says, & have a better program to offer the people. Also, their morale is much higher. In the Kuomintang, he says, there are too many corrupt officials. His only objection to the Communists would be if they are governed by Russian influences.

Incidentally, we had dinner at a Chinese restaurant & I learned to eat with chopsticks! It's really quite simple. Have you ever tried it?

Oh, darling, I hope you can come home soon!

All my love, Marian

⚘

August 12, 1945

Hello, Sweetheart,

This suspense is as bad as V-E day, isn't it? Ed said last night that he thinks they have the whole thing settled but are purposely trying to make it another anti-climax. I hardly think he's right, though.

Ruth's husband got here about 9:00 last night. He's a bombardier, Capt. Jack Griffith. Ed had brought over some bourbon and ginger ale, and the five of us really had a lot of fun. Only I was awfully lonesome—for you, as I always am, & especially when I'm with couples who are so obviously in love—and for Franklin, because it was the first time in months that I've heard so much Air Corps talk. We had a couple of good arguments on education, on Russia, & on the New Deal, which you would have enjoyed.

Haven't heard from you for about four days, so I assume you did get that 5-day leave. Hope you can tell me a little about it.

Have I told you, Gene, that I've been thinking of quitting my job & going home for awhile, possibly until you come back, at least. Think it might be a good idea? I think my folks might like it, and it wouldn't be so bad up there now that Jane is home, too.

It's such a nice day I ought to be doing something, but the music on the radio is so good I hate to go out. Right now they are playing Rachmaninoff's second piano concerto. If I go home, I would like to find someone to take piano lessons from again. Mother & Dad don't seem to mind listening to my playing, although it sounds like hell most of the time.

Darling, it's wonderful to think you might be home soon. I love you very much.

Marian

❦

August 13 '45

Hello, Darling,

Ah, some mail today! Your V-mail of the 5th & airmail of the 7th. I'm glad you had a good time—just so you didn't enjoy those dates <u>too</u> much!

The phrase that there are different ways to fight a war is apt. I just hope it doesn't have to be done the hard way again.

The suspense is still with us. Surely doesn't pay to get excited.

I started reading the latest of Upton Sinclair's novels this weekend. It's called "Dragon Harvest." Seems to me one of the questions you never answered was whether you had ever read any of that series. I like them very much.

Incidentally, in the part I read last night, this phrase was quoted: "Happy are they whose annals are tiresome." Ordinarily, that would not appeal to me, but lately I have been wishing that life, for a change, could be peaceful & happy enough to sound extremely dull. I suppose that is depression—you said I had sounded somewhat depressed recently. As you also said, it will pass—only being not so intense, it lasts longer. There is another quotation on this subject which I've always liked. It's Pearl Buck's, I think. "Sadness is the long reality, and gaiety is only for the moment. To know that is to know peace." It is, indeed. Agree? Just remembering it makes me feel better—much less impatient.

See you tomorrow, darling.

All my love, Marian

❦

August 14, 1945
V-J Day

My darling Gene,

It is so wonderful I really can't believe it. To know that there will not be another Iwo Jima, or even anything like it, is—how could I possibly express it? Very likely you feel it more deeply than I do.

Of course, the uppermost question in my mind now is: How soon can you come home? It seems that since you are so near, it should not be long. I suppose there is the possibility of the occupation, but perhaps with MacArthur in command it will be largely an Army job, I hope. More suspense! But with the world at peace, darling, the waiting will be so much easier.

I have not been doing very well at getting that holster for you. Guess I told you Ed was going to find out about it for me. He has evidently forgotten, & when he is around, I never think of reminding him. Now that the war is over (How good that sounds!), do you still want it?

Can't think about anything else tonight except how much I love you.

Goodnight, dearest—

Marian

✢

August 16 '45

Hello, Lt. Sweetheart:

No mail deliveries on these holidays, which is not so good—but I guess we ought to agree that the postmen deserve a rest. Right?

I have been doing practically nothing but reading this book I mentioned the other day. Murph & Ed have been out almost all the time, so I have been alone except for an hour or two which I spent with Al. He is of the school which prefers meditating to dancing in the streets. There are still many other kinds of wars to be fought, he says—not a pleasant thought, but certainly true.

What do you think of this article about China? The last paragraph in particular makes me furious. I showed it to Al & he said these puppets evidently hoped by this action to avoid punishment for their aid to the Japanese, but that they would be disappointed. If there are corrupt officials in the Chungking govt. as he says there are, it seems to me that is a naive attitude. To think that <u>anyone</u>, our own govt. in particular, should condone any sort of deal with Japanese puppets, absolutely burns me to a crisp!—Probably I should take some of the advice I give you and relax. Surely there isn't much I could possibly do about it.

Darling, you and I thought we might be able to celebrate this Victory together—and, as far as I am concerned, we shall, even though we may be rather late. In the meantime —

All my love, Marian

✿

August 18 '45

Dearest Gene:

I was very happy to get your letters of the 8th & 11th today. Had to laugh about your going to the show to keep from thinking too much about the war being over soon. It's a good sign when a <u>cynic</u> like you has to discipline his optimism—I like you, dear.

Before I forget, I want to tell you a quotation from this book "Dragon Harvest" which perhaps you ought to pass on to the pin-up lovers of your new Division. Just a gentle warning. This was in France just before the Nazi blitzkrieg: "Lanny thought that never had he seen so much of what the French called 'la belle poitrine,' and what current American slang knew as 'cheesecake'—meaning the semi-nude bodies of young females. He had the idea that it heralded the downfall of the nation or social class in which it prevailed."— Lanny's ideas are <u>usually</u> not to be taken lightly.

Getting back to your letters, it's really amazing how often we say the same things to each other, don't you think so? Sometimes I think we could almost eliminate them—oh, no, not that! Not while you're so far away.

The new Time really has an excellent section on the "atomic age." Right? I especially liked the part called "A Strange Place." "Life, as always, was irreversible." Too true, too true.

Incidentally, about the late Senator Johnson, I'd be willing to bet an atomic bomb would have to land on him to change his isolationist mind.

If there is another war, darling, I'll gladly go with you to that uninhabited South Sea Island—if you can find one.

Goodnight, Sweetheart. I love you very much.

Marian

✿

August 19 '45

Dearest Gene:

Someone has been shooting off fireworks tonight in a belated celebration. We could see them perfectly from our apt. windows, and it made a very pretty show. So we got a bottle of beer and celebrated, mildly, ourselves.

Poor Murphie isn't feeling very gay, though. She has been in tears all day over the state of affairs with Ed. It seems he continues to put off the question of marriage until she is about convinced he has no intentions but to postpone it forever. He has certainly not been very fair about it—never explains why he can't make up his mind. As you said when I told you about it before, I don't see why he ever suggested the subject in the first place. People are very peculiar and can get themselves into more complicated situations than even a Hollywood script writer could dream up!

I've been meaning to tell you another chapter in the story of Tyrone Power. When Ruth & Jack were here, she was telling us that Annabelle's secretary used to live in this bldg. The Powers used to come over here to see her occasionally, & Ruth had seen them in the lobby. She says Tyrone is not handsome at all— always looks as if he needs a shave—So now, Lt. Sweetheart, you'll have to think up someone else for competition.

Darling, I am beginning to wonder, when I write that I love you, if it seems insincere or monotonous with repetition. Each time I read it in your letters, tho, it seems equally wonderful—so perhaps you feel the same about mine. I hope so, because I do love you.

Marian

❀

August 20 '45

Dearest Gene:

Just now they are playing on the radio a new song called, "Till the End of Time." Have you heard it? The tune, they say, is from a Chopin Polonnaise (sp). Anyway it is a lovely thing. I like the words, too. My mother has an old Etude magazine at home (about 1917) in which there is a song with the same name. It has long been a favorite of hers—& mine, too. I'll play it for you some day if you'll promise not to be too critical. The words go something like this: "The fairest flower must wither & decay, but love like ours grown stronger day by day will live until the end of time." Like it?

Had a letter from Peg today. She's coming back from Washington a week from Friday & will teach at Stoughton this fall, as perhaps you already know.

We should be able to spend quite a few weekends together then—at least I hope so.

Your letter of the 14th came today. Needless to say, I am not very happy about the fact that you expect to be on occupation duty for sometime. I'm really quite impatient about it, but it isn't going to do any good, I know, so I may as well try to talk myself out of it.

I was just waiting for you to comment on that remark in Time about living conditions being bad "according to Air Force standards." Of course, being loyal to the Air Force, I have to remind you that they have their troubles, too. For one thing, the presence of possible death remains with them even after they're home—as long as they're still flying.

Peg told me Ray was in the convoy that took Laval to France. Wish I could tell you in detail all the stories about Laval, Petain, Reynaud, Daladier, etc., that were in "Dragon Harvest." They were very good.

Discovered today that Mr. Ripley's secretary is leaving. I am quite positive he will offer me her job & I definitely do <u>not</u> want it. 'Twill be quite a problem how to say no. I'll probably have to tell them I don't intend to stay more than a few months longer, and I don't imagine they'll like it. Oh, well—

Murph told me that Cal called one night last week when I wasn't home and sounded very unhappy, so I thought I'd better call him today. He's quite the opposite now, as he finally got that job he wanted so badly. Guess I told you about it a long time ago. He starts right after Labor Day. I'm certainly glad for him. Just hope it will be as good as he expects.

Guess it's time to say goodnight, darling. See you tomorrow—how I wish I could!

All my love, Marian

⚘

22 August 1945
[Hawaii]

Dearest Marian,

These are some rough days with more work than we can ever hope to do here in the office. I can honestly say that I never have worked so hard since I got in the Marine Corps.

Last night it was nice to go back to the tent, listen to the radio and dream of you and think about better days when I'll be home and all this just a memory. The war is over and that is wonderful. I feel that I never can appreciate that fact in one hour, one day or even a year—but gradually the feeling keeps coming back with all the memories—and then the realization is actually there.

Understand dear? That's why it is silly for all these reporters to go around and ask "How do you feel now that's it's all over?"

So much for the effects of V-J day. I see that we are going to be prohibited from fraternizing with the Japs. Right now I am not sure sure whether they will be bitter about the surrender and make it hard for the allies or bend over backward to be nice to us — sorta would bet on the latter tho — They are strange people — I still think that if it weren't for the atomic bomb that they would have fought to the end. It possibly gave them a face-saving excuse to end the struggle because the effects of the A.B. have been played up in the Tokyo papers. If I were to make a guess about the time I'll be home, it would be 6 mo. Nobody knows I guess — But we can hope — and dream and that's what I am going to do now.

All my Love, Gene

✢

23 August 1945

Dearest Marian,

Nothing much in the line of real news today that you don't know from reading the paper. Censorship is still in full effect and that of course limets the things that I can talk about and say for sure.

Had today off and spend most of it sleeping and listening to the radio. Johnson, my room mate, has left so I have his radio temporarily till he gets back. Also went over to viset George and Demmy this afternoon and they seem to be the same as always. Merle wrote a letter a few days ago and said that Demmy was not very well liked back there. This is something that I suspected but never bothered to find out how many people didn't like him. I suppose that he is harmless tho —

It felt good to have the day off after a week in which we had really worked hard almost all the time. The situation stands the same as it did in my last letter — as far as my getting home, that is — It looks like six months with the discharge probably being based wholely upon the point system. I can't complain about that because the point system seems to be the most fair way. The AAF came out with an extremely low point discharge affair as far as officers are concerned which doesn't help the situation very much as far as our morale is concerned. At least when we do get back the reconversion era should be on the way out and things should be more like the way we left them as civilians.

The Japanese seem to be cooperating very well so far and their genialty seems rather ironic after Bat-ta-an as our general says. Oh it is a strange life.

Just received your letter of the 18th and it was <u>very</u> nice. I think that they are all that way but some I appreciate more that others. Undoubtedly you must have found that the case too—Right??

The quotation from "Dragon Harvest" is something to tink (sp) about insomuch as <u>we</u> seem to be living under the same circumstances as some people characterized the 1940 France. Tho I don't agree entirely with that solution which was supposed to explain why France fell—I don't on the other hand, like this era of semi-nudism and all it stands for either.

It will never cease to amaze me when it comes apparent how America really got into the spirit of the war and did the job that she did these last 4 years. I don't think that the difference between France of 1939 and the U.S. of that same year as far as "social thinking" was great. The differences lie in the fact that France didn't have the time to convert to war and we did—and then there was the "outrage" of Pearl Harbor which sorta snapped us into the spirit. Want to argue dear????

We do often say the same things but undoubtedly there will be things we differ in when we start to reconvert. I like that word "reconversion"—it means so much—especially the social part of it.

24 August

Back again after another hectic day. I will finish this now and probably start another letter to you later on this evening to answer yours of the 20th which came today. I spent the last 6 hours auditing the books of the Wine Mess—a job I got quite by accident. My arm is sore from pulling the lever of the adding machine. More later then darling and

All of My Love to you,

Gene

⚜

25 August 1945

Hello Miss Smith,

I feel rather romantic and playful tonight. Think I ought to go to bed. Just sealed the other letter to you I finished earlier this evening. In the meantime, tho I wrote a long letter to Marty in answer to one of his I received today. He, too, believes that we should hang the emperor, but looks at it a little more farsighted and has come to the conclusion that the U.S. did the right thing—me too—

Your letter of the 20th came today. I'm sorry about Murph and marriage troubles again. What will she do if she becomes convinced if he is going to postpone marriage indefinitely? Darling, there may be a good reason for him not wishing to get married now. Because two people are in love is no foolproof argument why they should get married at some definite time in the future. Is it? A man can't say, "We'll be married 3 years from today." You don't have to answer these questions because it all revolves upon "security"—and you answered that very well some time ago. You are right about people getting themselves into peculiar situations, dear—

It has taken me the longest time to write this page and a quarter—I have a shoulder holster now so that is all settled—thanks for trying tho.

To change the subject for the fifty-second time—Tyrone Power has been based on Saipan and somebody from there says he has a handlebar mustache. I think that <u>he is</u> handsome—at least his eyes are big and brown which always is appealing to me.

I like to hear the "I love you's" probably as well as any normal human being and like to say it to you too which is just as important. I think that I have "met you" a million times in the last 10 months. All of them were very nice, but when it actually happens, I know that it will be wonderful. We do have much to learn about each other but we have a good start. Goodnight sweetheart and

All My Love, Gene

⚜

28 August 1945

Hello darling,

These are terrific days without hardly time to collect my thoughts and decide what I really am doing. I have not moved.

Finally managed to get a copy of the victory edition of "Time" and between jobs have managed to read most of it—a sentence at a time. As you said a couple of letters ago, the section on the atomic bomb <u>is</u> very good. It makes one realize that science, as with some of the liberal arts, the field for reasearch is almost unlimited. I don't have any patience with those who say that the discovery should have been destroyed instead of brought to light. It appears to me that these foolish people are the ones who are convinced that there never can be peace in the world and are attempting to make the next war as "humane" as possible. Seems to me that they should be convincing themselves that we never can allow another war and directing their actions toward world cooperation to make that possible. Right?

This typewritter is really remarkable—the lines are not much more straight than my hand written letters.

Getting back to the situation here at Camp Tarawa, (that's the name)—I have got a jeep now which was necessary due to the great amount of running around I have had to do—Have been sitting here for 15 minutes trying to think of something I can tell you—which I find is very difficult to do. I have not had any letters from you for 4 days now and what is worse—I don't expect to get any for quite sometime. It will be only a matter of weeks now till censorship will be lifted almost entirely. That will help matters considerably—at least my conscience anyway.

The Navy and Marine Corps has been sending out beautifully worded dispatches in an unveiled attempt to get as many of the reserve officers to stay in the regular service. We just smile and say "We know we know—," and think pretty much like that Naval officer quoted in "Time" a week ago who said "I wouldn't stay in this damn Navy if I starved to death on the outside." The Navy has probably realized that it doesn't take an Annapolis man to make good when the chips are down.

That is all the time I have now. Will try to write more tonight whenever I finish work. These are going to be rough days on both ends of the line but bear with me and I will try to get off some sort of a letter even if it is only to say that I love you—

Gene

30 August 1945

Dearest,

Don't know why I always pick on you—to write a letter to—after I have had something to drink. Well anyway—Just finished talking to Lt. Col. Quickly who is div. Q.M. and have had four "Old fashioned's" "Old fashion's" whichever it is—Started this about 5:45 PM tonight at the bar when he asked if I'd like to "roll" for a drink and I of course had to say, "Yes Sir." I lost the first 3, and that gave him a great laugh because he said he only had $2.00—after a rather strained conversation—you don't know what to say to a Lt Col, do you?—I finally found a friend of mine from the 34th R.O.C. and gentely broke away from the Colonel. But a few minutes later he came back to "roll" again and I finally won—and by the end of the fourth drink before chow—I was extremely dizzy which I still am. In the meantime we fought the battle of Iwo Jima again and other odd subjects the colonel wanted to talk about. I think he became very angry when he recalled the paper saying the "famous" 27th Army division was occupying Tokyo or thereabouts—which made me recall a issue of "Time" about June of 1944 and the account they had about the 4th Marine Div and the 27th at Saipan. Oh well—they are probably good—I don't take anything away from them.

The "Pearl Harbor revelation" was pretty much the way I had figured it would be—their desire not to reveal the "facts" indicated it probably would touch some of the high rankers still in important positions. I agree most whole-heartedly with Truman in his declaration that the American people were to blame ultimately. However it seems to me that commanders like [Admiral Husband] Kimmel & [General Walter] Short were responsible for their own security irregardless of any information they may not have had.

The fact still remains that the Pearl Harbor leaders were caught unawares—which is inexcusable as far as the military situation is concerned. If they had had only 2 destroyers—those 2 should have been alerted because we did have means to detect an approaching enemy force. Somebody was sleeping at the switch and as always the C.O.'s have to take the blame—because the first rule of military action is you can't delegate responsibility. So it seems to me at any rate.

Was extremely happy to see that Boyington[59] has been rescued from the Japs after apparently being dead. His story of the hardships he and other flyers had to undergo should [indicate] that someone ought to be punished for the those inhumane actions—but I still claim more can be done with a revised system of Jap education than making the whole nation suffer for crimes committed under a false philosophy. Agree?

Sat 31 August—

The morning after and I almost am afraid to read this—Well anyway I'll send it this morning. It appears that we are going to keep getting mail which is a great help to the morale.

More very soon darling—the work is beginning to slack off a little.

All my Love dear

Gene

✣

August 22 '45
[Chicago]

Hello, darling—

No letter yesterday, no letter today—and impossible as it seems, I keep wondering if you might be enroute to Tokyo. Unpleasant thought.

Speaking of Tokyo, this editorial by Shelton is pretty good, I think.

And Landis I like very much, as usual. In spite of the sarcasm, this is a nice piece of good humor; don't you think?

I was very glad to read that Ernie Pyle's wife is objecting to the grandiose plans for memorial parks, etc., for him. I don't understand the psychology of people who think million-dollar expenditures are appropriate memorials to such men.

What do you think of the end of Lend-Lease[60]? If it is true that it will now be impossible for those countries to obtain necessary food supplies, it is surely a tragic mistake — & one which I believe Roosevelt would not have made. For the first time, I wonder about Truman & his Missouri advisers.

Incidentally, perhaps I've told you Ed knew John Snyder & thought he was rather stupid. He didn't know him well, however.

That's enough about the day's news —

Last night I went down to the Union Station with Murph to pick up some tickets. I really enjoyed being there & thinking about the day we had breakfast there. Remember how you scolded me because you almost forgot to see about checking your baggage? It's wonderful to know that there will be another day like that.

Goodnight, sweetheart. I love you —

Marian

❖

August 25 '45

Dear Lt. Sweetheart:

Ah, a letter today — and a nice long one, too. It's amazing how much I miss you in the spaces between letters.

About the stars & all that stuff, I certainly share your skepticism, but how I'd love to believe that "character" who says you will be home by Oct. 26.

Wonder if Demmy's mother actually did tell him the war would end Aug. 15. Probably an accidentally good guess if she did. In Upton Sinclair's books Lanny frequently experiments with mediums & that sort of thing. He is skeptical, but curious. Some of the books on psychical research that he mentions I would really like to read — except that they sound so horribly complicated.

I had a letter from Mother today which worries me a little. She says the doctor who operated on her eye this spring has suggested that she should have a "thorough health check." So she is going to Madison sometime next month. She has been so nice lately, I wondered if something was wrong. That's a flippant remark — but, seriously, if she isn't caustic, something is wearing down her spirit. It makes me feel guilty because she's usually so self-sufficient I don't even think of being considerate.

She also told me one of the fellows, Ray Plesser, who went to high school with us is home. He had been in Hawaii (Oahu) with an anti-aircraft outfit for about three years. I'd like to see him. He used to help my dad quite often when

Franklin wasn't there. Liked it much better than Franklin did, too. They are quite pleased because he's going to help Dad tar the roof while he's home. Nice way to spend a furlough, hm?

The new Time answered my question about Wilson's wife. She was at the White House last Sunday.

See you tomorrow, darling.

All my love, Marian

❖

August 25 '45

Hello, Darling —

Rec'd your letter of the 18th yesterday, and I see that we have a few things to argue about — amicably, of course. (I hope.)

I am inclined to disagree with you about Grew. Undoubtedly his experience with the Japanese should make him of value in dealing with them, but from what I have read, I would prefer that he didn't have too much to do with formulating policy. Perhaps I've told you about having read a review of his book on Japan which said he seemed to have been impressed with the social life there & had little understanding of the basic problems of the people. Suppose I ought to read the book instead of taking someone else's word for it. He was also involved in what seemed to me the wrong side of that controversy involving the arrest of several journalists accused of using illegally State Dept. info. in writings which were more or less favorable to "Communist" China.

This other argument is one on which I have no convictions. I'm merely arguing to be contrary — and because I like to hear you defend the Marine Corps. There is no love between me & the General, either, & I understand the Air Corps is not exactly fond of him. But, aside from the fact that he advocates it, do you really think a unified command for all the services would detract from the spirit or change the caliber of the individual branches? I should think that ideally it would affect only such matters as procurement of supplies (which could surely be more efficiently handled by a single organization) and over-all strategy. It seems to me the fact that the Air Corps and Marine Corps, neither of which is wholly independent of a larger organization (or am I wrong about that?), are the proudest of the services, refutes your argument fairly well. That is certainly a complicated sentence. If it's too bad, send it back & I'll do it over.

To get back on safer ground — Murph & I went to the show this afternoon, and it turned out to be exceptionally good. "Roughly Speaking" with Rosalind Russell & Jack Carson. Have you seen it? It's a story of a woman who lives with jaunty courage & good humor a life that seems to be one disappointment after another. An admirable character. I'm sure you'd like it, too.

I hope your cold was not serious, dear.

Guess I'd better say good-night. In spite of the controversial tone of this letter, I still love you.

Marian

❀

August 27 '45

Hello, Darling —

Quite a collection of clippings today. I wonder if the newspaper is really much more interesting some days than others — or if it's just that I am sometimes more alert & able to appreciate what I read?? A little of each perhaps.

One of the minor items in the news which gives me much satisfaction is the prospect of nylons — possibly by Thanksgiving. Of all the unimportant comforts of living that disappeared during the war, nylons — & good chocolate — are the only ones I missed.

Getting back to something that will interest you, too — this Russian-Chinese treaty pleases me because it indicates that most of the accusations about Russia's ambitions in the Far East were untrue. Also, it seems the Chinese Communists could hardly have much of a connection with Moscow. In a way, I'm sorry about that because I don't want to see them kicked around. This article of Mark Gayn's is encouraging, tho. I hope the reforms of which he speaks will be carried out. Am anxious to learn the outcome of Mao Tse Tung's visit with Chiang. It looks as if we have our fingers in it all right with [Pat] Hurley acting as "escort."

The storm broke at Reliable today, & I had a long talk with Paul & Ripley about being "promoted" to secretary to the assistant to the president. Sounds like a Republican's conception of a Govt. job, doesn't it? I told them I couldn't make any promises about how long I'd be here, but they didn't seem properly upset about that. Paul seems to think I ought to make the change & work for Rip. I know he doesn't like Rip any more than I do — He says the important job for the next year will be obtaining materials, etc., for reconverting, and that's Ripley's dept. Paul said, "Frankly, you're too damn good to be doing the routine work they'll be giving you over here now that we're out of the turnbuckle business & I'll be traveling most of the time." Coming from such a noncommital person as Paul, that really pleased me. I still don't know what I <u>should</u> do, but I can see what I'm being talked into.

Incidentally, Paul has acquired a moustache. Ordinarily, I don't like them, but his is really becoming, I think. Somehow it seems as if he looks taller. Sounds impossible, doesn't it?

I can well imagine that work is exciting for you these days. Surely wish I could hear a little about it. Six months doesn't seem so long—I hope it won't be any longer. But when I think of these fellows who have been gone three years & more, we have been lucky, dear.

I think I do understand how you feel about not being able to realize that the war is over. It's hard for me, too. In a way, I feel that it won't be over until you come home—& in a way, it seems it will never be over. Probably because it seems so clearly evident that the underlying conflicts are still there & will remain for a long, long time. Someone has said that war is politics continued by another method, & the saying is probably true in reverse. That is not a very pleasant fact, but we can never keep the peace by ignoring it. Right?

There is more to say, but it will have to be postponed until tomorrow. In the meantime, darling—

All my love, Marian

⚛

August 29 '45

Dearest Gene:

Talking about the lack of chocolate last night reminded me that we solved our own little race problem with it. Our colored maid, Ellen, was so sullen & disagreeable that we really hated ever to stay home from work—simply because it was so unpleasant to be here when she came in. One time when I had a cold, she came in here three times & finally, about three in the aft., bawled me out for being in bed. It happened that she wanted to change the linens. One time not so long ago, I happened to be here when she came in & offered her a piece of candy. From that moment on—we've been friends. She buzzes around here like a ray of sunshine, & talks about everything, including Roosevelt. "He was a good man. I don' know what us po' folks would 'a' done without him!" After that, I began to like her, too.

DeGaulle is in town today. Would like to have seen the parade this afternoon—from a window somewhere above the crowd.

I have a new book—new to me, that is—by E. B. White,[61] which Julia suggested. It is a collection of essays which appeared originally in Harper's, I believe, & is entitled "One Man's Meat." Have you ever read any of his stuff? I like this book very much. If I were ever to make an attempt at writing, this is the sort of thing I'd like to do. He has a marvelous sense of humor. Guess I'll have to copy one of the paragraphs for you. This is a part of his light-hearted lament on hearing that New York's 6th Ave. El was to be torn down ('39). It applies to Chicago's El's also, rather it could. . . .[62]

That last sentence I love.

'Tis getting late again; so goodnight, darling. I love you, too—but <u>different-ly</u> than the sentence.

Marian

✤

August 30 '45

Hi, Lt. Sweetheart:

Your letters of the 23rd & 25th, which came today, were of the especially nice variety.

I have been laughing all evening about Tyrone Power's big, brown (& appealing) eyes. You won't give up, will you? Well—I suppose it is a matter of personal preference. I like blue eyes myself, darling.

About Murph & her problems, I agree that being in love is not the only thing to consider in getting married. But I do think that if there is some good reason why Ed wants to postpone it indefinitely, surely she has a right to know what it is. Don't you think she has? It seems the trouble is that he would like to have his cake & eat it, too, as the saying goes. I gather he has managed that in the past & is a bit upset because it doesn't work so well with Murph. I would tell you more about this if you were here—or if I had more confidence in my ability to say what I mean.

In the matter of my so-called promotion, I was maneuvered into a corner yesterday & agreed to work for Ripley. I had wanted to talk to Paul about it before deciding, but there was no opportunity to see him alone until today. However, what I wanted to know was whether or not he honestly thought it would be the thing for me to do & apparently he does. He explained today that the reason he approved was because I could get a better salary. ("After all, that's what we're working for," <u>he</u> said.) He has already talked to Mr. Cook about it to be sure I would. Darned nice of him, wasn't it? I told him I thought he knew I didn't like Rip very much & would probably be losing my temper every once in a while. He just nodded his head & said, "Well, take it easy!"—So, my dear, after the 15th of Sept. I shall expect to be treated with added respect. The whole thing will probably be just as hard on you as it is on me, if not more so, as you will be hearing all my complaints.

I like your application of the word "reconversion" to our own not-too-distant future. It sounds wonderful. You know, darling, sometimes I think both of us must have imagined those first few minutes so often that they could hardly help being anti-climax, in a way. Or is that a device I use to invite patience? Anyway, I would rather have it that way & improving with time than have the beginning better than the ending. Agree?

Goodnight, sweetheart, &

All my love, Marian

⚜

August 31 '45

Hello, darling—

Just after five tonight, someone brought a bottle out of the vault at the office, and each of the 5 or 6 of us who were still there had a rather stiff drink. Mine had the usual effect, & I'm lonesome.

Peg came in about seven this morning, but she couldn't stay over tonight, so I stayed home for about an hour this morning to talk to her. We had a good time, of course. She has to start teaching Tuesday. I was really disappointed that we had so little time. However, she's going to come down for the weekend early in October—when the Ballet is here. (She likes it as much as I do—or more.) When she came this morning, she called from the lobby first. Murph thought when the phone rang that it was our usual 7 o'clock call &, without listening at all, she said "Thank you" in her usual semi-conscious state & hung up. We had a good laugh over that. It's fortunate Peg used to live here & was not insulted.

If it doesn't rain tomorrow, I'm going to take a boat trip over to Benton Harbor with Lee, one of the girls at the office. We were both complaining today because we had nothing to do & no one to visit over the weekend, so it seemed like a good idea to do something together. I've never been out on the lake like that except once or twice on that old thing that used to go out for a couple of hours in the evening in Milw. It wasn't so bad as long as you stayed on the deck. Remember it? Did you ever try dancing on that ship? "Trying" is as far as we ever got.

It seems I've been writing such long letters this week—guess I'd better end this one here and do something else for a while.

See you later, darling. I love you very much—

Marian

7

"I really believe ... that the things you have to do now are as important, in a way more important, than the battles."

EARLY IN SEPTEMBER *we listened to the official surrender of a Japanese delegation on the deck of the battleship* Missouri *under the watchful eyes of General Douglas MacArthur. While Marian wondered how soon I would come home, I learned the Fifth Marine Division would soon be heading toward Sasebo, Japan, for occupation duty at the great naval base on Kyushu. However, I was assigned to the rear echelon and stayed in Hawaii. Unfortunately most of Marian's letters during the next month were forwarded to Japan. With the war over, there was much talk in Washington about a future "Unified Command," a move both the Navy and Marine Corps strongly opposed. When censorship was finally lifted on 7 September, I wrote my first overseas letter without restrictions from Hawaii's Kona Inn.*

---

1 Sept 1945
[Hawaii]

Dearest Marian,

It looks like V-J day is finally upon us after many false starts. I have the duty tonight but it doesn't make much difference insomuch as there will not be any great celebration here. The Marine Corps announced that they will go down to 200,000 in another year so our hopes rise once again. By Jan 1st I will have 60 points and I figure will have a good chance to get back and out.

The occupation appears to be moving along in great style so I hope the Marines will not see too much guard duty there. The 4th Marines have landed— probably they were chosen because the old 4th Marines were on Bataan.

Later—I am up here at hdqs on duty now. Since the first page I have heard the official surrender aboard the Missouri, MacArthur's speech, and the talk by Truman. It seemed like a sort of anti-climax, don't you think? Also have just read your last 2 letters from the 26th & 28th. For a change I will be able to comment upon them tonight because I should be fairly inactive as far as routine matters are concerned.

I hope that you have nylons when I get home—like most men I appreciate them too. That reminds me of that parachute we had as a ceiling back at the tent in the 3rd. I could have knit you a couple pair out of the nylon—you will have to blame the Air Corps for using all the nylon dear. I see that you definitely don't agree with me (and the Navy & Marine Corps) about the unified command. That's all right, dear, I still love you—The question you have brought up concerning whether the change will detract from the spirit of the individual branches is of course the big question. I think that perhaps those against it believe that it will for the most part. I believe that a unified command implies the "wearing of the same uniform" which probably would put a dent in the morale. So long as all jobs in the services are not and never can be equal it seems strange to me that people suppose that the spirit in a intra service organization can be high. The Blackhawk division protested to congress about being sent overseas after 20 days of combat duty and few casualties—never could I imagine a Marine division doing that.

It is true that the M. C. & the Air Corps are dependent to a great extent upon some higher unit but they have a sorta semi-independence which they wouldn't have otherwise. At least the Navy has a cabinet post which puts it on a par with the Army. Perhaps all this argument is stimulated by a typical Marine spirit which we don't think the Army has. In that respect it may be based upon error or a sorta selfishness. Seems to me it is similar to combining 2 colleges of great rivalry into one institution—the spirit is gone. Oh well—We feel, to sum up, that we are going to lose something—the Army doesn't give a damn about it which should mean something.

New subject—I guess that I have liked Grew mainly because he has expressed my feelings toward the Japanese. I never thought that they would surrender and I still believe that the Atomic bomb gave them a good face-saving excuse to get out. And if we hadn't agreed to letting them keep the emperor it would have been a fight to the bitter end. Maybe I was carried away by the "stupidity" of people who claimed the Japs would surrender right after Germany quit. Outside of that I know very little about Grew so what you say may very likely be true.

Have not seen "Roughly Speaking" but several of the fellows say it is good. I liked "Without Love" shown here a few weeks ago—The new "Time" mentions something about a Corwin "flop"—have you heard anything about it? Also in the "Letters to the Editors" is the usual sense and nonsense as far as the atomic bomb. Giving it to the international security council has good possibilities insomuch as it would more or less indicate our good faith in that organization.

Here it still looks like 6 months but I wouldn't be too surprised if it came sooner—provided the Marine Corps returns entire units to the states. Had I chose the 4th Division back in June instead of the 5th I probably would have come home sooner.

That's all for now dear. Goodnight sweetheart and

All my Love, Gene

⚜

3 Sept 1945

Dearest Marian,

The radio today said that the armed forces are no longer under censorship regulations so we are waiting for some official word on it. I hope it's true.

My work has squared away to a great extent and I am more or less taking it easy now. Yesterday was probably the worst however. I am living in a sorta house now with 2 Lts from Jasco. They are both from Chicago and in a discussion this noon, they both told me in great detail that you live on Chcago's "Near North side." Right? Wherever it is I wish I were there tonight.

They had a parade out here today which we listened to most of the morning—the army mostly I think, because the announcer only mentioned the Marines in passing. He said "and here come some soldiers—their chests covered with ribbons—everyone one of them well earned etc." I was thinking of the Army "Good Conduct" fiasco and wondered. Guess that I might as well get used to a lot of foolish talk about the war and everything pertaining to it—because apparently anything goes now that it is over.

I am in a peculiar position to tell you what is going on here so my letters will continue to be necessarily (and unnecessarily) confusing. When censorship stops, I'll have no excuses tho.

No letters for the past 2 days which isn't too good so I have to contend myself with reading your latest. Have not been on liberty since I came back from leave. Last night we saw, "My Man Godfrey" C. Lombard W. Powell It was old but good—seems that it was one of the best around 1936.

"Barnaby" seems to be doing good altho I thought that the part where he was supposed to meet the family was very weak.

It appears Chungking and the "Reds" have got together after a fashion probably due to a great part in Russia backing Chang. If he had made the mistake to back the "Communists" it undoubtedly would have meant civil war. Russia seems to have developed the habit of doing the right things at the right time.

Hope that your job difficulties clear up soon. If you are half as important to "Reliable" as you are to me—they should make you president instead of the Great White Father. You are doing good on this end and I love you—

Gene

❀

7 Sept 1945

Hello dearest,

Am down here tonight (at the Kona inn) with another fellow who lives in my tent. He has taken off to viset friends and I am stuck here in the lobby. I don't know why he ever managed to talk me into coming tonight but I sorta felt like getting away for awhile. Nothing much accomplished except reading "Time" and listening to the late news.

This is an attractive place with a rather peaceful atmosphere suited definitely to honeymooning. It doesn't compare with the Royal Haw—hotel over on Oahu (which incidentally is a submarine rest camp) but it is nice. Except for the Marine officers' beach and an enlisted one, the swimming here is highly overrated, I think.

There are 2 large mountains in the center of Hawaii which are about 13500 ft and formerly active volcanos—Mauna Kea,—Mauna Loa—the latter still pours forth at regular intervals. These lava flows are interesting but rather silly to explain in a letter. The whole center of the island is an enormous ranch consisting only of dust, cows, sheep and the 5th Division. The Parker ranch is supposed to be the largest in the world and lies between the two above mentioned mts. The principle occupations seem to be cattle raising, sugar cane and compiling tourist propaganda for romantic mainlanders. The people are mostly Japanese, Portuguese and a few Anglo-Americans in that order—more or less friendly but definitely "tourist-wise."

The Kona Inn is 45 miles from Kamuela and Hilo 65 miles. The latter was shelled by a Jap sub on Dec 10, 1941. Civilian products have been plentiful all during the war which is sort of surprising insomuch as shipping out here has been curtailed almost entirely.

So much for the situation and terrain—but I'll add "I wish you were here."

Next Tues. we move down to Hilo to await transportation to the rising sun land. Wish that it were in the other direction tho—I have been sitting here hoping that by next Sept I will be back in school. I think that I will.

I haven't received any mail for the last 6 or seven days—I believe. It seems longer—

Well it is almost 900 PM and I think I'll go and look for Lennin and drag him home.

I love you tonight too and goodnight sweetheart

Gene

❀

8 Sept 1945

Darling,
No letters in 8 days which is really bad—the sad part is that I am the only one in the Signal Co. not getting my mail.
Work here suddenly started again after a couple fairly easy days and so today I am tired again for a change. Wonder what really would happen if I had a civilian job.
The order came out this morning stating it will be necessary to have a driver accompany officers on all trips using government vehicles. It hit us somewhat of a blow as we had just become used to jumping in our jeeps and going on liberty. It will be particularly bad when we go down to Hilo. I am getting extremely tired of: (1) the rear echelon, (2) being overseas and (3) the Marine Corps. Usually it doesn't bother me too much but today I particulary would like to be stretched out with my head in your lap and forget all this confusion. I have found that investigating an accident to a M.C. vehicle is probably the height of paper work. We have had 2 Summary Courts Martial this week but thank goodness I have not been asked to be the recorder—that too, is a headache.
Wish that I knew exactly when I'd come home but there has been no definite word as to that. Good afternoon sweetheart—I hope I get a letter tonight from you.

All my Love, Gene

✾

9 Sept 1945
Hawaii TH

Dearest Marian,
Last night I heard, "Till the End of Time," on the hit parade. It was the first time and I thought rather appropriate insomuch as I had not received a letter from you for 9 days. It did make me feel better.
Today is Sunday and very peaceful at this particular time. The "Contented Hour" is on the radio and we have just finished a wonderful dinner—fried chicken—which reminds me that the meals here have been perfect, due I guess to the large amount of fresh meat and other foodstuffs left behind in the various units. We all eat at the Staff off. mess and I live nearby in a sort of hut affair, really quite elaborate compared to the tents and cots I had become used to in 9 months. It is amazing how much a person can take if it becomes necessary. I don't think that I ever will forget the "little things in life."
About a month ago I started to write some of the things I saw & felt while being overseas but have never got any farther than the Marshall Islands. I was

amazed in a way to note how much I had remembered about the departure from San Francisco, the trip over here and subsequent events on Guam. Perhaps I will gather enough energy to finish it some day. It probably will be the subject of conversation for sometime to come (being overseas etc) so I should have something to refer to. I imagine that these prisoners of war will have some interesting stories to tell—even tho most of it will be unpleasant.

We are just about ready to move to Hilo. I have sent 10 of my men down to establish some sort of telephone system before the main party arrives. My sgt called up today to tell me we had to have a BD 96 in order to tie in with the Army system on the island. I thought of you—The whole unit is called a TC-4 if it makes any difference to you.

We still do not know when we will go forward to join the main forces. I hope that it is soon as I would just as soon spend my time in Japan as here in Hawaii. [General] Wainwright was here a few days ago (i. e. Pearl Harbor) to lead a parade and now is apparently in San Francisco.

I am getting tired of all this—Wish that I could come home. The large number of strikes are a little disappointing but inevitable. Labor has cooperated more or less during the war but now it is the same old story again—employer vs labor. It is rather disgusting to note the obvious selfishness on both sides but it seems to me that is the whole social structure Your economics will have to change in keeping with the times—and that means more rights for labor. We can't go back to the pre-war days of low wages and minimum wage scales. This has been evident in England.

Well, so to bed for tonight. Eventually I must receive your letters, but the lapse makes me realize how much I do miss you darling—but I know that already so I hope there is one tomorrow.

All my Love, Gene

✧

September 2, 1945
[Chicago]

Dearest Gene:

I don't like these holidays when there are no mail deliveries. Since there were no letters Fri. or Sat., there will be at least four days without any—& that's too long!

As you may have assumed from the enclosed post card, it didn't rain yesterday, and we did go to Benton Harbor. During the two-hour stay over there, we followed the crowd to the House of David [retreat] and found it a much more pleasant place than I would have expected. This little train is the cutest darn thing! It takes people from the entrance to the amusement park to the restaurant and to the zoo. The grounds are quite attractive, and the food is wonderful—that is, if you don't mind the absence of meat.

On the boat we didn't do much of anything but sit on deck & enjoy the sunshine and <u>clean</u> air. We really had a good time, though.

Later—Took time out to listen to the special program on which Pres. Truman spoke to the Armed Forces. Did you hear it, dear? I thought it was very good, but somehow these programs of thanksgiving make me extremely sad.

Better to talk about something else, I guess.

There's an article in today's paper about Hong Kong which I think you will like. Mark Gayn again.

I read another of E. B. White's essays tonight. This one, on "Freedom," was written in 1940 & I gather that he would agree with what you said about the situation here before the war being similar to that in France. I think you are probably right, too. No arguments, dear. It must have been somewhat worse there, though, because their government was so unstable.

Well, darling, I guess I'd better go to bed.

I surely wish you were here this weekend—but that is not unusual.

All my love, Marian

❧

Sept. 4 '45

Hi, Genie—

With the light brown hair, <u>and</u> blue eyes!

No, I haven't been drinking. This gaiety is spontaneous & unassisted—also without any cause that I know of. Unless it could be your letter, which is surely cause enough, but somehow they don't always have the same effect. Maybe those Old Fashioned's were of an exceptional quality.

Some day I would like to have a discussion with you on why it is so uncomfortable to converse with a Colonel. That's a little hard for a civilian to understand, I guess. You don't feel so superior when you talk to a sergeant, do you? I should think a Colonel talking to a Lt. would be a fair comparison—All right, tell me I don't know what I'm talking about! I can't argue with that.

I was glad, too, that Truman told the people, including me, that Pearl Harbor was our own fault. It's about time someone told us we couldn't blame it all on the other fellow. I see Sen. [Robert] Taft is still insisting on a scapegoat. Evidently he is not accepting his own share of the responsibility. The rule that you can't delegate responsibility is one civilians should learn <u>and apply</u> also.

There is an excellent article in the Sept. Atlantic, "A Serviceman looks at the Peace," by an ex-Marine Lt. (that alone would make it good, dear.) He was one of Stassen's aides at San Francisco, & he seriously criticizes the Charter for being entirely dependent upon voluntary cooperation rather than setting up a real world government, which he believes is essential to peace. His arguments are convincing.

I like Barnaby today. That "8 minute day—very little overtime" is a prize!

I is weary—guess I'll go to bed and dream of Genie. That's a horrible pun, but it's so appropriate I can't help it. 'Scuse please.

I love you, darling,

Marian

�֍

September 6, 1945

Hello, Darling,

Since Paul is out of town again, the days are quiet, and I can write to you without disturbing my conscience.

Our desk clerks at home seem to have some method of misplacing your letters occasionally. Last night I was so disappointed because there wasn't any, and this morning (with no mail deliveries between)—there it was! It probably should have been here several days ago, as it was dated earlier than the one I had yesterday. Oh, well! It's very pleasant, anyway, to find a letter there when it is supposed to be impossible. Especially at that hour in the morning it does a lot to improve the aspect of the day—to say it conservatively.

My friend Grafton just returned to the editorial columns after about a month's vacation, and I am glad to see that he is still "emotional." I like what he says about the gas.

When I came back from lunch this noon, there was an old Buick parked just down the block, and it looked exactly, to the last dented fender and cracked window pane, like the one Franklin and I had when we were in L.A. I keep expecting him to walk in any minute. Makes me so damn lonesome.

Did you ever hear that theory about men swearing about the things women cry about? It's a useful idea to reverse.

I see that the Air Corps is agitating for a unified command and favoring MacArthur (!) to head it. Methinks it is a good thing I'm neutral.

As long as I am typing this, it should be an opportune time to copy a few more pages from E. B. White I get more enthused about this stuff every day. This first part was written in November, 1941, and the rest in December of the same year. The first is about a civilian defense meeting. . . .[63] [This was a story about a prank played on a local Jewish merchant. It concludes with the comment that we had failed to recognize the enemy in our midst.]

The comments on all this feverish typing—out of a book—are becoming too numerous. I'd better finish a little later.

Later—I surely agree with these ideas, particularly that there is a need for people big enough to love the whole planet. A difficult thing—but I believe it should be less difficult as more and more people travel in other countries, etc. His thought about the scientists is interesting. Also, its reference to the atom. I have the feeling this is something that ought to have been written very recently rather than in 1941. A far-sighted man, Mr. White. Yes?

It's almost five, so I'd better quit and put this in the mail. See you later, dearest.

Much love, Marian

⚘

Sept. 6 '45 [2]

Dear Lt. Sweetheart,

I just finished another letter to you about four hours ago, but I don't suppose you'll mind if I start over. Besides, that one was mostly in quotation marks. Of course the quoted paragraphs were far superior to anything I could write, but Mr. White can't tell you that I love you—so I have one advantage over him.

Rec'd your letter of Sept. 1 tonight & have decided all over again that you are wonderful. Even when I disagree with you, I think you're wonderful—and that seems rather important.

About this "unified command," as I said this aft., I really am neutral. I don't know enough about it to have any definite convictions. I like to argue with you about it just to tease you—& because I like to hear you expounding the pride of the Marines.

Incidentally, I'd like to see the movie of that name.

I notice the new Time says the same thing you do about the official surrender—anticlimax. I missed the speeches somehow—just neglected to listen, I guess. It seemed like a routine matter almost.

Your interest in nylons rather amazed me—altho I don't know why it should. It never occurred to me that men appreciated them—probably the reason I like them hasn't much to do with the reason you like them.

All I know about that Corwin thing is what Time said. Haven't heard the program.

There's a letter to the Editor which impressed me considerably in the new issue. It's about Ken Murayama. You will probably have read it by the time you get this letter. It's a subject I've thought about a good deal, since I've known Al, particularly. I think it has a significant relationship, also, to Mr. White's ideas about internationalism and people who can "love the whole planet." What do you think about it?

Darling, the next six months can't possibly go by too quickly to please me.

All my love, Marian

✤

Sept. 8 '45

My darling Gene —

It seemed rather nice to change that dateline from Aug. to Sept. I have been thinking that, on the theory of 6 mo., you might possibly come home in February, which would be just two years after that wonderful trip on the El Capitan. It's hard to realize that we've known each other nearly two years & been together only seven days. The whole thing is fantastic when you stop to think about it. But, darling, if you are but a dream —

There is an exhibit at the American Artists gallery on Mich. Ave. of drawings by one Kerr Eby called "Marines in Action." I went to see it this afternoon and brought home the "catalog," which contains reproductions of several of the paintings. I think you will appreciate them. Will save it for you. The artist was with the Marines on Tarawa, Bougainville & Cape Gloucester, I believe.

Murph & I went to see "The Corn is Green" last night. I liked it very much. Wish I had all your letters indexed now so I could find the one in which you mentioned it. My favorite scene was where Morgan Evans came back from Oxford, having discovered a new world.

In the newsreel they said Marines of the 4th Division landed in Japan. Are the 4th Marines part of the 4th Division, or is someone ignoring the distinction again?

Oh, incidentally, there was a sketch of Boyington in that exhibit. Very good.

For some reason, I'm extremely tired tonight. Should write to Mother, too. Until tomorrow, then —

All my love, dear,

Marian

✤

Sept. 9 '45

Hello, Sweetheart —

This may not be a very coherent letter, as Murph is home today for a change & we are busy catching up on our conversations. Seems good to have someone around again. Ed has gone to New Orleans for the week.

Time's account of the Pearl Harbor report started me thinking about this unified command again. Apparently lack of cooperation between the Army & Navy was an important factor. It seems they've learned to cooperate well during the war, but how long will they remember? And can we afford to base the nation's security on a voluntary arrangement? I don't question that the spirit of the Navy & Marine Corps is a valuable thing, but somehow in looking at that side of the question I keep running into the same arguments we use when we talk about the need for nations to relinquish some of their sovereignty to form a <u>strong</u> international organization.

I'm not sure whether I should change the subject now before I have thoroughly convinced myself—or continue & try to convince you, too. Better a new subject, I guess. But first, I do agree that the idea of the same uniform for all the services is definitely ungood!

Murph told me an interesting story today that would do a lot to renew anyone's faith in humanity. All the medical supplies the Army purchased from Eli Lilly Co. were sold to the Army at cost & they took as many contracts as they could handle. The company was able to do this unorthodox thing because it is owned by the Lilly family—no stockholders. Also, their only son went overseas instead of taking the desk job he could easily have had under the circumstances. It made me feel good to discover there is such a thing as a businessman who thinks of something besides his profits.

It is rather unfortunate, for me, that the cigarette shortage is over. I've smoked three packages this week. Very bad habit! Oh, well, if I go home for a week or two, that will put an end to it, for awhile at least. I could never stand the look of heartbreak on my dad's face if he saw me smoking—nor the storm of fury if mother did. The fury would be far easier to take, though.

I just said to Murph that I never can think of good endings for these letters & she suggested saying, "Hurry home!" Good idea—but it seems rather pointless as there's nothing you can do about it.

Good night, darling. I love you very much.

Marian

❦

10 Sept 1945
[Hawaii]

Hello dear,

I should really write something cheerful because I did get a letter from you about 10 minutes ago. The last letters I've written were probably pretty depressing.

I think that perhaps I appreciated this letter more than any others because I had to wait 10 days for it. The rest should catch up sometime soon. The letter

was from the 4th of Sept—the ones in between then and Aug. 25 and are probably floating around between here and Tokyo.

Glad that you appreciated the "Old fashioned" letter—it seemed a little silly
the morning after and I hated to mail it—as a matter of fact I hate to proofread
any of my letters—and so I usually don't—I have often wondered why one feels
so lighthearted after having something to drink. I don't like the taste of liquor
and definitely don't want to develop a liking for it because frankly I am afraid
of the results. In the service that realization becomes more apparent than ever—
too often there is nothing to do but drink and feel sorry for yourself which are
2 habits easy to carry over to civilian life methinks.

I wish that you were here tonight. I believe that since the end of the war I
have been thinking more of coming home and seeing you than I did before. I
think that I have met you a million times.

I am going to stay up here until Friday but all my men are down in Hilo
installing a telephone system. At present I am Signal officer, C.O. of signal co,
Records officer and coding officer. No increase in pay however—it's all done for
"old glory." Oh well—the war is over.

⚜

13 Sept 1945
Hilo Hawaii

Dearest Marian

Decided yesterday after a trip down here that I better establish my office at
this hdqs insomuch as I am signed out for about $10,000 worth of Comm.
equipment. My men have done a swell job and I really am proud of them but it
is pretty much of a headache for me—and them also probably. Gosh I worked
today—occasionaly I do earn the money they pay me. Mostly tho I am a little
embarrassed about taking it.

Rec'd 2 more letters from you in the last two days which makes it 3 out of
11 days. As usual they were very nice and I hope that tomorrow I'll have time
to write a long reply.

Mr. White writes very well—the part on internationalism especially was
good as you said. It would be better if we forgot a little about nationalism and
stressed internationalism—particularly in the schools. But there are still many
people who are distrustful of the world and believe we should "be the strongest
power on earth." I don't know what for—with the Atomic bomb and stuff. All
this talk about "not being caught flat again like in 1941," is just the 1945 version
of isolationism. Sometimes I wish we'd get a threat from some other planet—as
of Orson's [Welles] program—just so that this world could become unified. If
more people would know more about science they probably would realize how

stupidly insignificant we are—thus I was glad of White's reference to progress of Science independent of nationalism.

Darling, I am going to bed—just enough strenght to say I love you—and that I do.

Gene

❧

16 Sept. 1945

My dearest Marian,

Only 3 letters from you in 16 days which is bad—nothing in a month from Marty. It is a good thing I have been busy and so have not had time to feel sorry for myself. What is worse—nobody knows where the 5th Division is so we have been wondering about a lot of things in the last couple of weeks.

No definite word on when we are going to leave Hilo but it will probably be in the first week in Oct. We have had a good deal here ever since the usual confusion lifted. Our area is right in the middle of the N. A. S. [Naval Air Station]—everything strictly stateside even to the Waves and barracks.

Later—The paper tonight said that the 5th Div is going to land at Sasebo on the 22nd which sorta knocks out the scuttlebutt that they were on the way to the states. I still feel that we'll be home by March or April. This life is wonderful but only succeeds in making me want to come home—can understand why fellows got tired of this "stateside duty" but at least most of them have their necks.

The Submarine P. X. at P.H. is probably the most complete store I have ever seen anywhere—anything you can think of is available there. There are quite a few Bams & Waves out here which looked good to us when we arrived from Guam. Field scarves are necessary downtown—so much for that—

I have missed receiving your letters darling but eventually I'll catch up to them but meanwhile I love you.

Gene

❧

17 Sept 1945

Dearest Marian,

It has been a hot lazy day so far and I haven't had too much ambition Think perhaps that I'd better write you a letter however. Everything as far as communications is concerned has been going so smoothly that I have set up my other office here in the barracks which consists of a bed, radio and telephone. I wish that I could call you—incidently I made an attempt when I came thru Pearl Harbor last June but was not there long enough to get through the necessary red tape.

The P[earl] H[arbor] report seems to appear that the unified command is something certain to come—so long as that is the case I might as well get used to the idea and just worry about the implications that will arise. What I'd really like to know is why Navy men fight it and the Army backs the idea—

The letter you mentioned about Ken Murayama was <u>excellent</u> and I was much impressed with the one just above it—can't thing of what it was about for the life of me but I know that I liked it. Somebody stole my "Time" which is not uncommon here. I found out that my Sig Qm. sgt. is an avid "Time" reader also and really has a good background so in order to make life a little more interesting I made him my official driver. We have had some good discussions and I have him about convinced he should go back to college. He is quite good looking and has an exceptional personality. We have had some discussions in which we don't exactly agree—his cousin is Patterson of N.Y. "Daily News" and Bill likes him—good heavens—He is from Ossing [sic] N.Y. My other Sgt. is an Italian—Santora—and one of the best N.C.O.'s I have ever seen. I like to see someone make good despite his name or background The other fellow—Bill— just heard that "his" girl got married to a SeaBee on Tinian.

[Lt. Jim] Jackson[64] is here and wants to go swimming so I think that I will. No letters today either darling—so now I <u>am</u> complaining. Wish that I were home.

All my Love darling,

Gene

⚘

20 Sept
Hilo Hawaii

Darling,

Still no mail—It seems that the whole discharge system is moving faster than I can keep up with it. The army announced that all men with over 2 years in the army will be out soon. I am presuming that the M.C. will follow but probably a little later than the army. Also it says that only one Marine Div. will do occupation duty which, if true—means the 5th. They should be there now. I wouldn't mind if I knew that I was going to get out just as soon as the others. Oh well—

Nothing much doing here in the line of recreation—no dates, no letters, nothing! In fact I am leading a very lazy life just dreaming and sleeping most of the day—our work is becoming routine now which means just sweating it out until they decide to send the ships to pick us up from Hono.

I have read absolutely nothing and feel than am truly wasting my time but it is nice. Got a lot of shots a few days ago which made us all somewhat sick—plague, typhoid, scrub typhus etc.

Tomorrow I am going to start doing something useful. Jackson took me up to a friend who lives on a plantation and by making use of her phonograph we hear some good recordings of M[aurice] Evans in Richard II. That I liked—and decided that I am going to get some records of Shakespeare's plays when the civilian days come again. So long dear. I miss you and I love you very much.

Gene

⍝

September 11, 1945
[Chicago]

Darling,

Such exciting letters last night!!!!!!!! Would like to have answered them right away, but we had a party for Lucille (Mr. Ripley's departing secretary), and that sort of used up the evening.

On that subject, apparently I am not as important to Reliable as to you, dear. It makes me very happy to know that you would let me be president, but since it's going to be a man's world (unquote), I really don't think I want to be president. More about that later.

Evelyn (Mr. Cook's secretary) and I have just decided that we are going to start our own office. She can work for George, and I can work for Paul. Utopian!

I am so glad the censorship is off. Going to Japan should be interesting, and it will be good to be able to hear about everything as it happens. Makes me sad to think of your going so far away again, though. Guess it really doesn't make much difference, as long as you are not here anyway, but somehow it seems the distance is less real when you are in Hawaii.

Knowing how soon you would have been attacking Kyushu makes me even more thankful that the war ended when it did.

I thought you must have flown from Guam to Hawaii, but had been wondering about it. Wish I could have been with you, especially with that El Capitan atmosphere. For all my love of flying, I never have been up in a plane. It's sort of what you might call "worship from afar," I guess. Franklin promised to give me a "piggy-back" ride in his P-38 when he came back, but I'll have to find a new pilot. I would really have been a little afraid to go up with him. He would gleefully have given me the whole works in one ride, and I don't know if I could live through it.

I was telling Santa (the girl whose brother was lost for a few months in Yugoslavia) about the airmen getting credit for two missions for every flight to Japan before Iwo, and she told me the Air Forces in Italy used to get the same for each flight over Germany, also, until about November, 1944. Flights over Northern Italy counted for one mission only.

Can you tell me <u>why</u> those restrictions were placed on the bombing of Rota? Sounds very peculiar, to say the least. Incidentally, there were some pictures in this morning's paper of the Rota garrison now in a prisoners' stockade on Guam.

That story about Tokyo Rose gives me some conception of the meaning of psychological warfare. I used to think warfare was too strong a word, but I don't know—something like that could damage my mental attitude considerably.

Guess I'll have to finish this at home—much later. Marion, the switchboard operator, is coming over to have dinner at the apartment with us tonight, and we are going down to see the LST on which they are having "open house" near the Michigan Avenue bridge.

10:45 P.M.—It was all rather interesting, but nothing you couldn't learn as much or more about from pictures, etc. Reminds me that one of the things I'd like to know is how you landed on Iwo Jima, that is, from what type of ship, etc.

Another is something I asked about a long time ago, but I guess you couldn't answer then. When you left the States, did you sail from Point Loma?

Wanted to talk about that discussion you had on the post-war world, but it will have to wait until tomorrow. There's just about time enough now to say "goodnight"—and I love you, darling.

Marian

❧

Sept. 13 '45

Hello, darling—

Writing letters at work again. I'm <u>almost</u> glad to be going to work for Ripley Monday, as there has been so little to do the last week or two—& there's nothing I hate like doing nothing!

Rec'd your letter of the 7th from Kona Inn last night. Just like a travelogue it was—only much nicer.

I am sorry you have not been getting any mail, dear. Suppose they've been sending it all to Japan. Exasperating, isn't it? I hope it doesn't take you too long to get there—I hate to think of spending a couple of weeks without mail, too.

Would like to have heard your discussion on the post-war period. I won't argue about its being a man's world. I think it <u>should</u> be, and I believe there are very few women who would object, as long as they could find a place in it. Does that seem old-fashioned? "A woman's place is in the home." I do believe that, too, but would like to qualify it with the idea that it is also her place to know what's going on outside the home. It seems to me much of the difficulty in marriages in ordinary city life is due to the fact that husbands & wives live in two different worlds, so to speak. Know what I mean? Have been trying to elaborate on that idea, but it has too many complications & exceptions.

You are probably right that most men (those in the service at least) have learned a lot more in the past few years than the women have. How could they help learning from all the experiences they have had? However, when you consider that servicemen's wives, for instance, have had to be a good deal more self-reliant, I imagine there could be considerable argument from that standpoint. We'll leave it to someone else, though, shall we?

You said you wished you were more of the opinion that we could go back to the 1941 era in our social life. You don't really mean that, do you? You sound like an educator disowning progress. Elucidate—please!

Have you seen any of Bill Mauldin's cartoons lately? There was one the other day that I wanted to send you. I don't know whether it's still around or not. Had been wondering what would happen to him when the war was over. I'm glad to see that his talent & insight are not limited to the "GI" on the battlefront.

Until later, darling—

All my love, Marian

⚜

Sept. 14 '45

Darling,

I haven't been doing so well at writing this week. Knowing that you aren't getting any mail anyway makes it rather discouraging. Wish I could write on the envelope, "Please send this to Hawaii, <u>not</u> Japan—yet."

Murph & I saw "A Song to Remember" last night. We enjoyed it so much! Both of us came home wishing we knew, or had time to learn, to play the piano well enough to play Chopin with at least some success. We certainly did not understand George Sand, or is it Sands. What a cold-hearted gal she was! The scene where Liszt and Chopin played together for the first time was terrific. I would like to find a good biography of Liszt sometime. Have always been interested in his life, & his occasional appearances in this movie made me still more curious.

Murph just came in & we're going out to eat. Guess I'll mail this & start over a little later this evening.

Much love, Marian

❖

Sept. 16 '45

Hello, darling —
That letter I was going to write after dinner Friday night has been some-what delayed. Murphie was in such a state that night about her love life that it was difficult to think about anything else. Today everything is fine again. If it doesn't drive her crazy, it will me, unless they start being consistent pretty soon. I guess I haven't told you yet that she will be out of a job the 25th. Ed seems to be trying to get her a job here in Chicago, & as he is now expecting to return to St. Louis soon, naturally that hurts her feelings.

What do you think of this editorial called, "Darlanism in Japan"? Seems to me it's a little early to get excited about it, but then it's probably just as well to keep reminding the officials that <u>democracy</u> is our aim.

Did you read the review in this week's Time of that book by Andrew Roth? You see from what sources I get my opinion of Grew.

Incidentally, I'll start sending you pages from Time again, about next week.

Oh, this damn pen! Every once in a while it has a spell like this when it doesn't want to write. I just filled the darn thing! It's just being stubborn. Now what the hell will I do with it?

Spent the morning yesterday moving to my new desk. It's going to be sort of fun having new things to do. (I give up!) Writing all the purchase orders is rather interesting. I'm glad there's not much to do with priorities anymore, though.

June came in unexpectedly yesterday aft. She had been home on vacation & was on her way back to Cleveland, where she is in nurses training, as you may remember. She's the girl whose husband was lost in India two years ago. The sus-pense, now that they've been finding so many of those fellows, is pretty awful.

Guess I'll finish that book by E. B. White today. Haven't had a chance to look at it all week. One of the last pieces I read was about his wife's aunt, who married a Japanese named Omori back in 1905 or so & went with him to Tokyo to spend the rest of her life. They founded a settlement house, "the Hull House of Tokyo." Mr. Omori died five years after the marriage, & she continued his work, devoting her life to the poor. She died sometime during the war, presum-ably of natural causes. Must have been a very interesting woman.

The paper said the other day that the Marine Corps had reduced to 70 the no. of points required for discharge — for officers & men. Does it actually apply to officers? Sounds encouraging.

Darling, I wish you could be here today, as you said, with your head in my lap—wonderful dream—

I love you, dear,

Marian

❖

Sept. 16 '45 [2]

Dear Lt. Sweetheart:

Decided I would like to send you this book review from today's "Sun;" so I will write a note to go with it. Not with this pen, though, apparently.

Doesn't this sound like a good book? I am curious to know about his scheme for labor-management cooperation.

Mr. White said, in one of the essays I read today, that the trouble with private enterprise & the profit system was that the "common man" never had a chance to participate in the profits. He is paid for his work at a flat rate & <u>life</u> is flat. It's not a particularly new idea, but his emphasis on the desire for participation rather than the desire for money is different. I rather think he has something there.

The weather today has been perfect. It's been rainy & cold for the last week or two, so it seemed almost like Indian summer. I went for a brisk walk along the lake, &, for once, didn't even envy the young couples who were strolling there. It seemed as if they were so busy gazing at each other they were missing the rare beauty of the world. But then I would trade even a day like this for an afternoon with you, dear, so I shouldn't criticize.

Much love, Marian

❖

Sept. 17 '45

Hello, Sweetheart—

I can't decide tonight which makes me happier—your letters or the news MacArthur says he thinks all the draftees in the Pacific can be released by the end of six months. Now <u>that</u> is what I call good news! Somehow I mistrust it, though. Just hope he isn't getting too eager.

After something like that, I suppose I shouldn't be sending you a cartoon like this one by Mauldin—but I <u>know</u> you'll love it. I do. Those expressions!

I'm very glad you finally rec'd at least one letter, dear. I was really worried about that.

There was a map in the Chi. "Times" this afternoon showing what approximate areas in Japan are to be occupied by what troops. The "5th Marines," it said, would be at Sasebo on Kyushu. When you find out how to pronounce that, let me know, will you? I got a kick out of what Time said about the signs on the Ginza in Tokyo, especially the "Milk Snop." Have to laugh every time I think of it.

I'm glad you are writing down some of the things you remember about events since you've been overseas. There are millions of things I'd like to hear about, & most of the subjects are too broad or too vague to ask questions about now. I think if we had 42 hrs. to spend on a train now, we could, if we wanted to, spend the whole time talking — Darling, maybe it isn't so wise to let ourselves think about that so much more now that we can count on being together again in the foreseeable future. (That's a nice complicated word, but I couldn't think of the right one.) I don't care if it isn't wise, though — I like to think about it.

This was my first day as Ripley's secretary. Guess I'd better not be too proud of my new prestige. As Signal Officer, C.O. of Signal Co., Records Officer, and Coding Officer, you are definitely outshining my accomplishment. My one claim to superiority is that I get an increase in pay (I think). Seriously, it was a very pleasant day. Fun to have new things to do. And Ripley behaved amazingly well. I'm even beginning to hope we might get along ok. There are some things I like about him. See you tomorrow, dear.

All my love, Marian

❧

Sept. 18 '45

My darling Gene:

This is one of those nice quiet evenings when I miss you most. But if I concentrate on that, I will be dreaming instead of writing to you — so —

Had a letter from Mother tonight saying she still doesn't know when she can go to Madison. The longer it is delayed, the more anxious I am to go home. The leaves should begin to turn soon, & it's so beautiful up there in the fall.

Decided I'd better do some sewing while I'm up there, so I bought a pattern and some material for a blouse. I like it so much I think I'll send you a sample. This is probably not the least bit interesting to you, but you will just have to put up with it, dear, 'cause I can't keep it to myself.

I like this article by Lippmann & surely agree that "the disadvantages are a small price to pay for not having to invade Japan." It seems to me that people are always expecting miracles of the Armed Forces and of the government, without stopping to consider the enormous problems involved.

I'm almost afraid to mention it, but this pen has written a whole paragraph smoothly. I must have done the right thing with it at last.

Peg is planning to come down the weekend of Oct. 13. There are three plays, etc., she wants to see. "We can go Sat. aft., Sat. eve. and Sun. aft.," she says, "If that sounds like too much to you, we'll skip one of them." Well—I like her enthusiasm anyway!

This is getting to be a long letter, & it hasn't said anything of importance— Guess I'd better quit & go to bed.

Goodnight, dearest. I love you very much,

Marian

❀

Sept. 19 '45

Hi, Darling—

Had a note from Mother tonight saying she has to be in Madison Monday; so I'm going home Sat. aft. Wish you were going with me—

I think Barnaby is adorable today. Especially when he says, "All the ceilings fell down a long time ago." His father's pretty sharp, too, don't you think?

Rec'd your letter of the 13th tonight. I'm glad you liked Mr. White. You are right about people who believe we should be the strongest power on earth. I don't see what for, either. Ed is one of those people. "We've got to be the best," he says, "And we've got to be sure everyone knows it, too." But ask him why & his most sensible reply is, "Because we've got to be." To comment in kind— Phooey!

Since that last sentence I have been just sitting here for half an hour, trying to concentrate on something to talk about. Have finally come to the conclusion that I don't feel like talking. I would rather be gazing—Love may not consist of it, but it's surely a wonderful "added attraction."

Goodnight, Sweetheart,

Marian

❀

21 Sept 1945
Hilo Hawaii

Dearest Marian,

Another uneventful day characterized only by an increasing laziness on all our parts. I think that this heat has something to do with it.

This morning I read Romeo & Juliet again—I love it—Tomorrow I am going to start on Hamlet.

—Listen darling—

Will you write <u>one</u> letter to General Delivery here at Hilo? If you write fairly soon after receiving this I'll be able to get it before we leave. If I don't hear before we embark, it will be another 20 days before I can look for any letters— Oh, unhappy day!! Well at any rate here is the address

c/o General Delivery
Hilo Post office
Island of Hawaii T.H.

O.K.?—

I am also going to write to Marty and get these letters out in the civilian mail this morning so—Write soon.

All My Love, Gene

P.S. We should leave here during the first week in Oct—

✤

23 Sept 1945
Hilo Hawaii

Hello Darling,

Another Sunday and nothing much doing here at the base. They had their weekly dance at the N.A.S. off. club last night and Jackson brought a date for me—some friend of the girl Jim is going with here at Hilo. She is a nurse and has just been out of the states about 5 days, having come over on the Matsonia. We had a fine time but of course I kept wishing it were with you I was dancing—but I was dancing and that in itself was unusual. I wish that I were home.

"Time" this week had some good articles—the letter from the Marine probably tells the story we are all concerned about out here. The section on Surplus Property was extremely funny—as is the whole story on surplus war goods and the adaption to civilian uses—"little pigeons being born every minute."

Bill Mauldin's cartoons have appeared in the "Star Bulletin" (Hono) and I have liked them very much on the whole so don't quite agree with "Time" on that count—some are better—some worse—One of the best I thought was one where these 2 characters are standing along a newsstand and the proprietor is saying "The Stars and Stripes? Never heard of it." Also liked the blast at the N.Y. "Daily News" when they spoke of the N.Y. mayor race.

I hope that your letter arrives here at the Hilo Post office before I leave—
Gosh, how I <u>miss</u> you.

All my Love, darling—more tomorrow

Gene

❖

24 Sept. 1945

Darling,

Jackson (one of the fellows here) & I had a rather long discussion about various items that came up—he is quite a character—very talented, brilliant, and world-wise. Made me feel good to find that somebody here thinks primarily the same as I do concerning the post war period. I have often wondered about how these fellows in the service are going to fare in the world after they get home to a pre-war world. Often you hear the phrase that "I want things to be just as I left them etc." It has been my opinion that the men actually do <u>not</u> want things the same as they left them but what they really want is for the folks back home to have changed in ratio to how they have changed. This probably most of them don't realize.

I guess the whole subject came up in a discussion of husbands and wives not being true to each other. We both agreed that insomuch as this is going to be a man's world, (argument?) the wives must, by an understanding and intelligence, use those means to keep their husbands happy. It appears that the facility that men (& women) have to get divorces makes this all the more a fact. Now all this works from the woman's angle too and I don't want to argue to what extent each of them have to go to reach happiness but it probably is a fact that more men have become "more educated" than the women in the last war days. I am treading upon dangerous waters I realize, but I wish I was more of the opinion that we could go back to the 1941 era in our social life.

—More later—

Back again one of my men tipped over in a truck last night and I have been busy investigating all day. There are about 9 reports to be filled out etc which becomes pretty much a pain after awhile. He only broke a leg and did minor damage to the truck so the repercussions (sp) shouldn't be too bad.

We are all planning on moving down to Hilo sometime this week after we have all our gear stored in the warehouse down at the dock. Hilo is a fairly large town (smaller than Honolulu, however) and has all the conveniences of a stateside city. I spent my 5 days leave in Honolulu but it is such a madhouse that I was happy to come back to the peace and quiet of Hawaii. I flew over there in a Naval transport, but the trip was nearly as nice as the flight from Guam back in June. We had a beautiful four motor plane with the El Capitan atmosphere that is, seats etc everything but you. It was the first time I had flown since my dad took me up about 15 years ago. It took 8 hours to the Marshall's—8 more to the Johnsons and 4 from there to Pearl Harbor N.A.S. Really wonderful in every respect.

The only transportation here between islands is by air—I am writing these things as they come to mind—not much sequence or reason.

Also on the trip from Guam I met an AAF pilot based at Saipan who was going home on rotation after 6 months out here. He had completed 50 missions, I think and had been given credit for 2 missions every trip over Japan before Iwo was taken. Needless to say he appreciated the Marines. He also told some interesting stories about Rota—the island off Guam, still (?) held by the Japs. It seems that previously the bombers used to dump all their excess bombs on that island after a bombing run but lately they <u>had</u> to radio in to tell the Japs they were coming and then only release their bombs on a certain part of the island. That appealed to my sense of humor—I may have told you this before. If I did, I shouldn't have.

One of the interesting sidelights of the war was the ability of American subs to rescue our fliers within a couple of miles offshore Japan—over a <u>year</u> ago. That never ceased to amaze me. This rescue work of the Navy has been one of the best of their "well done" jobs.

I see that somebody has located <u>a</u> Tokyo Rose—she interested me ever since the time we were aboard ship in the harbor at Guam on Feb. 9 and we listened to her say, "The 3rd Marine Division is in the harbor of Guam and going to attack Iwo Jima—it is cold up there fellows but we'll have a warm reception for you—" That campaign was probably one of the worst kept secrets of the war.

I guess I better quit less I tell you everything and we won't have anything to talk about after I come home. Oh well, we can sit and look at each other and say, "Yes dear."

All my love, Gene

Is there anything you particularly want to know?

25 Sept 1945
Hilo Hawaii

Hello darling,
   Think perhaps that using these ruled lines I should be able to keep them straight—right?

I have no ambition to write letters these days—it is an awful problem to write something intelligent—I have the feeling that I am absolutely wasting my time in every respect because all this work I am doing now seems so futile—the war is over and there is no reason in the world why we shouldn't be out of the service. I approved of congress (very unusual) trying to speed up the releasing of men. Out here we still have men with 120 points around with no immediate prospect of going home. Usually I accepted this confusion and inefficiency good naturedly but now this release program is affecting me and seems so hopelessly confused. Oh well—

There certainly are enough men with 30 points or less to provide occupation forces so why don't they come down to that level immediately and start to send men home and fellows in the states out here. I am not happy—

We should start loading soon for the trip to Tokyo or (Sasebo). Hope that we don't travel on LST's at 6 knots that would be terrific. Oh, I have lots of complaints—I wish that you were here to hold my hand and cheer me up—or at least a letter from you. War was never like this!

The strikes back home seem to be more or less out of hand which proves that despite what the capitalists think—we are not going back to the old wage standards.

Goodnight sweetheart and I love you today.

Gene

❖

28 Sept 1945
Hilo Hawaii

Darling,

These are poor excuses for letters but as yet I haven't determined just what the trouble is—guess that perhaps it is a combination of not hearing from you—and the fact that the war is over and I am awfully tired of the service. Hope that you understand.

I think that I pulled a foolish stunt last week when I wrote that letter asking you to write to General delivery Hilo Hawaii because I didn't put a return address on my letter and mailed it down at the city post office. Just found out today that if we do that we must put on a 15 cent airmail stamp.

So anyway I wish that you would write there starting as soon as you receive this letter until the 13th of October or unless you hear from me saying that we have moved out. We still have no definite word as to when that will be.

They are trying every conceivable means to try and get us to stay in the regular Marine Corps—if the Marines are going to be used as an international police force as the paper said yesterday I can understand why they want so many to remain in the service. Not me tho—I am coming home.

I hope that you are all right and everything is going well in Chicago. Out here we are getting increasingly restless and impatient with the slow—fouled up discharge system. I am thinking about you as much as ever and I <u>do</u> love you.

Goodnight sweetheart,

Gene

❧

1 Oct. 1945
Hilo Hawaii

Dearest,

How are you? OK I hope. We are entering the 2nd month without a letter from you and undoubtedly it has been the worst month I've put in overseas. Think perhaps that your letters not arriving has a great deal to do with it.

I think that we will probably leave after the 2nd week in this month—then after a 25-day voyage will arrive at Japan and I can get my mail. That at least is the situation at present. I have come to the conclusion that it is probably the most difficult thing in the world to write letters when none are coming in—oh brother—

Been wondering what you have been thinking about concerning the world picture—and especially the foreign ministers' meeting in London. It is rather discouraging—don't you think? If that is the preview of what we can expect along the line of "world cooperation" it looks like a stormy trip ahead.

I believe that we should give Russia the secret of the Atomic bomb—would like to see some United Nations scientific council set up to do research along those lines.

I've been wondering what the solution for all these strikes would be—undoubtedly there should and will have to be eventually some government control which we in the U.S. are not accustomed to—Labor is probably demanding too much but it is in a position to get most of it. The extent to which the U.S. is reconversion happy is rather alarming, especially when coupled with the lack of interest in what we've won.

Goodnight Miss Sweetheart and
All of My Love,

Gene

❧

6 Oct 1945
Hilo Hawaii

Dearest Marian,

If I had a one wish that could be granted immediately—it would be a letter from you tomorrow. It is rough as we are in the 2nd month without mail. I just hope you are O.K. and still with me thru these days. I have found that the hardest thing to do is to write letters without receiving any—seems like throwing a rock in the ocean or something.

I am sorry tho that you have to suffer too because I know these letters are not up to par—about all I can do is grumble and tell you I still love you—that I do—I am not too interested in anything these days—We are loading some of our ships and should get out of here by the 5th of this month. I think that most of us will be happy to leave. This "stateside" duty just makes us long for the real thing all the more and somehow makes us realize all the more how futile this waiting and working really is. There doesn't seem to be much chance that we can discharge our "point men" at Pearl so it will be necessary to take them along to Japan and then send them back. In a few months they should be down to my level of 54 points.

Time to close again dearest—I love you.

Gene

❖

Sept. 23, 1945
[Wittenberg]

Dearest Gene,

I'll have to write this letter in a hurry and go to bed. Have a cold again, dammit! It seems every time I'm going home I have one—and then Dad tells me all about how unhealthy it is to live in the city. Maybe he's right!

I see that Pres. Truman enjoyed the cartoon about MacArthur and Eisenhower, too. That really pleases me.

One of the older women at the office, of whom I am very fond, is married to a Seabee. (She's the one who went on a couple of drinking sprees last winter.) She let me read one of his letters today telling about their landing on Okinawa. "We were attached to the 2nd Marine Div.," he said, "Thank goodness it wasn't the Army!"

They're playing "The Atchison, Topeka and the Santa Fe" on the radio just now. I like that. Reminds me of the El Capitan, etcetera. Especially the etcetera.

Darling, I am sorry you haven't been getting your mail. Wish there were something I could do about it. It's good to think that in a few months we probably won't have to worry about the mail anymore. That will be so wonderful I can hardly believe it will ever be true—Goodnight, Lt. Sweetheart—

All my love, Marian

❧

Sept. 24 '45

Dearest Gene,

I'm sitting in the store waiting for Dad to come back from Stevens Point. He took Mother over there this morning to catch the bus for Madison. Have just been wondering how a man with such a passion for "system" manages to live in this confusion. I guess maybe it doesn't seem confusing to him, but you never saw such stacks of dusty old papers, magazines, advertisements, catalogs, letters, freight bills, invoices—Lord!

I have spent most of the time thinking about how nice it will be to come home when you can come with me. I think Mother has about decided that she likes you. I get a kick out of that. Was thinking again on the way up here that I ought to warn you not to talk politics with either of them—but decided after I'd been here a couple of hours that I should follow that advice myself before offering it to anyone else.

Haven't seen any of the kids yet. Jane has gone to Neenah for a week, darn it! We always seem to get our signals mixed somehow.

I was glad to hear that you tried to call when you were in Pearl Harbor. That would have been wonderful!—wish I could remember how your voice sounds. I think I'd recognize it, though, if I heard it.

"Sgt. Bill" sounds very interesting—and Santora. I agree that it's nice to see someone like that make good. Had to laugh at your comment on the fact that Bill likes his cousin, Patterson. I suppose he <u>could</u> be a nice guy, personally.

Dad is back so I'd better finish this & take it to the Post Office & go to the store & get dinner, etc., etc.

See you tomorrow, darling.

All my love, Marian

❧

Sept. 25, 1945

Gene, darling,

I wish you had been here this noon. I needed some assistance. Ray [Plesser] came over this morning to help Dad move some furniture & stuff. Perhaps I've told you he came home recently after about 3 yrs. in Hawaii & a few months on Tinian. He told us that his brother, who has been with the Army Air Corps in Germany, is on his way home, too. It happens they are Catholic. So my father (Damn that Hearst press he reads!) is telling me now that the Catholics have had all the good spots and all the "breaks" during the war. And I can't convince him that Roosevelt wasn't a Catholic. Lord! Also, he was telling me what low-down heels officers are. He claims Franklin never could have been an officer in the ground forces. I told him about the argument you had with your sergeant on Iwo & he grumbled, "Yeah, but how many of them would do that!"—Well, I guess you just can't start educating a man out of his prejudices after he's 60.

Incidentally, Ray says Hawaii is run by the British. We protect them & they take the profits, says he. ???

Otherwise, things have been very peaceful around here. Dad & I delivered a crib last night to some Polish farmer way off on a back road. It's more fun trying to find someone whose name you can't pronounce.

This morning I made 2-1/2 jars of jam. I wish there were at least twice that much because it tastes pretty good. I did this on my mother's instructions—not because I feel that ambitious!

Right now I think I will go out & sit in the sun & dream about you, darling. Can't think of anything nicer, except to have you here with me. I love you very much, dearest—

Marian

❀

Sept. 26, 1945

Hi, Darling—

Dad has gone to Stevens Point again this morning—this time to pick up some furniture—so I am the storekeeper. 'Tis a job I don't like at all because I never know anything about anything. Dad said he wished I had been driving more so he could let me go after the furniture. I wish so, too.

We played a couple games of cards last night. We get along better at that than at conversation.

Yesterday aft. a young couple stopped in who had been in Venice, Cal, when we were in L.A. They have a little boy about two years old. He was very ill a couple weeks after he was born & it has left him with what I believe they called "spasmic paralysis." He can't control his muscles at all—can't sit up, can't walk, can't talk. I feel so sorry for them. The doctors say, however, that when he gets a little older he may be able to overcome it.

I saw Jane's little boy yesterday, too. Eric is about a year & a half old & he is the most adorable child! You would like him, too, because he has big brown eyes & long dark eyelashes—& a smile that would break your heart!

It seems all I have been talking about the last few days is home-town stuff. The trouble is I don't know what's going on in the world otherwise. Our radio doesn't work, & the only newspaper I've been able to get is the Milw. Sentinel—& that is worse than nothing!

Later—Ah, a letter today. I wish your postmen were as good as Murphie, darling. You're going to have an awful stack of mail to read all at once.

Those Maurice Evans recordings sound very good. Wasn't he playing in Hawaii for some time?

It's a good thing I didn't go to Stevens Point this morning. One of the front tires blew out. Daddy said he went all over the road before he could stop. Fortunately there were no other cars near. I can see myself trying to change a wheel on a truck loaded with furniture! I'd be there all week.

Darling, since I have nothing more intelligent to say, I guess I'd better quit. Until tomorrow, then—

All my love, Marian

⚜

Sept. 27 '45

Dearest Gene,

Did I say life was peaceful around here? I came within a quarter of an inch of losing one of my little brown eyes this afternoon. Dad & I were cutting some linoleum & accidentally dropped a 6-ft. steel rule. The end of it hit me just below my left eye & cut a gash that had to have three or four stitches taken in it. I sure am going to look funny for awhile, but I'm thankful it isn't worse.

Finally managed to get a few copies of the "Sun." Jane's father gave them to me. About all I've read yet, however, is Barnaby—& Gracie Allen. Wonder how Mr. O'Malley will fare in his contest with the Swami. That should be good!

I guess Mother will be home in a day or two. I'm going to stay here until Wednesday anyway. Jane is going to have a shower Tues. eve. for Melitta [Kersten Hyland], who is expecting a baby soon. Honestly, all these infants around town make me feel that I belong in a different society. Can't say that I envy any of these gals, though. If & when I have children, I'd like my husband, & not my parents, to help bring them up.

My dad thinks it's terrible that Jane went away for a week & left Eric with her folks. "People just don't care anything about their kids these days," he said. "I should think she'd want to know every day—." I don't think I exactly agree with him, but I do appreciate very much the fact that he felt that way about us.

Guess I'd better get busy & do a little reading & hope that I can write a more interesting letter tomorrow.

I love you, dear—Marian

❁

Sept. 29 '45

My darling Gene,

I'm beginning to feel as sad about the mail situation as you have been. Only one letter all week. Woe is me!

Mother will not be back until Thursday at the earliest, so I am going to stay until Saturday. They have told her she has high blood pressure & is overweight (which she already knew) and they've put her on a diet—no sugar & only a teaspoon of butter for each meal. That she doesn't like.

Had a letter from Peg yesterday. She has been reading a book on psychology by Horney & Menninger & is bubbling over with new ideas. She is a darling! Two of her choice statements in this letter are: "If psychologists can explore a little more & then find methods of teaching—especially parents—we might have happier people." And: "I'm becoming rather disappointed in Communism as the Salvation of the world." I like that "especially parents." That's just the way I feel right now, being confronted continuously with the reactionary (& worse) ideas of mine. I was going to tell you a few of them, but have been ignoring them so successfully the last couple of days that right now I can't recall any in particular.

Ray was here for a while this afternoon, and we had rather an interesting talk about the places he has been, etc. Their outfit had a good band, & when they were on Tinian, the officers at the air base used to have them come over & play when the fellows came back from a mission. They paid them $3.00 ea. for a night. Finally they decided they couldn't afford that any more & asked if the fellows would play anyway & they'd take up a collection. They took the collection when the party was in full swing & ended up with $15.00 apiece. Not bad, hm? Anyway, Ray believes in drinking—once in a while. When we were in h.s., he & Jane's husband used to spend hours trying to convince me that it's necessary for people to get drunk about once a month. Have to laugh now when I think of how angry I used to get.

Darling, I miss you so very much tonight—maybe it's being Sat. night that has something to do with it. Sat. night here always seems as if it ought to be exciting. It used to be—half the kids in town would be up here listening to the hit parade & my dad would be calling at intervals from downstairs to ask if we couldn't make a little less noise. What were you doing then, I wonder—That reminds me of one of E. B. Browning's sonnets. It ends, "Atheists are as dull, who cannot guess God's presence out of sight." I wish we could read those Sonnets together tonight. Would you like to, dear?

All my love, Marian

�֍

8 Oct 1945
[Hawaii]

Dearest Marian,
How are you? It has been 5 weeks since I received your last letter and it definitely is not good. I have given up all hope of getting mail until we reach the forward echelon and that will probably not be for another month at least. It seems that the idea of writing to General Delivery Hilo Hawaii never will succeed because I now find out that it is necessary for you to use a 15 cent airmail stamp—well anyway try that, will you?? I am almost sure that it will be almost 2 weeks before we leave here. By that time maybe something will arrive.
We have been working fairly long hours the last week and I am beginning to feel the lack of sleep. Also to make the situation more snafu I fell down last Sat night and sprained both of my ankles which is quite a feat—don't you think? Considering the situation and the terrain it was a miracle that I didn't break my neck.
The Marine Corps is down to 60 points now so I have hopes of getting out and home sometime around the first of the year. Haven't been thinking quite so much about it lately because nothing is being done about the high point men in this outfit. Wish that the people delaying their discharge would get strung up or something like that.
The London conference appears to have been quite a failure. I feel sorta responsible for that because of the lack of interest I have had regarding it. I think that that is indicative of the attitude of most people—and perhaps the governments too. We are all probably more interested in getting nylons than working out a system of cooperation and consolidating our winning principles. Frankly I don't know who is to blame but I hope that we don't go back to the old pre-war policy of nationalistic politics and isolationism. The seeds of distrust are unfortunately quite evident.
Darling I wish that I were there with you tonight. Despite the long time that I haven't heard from you, I still feel the same toward you Marian. Goodnight sweetheart and

All my Love, Gene

❖

October 1 '45
[Wittenberg]

Dear Lt. Sweetheart —
Today I am a sorry character on account of there's no mail yet. Now I have a long face in addition to my black eye. Dr. [Evenson] took the stitches out this morning & took the patch off. So it's black in one place, red in another, & yellow in between. A very colorful display!
Jane came home Sat. night. She & Eric were here yesterday afternoon. Conversation is rather difficult as it's interrupted, always at the most interesting point, & frequently, by Eric's attempts at talking, playing ball with a tomato, trying his mother's lipstick, or in general exploring where he gets into trouble. You should hear him talk! He lacks nothing in quantity or volume, but it's absolutely unintelligible. He shows promise of outdoing the escapades of his father, even — and Eddie fell in a tar barrel once! I don't know how they ever got him clean again.
I'm glad I can stay here another week, as Jane & I have seen each other so seldom in the last few years that we really need to get acquainted once more.
I like this article by Walter Lippmann from the "Sun," especially the paragraph marked. It surely seems to me that the Hearst press, with which I am plagued every morning here, is doing its best to convince people that Russia's intentions are wholly dishonorable — & is thereby undoubtedly doing a better job of convincing Russia that our intentions are far from friendly. Guess there's nothing new about that observation.
It has been unseasonably cold the last few days — even snowed a little, but of course the snow melted right away. Do you think Spring will ever come, darling? Reminds me of Shelley's, "If winter comes, can spring be far behind?" That's encouraging, anyway.

I love you, dear — Marian

❖

Oct. 3 '45

Darling,
I just got your letter today — don't know whether the mail was delayed or whether Murphie neglected to forward it. Wish I could send this by rocket or something, as the chances are very slim that you will receive it otherwise. I do hope, though, that a "wing & a prayer" will get it there before you leave.

I've been at home since Sept. 22. Mother is at the hospital at Madison trying to find out what is causing all the trouble with her eyes. So I am the chief
cook & assistant undertaker, the former with pleasure & the latter reluctantly.

Jane is at home with her little boy, and there are a couple of the kids here
who have been discharged from the service, & of course it's good to see them all
again.

Expect to go back to Chicago this weekend & resume my new job. Just in
case you haven't heard—I'm Mr. Ripley's secretary now. It is supposedly a promotion, but I'd rather work for Paul. Ripley is such a drip!

Darling, it's hard to know what to say in a letter like this—I would like it
to be one of those especially nice ones, and the ordinary topics of conversation
don't seem to fit. I only want to say how much I love you & how I wish you were
sailing to San Francisco instead of Japan. I really believe, though, that the
things you have to do now are as important, in a way more important, than the
battles. We can't win the peace if none of us are willing to work for it. I'll remind
myself of that & try to wait for you patiently, dear. We have everything to look
forward to, & that is the important fact.

All my love, sweetheart,

Marian

✣

October 4, 1945

My darling Gene,
    Your letters of the 22nd & 23rd did not get here until yesterday morning.
Don't know whether the mail was delayed or whether Murph didn't forward
them. Anyway, I sent a letter right away o / o General Delivery, as you requested. I surely hope you get it before you leave Hilo, although I think it will be
miraculous if you do. I could—I don't know what!—for not sending any that
way before. I had thought of it & then decided it would be useless because there
would be no way of letting you know you should look for them. I'm terribly
sorry I didn't anyway.

We have been busy the last few days. Dad took a man up to Wausau in the
ambulance Tues. morning & brought him back that night in the hearse (same
car—different personalities).

Jane had a baby shower for Melitta Tues. night. I think I told you about
her last winter sometime. Her husband, John, is in the merchant marine. We
had a good time, but Jane & I agree that a party like that is ok once in a very
long while. Most of the girls seem so young & naive, although all of them are
married & all but two have children. Jane thinks that the things they seem to

consider of highest importance—such as whether or not their husbands should wear wedding rings & whether or not they should have to witness the delivery of their children—are utterly ridiculous. I agree with her. You should have heard the discussion on that second subject! One of the girls insisted that her husband, being equally involved, should have to suffer as much as she did. How silly!

All this reminded me of what you said sometime ago about its being a man's world. Here is a paragraph on the same subject from an article called "Return" in the Sept. Atlantic:

"Maybe the returning soldier will not want to find his way back. Maybe he will want to take his wife & find a new way of living. Maybe the whole American idea of living will change—to an insistence on time to think & learn beyond the acquirement of symbolic possessions. . . . Or will women push their men back into this? A lot of our men have seen the world for what it is & have captured a freedom of decision they may never have had before. Who shall persuade them now to repeat the old pattern if they can see a better way to spin lives which have become so especially important from having been so nearly lost? We may even have a new national pride in government service, greatest of all the professions."

I like that very much. The whole article is good. I wish the idea in that last sentence could be achieved. Perhaps pride in government service would bring efficiency, too.

Changing the subject slightly, Jane was telling me one of the tales about Surplus Property that is not very flattering to the administration, I'm sorry to say. They had quite a number of ships in Seattle which some of the fisheries (Eddie's uncle owns one.) would like to have bought. However, the Govt. would sell to wholesalers only—quantity purchases at a very low price. So the individuals had to buy from the wholesalers, who naturally made extremely high profits. Can you figure out the explanation? My dad would say the politicians got a big rake-off. He thinks somebody ought to take Washington like we took Berlin & find out how the Politicians have been putting away all the money for themselves like Hitler did! Oh joy!

There's another article I just read in the Atlantic called, "Why I Read the Bible." It criticizes liberal arts colleges for overlooking religion in their curriculum. "Excluding" would be a better word there than "overlooking." There are a dozen angles of the question I'd like to discuss with you. Was religious instruction "required" at Marquette? Do you think it should or shouldn't be? I can see good reason for his suggestion that the Bible should be required reading—but beyond that it seems to me religion is too controversial, & secular instruction doesn't exactly belong in colleges. I wish that in my own mind I could separate the Bible from the Church. Organized religion, as I have found it, has too many laws & too little understanding. Of course it may be that I have wanted more understanding than I should have—but I have found many not particularly religious individuals with greater kindness than the Church. It has made me feel, at times, that there is more truth in the Rubaiyat of Omar Khayyam. This is getting rather long and confusing—as do most of these topics we ought to be talking about instead of writing about.

I really envy the nurse you had a date with. Imagine being out of the States only 5 days & dancing with the best-looking Lt. in the M. C.! (I can abbreviate that now—you've heard it often enough!) Well—just so she wasn't the best-looking Lt. in the Nurse Corps—

Jane & Melitta & Eric are here, so I'll have to quit. Guess it's about time anyway.

All my love, Marian

⚜

October 7, 1945

Hi, Darling,

This seems to be the only thing I can find on which to write, so I hope you don't mind the shorthand practice on the other side. It's nothing very interesting—about farming, banks & credit.

I think this collection of Barnaby strips brings us about up to date. I got them at Jane's last night. Gus's reluctance to join in this escapade is very amusing, don't you think?

These last few days have been a mess! Between midnight Fri. and 9 A.M. Sat., Dad made three trips to Wausau—two ambulance and one hearse. The corpse really ruined our plans for the weekend, too. They always do. We were going to drive to Madison today to bring Mother home, as she was afraid to take the bus in case she might have to stand. Then I was going on to Chicago from there—& I had tickets for the Ballet tonight. With funeral arrangements to make, Dad couldn't leave today, & he won't let anyone else drive his precious automobile that far (!!XX!!), so now I have to take the all-night train tonight, miss the Ballet, and I don't know how or when my mother will get home. I was so disgusted last night. Ray reminded me that Franklin's favorite phrase in discussing my Dad was, "Damn fool ideas!" Too true, too true! Much as I like him—after living with him for 28 yrs., I don't wonder that Mother has high blood pressure. Jane says her father is just as bad & she thinks we ought to train our husbands differently. Her mother agrees wholeheartedly. Ray says they'll be different anyway because they belong to a different generation. I'm glad of that.

Ray is different to the extent of being puzzling. He's a swell fellow, fun to talk to because he's interested in things like poetry & good music. He's interested in girls, too, but I would be amazed to learn that he had ever so much as held hands with anyone. Independent as hell! I'd be sorry for any girl who ever fell in love with him.

We had more fun last night kidding Jane about Eric. He took a notion to lift up her skirt & tickle her knee when they were down here the other day. We about died laughing, so of course he was much pleased with himself for being so amusing, and now she's worrying about how to keep him from doing the same thing all day! We all agree that he's taking after his father.

It's been so nice to be up here these two weeks that I hate to go back. Especially on that night train. Guess I'll go in the morning instead. One day more or less can't make much difference. I surely am an unreliable secretary.

I'd better go & mail this or I'll be an unreliable correspondent, too.

Goodnight, Sweetheart. I miss you.

All my love, Marian

⚜

9 Oct 1945
Hilo Hawaii

Dearest,

You are wonderful! Today I love you because you were intelligent enough to put a 15 cent airmail stamp on that letter of Oct 3d. It made me very happy — more than I can say.

I am glad that you are well and happy — congratulations on the new job. I see that you are still undertaking in your spare moments also. I'd like to see you at that but then I'd just like to see you — anyway.

I have been washing clothes and pressing shirts all night — mostly because the laundry situation is rugged and then it is something to do and I don't mind the work. Have found that shirts are quite a problem but an excellent way to relax and sorta think things out.

Some newscaster was just on and built his whole program around the announcement that the Japs had perfected (to some degree) a death ray [unfounded rumor]. It is rather profound I suppose but as he said — it's 3rd page news now. It all makes me anxious that the United Nations stay united in their determination to prevent wars. Refusing to give Russia the secret is not my idea of stimulationg good feeling between the countries. In that way the more or less feeling of animosity toward Russia in the U.S. is responsible for the London conference failure. Wish that Truman had been a little more concerned about it publicly — that's too much like the false and stupid optimism of the Hoover era. We can not rely on our scientific intelligence and production capacities to prevent future wars. Perhaps it would be well if more people (like [George] Patton) would say that there will be another war.

You of course are right about winning the peace and that means sacrifices for all of us. I hope that feeling is prevalent.

We have much to look forward to darling and the time will come when we can be together. I hope that it is soon—I can't help but be impatient. Goodnight sweetheart and your letter <u>was</u> wonderful.

All my love, Gene

P.S. Would like you to write to General Delivery till about the 20 of Oct or before if I let you know.

☘•

Navy day
Hilo Hawaii

Dearest Marian,

Just finished listening to Truman's speech in New York. It was very good but I wonder if it wouldn't be somewhat better if he had frankly told the people that things are not going too well on the diplomatic front. It appears that we are going to demand peace by use of military power—certainly something new in a foreign policy of the United States. I liked that portion of the speech in which he said words to the effect that lack of cooperation in the atomic age would be hell—wish that could be stamped on the hearts and mind of all men.

At breakfast this morning the Colonel told us some of the background of the black market expose of Pearl Harbor It seems he is a personal friend of Col. Stickney and helped draft the letter to the president (or senator) revealing the Navy (& M.C?) dealings along the marketing line. According to Col. Davies there are relatively few Admirals and JG's sleeping well over on Oahu these nights. How much of it will be presented to the public is questionable but it should compare with the Paris affair of a year ago. I had to laugh at the Commander's extreme irritation that Col. Stickney weighed <u>each</u> piece of meat he found in the routine inspection.

I have high hopes of leaving Hawaii (Hilo) for Oahu sometime after the 5th of Nov and then it will be only a matter of waiting transportation back to the states from the transient center at Pearl. I guess that I have already told you we are a separate organization now governed directly by FMF [Fleet Marine Force]. 250 men, 60 pts or above, left yesterday and there are about 150 more qualified to get out next week under the new lowering of the points. It <u>is</u> wonderful but I shall be sorry to leave the service in many respects. There are many tempting offers—one of which is the offer of flight training to all those wishing to stay in.

Time enough to discuss that when I get home. Good morning darling and

All My Love, Gene

❖

12 Oct 1945
Hilo Hawaii

Dearest Marian,
 A couple of bags of mail came in yesterday but none of it was for Hdqs Bn. So now the scuttlebutt has it we are getting some today—hope that it's true.
 Last night one of our men was killed down at the dock when a cable broke and hit his neck. Loading however continues and we should be ready to leave in 10 days or so—probably longer. A couple of Sgts. came back from Sasebo to report for loading help—they paint a horrible picture of conditions there. There is no food or water outside of what the division brought along. Rats, fleas, bedbugs, etc. are common everywhere but the population seems extremely cooperative in their stupid way. I thought that the statement some army officer made characterizing the Japanese was good—"When you tell them to do something, it's like telling your stenographer to bring her pad in and take some dictation—and she promptly forgets her pencil—"
 There is still a feeling in some parts that we are going home as a unit but I doubt it. I think that points alone will determine when we reach San Francisco The 200,000 occupation force seems too small but MacArthur should know.
 Saw the "Enchanted Cottage" a few nights ago and I liked it very much. I think that Hollywood would do well to produce more along that line that is, a love story of two <u>average</u> people. After years of movie going I had almost become convinced that love could come only to the handsome and beautiful.
 Time to go out and meet a couple army planes and pick up some officer messenger mail. Good morning sweetheart and I love you.

Gene

❖

14 Oct 1945
Hilo Hawaii

Hello darling,
 Mail finally arrived yesterday with a bang but it was a pleasant surprise to everyone—including me. Now I see I have a lot of questions to answer and

comments to make. The letters were old—from the 28th of August to the 13th of Sept. but nevertheless greatly appreciated and you are a darling. (Something I suspected right along) I had to laugh at you "being maneuvered into a corner" and then agreed to work for Ripley. I hope that it wont be as bad as you anticipate. Guess that you have been in that job for a month now. I will treat you with added respect and you can complain as much as you wish darling.

Also liked the reference of our relations improving with time rather than the beginning being better than the ending. I don't like that "ending" so maybe we can use the post- honeymoon period/era in place of it. O.K.?

As you suspected the 4th Marines are not in the 4th Div—they are in the 2nd div. It might be interesting for you to know that the 1st div was in the Russell Isles, Guadal. area (thence to Okinawa) the 2nd Div was based at Saipan, 4th at Maui, T.H. and the 6th organized the first of the year at Guadal. is now at Guam with the 3rd. Lately the 1st and 6th have gone to China, the 5th is definitely at Sasebo. Incidentally a couple of fellows returned from that place and called it a "dirty, filthy stinking hole." We have much to look forward to— should leave about the 25th or later. I don't care much for the 20-25 day trip by A.P.A. [a slow-moving ship] but I am hoping we stop at Guam so I can see Merle and Eddy. I suppose you read of the planned Amphib assault on southern Kyushu (Olympic operation). I am afraid that it would have been bloody. You were very nearly right in your letter in June when you said—Oct 1st.

Just had a chance to look over the new "Time"—in general I was impressed by the apparent indecisiveness as to what to do with the atomic bomb. The whole question grows more pessimistic every day. I don't think the world can accept the responsibility at this time. I am afraid that there are going to be too many disillusionments in the days to come. Sometimes I feel like throwing "Time" away and start reading comic books—people make more sense there. Somewhat along this line is John McGuigan's[65] who has the answer to the man of the year question—there is no question, 'tis MacArthur, the man who won the war against Japan." No, no, not that!

I'm glad that you had a pleasant trip to Benton Harbor—I remember that trip out of Milw. you spoke about—the dance floor was buckled in the middle.

Wish of course that you were going to Japan with me next week. We would sit out on the deck and talk about all the unimportant things of the last year or two. In a few days we can celebrate our last meeting (and parting) at Chicago— sometimes it doesn't seem like a year and now quite apparently we can see some definite landmarks in the future—somehow we can run our own affairs from now on without approval from the War Department. This is rather vague perhaps but it is nice to know that I'll still be around to love you tomorrow like I do today.

Gene

�֍

16 Oct 1945

Dearest Marian,

Didn't have a chance to write yesterday afternoon and last night we went to a movie downtown—I wanted to write because your letter of the 9th came General delivery yesterday. That makes about 17 in the last 3 days. It's wonderful and you are too.

I'm enclosing a picture taken last week of our Jeep, office etc. The only unusual thing about it is the fact that it is taken lately.

According to the latest info we should leave here between the 20th and the 25th of Oct so perhaps after the 21st you had better use the regular mail M.C. address again. On the trip over I should be able to write some sensible letters in answer to yours of the last few days. We are going to be busy tearing down our communications set up and packing the next week.

I don't like to think of the long boat ride—especially as it is in the wrong direction. Incidentally what you say about the importance of occupation is undoubtedly true—the only question is "Who should do it?"

The Indo China war is a little discouraging insomuch as it seems to symbolize the reluctance of people to be ruled by some foreign power. It is not consistent with our liberty sales talk of the past 4 years to stand by and let them fight it out. The sooner we decide it is our business, the sooner we will show the world that we fought for some very real ideals.

Good morning sweetheart and

All my Love, Gene

�֍

18 Oct 1945
Hilo Hawaii

Hello darling,

Your letters to G.D. Hilo are coming in fine shape, 9, 10, 11, 12, 14, 15—four yesterday and two more today. That of course makes me very happy but I'll say again that I like them a lot. Will have a lot to answer when we go aboard ship for the 20-25 day trip. I think that we'll get mail off at Pearl and probably at Saipan and Okinawa so there shouldn't be too long a stretch without you hearing from me. We are expecting a A.P.A. "Herald of the Morning," which took the 28th Marines 2nd Bat. back from Iwo.

To answer a question of long standing—we did sail from a part of Pt. Loma Calif. I thought that I had answered it already. Guess I have mentioned we were in San Francisco harbor a week under censorship however, and so couldn't get off the ship or mention the fact at that time.

I have become aware too that it only takes 2 years at Chicago to obtain a BA—seems that I read that the complaint of the U. is—too many uneducated BA's and too few educated Ph.D.'s. The idea of advancing at a comparative rate with your background sounds all right to me. I wish that you would go back to school—can't think of a good reason why I do except probably we would have more in common during the time I was in school but that is not too important.

Just found out that we probably will not leave until the 26th of Oct now so if you aren't running out of 15 cent stamps I'd like for you to continue to write until about the 22nd. This is wonderful—that is to look forward to receiving mail almost every day.

I haven't seen "Fantasia" but did attend the New World Symphony at L.A. in Jan of 1944. It was my first experience along those lines but I heartily enjoyed it. I can see where you are going to be a good influence when I get back but darling I am stupid outside of having an average college background. Hope that you bear that in mind because I don't want to disillusion you too much. Unfortunately too much of my education along the fine arts line ceased in 1942, but I am willing to learn.

I liked the cartoon of Betty Jane waiting in the railroad station. I hope that you are waiting.

More tomorrow sweetheart and

All my Love, Gene

❖

Oct. 8 '45
[Chicago]

Hello, Darling,

Back again in Chicago, & three of your letters were here, including the one in which you asked me to write to Hilo until the 13th. I do hope you get at least one of these letters. I'm glad you may be there a little longer than you had expected, as that should make it possible for some mail to reach you.

Don't worry about your letters to me, dear. I know how hard it is to write when there are no letters to answer. You sound so dejected—& I don't blame you. Waiting, with little or nothing to do, is the most discouraging thing in the world. I had an idea you would be feeling that it was all rather futile, which is partly the reason I said in my last letter to Hilo that I think the job of occupation is as important as the fighting was. I was thinking at the time that it might seem to you that my reasoning was not so good. I realize that the value of the whole thing depends on the over-all policies of the State Dept. & MacArthur, about which we can say & do very little. We can only hope that what they have in mind is in accord with our ideals, so that this time of ours is not really wasted. I talk as though I were in the same situation you are, which perhaps sounds selfish. (I can't think of the more accurate word.) However, I think you know that time for me until you come home is merely something to be counted off— so that, in a sense, what is good or bad for you is the same for me.

I have made this sound very confusing. Hope you understand, darling.

Mother came home last night, & I took the train this morning. She is awfully weak from having been in bed these two weeks and on such a strict diet. I hated to leave this morning as I'm rather worried about her. Also, I hate to go back to work after the free & easy atmosphere of life in a small town. Guess I'm really a country girl at heart.

'Tis getting late & they tell me there are stacks <u>and</u> stacks of work waiting for me in the morning.

Goodnight, sweetheart. I love you very much.

Marian

※

October 9 '45

Hi, Darling—

This will be rather brief, as I've had a busy day & it's late already. While there is still a possible chance of mail reaching Hilo before you leave, though, I don't want to miss a day.

I did about a week's collection of work today—which is a good indication of how simple my job really is. I just <u>hated</u> to go to work today. There was something so friendly & pleasant about being at home that I am about convinced I'd like to spend a few months there. I could work for Jane's dad, as he would like to have a secretary at least part time. He always has had, but this year has been unable to find anyone competent. Perhaps about the 1st of December. In the meantime, I'll change my mind several dozen times.

I am discouraged, too, about the outcome of the foreign ministers' meeting in London. It makes me feel a little sick to see how little the world seems to have learned about the necessity for <u>unselfish</u> cooperation. A few days ago the Sentinel headlines said something about "outlawing" the atomic bomb. It seemed so ridiculous. I have been convinced for a long, long time that laws & systems mean nothing unless the men & women who administer & live by them are good. I wonder why it is so hard to change human nature. That reminds me of the verse from Omar Khayyam about returning pure gold "for what he lent us dross allayed . . . oh, the sorry trade."—That's too long a thought for such a short evening.

Until tomorrow, then, dear—

All my love, Marian

⚜

Oct. 10, 1945

Darling,

The situation tonight is worse than last night—I'm too tired to think of anything to write, but I know I couldn't go to sleep without making some attempt.

No one has talked of much today except the World Series—& Chicago is one sad city. Murph has gone to all the Series games they played here. The Barrs, of course, were able to get tickets. It has been fun for Murph & a fine way to spend her "vacation." Probably I haven't told you—in any letter you've received—that she was all through working for the Army two weeks ago and decided to take a few weeks off before looking for another job.

Peg is coming down this weekend. She wanted to see a few plays, but I could only get tickets for one. No doubt we'll be busy enough talking anyway. She thinks Ray may be home by Christmas. If he is, they plan to be married during the holidays. There's an article in the Sept. Atlantic about "pioneering" in Alaska & what a wonderful life it could be for people who really wanted to settle there & <u>build</u>, in the broad sense of the word. It was just the sort of thing Peg would be enthused about, & I can hardly wait to see her expression when she reads it. I'd be willing to bet anything she'll want to go—That I'll tell you about Saturday.

Right now I <u>must</u> go to bed. Tomorrow night I should have time to write a good long letter.

Goodnight, Sweetheart.

I love you—Marian

⚜

October 11 '45

Dearest Gene,

The paper tonight says 1,250,000 troops will be home from the Pacific by March, leaving some 400,000 there. That should give us a pretty good chance, don't you think?

I haven't heard from you since Monday—which, compared to your situation, is nothing to complain about. But I do miss you, darling. Hope you are still in Hilo. By this time the first letter I sent Gen. Del. should be there.

These two clippings I cut out sometime ago, intending to send them to you. They are still interesting, I think, so perhaps it doesn't matter that I misplaced them for a while.

I appreciate Landis' remarks about Gabriel Heatter.[66] I just <u>hate</u> his commercials. They make everything he says insincere. Jane says her dad insists on listening to him every night & it's the worst 15 min. of the day for her.

"With Sirens Screaming" sounds like a gruesome story, but I am much impressed by it. Ripley was telling me yesterday about some of the racketeers & grafters he has come in contact with in business & govt. & I asked him if he didn't think they were able to get away with things like that because the average good citizen doesn't take enough interest in what goes on. He said, "Well, those things are so highly organized & deeply entrenched there isn't much anyone can do about them." Which seemed to me a good example of the defeatism I was criticizing—not that I have any right to criticize it. Some day, though, I would like to be a "reformer" of a different type than this story exposes.

Guess I'd better quit for tonight, dear. I wish you were here—

All my love, Marian

❧

Oct. 14 '45

Darling,

I am sorry I haven't written the last two days—just haven't had time to sit still long enough. Isn't much time now, either, as we are going to a concert in about 15 min., but I do want to get a brief letter in the mail.

We have been having a wonderful weekend, and your letters of the 6th 8th & 9th, which came yesterday, have made it even more perfect for me. I am so glad you finally rec'd a letter. Really, it is no compliment to my intelligence that I put a 15 cent stamp on these letters. It's just that I know a girl whose husband was with the Navy in Hawaii before the war & she used to get 15 cent airmail stamps for her letters to him, as this 6 cent stuff for service mail is a comparatively recent innovation.

There was the cutest story in this morning's Sun about the record no. of marriage license applications the other day. "242 hearts beat as 121," it said, and one of the bureau's clerks commented, "This reconversion is wonderful." Sounds good to me, too.

Peg was telling me that it is possible to earn a Bachelor's Degree in 2 yrs. at the U. of C. That interests me. Perhaps if you go there the second year, I may

study, too. Obviously that depends on a multitude of things, but I like the idea
and like to think about it.

'Tis time to go, darling. I'll have lots to write about tonight. Until then—

All my love, Marian

⚜

Oct. 14 '45
#2

My darling Gene:

The concert this afternoon was beautiful. I don't know when I have enjoyed
one more. It was the Chicago Symphony. They played Dvorak's Symphony
"From the New World," parts of the Wm. Tell Overture, some Sibelius, & the
"Sorcerer's Apprentice." I still can't remember whether you ever saw
"Fantasia." If you did, you will remember that the "Sorcerer's Apprentice" was
one of the selections included in that movie. Listening to it today, I could almost
see Disney's interpretation again, & I just loved it. I was thinking what a wonderful feeling it must have been to create "Fantasia."

Incidentally, we had no tickets for the concert & the box office was closed
when we got there. So Peg asked the usher if we could possibly get seats & he said
there were some in the balcony & we could just walk in—free! What a bargain!

Last night we saw Elizabeth Bergner in "The Two Mrs. Carrolls." She is a
good actress, but the play was lousy. There wasn't a single convincing thing
about it.

Peg says she likes Stoughton [Wisconsin] very much now. They have an
exceptionally good school system. They teach Shakespeare by recordings of his
plays with Maurice Evans & Judith Anderson. Also have recordings such as
Vachel Lindsay's readings of his own poetry. Isn't that marvelous? Peg says the
kids love it—& so does she.

Her reaction to the article on Alaska was exactly what we expected. When
she finished it, she sat for a minute looking thoughtful & then said, "You know,
that wouldn't be a bad place for Ray & me to go." At that point, Murph & I
burst out laughing. It's a good thing Peg has a sense of humor, too, & knows that
we really like her enthusiasm, or else she would get angry with us for teasing
her like that.

I really enjoyed what you said about pressing shirts being an excellent way
to relax & think. I have always liked to iron clothes—for the same reason. I also
like to hang them outside on a clear, sunny day, especially in California where I
can watch the P-38s in the sky at the same time—that is like Lin Yutang's list,
in "The Importance of Living," of all the simple pleasures which, to him, consti-
tute Happiness. Have you ever read it?

When you mentioned my efforts at undertaking, it reminded me of a story Ray told me about one time when he was helping my dad dress a dead woman. Maybe I told you before—Anyway, Dad put her slip on first and her brassiere over it. Ray said he didn't think it was supposed to be that way, & they argued at length until finally Mother came down & settled the question. Ray couldn't understand why my dad didn't know more about that than he did, but Mother says Dad never notices what she wears anyway. He is a riot!

We had quite a discussion this weekend about the strikes. Peg is completely in sympathy with them. She argues that the cost of living has increased so much more than wages that labor has a right to demand better pay. I think that's true, but I sometimes believe they demand too much. The tremendous cost of war cannot help but lower our living standards for a time, at least, & organized labor ought not to expect or ask wages that would permit them to maintain their wartime standards while the rest of the people's decline. That is an idea, not a conviction, because I don't know enough of the facts. One interesting thing Peg said was that some fellow from Kentucky who is manager of a coal mine or something like that told her the companies always know when to expect these strikes & see that they have sufficient stockpiles to carry them through. However, controlling the press, they tell the public there are serious shortages & thereby create public opinion antagonistic to the strikers. Could be—

Darling, I miss you so much tonight. Railroad stations make me lonesome, & having been at the Union Sta. with Peg twice this weekend makes me doubly sad.

I love you, dear—Marian

❦

Oct. 15, 1945

Hi, Darling,

How do you like the story of Senator Hamilton Horsehair? 'Tis very clever, but so close to possible realities, methinks, that I'm almost afraid to laugh. One editorialist in today's paper suggests that if we have not learned enough to avoid another war, the best possible use of the atomic bomb would be to blow ourselves up. If I were not so fond of living, I would agree with him immediately. He also suggests—& with this I definitely agree—that it is time to stop talking about democratic ideals (while acting like imperialists) and to talk about reality—The whole trouble is, as you so aptly said, that we are all more interested in getting nylons than in making a just & lasting peace.

I feel rather sad about the world tonight because it confronts people with problems so far beyond their capacities. Murph told me tonight why Ed doesn't want to get married. His mother was insane. It makes me feel so terribly sorry for both of them, but especially for Ed. And, except for one point on which I cannot agree with him, I am ashamed of having criticized him. I thought I had learned not to judge people's actions since the circumstances influencing them can never be fully understood, but apparently I had only learned not to criticize people who make the same mistakes I do.

Darling, when I am depressed by the seeming hopelessness of the world & my own ignorance, it helps so much just to tell you about it & know you will understand. I don't know what I would do without you, dear.

All my love, Marian

❧

October 16, 1945

Hello, Sweetheart,

Your letter of the 12th came today. I hope the service in the other direction is as good.

Hearing about that fellow who was killed down at the dock makes me sad. Life is so terribly insecure — in peace <u>or</u> in war. I think about the most heartbreaking story I've ever heard was that soldier who was flown home from Europe to attend the funeral of his parents & 6 brothers and sisters killed in an auto accident.

Oh, Marian, quit being so morbid!

Do you like the sonnet quoted in this book review? It expresses exactly what I believe: "The memory of us outlasts our breath . . . Giving . . . our death an uttered life longer than our living."

I don't know why I don't change the subject. Actually, I feel very good tonight and have for some time. Must be the cod liver oil I've been taking.

Had a letter from Mother tonight & she says she is getting along ok. I am glad of that as she really looked sort of pathetic when she came home from the hospital.

Have you had any mail from Marty? I hope so, dear.

I see that someone has already written "Time" to nominate for Man of the Year "Gen. MacArthur, the man who won the war against Japan." Obviously, the letter is from a civilian. That makes me furious! I think the Man of the Year should be a scientist, since surely the atomic bomb is the most epoch-making development of the year. I suppose it would be hard to choose which scientist, however. Anyone but MacArthur! Agree?[67]

Time to say goodnight, darling. I miss you and I love you <u>very</u> much.

Marian

☙

Oct. 18 '45

Dearest Gene,

The last couple of days have been rather hectic again. Ruth Griffith came yesterday & stayed over today to look for an apartment, which is a thing it's practically impossible to find. Jack is being released from the Air Corps & they plan to live in Chicago.

I'm glad they will be here because, if I decide to go home this winter, I'll not be so worried about Murph. That is the only thing right now that makes me hesitate about going—if Ed goes back to St. Louis & they don't get married, Murphie is going to be one sad & lonely little gal. I would hate to think of her living all alone with none of her good friends even in town.

Oh, honey, you should see the picture I just bought. It is Mother's birthday gift to me. (We are quite often several months late with things like that.) It's called "Mississippi Moon" & is a reproduction of an oil painting by Georges Schreiber. I love it—and so does Murph. We put it up tonight & she says it adds a "definite air" to our living room. Hope you will like it, too. When you are getting your mail regularly again, I'll send you the small picture of it that's in an advertising piece put out by the Assoc. American Artists, from whom I bought it. What a sentence that is!

This seems to me like a lousy letter. Guess I need some sleep. Until tomorrow, darling—

All my love, Marian

☙

October 19, 1945

Hello, Darling,

We just came home from the "Enchanted Cottage." It <u>was</u> a good movie. I liked especially the idea that they were seeing truth with their hearts rather than their eyes. And I agree with what you said about movies concerning average people.

This couple reminded me of a young farmer (I presume) & his wife who came into the store one day when I was at home. They looked just like the usual "dumb" farmers, but they had such a nice sense of humor & were so obviously happy with each other that it made me feel good just to talk to them.

I've had only one letter from you all week. Hope there will be some tomorrow. It seems for the last 3 or 4 weeks all the mail has come in a bunch on Saturday. Peculiar—

I finally got the raise that goes with my "promotion"—a whole 5 cents an hour! Only we're going on a 40-hr. week now, so actually I will be making $3.40 less per week. I might just as well go home. Guess I should be thankful that I can if I want to.

Darling, how I wish you could come home!

I love you—Marian

⚜

20 Oct 1945
Hilo Hawaii

Hello darling,

A dispatch came through about an hour ago which makes it quite certain that the rear echelon will <u>not</u> go to Japan. It is the speculation that we will either (1) stay here a couple more months (2) Move over to a demobilization center (Pearl) (3) go back to the states as a unit and receive the 5th. It of course was wonderful news and everybody is happy. Also now we have the authority to release high point (60) men for discharge. So that is the way it stands at present.

Later—just got a dispatch that we definitely are not going forward but probably will be split up. Everything is in an uproar—but it <u>is</u> wonderful. People are talking of going back to the states very openly now. It all sounds too good to be true.

I haven't much more time to finish this tonight as we have to prepare an inventory of all the gear on hand. The high point men are leaving next Thurs. for San Fran. I sure wish I were going along but nevertheless I am getting closer and my time will come. In a few weeks I'll celebrate 1 year out here—and a year since I've seen you. There is a dance here at N.A.S. tonight and I'd like to be taking you. I never have forgotten that night at the Schroeder. Goodnight sweetheart and,

All my Love, Gene

⚜

22 October 1945
Hilo Hawaii

Hello dearest,

Yours of the 16th came today via the city post office and of course was worth the trip down there.

I was sorry to hear about Ed's mother but I wonder if that "insanity in the family" business isn't carried too far at times. Undoubtedly it should be considered but in many cases there should be a reasonable doubt whether it would carry over to the next generations. I don't know tho

There are a few copies of the "PM" around the barracks and I had a chance to look them over this morning. It is an interesting paper and well written — I think I'd like to read it daily.

I liked your letter very much — especially the part on the world's hopelessness and our apparent understanding of each other. Perhaps I shouldn't have said "apparent" because I am convinced that it will be that way when I return. So when the world dopes off (according to our way of thinking,) we can very easily gaze at each other.

I felt somewhat that way today after receiving a letter from a girl back home. She had gone to a movie and had seen a Negro fellow and white girl together. Her comments could well have been written by Bilbo and unfortunately reminded me of the fact I had long suspected — that is, the narrowmindedness and prejudice of some people back there. I will not argue whether mixed races should marry or go out together but I hate the intolerance which always is present when people discuss those questions. "It was revolting," — "I shudder to think of it," etc —

I don't see how we can be concerned with what is happening in Indo China when we hold these ideas of racial prejudice in the United States.

It is about this time that I think we should blow ourselves up with the atomic bomb but perhaps that uninhabited So. Pac island deal would be better as far as <u>we</u> are concerned. "Senator Horsehair" article was amusing — unfortunately the way things look at present it could be true. The apparent distrust we seem to have developed for Russia etc makes us that much closer to hell.

Good afternoon sweetheart and I love you.

Gene

❁

October 20 '45
[Chicago]

Darling,

Still no mail — & how I miss you!

Have been meaning to tell you that Peg saw Gen. Vandegrift in Washington. She had gone to visit a friend of hers ("Bam") at the Marine Barracks. They went to a show there & the General was only a few seats away from them.

I just took some brownies out of the oven. Haven't made any for weeks & I can hardly wait for them to cool off so I can try one.

Another thing I liked about the "Enchanted Cottage" was that little story about the fellow whose hobby was making model ships & putting them inside bottles — they were so much like people, fit & seaworthy but stuck inside a bottle. Many's the time I've felt like that & I imagine you have, too, especially these last few weeks.

Unless I hear from you to the contrary, this will be the last letter I'll send to Hilo. This mail situation is making it difficult for me to write interesting letters, too. I am especially sorry because, since you will not be able to get any mail for some time, it <u>would</u> be nice if these last letters could be worth reading.

Hope your trip is pleasant, dear. I'll see you in Japan —

All my love, Marian

❖

October 23, 1945

Darling,

Your letter of the 18th came today. Since you may be there a few more days, I'll take a chance on sending one more letter to Hilo.

Have also rec'd your letters of the 14th & 16th, so I'm feeling very happy. I love you so much, sometimes I think it's impossible!

I am glad you are in favor of my going back to school. I really don't see how it could be done, but it's fun to think about — & miracles <u>can</u> happen.

Thanks very much for the snapshot. Needless to say, I like it. It makes me think that, in spite of the fact that you are so anxious to become a civilian again, you probably will miss the M. C. considerably. Ray said when I was at home that he couldn't write to any of the fellows he had been with because he'd get so homesick for Hawaii he could hardly stand it. Funny, isn't it?

Ruth & Jack are here so I'd better quit & be sociable.

Goodnight, dearest.

All my love, Marian

❖

Oct. 25 '45

Hello, Lt. Sweetheart:

This morning's paper carried the good news that the M. C. has lowered the number of points req'd for discharge to 50, effective Nov. 1. That sounds wonderful to me, darling. I hesitate to count on its making much difference in when you will be able to come home, but it is encouraging.

Margie called me last night to say that she & Rudy & his wife are driving to W'berg this weekend & to invite me to come along. I can hardly wait until Sat. aft. It will be so much fun — & imagine driving through Wisconsin at this time of year!

Listen, darling, how long will you have to go to school? I had been under the impression it would be four years — probably because you had mentioned something about 4 yrs. in connection with GI benefits. However, I understand it takes only 3 yrs. to earn a Ph.D. Is that correct?

As I told you in my letter to Hilo the other night (which you may not have rec'd), I am glad you are in favor of my going back to school. I don't see how it could be done, but it's nice to think about & I suppose it's not entirely impossible.

On this discussion of symphonies & the fine arts — please do not be under the impression that I <u>know</u> anything about either music or art — I merely enjoy them. I am very much pleased that you are interested, too. Life is going to be wonderful, Gene. I do love you!

To change the subject considerably, Paul's daughter (Gloria) just called & invited me to have dinner with her tomorrow night. I may have told you that she won a scholarship to the Art Institute and has been living at the Three Arts Club just a few blocks from here since school started. I feel rather silly because I've been telling Paul I was going to call her some day. I guess he decided I would never get around to it & told her to call me. Oh, I'm awful! I've never met Gloria, but if she is like her mother & dad, I'm sure I'll like her very much. I'm curious to know how she likes the Three Arts Club. It is the rule that only students of one of the three arts may live there. Jo Allen used to live there several years ago.

I see that the Marines in China have become slightly involved in skirmishes between Chiang's troops & the Communists. I had been sort of wishing your Division were there so you could get some first-hand information on the situation, but not if they're going to be fighting! I don't like that at all. Have been wondering what Al thinks of our aggressive interference in Chinese affairs. He said he favored the Communists if they were not dominated by Russia, and I hardly think he likes our domination any better. Would like to call & ask him.

This is getting awfully long. Guess it's time to quit.

Goodnight, darling.

All my love, Marian

✤

24 Oct 1945
Hilo Hawaii

Darling,

Oh happy day! The Marine Corps has come down to 50 points so I am really beginning to plan to be home for Christmas—or before if I am not "indispensable," which apparently I am at present. Don't think however that the Colonel will dare keep me too long—and if he does I think I can talk him out of it some way.

The news of all types hit here today. Mainly it consists of forming a new Rear echelon of 7 off. & 150 enlisted to stay in Hilo to transfer baggage to units of the 5th which are spread out all over the Pacific. The remaining officers who do not qualify under the point system will be transferred to other garrison units.

The Colonel seems to think I should stay but I think I can out-talk him—at any rate it shouldn't be too long before I see the golden gate again.

Your letters have been arriving in fine shape very regularly—something I should mention I guess insomuch as I haven't answered all of them. I am guilty of not writing to you but it hasn't been due to lack of interest in you or your letters—they are still wonderful and you too—

I'll let you know regularly now just what is happening altho nothing drastic will occur before the middle of November. The official notification of the 50 pt score is not yet in but it has been announced over the radio and probably authentic. I am happy and looking forward to a transfer to Pearl Harbor and then home.

Guess that I'd better get this in the mail tonight—that's the only important event of the day but the really important event of the year is that I love you.

Gene

P.S. Note the new address

❀

29 Oct. 1945
Hilo Hawaii

Hello dear,

I'm having trouble with this Sheaffer "Lifetime" [pen]—

I am seriously thinking of being home by Thanksgiving now inasmuch as we may leave directly from this island to San Fran instead of enduring the confusion at Oahu and the transient center. Also I don't think that I will be held long after next Thurs. the 1st of Nov. It all is working out so wonderful that I am expecting to wake up and find it a dream. No no not that.

Spent a quiet weekend after a rather nice Navy Day dance at N.A.S. off. club last Friday. This whole base is practically deserted except for the 800 RE Marines and the 17th Serv. bat. and a few pilots without planes (and flight pay.)

We hear that Oahu is really filled up, but at least when and if I get that far I will finally be on the last lap. Sometimes I become a little sad when I think of civilian life after being firmly entrenched in the M.C. 3—1/2 years. These offers the Navy has been making are almost too good to turn down but I have never really seriously considered staying in.

I expect to come in at San Francisco but I think that it would be wise if I met you in Chicago. I'll wire from there and I'd like very much if you'd be on hand to form a small welcoming committee of one (1) to greet me at the station. OK?

I am a little tired of struggling with this pen so that will be all for today. More tomorrow and meantime as usual

All my Love, Gene

❁

Oct. 27 '45
[Chicago]

Darling —

Just have time to write a short note & tell you how happy I am that you are not going to Japan. It is too good to be true! The possibilities make me so excited I can hardly think — especially since the discharge rate changes to 50 on Nov. 1.

I suppose I can write to you at Hilo again for a while, hm? It's getting so I can't remember what I've said in which letters, so you are apt to be confused by the lack of continuity.

I'm leaving in about an hour for Racine. Margie called the other night & said she and Rudy and his wife were going to drive to W'berg this weekend & would I like to come along. Naturally, I would. It will be so much fun.

Had dinner last night with Paul's daughter, Gloria. She is going to the Art Institute this fall and living at the Three Arts Club just a few blocks from here. I had never met her before. She's a cute girl & interesting, too.

Murph has a job with RCA Victor starting Monday. The salary is not what she wanted, but she thinks she will like the job & the people, which is really the important thing.

They had a Navy Day parade downtown this morning & there were Navy planes roaring over for a couple of hours. Murph counted 53 in the formations. They certainly looked good.

Guess I should get ready. See you <u>soon</u>, darling!
I love you very much.

Marian

✣

Wittenberg
October 28 '45

Hi, Darling —
Guess I should have time to write to you before the kids come down this afternoon. They stayed at Marcella's. She had a party for us last night, & we agreed that we hadn't had so much fun in years — not since the parties we used to have in high school. We laughed until our sides ached and our throats were actually sore. Sure was wonderful. Jane, Ray, Tup, Melitta & John were there, too.

Ray & Rudy discovered that they were just two blocks from each other on Tinian for a month & a half — & neither knew the other was there.

Rudy said Tyrone Power flew him from Tinian to Guam when he was coming home. (I can't get away from this argument.) So I showed him this last snapshot you sent & asked if you didn't look like Tyrone Power. He said yes, & then Ray wanted to see it. "Why sure, that's who it is!" Ray said. Ha! <u>Now</u> do you give up? Of course when I told them who it really was, Rudy said you couldn't possibly be that good looking — it must be the picture. But I know better, so he can't hurt my feelings that way!

Well, I'd better talk about something else so you don't get too proud! Oh, I like you, sweetheart —

Planning Department: I've quite definitely decided to come home to stay about Nov. 20. Mother is getting along fine, but she really needs some help & I need a <u>long</u> vacation. However, when you come home, I want to meet you in Chicago. OK? Perhaps you'll be here before the 20th. Oh, Mari-an, come down to earth!

Until tomorrow, darling,

All my love, Marian

✣

October 29 '45
[Chicago]

My darling Gene:

I couldn't have found here when I came back today anything more wonderful than your letter of Oct. 24—unless it could have been a telegram from
San Francisco. Surely hope the Colonel can be persuaded that you need not stay
there long. I still can't believe that you will really be home so much sooner than
we expected. 'Tis marvelous, darling!

I was a truant today & didn't go to work—didn't even telephone. We got
into Racine about 1:30 this morning & the thought of taking a train to Chi. at
that hour was pretty revolting. So I stayed with Margie & came back at noon
today. It's a good thing I've decided to quit & go home the week of the 15th. If
they fire me tomorrow, I can say that's all right, I was going to quit anyway.

Rudy and Nona (his wife) are going to W'berg again in a couple of weeks,
too, & plan to stay several days. He is one of those angelic people who will
arrange to go the same time I want to go home & will very likely come down
here to get me so I don't have to worry about getting my things to Racine on the
train. Darn nice to have friends like that.

Rudy would like to open a music store and wants to see if there are any good
opportunities in one of the small cities near W'berg. I hope he finds a promising
place. We had fun talking about it on the way back to Racine last night. We were
all wishing we could have stayed up there. We had the jobs in this music store all
figured out. I told them I wouldn't be the bookkeeper unless you could be the
radio man & you couldn't do that because you're going to school. So Rudy said
I should tell you that you can go to school after we go broke. More fun!

For a week I have been meaning to tell you about Peg & Ray's latest enthusiasm. Ray's Major is crazy about hunting & fishing—& I imagine it didn't take
much to get Ray interested. So now he's bought a collapsible canoe & is sending it home for them to use on weekend trips! I can just picture the canoe col-
lapsing in the middle of a romantic scene. Those kids are a circus!

There have been several things in the news that I meant to talk about, too,
but I am definitely not in the mood for making caustic comments today & can't
even think what the subjects were.

I liked what you said about our apparent understanding of each other and
your conviction that it is more than "apparent." I am so sure of it that I can't
even scare myself into thinking it might be over-confidence.

I like the "event of the year," too. And as for the "Man of the Year," as far
as I'm concerned, it's you, darling—& not only this year! Wonder if I could persuade Time to agree with me. You'd look wonderful on the cover.

Needless to add, I love you, Gene.

Marian

✧

October 30 '45

Hello, Darling,

I have just heard Congressman Emanuel Sellers of New York give a radio address on the Palestine problem. He spoke with great fervor, on the Jewish side of course, and I was very much impressed. He reminded me of the saying that "if a man in a garret burn brightly enough, he can set fire to the world." I wish this man could inspire the world with his recommendation that the Great Powers consider human decency & honor above such things as "Oil."

Did you hear Truman's speech on wages & prices tonight? I liked it very much.

I've been at home all day—again—with a cold. As I've said before, it makes me so darn mad! And lately I've spent a couple of days every two or three weeks fighting with one. That is one of the most important reasons I'm going home. I hope that I can gain some weight & some resistance.

On this cheery note, I'll say goodnight & go back to bed. Hope to be in better humor tomorrow.

All my love, dear,

Marian

✧

Oct. 31 '45

Hi, Sweetheart:

Rec'd your letter of the 27th today; so I'm in a better mood than yesterday. Also, my cold is somewhat improved.

I really have to laugh at you for being tempted by the offer of flight training. Can't say that I blame you. Let me tell you, though, about our weekend conversations on flying. For one thing, Mr. Haseltine (Jane's father) asked Rudy so many questions about their bombing missions over Japan that, for once, I heard all I could stand about flying. Rudy says airplanes are not here to stay. "The darn things just aren't safe." Coming home, he flew in a B-29 from Hawaii to Frisco. They lost two engines on one side just a few hundred miles out & didn't want to turn back because they thought they'd be stuck in Hawaii for several weeks if they did. The ocean kept getting closer all the way until, by the time they reached the Golden Gate, they had just enough altitude to clear the bridge—between the spans. Anyway, Rudy had a priority to fly from the coast to Chicago, but he wanted to get here for sure, so he took the train.

I've been saving these Barnaby cartoons for weeks, as you can plainly see. There is one important one missing, but you will probably assume from the others that Gorgon had an Indian up a tree instead of a deer "at bay."

Hope you don't mind the sudden change in stationery. The other stuff is all gone.

Would like to have heard the Colonel's comments on the black market at Pearl Harbor.

One of the minor reasons I'm glad you will be home soon is that now I won't have to have my picture taken. I've been postponing it on various excuses for <u>several</u> weeks.

One of the major reasons is that it will be so wonderful to <u>talk</u> to you!

All my love, darling—

Marian

⚜

30 Oct 1945
Hilo Hawaii

Dearest Marian,

Time tonight to write a few lines to you. The only important news to me it seems is—when am I coming home? Right now it seems as tho I may leave here in a week or 10 days for the transcient center at Pearl. It appears that I will not sail from here as I hoped yesterday. (This looks like invisible ink) The day after tomorrow I will be eligible to get out but unless I have some success with the Colonel, I'll be held here for another short period. If I do—it probably will be in "hack" cause I am going to tell him tomorrow morning that I <u>want</u> to go this weekend—or know the reason why—He is very stupid at times. At any rate I still have hopes of being in the states sometime next month altho I don't know what the situation is at Pearl—or in San Francisco.

Your letter of Oct 23th arrived at Hilo yesterday. I'm glad to see that they are arriving at such regular intervals and include all the things I want to hear—and I also am happy to have you to come home to—

I love you very much darling.

Gene.

⚜

Xxx   Oct 31 1945
D-1

Dearest,

'Tis the day before the day when I can start to complain in earnest about getting released. Also it is approximately a year since I last saw you—can't figure out exactly tho what day it was that I left Chicago.

The Colonel this noon sounded a little encouraging concerning my release—especially after I said, "Good God, Man, there is no reason why I should be held here." I shudder when I think about it now, but he just sat there as confused as ever. Did say that in a week I should be on the way to Pearl—and according to a report from Lennin who has just returned from there—transportation is no problem. I wish I knew just what to believe but at the worst I will be home for Christmas—perhaps Thanksgiving.

Mail arrived from the forward echelon today and so I had a pleasant half hour reading your letters dating from Sept 17 to Sept 26. And after that I became more convinced than ever that I am in love with you. I still think a little of the practical side of being in love, merely because I never have been in love in the states before.

In one of Marty's letters he spoke rather bitterly of MacArthur's "scoop" on the War department concerning the size of the occupation forces. Will have to send him that cartoon of Mauldin and the article of the Chicago Sun.

Also heard some more details of the wedding of Reuben. I should have been best man I guess—My mother also has found a girl for me. I like that—the last one she picked out was a farmer's daughter who lately quit high school to work in a pea factory. I have always kidded my mother along and she knows that I don't pay any attention to her. It is the only way I possibly can stand her for more than a few hours at a time. I think Marty is wonderful tho—

I'm glad you had a chance to go home to Wittenberg for a few days. It sounds like a rather peaceful town and I shall be happy to meet your parents. We will get along. Time to close darling. I am not making any attempt to answer your questions now or remark on the clippings and comments in your letters. Nevertheless I enjoyed them all and as usual your letters are perfect—no qualifications dear

All my Love, Gene

❧

1 Nov 1945
Hilo Hawaii

Dearest Marian,

I spent the majority of the day sleeping and taking a lot of kidding that I'm indispensible (sp?) But in a week or 10 days I should be nearly out or crazy.

Think that I'll have to fly over to Oahu on business this Saturday in connection with some registered publications on an LST that broke down 100 miles from Pearl. We have also sent a Lt. Col. to Sasebo to find out what is in the minds of the people of the forward echelon insomuch as they never answer our dispatches. We have quite a lot of their gear in our hands and don't know exactly what to do with it. There is a Major here who is quite a character and typical of the fouled up nature of the rear echelon. Bill Craven asked him a question the other day to which the major replied "How in hell do I know—all the mind readers are in the forward echelon!" Despite the clever answer he is extremely stupid.

Your letters of the 27 and 29th of Oct came today. Good time? I have almost decided for sure to go back to Marquette so I hope that works out O.K. with your plans to go home to stay. I think that it will all right but I definitely want you to meet me in Chicago. We have waited too long to miss that.

Goodnight sweetheart and

All My Love, Gene

⚜

November 1 '45
[Chicago]

Dearest Gene,

This afternoon I heard a broadcast of Frank Sinatra's appearance in Gary. For the first time, I really liked him. He's not a very smooth speaker, but his sincerity is unmistakable. I still can't understand what makes the bobby-soxers so wild about him, but I'm glad they are if his popularity will help convince them to follow the ideals he tried to express today.

Talking about speeches, one of the things I liked about Truman's Tues. night was the way he scolded Congress for side-tracking the Full Employment Bill. They've been so busy investigating & criticizing everyone else, it's about time someone reminded them of their own responsibilities. Right?

Had a letter from Mother today saying that Melitta had a baby boy Mon. night—& the next morning her father died. He'd been out in the yard raking leaves & just died. Security is where?

I liked the letter in the new Time from 16-yr. old Mary Lee Hogue, also the editor's comment: "There's no hiding place." He doesn't know about our island, fortunately.

See you tomorrow, darling.

I love you.

Marian

❀

Nov. 2 '45

Hi, Darling,

Peg & I heard this speech of Norman Thomas'[68] the weekend when she was here & were so interested that I decided to send for a copy. His criticisms of Roosevelt and of "PM" puzzle me. What do you think of it all?

In case it worries you, the shorthand on the first page says, "Post-war Asiatic Battlefront," which is a phrase some radio commentator used in speaking of events in Java. The irony of it amuses me. I put little shorthand notes like that in all sorts of peculiar places to remind me of things I want to tell you about.

I started to read some more of Time tonight, but the romantic music on the radio distracted me; so I decided to write to you instead. It seems, though, that most of the things I've been thinking about lately are subjects that have to wait until you are here. One small dream perhaps I can tell you about. It may sound a little ridiculous to you, being only a high school prom. It's the event of the year, though, in W'berg, & this year it's going to be real wonderful (I think) because it will be the first since '39 or '40 that we'll all be able to attend. Will you go with me, dear? Of course, it isn't until next April or May, but I'm having so much fun thinking about it.

Goodnight, sweetheart—I love you very much.

Marian

❀

Nov. 5 '45

Hello, Darling—

I'm still at home and complaining, but do feel reasonably alive today. Another day or two perhaps—

Julia is taking me to see "Anna Lucasta" tonight. It's supposed to be exceptionally good. I imagine I shouldn't go, but I want to, so I am. No self-discipline. I need someone to order me around. How are you at giving orders, dear?

Rec'd your letter of Oct. 30 today. I hope you had good luck in your talk with the Colonel. No doubt he would be extremely friendly & cooperative if he knew you said he was very stupid at times. I like you, honey—

The only important subject to me, also, is when are you coming home. However, there isn't much I can say about it that hasn't been said a dozen times already. Have you heard that song, "Waitin' for the train to come in"? 'Tis very appropriate.

Until tomorrow, darling,

All my love, Marian

❖

Nov. 6 '45

My darling Gene—

I have your letters of Oct. 31 & Nov. 1, and they are wonderful—even more so than usual. If I had any doubts about it, your conversation with the Colonel would surely convince me that you <u>are</u> anxious to come home. Why, darling, you're practically reconverted already!

I'm glad you told me what kind of girl your mother would pick for you— otherwise I'd have been somewhat worried about her latest choice. Seems rather strange. My mother would never be satisfied with <u>any</u> girl for Franklin. She isn't that way about me, though. I know you will get along with her fine. She likes you pretty well already, I think—She even uses those Iwo Jima postage stamps on all her letters. My dad is a totally different story. As I've probably said before, the workings of his mind are a complete mystery to me. I don't see how he could help liking you, though.

I'm glad you think your plans to go to Marquette & mine to stay at home will work out OK. I was afraid that last time I talked about it, I might have given you the impression that I'd want to get married as soon as you came home— which is not at all true. More accurately, I might <u>want</u> to (<u>IF</u> you asked me), but I don't think it would be sensible, & I'm sure you don't, either.

The play last night was very good. Remind me to tell you about it when you get home. It's wonderful to think you <u>could</u> be in Pearl Harbor now—or even on board ship, homeward bound—

I love you, dear.

Marian

❖

Nov. 8 '45

Darling,

I'm sad tonight on account of it's Thursday & I haven't had a letter since Monday—& the suspense is terrific! I hope you are not indispensable to the Colonel, because you <u>are</u> to me.

You should have seen me dyeing nylons the other day. I discovered I had two—rather well worn & of widely divergent shades—left over from the days when. So I got some color remover & some dye & attempted to make them resemble each other. Murph didn't laugh when she saw them; so I guess they're OK. Such monkey business I wouldn't do for anyone but you, dear.

Here is the complaint I warned you of regarding my new boss. The first few weeks I thought he was going to behave, but he's reverted to type. Last Friday he brought my check to me here at the apt. (which was very kind of him, or would have been if he had done it purely to be kind), but then he sat around for two hours telling all about his "fatherly" affection for me. Makes me sick to think of it. Furthermore, when I went back to work Wednesday, he wrote & put on my desk a note which said, quote: "Entirely aside from business, I'm terribly glad to see you." Of all the <u>revolting</u> characters!

There! I feel better now.

Tomorrow night I'm going with Gloria Rhoads to see the "Student Prince."

Right now, I'm going to dream about you, darling. Goodnight—& I love you.

Marian

⚜

6 Nov 1945
Hilo Hawaii

Dearest Marian,

I was over on Oahu this weekend, supposedly on business but actually it was more of a a pleasure trip—if Oahu can be connected with the word pleasure. So I accomplished practically nothing and was glad to get back to the peace and quiet of Hawaii.

There is no definite word on when I'll leave here. . . . I am still "indispensable" in the eyes of the colonel which has ceased to be funny but there is nothing I can do until he makes up his one-track mind. As I tell everybody every hour—there is <u>no</u> reason whatsoever why I should be held.

I managed to read the latest "Time" over the weekend and liked the article on reconversion—and the letter from that 16 yr old girl. There must be a hiding place to escape some of the disillusionments and selfishness of the world and men. At present it looks very much like we have accomplished practically nothing in this war except the opportunity to make the same mistakes again.

A few weeks ago I bought a radio in the expectation of coming home soon—I sent it to you last week and I hope you get it all right and in one piece. It is <u>yours</u>.

More later sweetheart and

All My Love, Gene

8 Nov. 1945
Hilo Hawaii

Darling,

Rec'd mail Tuesday with a bang again—only 3 times in 9 or 11 weeks was not good but I really got caught up with the news back there. I have been receiving yours regularly through the Hilo P.O.

In the last batch you mention getting a cut on your eye—good heavens, be careful! I hope it is cleared up now. I liked the letters you wrote from Wittenberg despite your apology that it was only home town news. It was different from what you regularly write but I enjoyed it—and wholeheartedly agree with you say about some of the people being <u>too</u> naive. Perhaps it would be good if "Forever Amber" were required reading for your home town and mine.

I spent all day yesterday opening up a field safe by drilling out the back and then in the afternoon we had it welded together. As I watched this fellow weld it I realized again that perhaps to a great extent fellows have picked up a trade in the service. I'd like to be a welder. They have also learned how not to be naive!

Bill Carey, Santora and the other 50 pointers are leaving for Oahu Saturday. Wish that I were among them but talk as I will the Colonel is definitely going to hold me for a "couple of weeks" he says. I talked to him today again but to no avail. I <u>will</u> be home for Christmas if I have to swim or steal an LSM. Col. Davis said that he wants to get home too but that's a dirty lie. He's got some maiden from one of the plantations on the string, and I know he isn't too anxious to see his wife. I told him that he's a regular and can expect to stay over here a long time—he thought that was funny.

We have a Colonel from an outfit who has gone to Japan and is expected to be back soon with plans for disposition of the rear echelon When he returns I'll be free to go—or so the story goes at present.

This noon I listened to the "Schoolroom of the Air" and I surely am impressed with that program. It's wonderful—"Pilgrims' Progress" today. In general these AFRS [Armed Forces Radio Network] programs are excellent and quite welcome after these Hawaiian musicals.

Good afternoon sweetheart—I love you.

Gene

�֍

November 13 '45
[Chicago]

Darling,

I'm sorry I haven't written the last few days. It had been so long since I'd heard from you that I thought you <u>must</u> be on the way home. However, your letter of the 6th came today & I see that was merely wishful thinking. Except that it seemed so good to get a letter again, I'd probably be feeling very deject-ed. If you are still in Hawaii when this letter reaches you, you will undoubted-ly be feeling dejected, too—all of which proves nothing we don't already know.

My Lord, what a paragraph! Could be that I can't afford to get out of prac-tice.

I am very much pleased about the radio. 'Tis real wonderful of you, dear. I hope it does get here ok. I should have told you long ago that it would be better to send any sort of parcel to W'berg because we have never yet received a pack-age here that was not insured. At least half a dozen in the past two years have failed to arrive. Apparently something is wrong somewhere.

The girls at the office are having a party for me tomorrow night. They always do for anyone who is leaving—& it's always fun. Every day I am more anxious to leave. I shall not miss a thing—except Murphie.

My boss is more annoying every day. Bach gave me a bunch of silly little verses (clever ones) today, which he had written about the people in the office. Not to be outdone, Ripley offered this disgusting contribution:

"And here's from one who should be at your head
But found you were so altogether sweet
That he prefers the moment which instead,
Found him there sitting, wistful, at your feet."

(Referring to the day he brought my check over here. He was sitting on the floor, the big goon!)

Someone else who dislikes him (nearly everyone does) suggested that I send the note in his handwriting to Wallace Cook with a brief explanation of why I don't like working for Ripley. If I thought Mr. Cook were any better, I might do it.

Still don't know exactly when I'm going home. I'm waiting to find out if & when Rudy & his wife want to go.

The future is looking brighter for Murph. It really seems as if Ed will get around to making up his mind soon. I hope so.

Did I tell you about seeing the "Student Prince" Friday night. It was not especially good, but the Prince was handsome—almost as handsome as you.

Goodnight, darling. I love you very much.

Marian

✧

Nov. 14 '45

Dear Lt. Sweetheart—

I came home from the party tonight & found your letter of the 8th. Although the party was nice, I liked the letter much more, except the part that says you have to stay there a couple of weeks yet! I'm getting disgusted with the Colonel, too. Guess there is nothing to do but be patient—it won't be so very long.

Had to laugh at you for saying you would like to be a welder. That sounds like Peg! I think I know what you mean, though.

Guess I should tell you about the party. This afternoon they gave me an orchid—which is a lovely thing, but somewhat conspicuous in an office. Do you remember in "Wilson" that he sent an orchid to his wife & told her that she was one woman who could wear an orchid—that usually the orchid wore the woman? Julia had mentioned that with some sarcasm when one of the other girls left & was given an orchid. I guess she thought I would remember; so she told me today that she thought I could wear one very nicely. I got a big kick out of that. As I told her, I really felt as if I were being worn by the flower. No real sophistication, I'm afraid.

We had cocktails and dinner (delicious steak) and a very pleasant time. No one even had an argument & that is definitely unusual.

I'm glad you rec'd the rest of your mail—& I'm glad you enjoyed those letters from W'berg. One of the innumerable things I like about you, darling, is that I can tell you about anything & know that you will understand.

It is late, so goodnight, dear.

All my love, Marian

❖

November 15, 1945

Dearest Gene:

I haven't heard from Rudy or Margie yet and, therefore, don't know when I'm going home. Have about decided to go up on the train Tuesday unless they make some definite plans before then. Ed is going to be in town over Thanksgiving & I have no desire to spend the holiday alone.

Had a letter from Peg last night which I didn't have time to tell you about. It was, as usual, entertaining & very welcome. This is the paragraph I liked best:

"I have been very unhappy lately because I am getting even more disillusioned about people. There was a girl here who I thought would be a fair friend, but she wants to reform me first, and that is no foundation for friendship."

I'm sure I wouldn't be nearly so fond of Peg if she "reformed."

Ray is supposed to come home sometime after Jan. 10.

Since I wrote that last sentence, Murph & I have spent half an hour or so worrying about Ray & Peg because they are both so impulsive & impractical. I'm afraid neither of them thinks their wild enthusiasms are funny—& they ought to realize it or they are likely to lead a mad existence.

I don't seem to be able to concentrate on anything else to write about. Guess I'd better quit for today. Every time I think of a subject, we start talking about something else. Wish you were here with us.

Goodnight, darling. I love you very much. (That I can always concentrate on.)

Marian

❖

November 17 '45

Hello, Darling,

It surely seems good to think that I will never have to go back to work at Reliable. Yesterday was my last day, and I didn't feel the slightest tinge of regret at leaving, although I like most of the people there & will probably miss them.

Murph & I went shopping this afternoon & had a lot of fun—something not ordinarily included, in my opinion, with shopping. I bought a new hat which I hope you will like as well, or nearly as well, as the brown one. Murph likes it better.

We found the book "Not in Our Stars" at the rental library today. I'd like to finish it before I leave Tuesday, but that is probably a forlorn hope.

Don't you like this article of Grafton's? I think it is one of his best. Sort of scolds us, doesn't it, for our South Sea Island dreams. I was thinking the other day that perhaps too many of us attempt to escape from the world's problems by making our own lives as comfortable as possible—and the measure of our success merely complicates the problems. Could be?

Until tomorrow, Sweetheart—

Marian

❀

12 Nov. 1945
Pearl Harbor

Dearest Marian,

About the time you receive this I should be on the west coast. Rec'd my orders Sat. on mighty short notice transferring me to P. H. to await transportation to the states so I flew over to Oahu and reported in that afternoon. This is my 3rd day here and from the looks of the situation—I should get a berth tomorrow or Wednesday. I am only 14th on the officers' waiting list which looks very good. This place is efficient and very satisfactory in every respect. I don't know what port I'll come in at on the west coast but probably it will be San Fran, San Diego or San Pedro. I hope that it is the latter insomuch as I'll be able to see my uncle. From there I'll be sent to a separation center with Chicago being the most likely. Now you know just about as much as I do about the situation.

I'll wire or call from the states as soon as I know a little more about what is going to happen. There is a possibility that I'll come back on an aircraft carrier as it seems there are several in the Harbor. It would take about 4 days—if it's an L.S.T., about 12-14.

I don't think that I'll write again unless I don't leave in the next 2 days. You had better hold your letters too—and meanwhile I will see you soon.

All my Love darling,

Gene

❀

WESTERN UNION
CK390 10 TOUR=SANFRANCISCO CALIF 20 33 OP
1945 NOV 20 PM 6 13

MARIAN SMITH=
14 WEST ELM ST=

LEAVING SAN FRANCISCO 21ST EXACT TIME ARRIVAL CHICAGO
LATER LOVE=

GENE

❧

WESTERN UNION
KHA457 NL PD=CARLIN NEV 22
1945 NOV 22 PM 11 43

MISS MARIAN SMITH=
APT 1503 14 WEST ELM ST CHGO=

OVERLAND DELAYED FOUR HOURS SAN FRANCISCO CONFIRM
ARRIVAL TIME NORTHWESTERN STATION PLEASE=

GENE

8

"I am anxious to get away—and doubly anxious to be with you."

THE OVERSEAS LETTERS *ended a few days before the telegrams. I was sent home on an aircraft carrier with orders to report to the Great Lakes Naval Training Center for discharge from active duty and into the Marine Corps Reserve. I was now almost home after three and a half years, but whether home was in Milwaukee or in the Chicago train terminal I was not sure. Gone was the loneliness of military life with its regimentation and the uncertainty I might never make it. Now my life was once more my own and the future was in my hands. I could do what I wanted, live where I wanted, and spit at a colonel if I wanted. The shackles of military life with its artificial and undemocratic hierarchy would never frustrate me again.*

I had never completely adjusted to military life. I was not comfortable with weapons despite exhaustive training with them. While some of my comrades enjoyed the feel of their M-1 rifles, liked to break them down and reassemble them—and many could do that blindfolded—I looked at mine as a piece of dumb metal and wood. Firing it brought little satisfaction and probably that is why I never learned to shoot straight. I hated to think of my life depending on killing an advancing Japanese soldier.

I made the best I could of the social life. Macho talk, much of it about women, did not appeal to me, and as Merle and Eddy felt the same, we naturally spent our free time together. Movies, which played such a big role in our overseas life, were an escape from boredom. Alcohol served mainly as a stimulus for discussion.

Yet we often discussed the attractiveness of military life. The pay wasn't bad, especially for the higher ranks, and except in combat there was little personal risk. But we agreed the security that service life offered was the major attraction. The Marine Corps furnished our clothes, a bed, and fed us seven days a week. We got free mail, entertainment, transportation, vacations, and alcohol and cigarettes at bargain prices. They fixed our teeth and kept our bodies healthy, and if you died, they buried you. Not many civilian jobs offered more.

Even the awful boot camp, which humbled us and stamped out any vestige of individualism, taught us the discipline that was essential in war and useful in peace. Big battles are not won by armies but by small units of men working together in dangerous situations. Many of us would have laid down our lives in combat to protect our comrades. We had discovered a camaraderie we had not known before and, for most, would never know again. Grudgingly we acknowledged the old saying, "Once a Marine, always a Marine."

Like every other returning serviceman and woman I faced the terrible adjustment we called reconversion. In some ways we wanted to pick up where we had left off, but if we gave it some deep thought we knew that was not possible. Before enlisting in July, 1942, I had finished my undergraduate work at Marquette University but it did not mean much. I suppose some of my family were proud of me. I was the first Petersen to attend college and the second Staab on my mother's side to get a bachelor's degree. But I knew my mother would have gladly traded it for a defense job for me at Allis Chalmers, and my father, for reasons best known to himself, preferred I had never set foot in college. Under these circumstances I didn't even bother to go to graduation but simply picked up my diploma when it was available, took one look at it, showed it to my grandfather, and put it away with my other childhood mementos.

I had never agreed with the old adage that "money can't buy happiness." I had some, and it was going to buy me the opportunity to go to graduate school, which I wanted more than anything. My father's reluctance to pay my semi-annual $100 tuition was such a painful and embarrassing memory that I had determined to be financially independent. Before I left home, my grandfather and I had established a savings account at a suburban bank with the money I had saved with my part time janitorial job and there was $750 on the bottom line. He periodically deposited the money orders I sent to him and twice a year drove the six miles to have the interest entered in the passbook. By now it had grown to nearly $3000, a respectable sum considering in the first eighteen months of service life I made less than $60 a month and the last two years never earned more than $200. I did not spend much in the United States Marine Corps. I was confident that with a part time job I could easily support myself in the pursuit of both a master's and a doctoral degree.

But now my life was pleasantly complicated by the girl with whom I had fallen in love. It was hard to imagine it was only a year ago, in October, 1944, that she had answered my request for a date with, "Of course I want to see you," and had signed the letter, "as ever, Marian," with the "a" underlined to remind me of something. A few weeks later as I was headed overseas, she had written that we had "a wonderful chance for love." How things had changed in a year! In that time the words above my signature had evolved from "love" to "love?" to "much love," to "all my love," and finally, "I love you," but by then we had written over 400 letters.

The train was crowded with servicemen, and when the doors opened in Chicago's Union station, we all poured out with our suitcases and seabags. When we reached the lobby, the place was jammed with friends and relatives of returning servicemen and women, and I wondered if I could find her. However, she stood alone in a far corner of the station and was, I thought, prettier and thinner than I had remembered. She wore a tailored brown suit that befitted late fall in the Midwest and the same hat I admired at our first meeting on 18 February, 1944. I kissed her.

The next day we boarded the train to Milwaukee where she could stay with a friend. I called from the station and told my stepmother I was in town, but as my dad was at work, it was not convenient for them to pick me up. Gwen and Marty were pleased to see me. My two young half-brothers were in school. Of course my mother was anxious to see me. The following day I borrowed my grandfather's 1931 Pontiac and made the sixteen-mile trip to Waukesha. It had been over a year since I had seen her and my stepfather, Ray. My mother thought I looked thin but then she always did. For the next two days I was paraded before my many aunts and uncles, which as usual I found exceedingly boring.

"Did you have a hard time?" my uncle Bill asked. "Not very much," I said. "But I thought you were in a battle or something." I explained most of military life was pretty boring and other than a month on Iwo Jima, I could not really complain.

"Myrtle's boy was in the Marines, too. Did you see him over there?"

"Where was he stationed?" I asked.

"I don't remember, it was a small island with a lot of jungle. He got malaria. Now he's working for the Motor Works and is going to get married." With that, Bill's attention wandered and I was glad to get out of it.

I could not blame the civilians for showing little real interest in my life in the Marine Corps. Their questions were perfunctory and my answers lacked much enthusiasm. I would like to have talked about foreign affairs, but when I tried to elicit an opinion on the United Nations, I drew a blank. The few who had given the organization any thought were suspicious of an international body where Russia had an equal voice with the United States. The old pre-war isolationism in the Midwest had never really died. I realized that other than a blood relationship I had nothing in common with these people. My father wanted me to get a job. Only Marty gave me quiet encouragement to go back to school. Frequently I became depressed in my new freedom and for brief moments found myself envying the guys who had stayed in the service.

There was much talk of us young people having wasted the best years of our lives. My mother especially played this theme. I tried to explain I did not feel that way. I helped defend my country from the German and Japanese military threats, but I believed I had also aided less fortunate peoples to obtain the blessings of democracy. My military service had brought many benefits. Socializing with young men my age from all over the United States and learning about them from endless censoring of their letters had broadened my outlook. Certificates awarded by those boring communication schools were worth more than the paper they were written upon, and I had seen a part of the world I might never see again. Nor was I the same youth after living with death on Iwo Jima. Even if I could have found someone to listen to me, these were concepts I found difficult to explain. I bore no resentment for those who had not served, nor envied them the fruits of their wartime labor but was dismayed that the idealistic objectives of our national war effort somehow had escaped them. Perhaps I did not understand them, and certainly they did not understand me.

My orders directed me to the Great Lakes Naval Training Station near Chicago, which handled separations for Midwest Marines. When I reported a week later I found utmost confusion as hundreds of Marines and sailors filled out the required forms, took their final military physical, and waited for release, a process that took several days. By that time I had come down with a bad case of flu and was torn between sleeping in a drafty naval dormitory *or taking the short train ride back to Milwaukee and spending the nights at home. I ended up doing both and was miserable in both places. Finally at the end of November I was awarded an honorable discharge from active duty. As an officer I remained in the inactive reserve for an indefinite period. Presumably if Hitler surfaced or the Japanese Emperor decided to resume the war, I would be yanked back in. In the meantime my only real joy was thinking of Marian in Wittenberg. If there had ever been any doubt, I knew now she was my future.*

Marian and I had confided little about our relationship, so introductions to our parents were of immediate concern. My mother took a dim view of Marian, whom she had hardly heard about, and like most mothers wanted me to delay marriage and hopefully settle in with a more familiar face. Marian's mother took a more helpful and realistic view based on our obvious love for each other. Her father accepted it gracefully but harbored the hope that a son-in-law would help him in his business. I found myself once again debating my own father on the wisdom of going back to school rather than "finding a real job." After three and a half years away from home and some inevitably acquired sophistication, I found I was still defending my decision to get additional formal schooling. When Marian went home to Wittenberg early in December, we continued our correspondence.

7 Dec 1945
Milwaukee, Wisc.

Hello Sweetheart:

Feel slightly improved tonight so will get off a few lines before going back to bed. Took a strong dose of Southern Comfort this noon but couldn't sleep. Undoubtedly, I have the grippe which makes me feel as tho I've been hit in the chest with a hand grenade. I'm sorry I couldn't see you off down at the station but figured that insomuch as I have some rough days ahead down at Great Lakes, I had better take it easy today. O.K.? So I'll have to love you in silence (& absence) for the next few days.

The situation at present looks something like this. I go down tomorrow and probably will start processing on Monday & finish Wednesday. Then after a stop at home if I feel better I'll come up to Wittenberg. There is not much sense to come up if I don't feel in tip-top shape despite the fact I'd like you to be my nurse. Marty has been doing everything to keep me comfortable and is a good nurse and as usual we have been having some good discussions.

I hope you are having a pleasant trip—imagine that you are about in App.[leton] Junction now. Darling these last two weeks have been wonderful in every respect which makes me feel as tho I was pretty smart in falling in love with you on Guam. You are everything that I have ever desired and I know that we can be happy. Goodnight and I love you.

Gene

Address letters
3137 — So 31st
Milw. Wisc.

�֍

8 Dec 1945
Great Lakes,

Hello darling,

I checked in this morning down here but will not begin processing until Monday morning with the possibility of finishing Wednesday. It is only a possibility tho.

The cold has apparently settled down to a long fight but today I seem to be holding my own (at least) — still have a headache and general body pains. Have stayed in bed all afternoon but tonight I think I'll . . . get something to make me sleep. So much for the health situation —

Got two books at the library this noon which I'll attempt to read tomorrow (in bed) "A Short History of Russia" Sumner and Lippmann's "Preface to Morals." Also procured "Time" & "Life" so that solves the recreation problem.

Needless to say (but I will) I <u>do</u> miss you very much darling but I hope that I can get up there sometime before Christmas.

Even tho we can't (?) have everything, I wish that you were down here during this first stage of reconversion. I hate to face these stupid civilians all alone. Marty & I were alone last night and had a long discussion concerning the events of the last 10 years. He still believes in me which I appreciate & is fond of you too.

I think that I'll probably get a job somewhere until March (full time) and then concentrate on a good part-time affair after I start school. Will also drop in at Marquette when I get home so that I can be sure to get in there in March.

So much for today sweetheart. If you were here, I'd probably gaze into your pretty brown eyes & say I love you.

Gene

✖

10 Dec 1945
[Great Lakes Naval Train.]

Dearest—
The cold feels no better even after a quiet weekend in bed but I am trying to hold out until Wednesday when they say I will be finished. If no better by then—I'll go home and stay in bed until I have it licked. I feel miserable! Take my physical this aft. & will try and talk the Dr. out of some sulfa drugs which are supposed to do wonders for the Flu—grippe etc.

Started processing this morning—the general situation is snafu—nobody knows or cares much what is supposed to be going on. Despite the confusion they seem to muddle thru somehow.

Have been reading a lot this weekend (& sleeping) Got through 1/2 of "Russia" & all of "Magnificent Obsession" which I liked—never saw the movie tho.

Am sending some of the Sunday "Sun" which should be a pleasant relief after the Milw Sentinel.

Hope all goes well in the little town—will eventually be up but it all depends on this cold. I miss you darling—more than ever I guess but it's not like being 6000 miles away.

Goodnight my sweet &
All my Love

Gene

❖

11 Dec 1945
Great Lakes

Hello darling,
Decided to go home last night in order to get <u>warm</u> again. This is the coldest place in the world undoubtedly. My cold is somewhat improved and I think that I have it licked now—however when I finish here tomorrow I am going home and stay there (in bed) until I feel natural again. I think that I will get out about noon tomorrow despite the confusion. I don't believe they can hold me any longer.

Yesterday I accomplished a great deal even tho I felt rotten. After trying to keep warm for the last week, I had to stand semi-nude in some windy barracks for almost 2 hours while taking my physical, "to determine whether I was physically fit to be returned to inactive duty." Like most physicals this one was a farce—some stupid corpsman jabbed me 5 times before getting a blood sample. So when I finished I decided to go home in order to get a good rest in comfort.

Kreils[69] had been out one night over the weekend—he said he remembered you. "Isn't she from Wittenberg?" We'll have to call on them when you get back.

There were no letters from you yesterday but by tomorrow I should have some. Marshall Reiboldt called last night & we talked for 1/2 hour despite the fact he had got me out of bed. Says Reuben is in Memphis and he (Marsh) had got out around the 15th of last month. The housing situation is troubling them too—also plans to go back to school for 3 years—he lacks 2 years for a B.A. Reminds me that I am all set as far as schooling is concerned under the G.I Bill. I'll go down to Marquette as soon as possible in order to register for the March term.

That about concludes all the news for today. Hope you are O.K. and haven't caught a cold etc! As usual I do miss you darling. I hope that I can come up in about a week and if the cold continues to improve it is probable. If not I will be up shortly after Xmas.

Goodnight dear & I do love you.

Gene

⚜

December 8 '45
[Wittenberg]

Hello, Darling—

How are you? I hope that staying in bed yesterday cured your cold—or at least improved the situation considerably. I've been worried about you. Did Gwen's mother tell you I called just before I left? I was wishing after I talked to you that I had said I would come out to see you—I felt so lost.

Kathleen had stayed home, though, trying to get rid of her cold, and she complained when I suggested leaving; so I thought I'd better stay there until train time.

I've been so busy today I've hardly had time to think. Things are fairly well organized now, though. Tomorrow I can start making that yellow blouse.

It's cold up here—or rather it looks cold. There's quite a bit of snow & ice. Seems rather good. Listen, dear, if you want me to wear stadium boots, bring some along for me if it's convenient. Otherwise, I'll have to find something up here, I guess. In the meantime, I'm wearing Mother's.

That last paragraph reminds me that you have been almost <u>too</u> good to me. Don't let me take advantage of you, darling. I'm afraid I might—and I surely don't want to.

Oh, honey, I love you so much! And miss you!

Marian

✤

Dec. 9 '45

Hi, Honey,

Mother told me at 5:45 last night that the mail doesn't go out at all between 6:00 PM Saturday night and 8:25 AM Monday morning; so I decided I might as well send these two letters together. I hope you won't be at home tomorrow and wondering what's happened to my "letter every day."

Almost all I can think of to write about is how much I miss you. In spite of the numerous odds & ends I have to do, the time drags. It seems like a week since Thursday night instead of three days.

Jane came down for dinner this noon. (Dinner is always at noon here.) We started to go for a walk this afternoon, but a couple of blocks was far enough. The temperature was 8° above.

Tonight we're going to play "sheephead" [card game] with my dad.

That is my day, play by play! Nothing much interests me except the state of your health and when you are coming up here.

Until tomorrow, then—

All my love, darling.

Marian

✤

December 10 '45

My darling Gene—

Your letters of the 7th and 8th came today. I am still worried about your cold. I'm glad you stayed in bed because that is the best way to get rid of one.

I've had a busy day again. We washed clothes this morning, and I nearly froze my fingers hanging them outside. Had to come in every few minutes to thaw my fingers out. It was fun, though.

The yellow blouse will be finished sometime tomorrow; so you can come up any day now, honey. I hope you will like it.

Your reading schedule for Sunday was rather ambitious, wasn't it? I would like to read Lippmann's "Preface to Morals" sometime. I started it once and, for some reason, didn't have time to get far.

I think you would be wise to take a full-time job until March. The sooner you find something to keep you busy, the easier the transition will be, I believe. The more time you have to worry about possible difficulties, the more exaggerated they become. Really, you have <u>nothing</u> to worry about, dear.

I was telling Mother what Les [Larson] said about not being able to retain anything when he went back to school. She told me that after she had been teaching for three years, she went back to school and had the same difficulty. But it took only about six weeks to overcome it. That wouldn't be bad, would it? "All you have to fear is fear itself." Unquote.

Goodnight, Sweetheart. I love you so much!

Marian

❖

December 12 '45
[Wittenberg]

Darling,

Your letter of the 10th came today. Apparently what I told you about the length of time required to get a letter here was not very reliable. The Christmas rush, I presume.

I hope the doctor gave you sulfa or <u>some</u>thing to break up that cold in a hurry. — I don't like being a mere 200 miles away, especially when you're not feeling well.

The "Sun" will surely be welcome. In yesterday's "Sentinel" under the head-line, "Hitler 'Tipster' Jailed as Fraud" was an innocent article stating that Truman had spent a day or two on his yacht. Some character must have been drunk that day.

I finished the blouse yesterday. Have been ironing all day today. Incidentally, Mother says she thinks there are a couple white shirts of Franklin's here which you may have if you can wear them.

I think I'll go over to the library this afternoon if it's open and see if they have a copy of the "Citadel." No doubt you will approve of that.

I hope you will be here soon, darling. It's so lonesome without you.

I love you very much.

Marian

❖

Dec. 13 '45

Hello, Sweetheart —

Today I am in bed, too. Isn't it disgusting? I don't feel so bad, but I have a cold (mostly in one eye), and I want to get rid of it in a hurry. It makes me so mad!

I did manage to get the Citadel [A.J. Cronin, 1937] yesterday and started reading it last night.

Your letter of the 11th came yesterday afternoon. I hope you finished at Great Lakes ok. & are feeling somewhat normal again.

I was rather surprised that Mr. Kreil remembered where I was from. I guess there is a logical explanation, though. Mr. Herzberg, the vice president at Frank & Co., has some relatives who live on a farm near here. I had forgotten about that until Mother mentioned it today.

Jane brought Eric down for a little while yesterday. He would have eaten all the cookies in the house if we'd let him. Jane thinks he looks like Thumper, the rabbit, because his cheeks are so pudgy.

Guess I'd better quit & go back to the Citadel. This is a lousy letter, indicative of the mood I'm in. Things will be better tomorrow—

I hope you will come up Sunday or Monday night—??? After Christmas seems like eternity!

I love you, darling—

Marian

✦

13 Dec 1945
[Milwaukee]

Hello Honey,

Just a note today before I go down to Marquette—didn't write yesterday but I <u>have</u> been busy doing a million odds & ends since I got back yesterday noon. Got <u>2</u> new tires on today so that helps the transportation problem considerably. Can't have a gal without transportation, can you?

Your 2 first letters have arrived which makes it appear that you miss me as much as vice versa. I <u>do</u> darling. Will comply as far as the stadium boots are concerned—guess I talked myself into that one but the snow <u>is</u> deep here today. Reminds me that Reuben & I never could figure out—when people would always say "Oh there's a lot more snow up North than here in the city." Some people <u>insist</u> it snows more in the country than in the city. Don't puzzle over that last sentence too much—just an idle thought.

Have some necessary Christmas shopping to do today—a viset to my mothers soon—also to Helgas—down to the school board about a job—get some stuff for the car etc!! and a million other jobs.

I feel almost normal—the cold has retreated so I plan to be up some time early next week depending largely upon how much of this running around I

have accomplished by then. Until then I'll have to go on missing you and all that goes with being in love (and being faithful I might add.) So till tomorrow
All my love to you,

Gene

⚜

14 Dec 1945
[Waukesha, Wis.]

Dearest Marian.
No letter yesterday . . . I have been doing a lot of necessary running around and getting my affairs in order which has been neglected for 3 years. These people I viseted in the last few days want me to stay—I can't tell them I <u>have</u> to get back to do something else like I would when I was on leave—so have to make it a long visit. This is particularly true out here in Waukesha—where I am now. This is organized torture.
The cold is much better so I am coming Monday night for sure—better meet me less I get lost in the metropolis. We'll have a lot to talk about when I do get there. Have been thinking (between answering a lot of stupid questions,) of what I'll write my Master's thesis on. I am expecting some suggestions from you. Thought of "The United Nations." What do you think of that??? I'll major in U.S. History I guess. Apparently I'll have to decide by April sometime—think that it will be fun to work together—don't you?
. . . I love you.

Gene

[Photo of Tyrone and Annabella Power enclosed with the note]

Stinking aeroplane driver. This has been a tough week for the USMC. This is the final chapter but I still say undoubtedly he is—

⚜

Dec. 13 '45
[Wittenberg]

Darling,
There are a dozen things I wish I could have said to you on the phone tonight, such as I miss you and I love you and Monday is four <u>long</u> days away.

But my mother, with characteristic lack of tact, sat right beside me through the entire conversation so that I had to be rather impersonal. I'm sorry, dear. It was good to talk to you anyway, and I'm glad you are coming Monday for sure. Hope the trip won't be too bad. The train is supposed to get here about 9:15, but it seems to be almost an hour late usually.

Have you seen Marion yet?

I was reading the Citadel all day. I do like it very much. Guess I've finished about half of it.

Listen, honey, don't go to a lot of trouble trying to get those stadium boots. 'Tis a matter of minor importance.

Fri. morning: Guess I'll stay in bed again today. I can breathe this morning, but I feel awfully weak.

Had a letter from Murph yesterday. She said Ed was at Camp Grant & expected to be out the same day you were.

Until tomorrow, Sweetheart—

All my love, Marian

❀

Dec. 15 '45
[Wittenberg]

Hi, Sweetheart—

How are you? Fine? My cold is much better today. I spent the morning doing odd jobs in the kitchen. We have two corpses downstairs so Mother doesn't have much time for housework.

She just put me in a cheerful mood with these remarks, quote: "Are you writing to Gene? Well, you'd better hurry up & then I'll mail it when I go downstairs. Otherwise it won't go out until Monday & then you don't need to send it."

I just love being told, in that dictatorial tone, something I already know!

Your letter of the 13th came yesterday afternoon. I enjoyed the clipping & your comments thereon. I agree it's been a tough week for the Marine Corps, losing its most handsome Lt., namely you, <u>and</u> most handsome pilot. How's that for a compromise, dear?

You do have a lot to do, but take it easy, honey—you have 27 days and you don't want to finish everything at once.

I'm glad to hear that you're being faithful. Not that I have worried about it. I may be naive in that respect, but you are so wonderfully sincere, darling—it's easy to trust you. And I love you for it.

I'll be waiting for you Monday night. It's been a long week.

All my love, Sweetheart,

Marian

✤

25 Dec 1945
Milwaukee

Hello my love,
Got home safely last night at 10:30 PM after a miserable repeat miserable trip. Among the amazing events were (1) No lights on the Appleton train (2) A 1910 coach which was uncomfortably cold (3) A breakdown at West Bend (P.S. The wheels went flat, believe it or not) (4) A cold 4-1/2 [hours] wait during which a couple of small children cried at regular intervals (they alternated) (5) A cold bus trip to Milwaukee from West Bend.

I made it tho & am not really complaining. Surprisingly the train was not crowded and I had a double set of seats. Ah yes—it was an experience. Looking over the paper today I see that transportation is really snafu throughout the nation. Would advise you to consider the "400" out of Appleton—think it's due there at 4:45 PM. I, of course, will meet you at the N.W. station Monday evening.

Oh—dropped in at the Danish Brotherhood Christmas confusion later last night and it turned out to be very profitable. Our friends the Jensens on Layton Blvd. will hold a room for you for the week of 31st to 6th or whenever you want it! Most of their stuff is apartments, which is good to keep in mind I reckon! Nothing much in the paper today—it will be a problem.

Told the family of our plans in very general terms & they approve—also mentioned the undertaker deal. It turned out pretty much the way I thought. Marty said nothing but they all approve of you which makes things much easier. Will be glad to see you next Monday as I am lonesome already. There is nothing to do today but tomorrow I'll be busy. Perhaps I'll call Marion II and (of course) get that settled. My conscience hurts a little. Jackson sent my blankets (We will have that anyway).

"Oh"—while unpacking I found my Xmas present. It was fortunate I had to open my Val-Pac to put in those blankets because I had missed it last night. I like the pocket book [wallet] a lot—and thanks much dear. I am terribly sorry I neglected to bring yours along but you should get it Tues or Wed. I hope that it is satisfactory. The smaller and more important things will come later. This has turned out to be long but there was a lot to say.

Till tomorrow then my darling all my Love and a Merry Christmas to all of you (also to any bodies you may have around)

Gene

✤

24 December 1945
Milwaukee, Wisc.

Hello again darling,

Tis the night before Christmas and all thru the house—it sounds like hell. Oh brother this is really something—The kids put one in the Christmas spirit however and it is good to have them around. This morning I mailed your Xmas present and also the stadium boots. Concerning the latter—I couldn't get exactly the same kind at the store so am hoping these are equally satisfactory. They are suede. At the postoffice this morning the man said that there was a good chance that you would get the packages today or tomorrow morning. I hope that he knows whereof he speaks. It still was stupid that I didn't bring your present along. Oh well—pretty soon you can do all the thinking for us.

Got an alarm clock this morning with a thought for the future—also checked up on the pay for working at school—will make about $53 per month if I work 3 hours per day. That isn't bad at all and I think we can manage o.k. At least it will make us financially secure some what and also may give us a chance to put away something for our idealistic future. As your dad says— "There are a lot of lawyers driving street cars in Milwaukee." I hope that he doesn't question you too much about my plans. Some of those farmer corpses would probably jump out of their caskets if they knew of our plans—to say nothing of your dad.

Christmas Day—

Will finish this now before I go out to my mother's. It is rather warm today but the roads are not too clear. Enjoyed hearing you last night again even if I couldn't tell you how much I actually miss you—& love you.

Went to Redeemer Church at 10:45 to hear their candlelight service. It was excellent—wish you could have heard it. Time to go now so

All my Love, Gene

✧

26 Dec 1945

Hello darling,

Didn't have a chance to write yesterday. Went out to Waukesha about noon and had a fair time but rather surprised them with our plans but I hope not too much. Would not make much difference but it would be better to get her consent. I know that she doesn't like the idea getting married up there—also heard about this gal she had picked out. It was a little rough and I wish Feb. were not so far away but everything will be O.K. I know.

If worst comes I'll come up there and kidnap you and we'll elope. I have been irritable and restless ever since I left your house—mainly I guess because I miss you so.

I am afraid to think of getting a place to live—it sounds so hopeless—and I suddenly can't see any reason to wait any longer (than Feb). We'll find a place tho. Jensens are coming over tonight and I'll explain that we do want an apartment—if one comes up before Feb I'll take it. Don't imagine that it is too bad there. They have cooking equipment just in case we can't live on love.

Christmas was pretty much like the pre-war days. The kids enjoyed themselves. Got a little civilian clothes so I think I'll convert one of these days. I figure I had better wear it (uniform) down to Chicago in order to get a room at the Knickerbocker.

Good afternoon darling—I'm glad that Monday is not too far away. I love you dear.

Gene

�֍

27 Dec 1945

Hello Honey,

Went down to Jensen's this morning and had a nice talk with her for about an hour. They are <u>very</u> nice people and good friends of my dad's. The room for you is secured and then she told me of another deal on a large room with light housekeeping opportunities that may be vacant next Monday. I didn't see the room and of course it all depends on you but it sounds like a good thing to grab just on general principles. I told her as much on the presumption it would be agreeable to you and she is going to let us know Monday or Tues. Now the disadvantage is—it is an old fashioned house with little of the modern comforts—on the order of the one on state street you stayed at. That isn't too good but the advantages are many—(1) The people are pleasant (Jensens) (2) The location is ideal—when I go back to Walker—and to and from work and school. (3) It will be economical—probably $40 or $45 at the most (4) It will solve our immediate problem of a place to live for the present.

But as I said, it all depends on whether you want to live there in a 19th century atmosphere. We will see when you come down next week.

Reuben & Phil came in Christmas night from Memphis and I saw them last night at a party Marshall had at his house. Also also saw Marion at church last night at the childrens' Xmas party and all seems to be O.K.

I am waiting patiently for Monday to come—and it will be good to see you darling. Still haven't heard from Chicago concerning the tickets. So long for now and

All my Love, Gene

✢

28 Dec 1945
Milwaukee, Wis.

Hello Marian,

I am glad that you liked the bag [purse] & stadium boots. Your letter came this morning so I read it during breakfast (at 10:30). Had received 2 the day before yesterday and none since then so I appreciated this one all the more. We can use 2 alarm clocks as you say—

Was down to the school board to see Hineline, the chief engineer-Janitor, and also Rilling the sec. of the school board and had a nice visit. My job at Walker is waiting anytime I care to go back. They are swell people in every respect and seem to appreciate the returning servicemen. I hate all the gush of some people—but when a sincere effort is made to give you something worthwhile—that I like. With the new 44 hour week of all janitorial full time employes, it is possible for me to work my 3 hours almost anytime in the early or late afternoon. The work does not have to be done by 5:00 PM as formerly. I'll try to arrange my program at M. U. so that I can start at about 2:00 PM and then be home by 5:10 PM.

Don't think that I told you that my dad will almost definitely drive up to Wittenberg if the roads are open—also Marty will come I think and Helga. Wish there were a way to bring my mother, but she . . . couldn't come in the same car—something which disgusts my grandfather to no end—and also me.

When we were alone the other night, I asked Marty what he thought of my plans, and he said that so long as I was certain of you, and that our views were primarily the same, I should get married. Couldn't help but think that it was another way of saying, "gazing in the same direction." That, coming from the two people I think most of in the world, I appreciated because to me that is the essence of married life.

I am getting tired of apologizing for wanting to go to school. The angle of wanting more education to become a college teacher does not half tell the story—you know but it seems to be the only language most people understand. For that reason it will be good to be alone together and we can choose our friends who do understand that a liberal education has a compensation not figured in cash or earning power. Whatever we do, we will do it together and in that there is strength and satisfaction. I want you to be happy and to realize from the start that it will not be easy. I know that you do. It will also be you who is going to school. I love you darling—every inch of you.

Gene

✦

Dec. 23 '45
[Wittenberg]

Hello, my Darling,

How are you? The village seems deserted since you left, dear.

I haven't told Mother & Dad about our plans yet. Thought it might be better—& easier—to tell them when I come back from Milwaukee. I expect they will object to our not waiting. Some sarcastic remarks were made tonight about a fellow who is going to Northwestern & got married. However, as we agreed yesterday—we are responsible for our own lives anyway; so we may as well live them in the way that seems best to us, regardless of the opposition.

Dad has not mentioned his "conversation" with you so I haven't brought up the subject, either. I told Mother about it, though, and explained why you want to go to school, including the factor of the security a Master's Degree would afford. She seems to think your point of view is sensible & perfectly natural. So far, so good. Oh, honestly, I wonder why parents have to be such a problem!

It is truly ironic that last night I was in Antigo. Irenus [Hoekstra], the fellow who had asked me to go to that banquet at the Chem. Engrs. Convention, called yesterday aft. and wanted to come down in the evening. In between times he met two other kids who have been discharged recently and promised to pick them up about nine. So the four of us, and also a girl who works at the Orphans' Home, drove up to Antigo in search of a place with an orchestra. We didn't find one, but we had a fairly good time. This one kid used to be extremely shy when we were in high school, and it was a pleasure to see how his ability to meet people has improved. I <u>wish</u> you had been with us, though, darling. Now that we are Engaged, I don't like having dates—even with reasonably harmless old classmates.

Did you find your Christmas gifts? They don't amount to much, but since it's your money I've been spending, I thought it best not to buy anything extravagant without knowing what you would like at least. Thought I'd give you that address book so you wouldn't have to keep the old one. <u>Some</u> of the names you may copy, of course.

I went up to Jane's for a while this afternoon. They all said they liked you very much. I'm supposed to tell you Mr. Haseltine was given another bottle of that brandy yesterday!

I love you, darling, and I do not like living without you any more. Goodnight, dearest—

Marian

❖

Dec. 25 '45

Hello, Sweetheart—

Merry Christmas again! I'm sorry I didn't have a chance to write to you yesterday. We really had a busy day. Daddy had a funeral in the morning, an ambulance trip to Stevens Point and several deliveries in the aft. Consequently, Mother was downstairs all day and I did the washing and the cooking alone— also scrubbed the kitchen floor.

It has been snowing ever since yesterday noon, and we have enough snow for two white Christmases.

Jane & Eric were down for a few minutes yesterday. Eric wouldn't touch the tree—in fact, he wouldn't go near it alone. He merely looked at it in rather delighted awe.

Of those two packages I told you about, one was from Peg & the other from Dad. He had put a $20 bill in a big box & wrapped it all up to look as if it had come in the mail. Peg sent a pretty black nylon slip. Guess she isn't angry with me.

I am listening to a Christmas program starring Eddie Dowling. It's lovely. Right now they are dramatizing the story of the writing of "Silent Night." The young musician's father is telling him he should go to bed—"There is no money in this tinkering!"

"Money, father?" Rather pertinent, is it not? I like Eddie Dowling. He played the lead in "The Glass Menagerie."

I told Mother something of what you had said about how impractical it sounds to say you want to go to school when you could have the "security" of a business. She said, "Yes, but you would not be wise to do anything else unless you were convinced you would like it." She hasn't the old-fashioned ideas daddy has, you see. She also said she had told Daddy you might go to school for three years & he said, "Well, then I guess if he wants Marian to be with him, she'll just have to get a job." I'm glad his attitude was resignation instead of revolt.

It surely is a good thing you have friends who own property! I'm glad you saw the Jensens and persuaded them to hold a room for me next week. The apartments sound interesting, too.

I knew you would call last night, darling. You are so thoughtful—& I love you so much!

Marian

❖

Dec. 26 '45

Darling,

I thought you said it wasn't much! It's marvelous! Absolutely couldn't be any better. I've always wanted a nice alligator bag, and this is exactly the style I like—and everything! You are just too good to be true, honey.

The stadium boots are also entirely satisfactory. Thank you <u>very</u> much.

This has been a pleasant day. This morning I did the ironing, and this aft. I went to see one of the girls I went to h. school with. She works in Rhinelander now, but was home for Christmas. Tonight Jane is coming down & we're going to the show, "Meet me in St. Louis." I've seen it, but Jane hasn't & I thought it good enough to see again.

Remind me when I come down to tell you about my talk with the bank cashier regarding Franklin's account in Santa Ana. It's too long to write.

Isn't this clever stationery? Jane gave it to me. I think she must have done the "decorating" herself.

Listen, dear, you'd better consult me when you buy these things for the future. We already have an alarm clock. 'Course it's usually a good idea for me to use two of them—just to be sure.

Oh, I've gained two pounds again—almost three.

Where did you get the typewriter?

Jane will be here any minute, so goodnight, darling.

All my love, Marian

❖

Dec. 27 '45

Hello, Sweetheart,

Some more new writing paper. This is from Murph. I like it better than the other, really.

There seems to be practically nothing to write about today. Haven't had a letter from you—at least not yet.

I finally invited Marcella over for dinner. She's coming tonight. I don't know what we'll ever find to do besides eat.

I am anxious for Monday to come. These three weeks at home have been long enough—and one week without you is <u>too</u> long, darling.

My new "Time" came today. There is an interesting <u>short</u> article on J. B. Priestley under Books. He says, "The chief freedom the English people need now is the freedom to have more fun, without regard to the feelings of sour-faced old women and envious old men." That applies not only to the English.

In the review of "Stuart Little" [by E. B. White], Stuart's comment upon his return from the bathtub drain reminds me of your dad. Yes?

Until tomorrow, darling.

All my love, Marian

⚜

Dec. 28 '45

Hi, Honey,

Your letters of the 26th and 27th came today, also Gwen's letter. Did you read it, or did you know she had written? It was <u>very</u> nice. I only wish all six of our parents would be as agreeable as she.

I'm beginning to feel rather guilty about not having told Mother & Dad yet. That will require some explaining when I see you again.

I agree with you, so far, regarding the place at Jensens. The atmosphere may not seem quite right for a honeymoon, but "we can't have everything." The important thing is to have <u>some</u> place to live. The location & the economy are big advantages, too.

How long will Reuben be at home?

I had a Christmas card today from Al from Costa Rica. I wish he had writ-ten a note with it because I'm curious to know why he's back there.

Had my hair washed & set today so that by Monday it will be the way you like it.

I surely hope your mother will not dislike me. She probably does not—just on general principles. Regardless of how much it matters, life will be a lot more pleasant if we can get along. Maybe I can try a little of my dad's "bedside man-ner," hm?

Goodnight, darling. I do love you.

Marian

⚜

7 Jan 1946
[Milwaukee]

Dear one,

Gosh how I miss you—and you have only been gone 3 hours. You should be on the Wittenberg express by now—if I can stay awake till 11:00 PM I'll be thinking of you during the crisis. You have my moral support but I definitely would not like to be there. Think perhaps, if there w[as] trouble, I'd snatch you away and head for Iowa.

My dad saw that article on suggested terminal leave for enlisted men and really expounded at great length on why they should have it (something to which I and most people agree) But much to my disgust he again tore into the officers presupposing that they would all be against the idea. Oh brother—It is however a relief from the old college angle folly.

It's times like that when I appreciate you most—and also the fact we are going to be alone. Oh darling it is going to be wonderful no matter what we may run against. I feel so confident and optimistic and oh so much in love.

Have made a list of all the things that I am going to do. Forgot to tell you that Mrs. Jensen said that they may borrow a sanding machine if I'd help. Carl may paint the woodwork a sort of oak color—something which he is very adept at I hear. Both the men were washing woodwork up there today and Mrs. J. said it looks swell. I didn't go up. I definitely have the desk which Marty said is <u>mine</u>, so that solves that problem.

Helga stopped in tonight. It appears that the chickens got out of the coop and that was the reason they missed us . . . will definitely come to the wedding.

Well—I'll close for tonight. I am too tired even to feel the sparks fly but anyway—

All my love, dear—Gene

❧

8 Jan 1946

Hello darling,

Didn't accomplish much today except clean out the back seat of the car and write down the names to whom we'll have to send wedding announcements.

Marty and I had a good long talk today about how to bring up children. He believes none of his children really appreciates what he has done in the true sense of the word. I think (& he too) that I may be the only one—It's rather sad but actually is a fact. By "appreciation" we agreed that it meant—If he were not able to pay for his upkeep, he probably would have trouble living with them mainly cause they have forgotten all that he has done for each of us.

All this is something we know already but it makes me wonder just how you should bring up children.

I slept until 11:00 AM today which felt good but tomorrow I am going to start getting up at a reasonable hour instead of wasting time. There is so much that I want to accomplish in the next few weeks that I'll have to get busy soon.

Think perhaps that I'll drop in at Jensen's to see what can be done there. We talked about the furniture at the cottage this noon but everybody agreed that there was not much there that we could use. Helga may have my toaster & waffle iron out there & I'll try to get them if possible (to use till we can get something better.)

Meantime I love you more everyday darling. I hope you weathered the night OK. Will be waiting anxiously to hear from you tomorrow.

A. M. L. Gene

❖

9 Jan 1946

Hello sweetheart,

I must have checked the mail 10 times today but no letter—I hope that that is good news but I should get one tomorrow. Would like to call you tonight but it I guess that wouldn't be such a good idea in case you are having trouble. I hope not tho.

Nothing much in the line of news today. I stopped in at Jensen's and took stock of the things I should do there in the next few weeks The hallway looks excellent—the part they painted—a real light color and that brightens it up considerably. Mrs. J. just called and asked if I'd come over tomorrow to take the bed out. That will make it easier to see just what is to be done. The woodwork will be varnished and the floor also tho not sanded which I'd like better. It seems as tho the sanding machine jars these old houses quite a bit. They are trying to get a large linoleum rug for the floor so then it shouldn't be too bad. The cupboard is very large—which is good and the ice box is in good shape. Can we obtain ice in winter?? They are going to put a Yale lock on the door also.

Hope that you have made some progress on the studio couch but you can sleep on a little bed we can get from Jensen's when you come down for the license—insomuch as we are taking the bed out.

Gosh, I wish all these preliminaries were over and we were starting to really live together. I miss you an awful lot darling and I do love you.

Gene

❖

Jan. 8, 1946
[Wittenberg]

Darling,

It's all so simple I almost wonder if I'm not dreaming these episodes. The crisis went something like this:

Mother admires ring. Long pause
Me: " Would you like to know when the wedding will be?"
She: "Do you want to tell me?"
Me (With one eye on her & one on the ceiling.): "Sometime in February."
She: "Well, haven't you set a date?"
Me (Hopefully): "We thought either the 2nd or 9th."
She (Gaily): "Oh, that would be kind of fun if you had it the 2nd. That's the same day Jim is being married, you know."

From that point things have progressed harmoniously. She doesn't even object to my wearing a suit. Tonight, when we have time to discuss it with Daddy, she wants to get all the details settled. Happy day!

Some poor swallower of gossip said to my mother the other day, "Marian is engaged to Rudy Thompson, isn't she?" Imagine! Mother said, "Why, no! I wouldn't be at all pleased about that! Gene is much more stable than Rudy, if you know what I mean." I got quite a kick out of that.

I'd better get this in the mail. Will write again tonight probably. I miss you already, honey.

Much love, Marian

❖

Jan. 9 '46

Hello, Honey,

I just want to talk to you for a minute to make myself feel better. Had an argument with Mother tonight about who is & who isn't invited to the wedding. It was very silly, and she agreed in the end that harmony should be maintained at all costs, but the harmony here was certainly destroyed for a while & it made me wish, again, that we could go to Dubuque! I'm so glad we're going to live alone, darling.

Mr. Haseltine[70] called tonight & asked me to work for him for a couple of days; so I shall. He said you had called & told him to put me to work. I said I supposed you needed some money & he replied that that was what you had intimated. He says he'll send my salary directly to you.

Guess I'd better go to bed. I'm tired—but not too tired to wish you were here to keep me warm & happy.

I love you, dear.

Marian

❖

10 Jan 1946
[Milwaukee]

Honey,

Your letter with the good news came this morning and the one you wrote the 9th arrived this aft. Am terribly glad it went off as smoothly as it did—that was almost too much to hope for but at any rate the greatest job is done now—the rest shouldn't be too difficult .

The other details sound fine too—I hope that the dinner won't be too much for your mother. It sounds like a lot of fuss & bother. The wedding list is O.K.—don't know whether Charlie or Ray can come yet but as soon as I do know I'll inform you. Will take that health test on Monday—or possibly this Saturday. When do you plan on coming down? Either the 19 or 26 would be O.K.

As for the dinner again—we will almost have to have <u>all</u> the people I know who are there attend. Don't you think so???? If we invite those people from Antigo and my mother is there they will naturally want to be together awhile ("they" are Ray's sister etc.) If we don't invite them—and they live so near—I don't know what will happen. Why not have the reception <u>at</u> the hotel? Oh hell!!

Ya, better get a corsage for Gwen too. Do you need some money?

—The dinner again—why can't we have a heavy lunch of sandwiches at a buffet style and then have everybody? They won't starve!

—another thought—How about Dorothy? I will <u>have</u> to invite her also—and I have a sneaking suspicion she will want to go.

It took me an hour to write that last page—been thinking mostly of that damn reception business. I don't see any solution except to have them all for a lunch nothing more—to save your mother. Can't you explain that to her so that she'll understand I <u>must</u> invite these people up there and then it follows that they should be at the reception. I'd still rather elope in order to save us all some grief. Oh brother!

Well so much for that—

Washed woodwork all day today at "our home" and it doesn't look too bad. A coat of varnish will do practically no good so I haven't decided to do anything yet. Mrs. J. showed me a pattern of linoleum which looked good. It apparently has rather small blue flowers and is very light. There is another deal for a rug transfer which probably would be better and we should know in a few days. She wants to pay for the material for slip-covers but claims they aren't too hard to make. I don't know. We can decide when you come down. Also she says you can use her sewing machine whenever you like.

What color are the drapes?

That's all I can think about now—Some of the addresses are . . .

How are <u>you</u> otherwise darling? I hope O.K. I'd like to call you sometime next week if that's O.K. So for now all my Love sweetheart and good night

Gene

❦

11 Jan 1946

Cheer up Darling!

Soon the whole thing will be over with and <u>we</u> can start to work out our <u>own</u> problems. I am terribly glad that we are going to live alone and that's the way it always is going to be. This household is getting a little strained too—especially after a discussion yesterday about me going back to school. My dad sees <u>absolutely no</u> sense in it whatsoever—but it's actually the same old story we've gone through a dozen times. The only different aspects are—I am getting married and I have finished 4 years but the arguments are absolutely the same. It goes something like this—

Father: "What are you going to do?" (as if he didn't know.)

Me: "Go back to school for a few more years."

Father: "What's your goal in life?"

Me: "I'd like to teach college."

Father: "You better start to think of security and get a job."

Me: "As far as security is concerned, we've got that now with my job at Walker and the government support."

Father: "That isn't going to last."

Me: "I know that but at least we'll be happy and secure for a few years till I finish."

Father: "You can't expect Marian to work and slave to keep you in school."

Me: "She doesn't have to work unless she wants to—if she does, so much the better."

Marty: "Is Marian in favor of your ideas?" (The only sensible question asked.)

Me: "I presume so, if I didn't think so I wouldn't marry her now."

Father: "You are making a big mistake. I'll bet that in 15 years you still will be sweeping at Walker."

Me: "That's possible. (a stupid answer to a stupid question.)

Me: "The fact remains that anytime things get too bad I can get a job teaching to support us. I don't want to teach high school however and so long as we can get along all right financially, I can't see any good reason why I shouldn't go to school for awhile to get those qualifications it is necessary to have to teach college. If I wanted security so badly I should accept Marian's father's offer to go into his business."

Father: (very excitedly) "Yes! Yes! Yes! That's exactly what you should do. You are foolish if you don't."

Me: "Perhaps I am—and I admit that it's a gamble I'm taking, but so long as Marian is agreed to marry me under those circumstances, I'll try it."

Finis

A good title to this short play would be, "I didn't raise my boy to go to College—or there are a lot of college men driving streetcars in Milwaukee."

Oh well.—Went shopping today & got a blue shirt and pair of $13.50 shoes. I am really going to look sharp!!—also got a cheap watch band. Will take that blood test today or tomorrow for sure.

Wish you could come down the 19th. If you wait until next Saturday, we can just barely get the 5 day waiting period in before the 2nd. Besides, I want to see you soon.

Good-by for now sweetheart—

All my Love.

Gene

❖

13 Jan 1946
[Milwaukee]

Dearest,

I was especially lonesome today—perhaps because I didn't get a letter. It is Sunday however and nobody is to blame except the post office—and the government. I think I'd vote for anybody who promises to have mail delivered on Sunday.

Played schvensel (sp?) last night with the family and won 13 cents. Today I went out to Waukesha and spent a few hours with my mother. Apparently she likes you—or I would have heard. Ray, too, but he still favors the strong ox-type farmer gal who can "work."

Later (Monday morning): Marshall called last night (he has a dial phone) and wanted me to come over for awhile. All is going well—he is definitely coming.

There is so much to write today, but I'd better mail this this morning so you get a letter today, such as it is.

Will write a long one today sometime. Am going to try and get a blood test this aft.

All my love, darling,

Gene

Did you get your blood test?

❖

14 Jan 1946
[Milwaukee]

Darling,

Time for a few lines before I go to work. Just finished taking a blood test & I'll get the certificate in a day or so. They don't send them to Madison from down here, just to a Milw. Lab. Bob's & Rita's [Poeppel] [71] took only 3 hrs —

Then I went up to Sealy's to look at some studios but didn't accomplish much outside of seeing them. They looked all right to me, and the colors were nice. (1) a sort of wine flowered (2) a light blue (3) a bayge (spelling may be wrong). The latter I liked tho it is light (a tan tapestry appearance). The fellow in the warehouse said I couldn't do better anywhere but didn't try to "sell" me. They have springs & a wooden frame. He didn't know the cost. Now we can either wait till you get down (as we probably can get almost immediate delivery) or I can get the color you like. What color are the drapes?

Stopped at Jensen's — they have put on a Yale night lock — nothing else of any importance has been done. I wish you were down here so we could determine what to do in the line of major changes, if any. If I can paint it — what color would you like? Maybe a light cream?

Ray is sort of undecided about coming, but I'll find out soon. Marsh & Kay [Rieboldt][72] want to stay in Wittenberg that night, if possible. How many single & double rooms have you reserved?

See you later, honey. I love you.

Gene

❖

14 Jan 1946 [2]

Dearest Marian,

Would like to call you tonight now that the strike is over and perhaps I will later on. Gwen is being installed as Cominch of the "True Kindred" tonight. Don't know what it's all about, but I guess I'll attend the installation. Dad asked whether I was going to join the Masonic order. I told him I wouldn't until I had time to get something out of it. Don't know whether he liked it or not.

Have been reading "One Man's Meat" and I really enjoy it. It's so light and at the same time "profound" in parts. In "Religion" he said, "My father was a God-fearing man, but he never missed a copy of the 'New York Times' either." That I like.

Studying has not been going too well mainly because there always seem to be other more urgent things to attend to. Have located my old French books which will come in handy for these comprehensive exams next fall.

My mother has some pillows for us and also a rug. If we can't use the rug, I'll give it to Mrs. J. Will get it next Wed. when I go out there. Incidentally, she wants to have a shower for you—tried to stall her off but she insists. It would have to be when you come down. There won't be too much to do—will there? Actually just get the license, order the cake, look at studios—and gaze into each other's eyes—which I'd like to be doing now. Well, it won't be too long according to the calender—but every day seems like 10—

Goodnight my love

Gene

⚜

15 Jan 1946
[Milwaukee]

Darling,

A couple more wedding presents today which I <u>know</u> you'll appreciate. Jensens are going to paint the walls (real light tan) and refinish the woodwork! That is something I'll like very much as it sure will make a decided improvement. She said it's our wedding present. Tonight when I got home Marty showed me some pictures in a magazine of midget washers which impressed me to a great extent. I said that they probably would not be on the market for 6 months but then my dad popped up and said he had one about the same type in the basement which we could have! Sure enough and it's a honey!! It's round, 1-1/2' diameter, and about 2' high. It looks amazingly practical for us—we can put it in that closet. So that takes care of 2 of our great problems as far as living conditions are concerned. Isn't it wonderful??

Everything is working out so well down here I am extremely happy. Now if you arrive Saturday, it will have been a very pleasant week. I'll be down there at the station at 1:30 PM & again at 6:30.

I like the drapes (color, that is) I think that they will go well with the color of the walls—also probably we can get that "bayge" studio couch.

My dad is going to work on the recreation room tonight, so I guess that I'll help him.

I like being in love, don't you? Couldn't tell you how much I really missed you on the phone last nite. How are you, brown eyes?

Gene

❀

16 Jan 1946

Dearest Marian,
    Just finished a long "discussion" with the family on education & am so mad, so damned mad, that my blood is boiling. It is a long story and one of the most unpleasant I can remember. If we weren't getting married, I would leave here tonight. I always have tried to avoid such stupid arguments, but after some of the accusations my dad made tonight, I couldn't hold my tongue.
    "<u>Anybody</u> can go through <u>any</u> college."
    "The private colleges, especially Marquette, want the money so badly that they'll keep all the GIs in school whether they fail or not."
    "A non-educated wife is <u>better</u> than one who has an education."
    "The GI bill of rights (schooling) is unfair because it favors 'a few'."
    "Oscar's daughter will get along better if she doesn't go to college."
    "Veterans are taking advantage of the schooling because they are natural loafers."
    "If a girl marries who has a college education, that time she spent getting it is <u>entirely</u> wasted."
    These are all <u>actual</u> <u>statements</u> and he is serious.
    Darling, those 2 weeks seem like eternity. I guess it's times like this when I appreciate you the most. All my work, all those evenings studying, all the things I went without, and now to realize again that my own father regards it as less than nothing. It is depressing.
    Think I'll do some reading.
    —I love you tonight—

Gene

❀

Jan. 9 '46
[Wittenberg]

My darling,
    There is so much to write about, I don't know where to begin.
    We washed this morning and also unearthed all my linens, etc. I may as well list the major items for you:
    5 Sheets
    6 Pillowcases
    4 Bath towels

7 Hand towels
3 Table cloths
2 Lunch cloths
3 Tea towels

Those drapes I told you about are practically made. There are only a couple of hems to finish, & Mother will be glad to get the stuff out of her way. It's the right length, too.

I cut out one of the shirts last night & should have it finished in a few days. If all the love that goes into this labor shows in the shirt, honey, it surely will be beautiful!

We looked through some of Franklin's things, too. He has two white shirts & three colored ones, but I don't think you could wear them. They're 14-1/2. I'll iron one of the white ones & bring it down for you to try, anyway. He has about a dozen pair of shorts & shirts which you may have, also.

As for the wedding plans, things are pretty well organized. Mother wants to serve dinner for the guests after the wedding, which will be at church at 4:00, Feb. 2, provided that's agreeable to you — & to the minister. Mother will see him at Ladies Aid Thursday & ask him about it. As for the dinner, she won't fix it herself, but will ask the people at the hotel to do it for us. If they can't, she will hire someone to cook & serve it in the church basement. I told her we'd rather have a reception & serve just cake & coffee, but she says everyone will have to eat anyway & coming such a long distance they should have a decent meal. Period! So I hope we can keep the number of guests limited. No one outside the family. OK? This is the list I have now, and these are the only people to whom I will send written invitations unless you think there is someone else we must invite: Marty, your dad, Gwen, your mother, Ray, Helga [Stubbs], Charlotte [Staab], Marshall, (Send me the addresses, pls.) Kay, Jane, the minister & his wife, John and Anna Schmidt (cousins of my dad's who are particularly dear to him.) That would make a total at dinner of 18 or 19. What do you think of asking Mr. & Mrs. Haseltine? As long as Jane is there, perhaps we should. Mr. H. probably wouldn't care much about coming, but Mrs. is a slightly different story.

I'm not going to write to Murph or Peg or Rudy & Nona & Margie. Wouldn't know what to do with them if they came. Which reminds me—the hotel rooms. Your grandfather will stay at our house, of course. But you'd better let me know whenever you can exactly how many rooms to reserve at the hotel.

Also let me know how many announcements you will need.

The wedding cake I am supposed to order when I'm in Milwaukee. The flowers we'll order in Wausau. Mother said to ask you about a corsage for Gwen. It's customary for your mother & mine to have one & I imagine you'd like us to order one for Gwen, too. Would you?

Tomorrow or Friday I'll see the doctor about that health certificate. If you go about the same time, that should work OK.

Now that you are informed of all developments, how are you otherwise, darling? Still love me? Sometimes I think that if we manage to get through all the confusion of the wedding without quarreling, we can live happily ever after for sure! We will, too, sweetheart.

I read Aage's letter Mon. night and enjoyed it very much. I like his ideals. A <u>strict</u> idealist and believer in Christian behavior would not be able to agree, though, with his desire to combat mud-slinging with more mud-slinging. We'll argue about that some day, shall we?

I miss you terribly, dearest. Those three weeks and three days until we'll be together for good seem like eternity.

All my love, honey—

Marian

❧

Jan. 10 '46

Hello, my love—

This has been a busy day. It's sort of fun working for Mr. Haseltine. All these characters come in to have him make out their income tax forms. I did six of them today at 2.00 each, so Mr. H. made a profit of 7.00 on me today. It's nice to know that I really earned my salary, anyway.

Went to a basketball game tonight with Melitta. We won, of course—45 to 18.

Rec'd your letter of the 8th. I'm glad to hear that you've cleaned up the back seat of the car. I told Mother we were going to throw all my stuff in the back seat to take it to Milw. and she said it might not look so good to throw in "all" the wedding presents & take them along. She suggested we go to Green Bay for a few days & then come back here to pick up the stuff??

She is taking the wedding plans well in hand. Four rooms are reserved at the hotel for the 2nd—and arranged to keep the Trapps & the Petersens apart, she says.

The dinner will be in the church basement.

I asked Dad about the studio couch & he says we should go to the wholesalers in Milw. & order what we want.

If you go to Jensen's, find out if we'll need pillows, please.

On the train the other night, I read a story in the Atlantic by Cord Meyer, Jr. called "Waves of Darkness." It was absolutely marvelous & I know you'd like it, too. Do you remember his last article, "A Serviceman Looks at the Peace?"

Time to go to bed again. It's really punishment to get up at 7:30 AM after all these weeks of leisure. Until tomorrow, then, darling.

Love & kisses, Marian

P.S. I like that abbreviated love with which you concluded your last letter. I like you, too, honey.

❖

Jan. 11 '46

Darling,

I am sorry you didn't get any mail Wednesday. I did write Tuesday and mailed the letter about 1:00, which should have been early enough for the train.

Working for Mr. Haseltine is delaying some of the other things I have to do—especially your white shirts, but I'll probably work only one or two days more. I admire his business ethics. He's really a fine fellow. Remind me to tell you sometime about my dad's idea that Mr. H. doesn't pay any income tax— strictly an unfounded suspicion. He, my dad, can make the damnedest accusations—for no purpose that I can see except to uphold his own stubborn pride. As you can plainly see, I was very much annoyed with him tonight.

Later—Marcella came over & we went to Melitta's to see her baby. He looks rather like John. His features, at any rate, are unmistakably boyish.

Yes, dear, we can get ice in the wintertime.

If the bed is gone already, perhaps you'd better see what you can do about the studio couch. I'll enclose a list of the places you could try. Dad says most of them have discontinued their showrooms, but you could go to the office & tell them you are his son-in-law & ask if it's possible to get a studio couch (<u>with springs</u>). If so, you can tell them to deliver it to Jensen's & bill it to A. F. Smith. If necessary, Dad will send them an order for it. Ok? Anything you decide on is all right with me. We could wait until I come down, but we may not have much time then.

Oh, honey, I miss you so! It seems like weeks since we were together & it's only four days. Must be love!

Goodnight, Sweetheart,

Marian

❖

Jan. 12 '46

Hi, Sweetheart:

I just came back from the doctor's office, and my arm feels very peculiar. The test should be back about Thurs. or Fri. If possible, I'll come down Saturday—perhaps on the morning train. It's been coming in the morning lately.

I was very glad to get your letters of the 10th and 11th today. Darling, it is good to know that our love does consist in gazing outward together in the same direction. Even in such minor controversies as these wedding plans involve, I'm glad you & I agree.

There is no point in even suggesting anything about this dinner. Mother will do it her way, regardless, and I only get into fights by disagreeing with her. The same is true of the invitations. She has decided Haseltines are to be invited and nearly bit my head off today for saying I'd decided it wasn't necessary to ask them. It's ok to ask Dorothy [Biederwolf][73] & the people in Antigo. If someone else wants to come, just say you'd like to have them but it can't be done. You can blame it all on her. The people who are on the list now, including Dorothy & Ray's sister & husb., will come to dinner, of course. Mother is not doing any of the work for the dinner except the planning. We couldn't have it at the hotel because the hotel-keeper's wife is in the hospital. It will be in the church basement & we already have the ladies to do the cooking & serving. Incidentally, send me the address of the people in Antigo if you have it.

It's very nice of Mrs. J. to offer to buy the material for a slip cover. I'd be glad to try making it if I can use her machine. She surely is a honey!

I'm enclosing a sample of the drapery material. It's awfully small but should give you an idea of what the stuff is like. Perhaps I'll bring them down Saturday.

Your account of your argument with your dad was entertaining—although I know it was far from pleasant for you, dear. It seems to me that since he never saw fit to assume any responsibility for your upbringing, he has no right to try to tell you what to do now.

Mr. Haseltine is very much in favor of your ideas. We had a good talk about it between clients today. He thinks there are two kinds of people—those to whom money-making is the chief end in life, & the others. It's pretty obvious he prefers the others. We, too. Yes, darling?

Of course it's OK for you to call sometime next week if you want to. It's so unsatisfactory when Mother & Dad are here, as they almost always are, that it hardly seems worth while. If I could talk to you, it would be wonderful. I love you so much, honey! You & your blue eyes.

Marian

❖

January 14 '46

Hi, Honey—

Thought you might enjoy reading this letter from Margie. I'm very much pleased that she & Les are planning to be married. He seemed such a nice fellow, and Margie is really not so flippant as she sounds most of the time.

Mother & I drove to Wausau today (much to my father's displeasure), and we accomplished quite a lot. We stopped to see the florist and settled most of the details regarding corsages, etc. Remind me to tell you all about those plans this weekend.

Jane has been working at the hospital in Wausau for a couple of weeks. She was home yesterday & today, however; so I had a chance to talk to her. She wants to get a green gabardine suit for the wedding. If she can't find one in Wausau this week, I'll have to look for one for her in Milw.

—It was nice to talk to you just now, darling. I'm very much pleased about the studio couch. The beige will be fine. We don't have to be practical about every_thing, do we? Let us know if Dad should send them an order.

I get so _mad_ at my mother I could scream! I think it's positively rude of her to sit here & listen when I'm talking to you on the phone. I'd better change the subject before I begin swearing out loud!

That wedding present from the General is lovely. Do you think I should send him a thank you note?

I hope your mother gives up the idea of having a shower for me. I'd feel ridiculous accepting gifts from a bunch of people I've never even seen before.

Listen, dear, why don't you write a note to the Northland Hotel, Green Bay, and ask them to reserve a room for you and your wife (That's me!) for Feb. 2, 3, and 4—just to be sure we won't be stranded. Think so?

No, thank you, darling, I don't need any money yet. Probably won't until after we're married, as that is one thing Mother is being very nice about. She will buy my suit & hat, and wants to get me a pretty gown, too. She doesn't like the one the kids at Reliable gave me.

Honey, I'll be _so_ glad when this is all over, and we are together for good. It will be for _good_, too. Everything is even more perfect than I dreamed it could be, darling, and I love you—all the ways there are!

Marian

❖

17 Jan 1946
[Milwaukee]

Hello, dearest,

Have been putting in some long hours working this week. I start at Jensens at 8:00 AM and work there until it's time to go to school. We are really accomplishing something, tho, and I think the room looks swell. You will see it Saturday, but sorta would have liked to surprise you when we came down. I am really thrilled over the improvements. Haven't done anything about the studio couch, but we can do that while you are here. You can't possibly go home before next Wednesday. O.K.? I think that we can get a lot of our work out of the way in four days. Gosh!! am I anxious to see you. I figure that I'll start out on the Friday before "the Saturday" and spend the night in Wausau or thereabouts. So if I get stuck with the car I won't leave you standing at the church. There will be time to catch a train or bus.

Dorothy is not coming definitely—makes me a little irritated because she has not got a good reason for staying away—and we are taking care of all the arrangements. Oh, well. Will find out about Charlie & Ray this weekend.

Received my certificates (2 for me) today, and everything is all set—just to get the license. Kreils have some sort of water container I am interested in—Will investigate that soon. I intend to start moving as soon as the room is finished. That probably will not be until the middle of next week, however.

I hope you get this before you leave Saturday. Until then all my love brown eyes.

Gene

❖

Jan. 15 '46
[Wittenberg]

Hello, Darling,

We played cards tonight to keep Daddy happy & it is now too late for more than a brief note. I worked today, & Mr. H. talked me into coming again tomorrow. That <u>will</u> be the last day, however. I asked him about income tax for servicemen & he says he doesn't know much about it except that you have 6 mos. to file and an exemption of 1500.00 (per yr., I presume). He suggested that you see one of the veterans administration offices about it.

I got my health certificate today. Was surprised that it came back so soon. I'll be down Saturday for sure now. I have quite a list of stuff to shop for, but it shouldn't take too long.

Guess I haven't told you Mother reserved four double rooms at the hotel.

Last night I dreamed I was so angry with my folks that I broke a wheelbarrow & then ran away from home. I am anxious to get away—and doubly anxious to be with you, dearest.

All my love, Marian

✢

Jan. 16 '46

Dearest,

No mail today, except a letter to you which was returned from Hawaii and which I threw in the stove. These three Barnaby cartoons were enclosed. As they are especially good, I decided to send them to you again.

I've been working on your shirt this evening. I should be able to finish it tomorrow. Will bring it along down Saturday. Only two more days, thank goodness! I'm so lonesome for you, darling.

I'm rather glad to be through working for Haseltine although it was very interesting. I didn't ask him if he knew the lawyer in Antigo, but I'm sure he must as some people were in today to get some information re a mortgage on some land they wanted to sell, and he asked if Mr. S—was handling the sale. He was.

I'm going to mail most of the invitations tomorrow. Guess I'd better go to bed now. I'm tired! Goodnight, sweetheart.

All my love, Marian

✢

24 January 1946
[Milwaukee]

Dearest Marian,

First chance I've had to write since you left last night. Nothing much new today either but I did work at Jensen's all day assembling latches, door plates etc. and finished the cupboard. So now tomorrow I'll scrub the floor and varnish it if possible. Also attempted to shine that 19th century light fixture. It looks slightly better—got the drape fixtures up, too. Will be anxious to move in when the floor is finished and the time is getting short too—

Can't imagine what it's going to be like to have you around <u>all</u> the time to work out our problems together. I believe that the actual reality of it will be just as pleasant as our anticipation. I am really happy, darling, in a realistic manner.

Met Wiebeck, the teacher, down at the auditorium last night and heard Deans Holt & Little from Madison explain Why & Who should go to college. Nothing much we could take home except more ideals of which I have plenty. Really expected something more concrete along the "techniques of study" angle, but it definitely was not a practical session. Holt (formerly of U. of W. Extension) is an excellent speaker but Little was boring. Never have seen an audience so eager-looking and apparently serious-minded in my life. Statistics show that the veteran does slightly <u>better</u> in college than the others. Rather encouraging, but I wonder about graduate work.

Father said this noon that taking advantage of government as per GI schooling is like "outdoor relief." Dean Holt said Ramona should go to college — (cited an identical situation)

They are having a party for Kreils the 16th of Feb. which I said we'd like to attend. O.K.? A sort of farewell deal and about 6:00 . . . . No more info on our reception and I'm afraid to ask. When do you want to send out the announcements?

That's all for tonight, dearest. More tomorrow and my love

Gene

❧

25 Jan 1946

My dearest Marian,

So we have got some more Pyrex—oh, well, I'm glad of the frying pan deal you made with your mother, however.

Bruce & Skip[74] have developed extremely <u>bad</u> cases of chicken pox—they look horrible and I sure feel sorry for them. I hope I don't get it—but I shouldn't insomuch as I have had it when I was about 9 years old.

I <u>have</u> <u>finished</u> the room now after scrubbing the floor and varnishing. Now there is nothing in the line of great tasks to be done. If I don't get a chance to paint & varnish the furniture before we move in, I can always do it then. Tomorrow I'll get the license and also the wedding ring which will be 2 more jobs out of the way.

Dr. Koepke[75] talked with me tonight and is extremely favorable toward our plans. He said I should attempt the Doctor's degree immediately (after the masters) and not worry about experience—suggested Minnesota, Columbia, and Stanford. Along the practical line he gave me a book listing various men who had received degrees throughout the country (and had gone into teaching). Particularly it shows some of the "big" jobs that they had stepped into within a few years after their doctor's degree had been earned. Rather encouraging that he agrees so much with my plans. I'd like to have you meet him sometime.

I see that [John L.] Lewis is back in the A.F. of L.—rather surprising—
So long for now, darling. Am going over to Oscar's[76] to a graduation party for Ramona. I bought her the "Immortal Wife" as a present from us.

Much love, sweetheart, Gene

❖

26 Jan 1946

Dearest,
Only one week to go darling and all the fuss & bother will be over—am glad that it's only a short while. Some more developments concerning our house which should please you, I'm sure. The linoleum is down and it really is a pretty pattern—am quite satisfied. The rug should be back tonight and on tomorrow. I had it cleaned as you know—and also mothprofed, as the cleaner said it turned out swell except that the moths had been there. So outside of a few small holes, the rug should be very nice. We have a new occassional chair which is a vast improvement over the other. Chris[77] is going to put in a wall socket next to the gas range <u>and</u> we have an electric refrigerator which is a honey. Isn't that wonderful? Gosh! Am I happy about that. We are getting it because I promised to mop out the bathroom once a day while we are there. Don't imagine that will be a great strain—will also give her a little extra money off and on to help pay the extra electric charge. She does not want any, but we can see—
I picked up our license today and also ordered a ring. Are you sure you only want a plat. ring with a "knife edge"?
I hope this cold weather ceases before next Sat. It is terrible down here. That's about all tonight. Went to Ramona's grad. party—nothing unusual happened. Also varnished the chairs & dresser at the house.
Goodnight sweetheart and I do love you very much.

Gene

❖

27 Jan 1946

Dearest Marian,
Just finished a long game of Monopoly and I am extremely tired. Went to bed at 8:00 last night and haven't done much of anything today but the bed sure looks good. This morning I was over at Jensens and put the rug down. It really looks grand—I am well satisfied with it in every respect (even the moth-

proofing). I can spell that today, too. Also spent 2 hours cleaning the refrider-atator [*sic*] and after the dirt was removed it looks better than ever. I sure am happy for that. In fact, the room is practically complete now except for the studio couch and you. I plan to move about Tues. or Wed. (that is, my belongings). Tomorrow I am going to work at school all day, as they don't have classes.

I even put the drapes up (OK??) to get the effect and they are very nice. The room is so bright that sometimes I am almost blinded. Couldn't help thinking when I worked over there this morning that I am extremely happy. That is, as happy as I could be without you. I feel so confident and optimistic with our future together that sometimes I don't seem like the same cynical person. It has all been due to you, and with you I could be happy doing anything. I guess perhaps that is just another way of saying, "I love you," but it is good to feel that I don't have any qualifications about it.

Goodnight, sweetheart,

Gene

✤

28 Jan 46

Hello dearest,

Your two letters from the 25th and 26th arrived today at noon and as always I was glad to hear from you. Today I worked 7-1/2 hours [at Walker] and I feel bad—no fooling—washed walls most of the day. It is really the first day's work I have done in several years I believe.

I will try to accomplish as much as possible in the next few days along the lines of things I should do. It seems however that I am going to be caught short on time and will have to leave a few things until you get down. It seems as tho every day brings additional tasks to be done—or which I'd like to have done before you arrive.

Tomorrow I am going to start moving and do some more shopping if I can before 2:30. I start work at that time now and put in 3 hours. Unless the weather turns extremely bad, I'll leave here Friday morning and should arrive in Wittenberg early in the afternoon. Will take highway 45, and in case I do have trouble with the car (heaven forbid) I can always take the train.

The kids have recovered from the chicken pox to a great extent but we do have a sign on our house and it will remain for at least two weeks. So far as I can gather, the reception will be held here, but Marty & I are still in the dark as to their plans.

So long, darling. It won't be long now.

All My Love, Gene

❖

Jan 24 '46
[Wittenberg]

Hi, Darling,

Guess what! We have some more Pyrex! But don't get excited, dear—it isn't <u>too</u> bad. When I came home last night, Mother told me Ramona [Bricco] (at the restaurant) wanted to see me & I should go right over there. So I did & of course it was a shower. She & Helen Schlytter gave it. There were about ten girls altogether & it was sort of fun. Here's a list of the gifts:

1 Pyrex loaf pan
1 Pyrex pie plate
2 Sets of bowls
1 Blue teapot (very nice)
1 Small stew pan (alum. I think)
1 Paring knife
3 Sets (2 ea.) of guest towels

Mother would like to have the Pyrex loaf pan & will trade her Pyrex frying pan for it. So you won't need to buy one, honey. Melitta gave me one of the sets of bowls, & she says I may exchange it if I wish; so I may try to get one of those Pyrex stew pans or else a muffin tin.

We washed this morning, & I fixed the collar on your shirt. Also, Daddy sent in the order for the studio couch ("Sofa lounge, deluxe") to be delivered to 940 S. Layton about Mon. or Tues.

This aft. I've been trying to get rid of the beginnings of a cold. It surely would make me angry to catch one now.

I asked Mother about when you should come up, & she seems to think Thurs. would be better. Will tell you definitely later.

Jane & Eric just stopped in for a few minutes. She likes her blouse. We've agreed to wear orchids.

I'm so glad it will be only a week, darling. I want to be with you <u>all</u> the time.

Much love, Marian

❖

Jan. 26 '46

Hello, Honey—

The minister was here a few minutes ago to discuss the plans. I told him, in answer to his question, that we wanted just the ceremony—no sermon. OK? We will practice Fri. night at 8:00. He says he doesn't like "Oh, Promise Me" or "I Love You Truly," and I assured him that I would want anything else but that!

There is a bit of a problem created by the fact that we have no ushers in the wedding party. He said we could arrange so that the best man would act as an usher if we think we need one. In view of the delicacy of the situation, I would say we did, unless we can let everyone know in advance where they should sit—all the invited guests, that is. What do you think? We can work it out at rehearsal.

We just heard that one of our very good friends died & Daddy should go after him. His two daughters are rather special friends of mine. They used to live on a farm when we were in high school & I used to spend weekends out there. Makes me feel rather sad. He hasn't been well for a long time, but Joyce [Schulz] was always very fond of her father & I can imagine how she feels.

Changing the subject again, I returned a set of bowls today & got a nice big steel skillet and a butcher knife. Mother informed me this morning that a loaf pan will not be sufficient to trade for the frying pan. She wants a casserole, too. So bring along one of our small ones for her, will you please, dear?

It surely is cold up here today, 24° below, this morning. I think I'm making some progress with my cold, though.

The party for Kriels will be fine. When are we going to see Peg, though?

I thought we might send the announcements about Monday, the 4th.

Listen, you pessimist, if veterans do better in college, it's logical that they do better at graduate work also! You haven't a thing to worry about, honey. What other student will have a special assistant like me? And what other special assistant will have a student like you? Oh, I love you, darling!

Marian

❖

Jan. 27 '46

Dearest Gene—

The event scheduled for yesterday occurred today & I felt like h___ this morning. Feel fine tonight, though, & my cold is also under control. By next Saturday, the situation should be ideal.

Dad thinks it's going to snow tomorrow. I surely hope we don't have any storms until after we are at <u>home</u> in Milwaukee, at least. It will really be home to me, darling, in all the best meanings of the word.

Mother said to tell you to come up Thursday. Of course, you don't have to if you'd rather come Friday, but we'd like to have you here Thursday. I would, especially.

Spent the afternoon up at Jane's looking for music and crocheting an edge on some pillowcases. Jane's suit is <u>very</u> pretty. She has a hat made of feathers, also. I think you'll like it better than mine.

We played cards tonight & Daddy won both games. Every time I thought I had a good hand, I'd get set. Bad night!

Guess I'd better go to bed, honey. Until tomorrow, then —

All my love, Marian

✢

Jan. 28 '46

Hello, Honey —

How are you? For heavens sake, don't get chicken pox! Not until the 3rd anyway! Hope I don't either. I've had it before, too — I guess we shouldn't worry.

Today I finished making arrangements for music. I found a lovely song called "The Prayer Perfect." The words are so nice. Hope you will like it, too. Walter Kersten & Esther Maack will sing it as a duet. I believe you met Mrs. Maack when we were looking for Xmas tree lights. They own the drug store.

Also borrowed an ornament for the wedding cake from Melitta. She gave me some place cards, too.

Am enclosing a sample announcement. I think they look quite nice.

Did some more crocheting today, and helped Jane take pictures to send to Eddie for Valentine's Day, which is their anniversary. We tried taking time exposures indoors. Hope they turn out OK. Took several with Franklin's camera, too.

Jane was trying to make some overalls for Eric & I nearly died laughing at her! She had sewed the trouser legs together all wrong. Instead of sewing the front of each to the back, she sewed the two fronts together and the backs together. The poor kid would have had a hell of a time trying to walk in that outfit. She said, "Oh, Eric, your mother is so dumb!" I can see why she doesn't like to sew, anyway.

Who is Dr. Koepke? Your talk with him sounded good. I'm glad there are a few people who encourage you, dear.

I hope you will be here Thursday. I'm getting awfully lonesome. Don't drive, please, unless the weather is good — and do be careful, darling.

I love you.

Marian

P.S. If you have time, see about tickets to the Ballet, will you pliz? Probably we could get them later.

❀

29 Jan '46
[Milwaukee]

Hello darling

Just a note before bedtime — Everything is progressing satisfactory except that I see that it is snowing again. Just returned from our house after some more varnishing and thinking — It is going to be wonderful dearest. Took my desk over tonight so I am practically moved now. The S. Couch came today and it is swell but I believe we definitely will need a pad — at least after the first week. Got a much better table today from Christ [Jensen] and also a couple kitchen chairs instead of those others. OK?

Darling, I don't believe I can come up before Friday because of my work at school. I will make another attempt to talk to Dad tomorrow, but he seems in a sort of ugly mood. Will be glad when I get out of this cage I've been in for the last 5 years. There is only 2 more days left and I'll be <u>free</u>. That's a rather different outlook from most fellows when they get married. I hope your cold is under control. Take care of yourself — you almost belong to me.

Goodnight, my love,

Gene

(Sent the shirt material today)

❀

Jan. 29 '46
Wittenberg

Darling,

I'm delighted with the improvements on our room — the new chair, the <u>wall socket</u> and the <u>refrigerator</u>! It's wonderful! I really think we'll like it as well, if not better than any apartment we might have found. It's so nice to have everything newly scrubbed & refinished. You are wonderful, dear! I don't see how you managed to put the drapes up, but of course it's OK.

Yes, dear, I only want a platinum ring with a "knife edge." I'm sure!

It seems that almost everything is done that can be done before Friday, and I'm getting very impatient to see you again and especially to have the wedding over with. Guess I'll see if Jane wants to go to the show tonight.

Darling, to say that you are optimistic & confident of our future together is about the nicest way you could possibly say, "I love you."

I love you, too—

Marian

We became man and wife at 4:00 P.M. on 2 February, 1946, Groundhog Day, in Wittenberg, Wisconsin, two years less 17 days after the train ride. The small Lutheran church was mostly filled with well-wishers, and the chicken dinner in the church basement went off smoothly. At the time we exchanged vows it was exactly 20 degrees below zero, and when we stepped outside to have our picture taken, Marian's orchid corsage instantly froze. My grandfather's 1931 Pontiac, despite over 95,000 miles on the odometer, was usually reliable, but as we prepared to make our getaway to Wausau, twenty miles to the west, I could not start it. My new father-in-law was accommodating, however, and pushed us with the hearse until the motor turned over. When we got to the hotel, the temperature had dropped to minus 25, but we did not care: We were together and the future, about which we had written so much, had begun.

Epilogue

I GUESS WE did look to the future, but the present was enough to keep us busy. Graduate school at Marquette led to a masters' degree in American history in 1947, and the thesis was written alongside our first gas plate, electric refrigerator and studio couch. If I hadn't realized it before, I now knew my wife was much more adept at putting a thought into concise and clear language than I, and when I submitted the Learned Document, what clarity it possessed was due in no small part to her gentle suggestions. I was not particularly proud that I had written with such authority about graduate school and girls being incompatible, but secretly felt rather smug to think I had picked one who was.

That fall I got my first real job teaching American and Modern European history at the University of Detroit, and a few months later Jay, our first child, was born. After three years I enrolled full time at the University of Michigan in Ann Arbor and in 1952 received a Ph.D. in American Constitutional history. In the meantime Todd had arrived in 1951 and our daughter, Marta, in 1953. Like so many others who had served in the military, the G.I. Bill had made it financially possible to study and support a family at the same time. When my student days were finally over, I had been in graduate school nearly four years under this extraordinarily generous government subsidy for education.

Marian and I had hoped I could find a teaching job in California but it was not to be. I accepted a position at the University of Michigan teaching American and Michigan history, and in 1954 had a chance to become the director of the State of Michigan's historical museum. Four years later my family and I moved to Mackinac Island in northern Michigan, where I directed the Mackinac Island State Park Commission's historical restoration and reconstruction program until retirement in 1985.

My old outfit, the Third Marine Division, had ceased to exist at the moment of our engagement on 31 December, 1945, and if memories of the Marine Corps returned occasionally, we did not talk about it much. Merle wrote occasionally in those early years and had gone to graduate school at the University of California at Berkeley as he so often talked about. Many years later I read a review written by a Merle Borrowman of a newly published history text. I wrote to the magazine but got no reply. I would have liked to have kept in touch. Thomas Edwards and I exchanged a few letters in the 1950's. After medical school in Colorado he set up his practice in Phoenix, Arizona. In 1993 we found each other again, and I learned that his love life, like mine, had turned out very well. He met his wife, Dottie, while in school in Colorado, and they had six children. In 1997 fifty-two years after I left Guam we finally got together in a joyous reunion in Milwaukee, Wisconsin at a 3rd Marine Division Association meeting. We had much to talk about.

❖

When Gene first brought out these letters and I saw, "Dear Lt. Sweetheart," I said, "Put them away!" Later when I had read a few , I suggested that if he left out the beginnings and endings, the rest was quite sensible. He thought for a moment and said, "But without the beginnnings and endings there wouldn't have been much love." After my son-in-law, Peter Olson, read them he said, "I don't know why you're worried. They're practically Victorian!"

I met Gene just a couple of months after my brother had gone overseas, but it was not until after Franklin was reported missing in June, 1944, that we began to correspond regularly. Gene, I think, felt a little guilty he had not answered my earlier letters. I had been hit hard with the realization that you could lose someone with whom you had shared most of your life, and that the rest of life could be quite desolate unless you could find someone with whom the same values could be shared. My involvement with Cal had been both exciting and disorienting, but I had always known it could not be lasting. So I began to worry a great deal about the dangers Gene faced in the Pacific. At some point in the winter of 1945 I wrote to my friend Jane Haseltine Basse, "I think if Gene survives this war, life may become worth living again."

And indeed it did. As I wrote a half century ago, I admired the philosophy in, "Love does not consist in gazing at each other, but in looking outward in the same direction." In 1958 when Gene suggested to his new boss that he needed a secretary, the Chairman of the Mackinac Island Park Commission, a very conservative Republican who didn't want to add to the proliferation of state employees, said, "Your wife can type, can't she?" This was the beginning of a professional partnership that was very satisfying for both of us and, I think, beneficial to the Commission.

On a personal level, we were fortunate to have the two boys and a girl I had always wanted. Jay Franklin, our first, is the problem solver; Todd Martin is the compassionate administrator; and Marta Jean, like her father, is both driven and creative. It is not yet the end of the story, but there is a bit more glory than my modest husband would admit, and surely there is much love.

❖

While our son, Todd, took our picture on a sunny December day in 1996, Marian and I stood in front of the Iwo Jima memorial in Washington, D.C. Its size and that magnificent setting overlooking the beautiful Virginia countryside impressed us. Not far away is the National Cemetery in Arlington with its rows of white crosses similar to those I had seen at Iwo Jima. Beneath most lay the remains of the military dead; others are reminders of those who gave their lives but whose bodies never came home. One of these markers remembers Lt. Albert Franklin Smith, United States Army Air Forces, who died when his P-38 was shot down over Romania in 1944. I know his sister.

Notes

1. This is a belt with a cross strap worn outside of the uniform jacket.
2. I had two younger half brothers, Thor (Skip) and Martin.
3. Antoine St. Exupèry, a French aviator and writer, was best known for *The Little Prince*. After the fall of France, St. Exupèry escaped the Germans and fled to the United States in 1943, where he became a close friend of Anne Lindbergh. He later rejoined his unit in North Africa and was shot down over the Mediterranean in 1944. Actually, this is misquoted.
4. Virginia Wilson was Marian's roommate in Los Angeles.
5. Paul Rhoads was a field engineer at Reliable Electric Company.
6. Since Franklin was known by his first name, Al(bert) in the service, Marian often calls him that in her letters, especially when she refers to his fellow pilots.
7. Henry Luce was the founder and publisher of *Time*, the weekly newsmagazine that pioneered short narrative articles and strong international coverage.
8. June Bumann Gowell was Marian's Wittenberg schoolmate and Chicago roommate.
9. Cordell Hull was Secretary of State, and Edward Stettinius later played an important role in the founding of the United Nations.
10. Power was a popular movie star.
11. In 1944, there was a struggle between Greek communists and royalist faction to control the government.
12. Award to Reliable for excellence in war production.
13. V-mail letters were written on self-folding onionskin. The addressee received a photocopy.
14. Arthur Vandenberg was a senator from Michigan and an isolationist until after Pearl Harbor, when he strongly supported Roosevelt and the war effort.
15. Merle Borrowman was one of my closest friends in the 3rd division.

16. This 1944 movie told the story of President Woodrow Wilson and his fight for the League of Nations.

17. Ernie Pyle was one of the most popular war correspondents.

18. Anita Colby and Jennifer Jones were popular movie stars.

19. *Thirty Seconds over Tokyo*, the story of the James Doolittle air raid on the Japanese islands four months after Pearl Harbor and a great morale builder in the United States, starred Spencer Tracy and Van Johnson.

20. The War Manpower Commission allocated people in the war effort.

21. Sewell Avery, head of the huge mail order company Montgomery Ward, challenged the authority of the War Labor Board and was carried bodily out of his Chicago office by the soldiers.

22. Roosevelt, Stalin, and Churchill met at Yalta in the Crimean peninsula in one of the most important conferences of the war. While it dealt mainly with establishing a new Polish government sympathetic to Russia and the role of the allies in post-war Europe, Roosevelt did get a secret commitment from Stalin to enter the Pacific war after the defeat of Germany.

23. Pace and Ray were two lieutenants who were in the 28th Replacement draft and who came to Guam with me.

24. Tokyo Rose was a woman who broadcast propaganda from Japan and played popular music for the American servicemen in the Pacific. It was her objective to undermine their morale.

25. William Randolph Hearst was the publisher of a newspaper chain and was often critical of the Roosevelt administration.

26. John O'Leary and I had served together in several posts including Officers' training in Quantico, Virginia.

27. Mohorovitch was another lieutenant who came to Guam with me.

28. This is a stanza from Walt Whitman's poem "O Captain! My Captain!"

29. Utley was a popular author and lecturer.

30. This was typed on a military typewriter that had only the upper case.

31. Julius P. Heil was a colorful Milwaukee industrialist and Wisconsin governor, best known for his promotional slogan, "If she's got dimples in her knees, she eats Wisconsin cheese."

32. Ione Q. Griggs was a *Milwaukee Journal* columist who gave advice to her readers.

33. Samuel Grafton was a syndicated columnist whose articles were carried in the *Chicago Sun*.

34. Walter Lippman was a popular columnist.

35. Lawrence was a popular English music hall entertainer.

36. *Esquire* magazine's paintings by Varga of beautiful girls were favorite pin-ups for servicemen.

37. This is from William Blake's *Auguries of Innocence*.

38. Lilienthal was head of the Tennessee Valley Authority.

39. The *Time* account of the discovery of the extermination camps for Jews was the first we had heard about it.

40. Paul Robeson was a black vocalist and actor.

41. Trieste in the northern Adriatic sea was long contested between Italy and Yugoslavia.

42. George Burns and Gracie Allen were a popular radio entertainment team.
43. *Barnaby* was drawn and written by Crockett Johnson and one of the best comics of the decade. It featured pre-schooler Barnaby and his fairy godfather, a fat man with a large cigar and pink wings.
44. Norris was a United States Senator from Nebraska.
45. Robert Hutchins was president of the University of Chicago.
46. Gerd von Rundstedt was a German field marshal.
47. Gen. Alfred Vandegrift was commandant of the Marine Corps.
48. The G.I. Bill originally provided $75 a month for living expenses plus tuition and books for any college that would accept the servicemen.
49. The conference was an organizational meeting of the United Nations.
50. U. S. Army General Joseph W. Stilwell served in the China-Burma war zone.
51. Gertrude Stein was a prominent American writer living in Paris.
52. General Simon Bolivar Buckner, son of a Civil War general, led the Tenth Army against the Japanese in the Ruyukus Islands. He was killed at a forward observation post on 18 June.
53. John Bradley, one of the flag raisers in Joe Rosenthal's famous Iwo Jima photograph, was from Antigo, Wisconsin.
54. United States Senator Theodore Bilbo, of Mississippi, was an outspoken segregationist.
55. An air force B-25 bomber hit the Empire State Building in New York City, killing thirteen people.
56. Claire Booth Luce was the wife of Henry Luce, publisher of *Time*.
57. I spent the leave on the island of Oahu, site of Pearl Harbor.
58. United States Senator Hiram Johnson, of California, strongly opposed the Selective Service Act.
59. Gregory "Pappy" Boyington was a Marine Corps ace pilot who shot down twenty-eight Japanese planes.
60. The Land Lease Act allowed the President to transfer military aid to Great Britain.
61. Elwyn Brooks White, American essayist and long time editor of the *New Yorker*, wrote a monthly column for *Harpers*.
62. The missing paragraph is from "Progress and Change," E. B. White, *One Man's Meat*, 31-32, New York and London: Harper & Brothers Publishers, 1944.
63. This was from "Coon Hunt," E. B. White, *One Man's Meat*, 267.
64. James Jackson of Evanston, Ilinois became a close friend on Hawaii.
65. McGuigan was an author of a letter to the editor.
66. Heatter was a political commentator on the radio.
67. President Harry S. Truman was *Time*'s Man of the Year in 1945.
68. Thomas was a socialist candidate for president.
69. Thorkild Kreil was a longtime Danish friend of the Petersens and executive of "Frank & Co." sausage company in Milwaukee, for whom Marian had worked before the war.
70. W. D. Haseltine was a lawyer in Wittenberg and father of Jane.
71. Rita was Gene's cousin, daughter of his Aunt Helga Stubbs.
72. Marshall Rieboldt was a close friend before the war and best man at our wedding.

73. Dorothy was a great aunt and Charlotte's mother.
74. Skip (Thor Petersen) was the older of my half brothers. Bruce was a foster child of my stepmother.
75. William Koepke was principal of Walker Jr. High School in Milwaukee.
76. Oscar Nelsen worked for my father at Walker Jr. High.
77. Chris Jensen was the apartment owner.

Index